THE CHANGING
POLITICAL ECONOMY
OF THE THIRD WORLD

THE CHANGING

POLITICAL ECONOMY

OF THE THIRD WORLD

edited by

*Manochehr
Dorraj*

LYNNE
RIENNER
PUBLISHERS

BOULDER
LONDON

Published in the United States of America in 1995 by
Lynne Rienner Publishers, Inc.
1800 30th Street, Boulder, Colorado 80301

and in the United Kingdom by
Lynne Rienner Publishers, Inc.
3 Henrietta Street, Covent Garden, London WC2E 8LU

Library of Congress Cataloging-in-Publication Data
The changing political economy of the Third World / edited by
    Manochehr Dorraj.
        p.   cm.
    Includes bibliographical references and index.
    ISBN 1-55587-554-8
    ISBN 1-55587-577-7 (pbk.)
        1. Developing countries—Economic conditions. 2. Developing
countries—Social conditions. 3. Developing countries—Politics and
government. I. Dorraj, Manochehr.
HC59.7.C3438   1995
330.9172'4—dc20   94-31378
                                                             CIP

British Cataloguing in Publication Data
A Cataloguing in Publication record for this book
is available from the British Library.

Printed and bound in the United States of America

⊗ The paper used in this publication meets the requirements
    of the American National Standard for Permanence of
    Paper for Printed Library Materials Z39.48-1984.

5 4 3 2 1

For Patsy and Katti

Contents

◆

Tables and Figures

◆

Tables

Figures

Acknowledgments

───────── ◆ ─────────

I would like to express my gratitude to the authors for their contributions, patience, and cooperation, making the successful completion of this volume possible. I owe a debt to several friends and colleagues who agreed to review some of the chapters and share their critical comments with me and the contributors. For obvious reasons they will remain anonymous. My heartfelt thanks go to Albert Harris, who initiated this project with me and assisted in editing some of the chapters and provided invaluable insights. Unfortunately, due to unforeseen circumstances, he had to withdraw from the project. I am grateful to my colleagues in the Political Science Department at Texas Christian University and to Dean Michael McCracken, Vice Chancellor Larry Adams, and Dean Joe Helmick, who provided me with the necessary financial assistance to do research at the OPEC library in Vienna, Austria, for this project. I would like to express my appreciation to Martha Peacock, acquisitions editor at Lynne Rienner Publishers, for her exemplary professionalism and cooperation, and to Michelle Welsh-Horst, also at Lynne Rienner, for her excellent editorial suggestions. Thanks are also due to the anonymous reviewer for providing insightful and constructive criticism. I must express my gratitude to Dr. Joe Law for his meticulous editorial assistance. Special thanks are due to Marilyn Eudaly for her computer assistance and Carmelita Shepelwich for her patience and diligence as she assisted me with the preparation of the final draft of the manuscript. Last but not least, I thank my wife and daughter for their love and support.

Manochehr Dorraj

1

♦

Introduction: The Changing Context of Third World Political Economy

Manochehr Dorraj

In the post–Cold War era, as the axis of global conflict has shifted from East-West competition to North-South confrontations, developments in the Third World have assumed a new significance. For example, in an increasingly interdependent world, developing countries import nearly one-third of U.S. exports and are the source of nearly 30 percent of total U.S. imports. More than 73 percent of U.S. petroleum imports originate in the developing countries, which also account for more than 40 percent of U.S. iron, steel, and electronic machinery exports.[1] Moreover, the rise in interest rates to nearly 20 percent during the first term of the Reagan presidency and the mounting debt crisis in Mexico, Brazil, Argentina, and elsewhere in Latin America substantiate the reality of global interdependence. Comprehending this global interdependence may also shed light on the change of course in those countries that embraced a socialist path over capitalist alternatives as an avenue to achieve economic growth and prosperity through self-reliance and central planning.

The globalization of industry and technology and the emergence of an electronically monitored financial system have allowed multinational corporations to move capital, labor, and technology across borders more rapidly. This new internationalization of capital, standardization of technologies, and universalization of labor processes has induced further integration of the Third World in a global capitalist economy. Driven by ever larger profit margins and intense competition, many multinational corporations continue to seek expanding sources of cheap labor, low taxes, and lax environmental and labor laws; as a result, they move their plants and operations to the developing nations. The old international division of

1

labor is disappearing, and a new one is emerging. The classical division of labor in which developing nations were the exporters of raw materials and importers of goods from more advanced countries may have ended. The mutual integration of production, migration of labor, capital, and transfer of technology has ushered in a new international division of labor.[2] In other words, with internationalization of domestic capital, universalization of labor processes and consumer taste, and the standardization of commodities, increasingly economic decisionmaking has also become transnational. The old ideas of national autonomy, economic independence, self-reliance, and self-sufficiency have become obsolete as the national economies become increasingly integrated and the state becomes the agent of the international system. To survive in this competitive and interdependent world, Third World economies have become more commercialized, mechanized, and standardized in the process.[3] The new international division of labor based on the law of comparative advantage has transformed many Third World economies from mere suppliers of raw materials into the manufacturing of counterparts already available in the North. The global assembly line, the global consumer society, and the unceasing march of new commodities that continue to alter and mediate human relations are also the realities that are molding Third World societies. This process, however, is an uneven one, as parts of the Third World, particularly East Asia, rank among the fastest growing economies in the world, while others, such as Africa, struggle to survive.

As the Third World—a label given to characterize developing countries in a bipolar world during the Cold War—itself polarizes into richer and poorer nations with widely divergent political systems and social agendas, it has become increasingly clear that the term has become obsolete. For example, the newly industrializing economies of East Asia (NIES) (Singapore, South Korea, Taiwan, and Hong Kong), are among the fastest growing economies in the world and possess higher per capita gross national products (GNPs) than Russia, Eastern Europe, and some Southern European countries such as Portugal. On the other end of the scale there are African countries whose GNPs are among the lowest in the world. Whereas the East Asian economies grew in the 1980s at the annual rate of 7.4 percent, Africa grew at a rate of only 1.7 percent.[4] Other statistics indicate that in the 1960s, South Korea had a per capita GNP exactly the same as Ghana's (U.S.$230), whereas today it is ten to twelve times more prosperous. In fact, South Korea is on the road to becoming one of the richest countries in the twenty-first century.[5]

The NIES of East Asia also enjoy some of the highest literacy rates in the world. The 95 percent literacy rate in South Korea, for example, is similar to that of Spain, while Nigeria's literacy rate is only 14 percent.[6] Such profound disparities permeate the entire region.

Mindful of the changes in global politics and the polarization in the political economy of the developing nations, but lacking a better terminology, we use the term Third World in this book to refer to the developing countries of Asia, Latin America, Africa, and the Middle East.

The colossal changes in the international arena in the past decade have transformed global and Third World politics fundamentally. The collapse of the Soviet Empire, the end of communism in the former Soviet Union and Eastern Europe, while depriving some of the Third World states of possible allies, has also created new competition for others as they find themselves competing with the former Eastern bloc for foreign investment, loans, and export markets. In the new strategy of Western powers, the integration of the former Soviet Union, Eastern Europe, and China into the world capitalist system assumes the top priority. Hence, the division of the world into trade blocs and the rise of regional economic powers (European community led by Germany, North Atlantic free trade zone led by the United States, and the Asian economic bloc led by Japan) pose new dilemmas and challenges to the Third World. How can they remain competitive when most of them, with the exception of the members of the ASEAN (Association of Southeast Asian Nations) trade bloc and Mexico, are not members of these trade blocs?

Two options remain available to the Third World. First is the South-South regional trade. In the 1980s there was a major reassessment of development strategies and trade policies. In Africa, the Middle East, and Latin America many countries have abandoned economic nationalism and import substitution and have opted for trade liberalization and outward-looking, export-led economic strategies. By the 1990s multilateralism was on the wane, and various less developed countries entered into bilateral and regional trading arrangements. The Southern Cone Common Market in Latin America, the Caspian Sea trading bloc in the Middle East, and the Central African Economic Community are a few examples.[7] However, the limitations of Third World economies, their need for high technology-driven industrial goods that can only be imported from the industrial nations, and the prevalence of war and conflict render the viability of regional trading blocs a problematic one. The second option is the possibility of siding with one of the three trading blocs: European Community (EC), North American Free Trade Agreement (NAFTA), or ASEAN. If this scenario materializes, the Third World is likely to play only a minor role in the partnership of this tripolar world.

As many Third World economies abandon the inward-looking nationalist, populist, and socialist policies of the past and embrace outward-looking approaches in their trade and development strategies, they will be further integrated in the world capitalist economy. While some may benefit from such integration and prosper, others may become more vulnerable to crises and fluctuations prevalent in capitalist economic cycles. Impoverished and dependent, with the exception of the newly industrializing economies, much of the Third World is ill-equipped to reap the benefits of global interdependence. As the source of wealth increasingly changes from raw materials to knowledge and expertise, other factors such as reduced economic importance of labor in the age of robotics revolution and information and service industries would lead to further decline in significance of many less developed nations.[8] The lack of necessary capital, high technology, skilled labor, and modern infrastructure make it difficult for many Third World countries to participate in the communication and information revolution and harvest its fruits. Hence, some of the traditional causes of underdevelopment, such as the flight of capital and excessive arms expenditure, continue to escalate. Each year $43 billion flows out of Asia, Africa, and Latin America to the First World. The adversarial effect of massive military expenditures continues to hamper economic development by devouring a large share of national budgets. The annual Third World defense expenditure for 1988 alone, for example, amounted to $150 billion. This figure has remained more or less the same in the 1990s. As the cost of high technologies continues to soar and the price of such raw materials as oil, copper, and coal either declines or does not keep pace, the pauperization of the region intensifies. Consequently, the South becomes even more dependent on the North than a century ago under colonial rule.[9]

Neither can the South hope for a trickle-down effect to benefit from the technological revolution in the North. The endemic poverty would not enable it to afford such technology. Hence, the mounting debt crisis in many parts of the Third World is another obstacle to development and economic growth. According to one account, "since the mid-1980s, the interest and principal on loan repayments from Third World to First World has physically exceeded (by $10 billion or more annually) the capital flowing into the Third World for development purposes."[10] The debt crisis exacerbates the endemic poverty of the region and has led to the actual decline of living standards.[11]

Nor can democratization or democracy act as a panacea for the problems of underdevelopment and rampant poverty. The recent wave of global democratization has had some notable success, especially in parts of Latin America. However, insofar as democratization is not accompanied with more equitable division of wealth, it is bound to remain short-lived and unstable. Hence, other correlates of democracy, such as a high level of literacy, the absence of internal strife and ethnic conflicts, and cultural norms supportive of democratic rule, are missing in many parts of the region.[12] These attributes render the present wave of social compacts and elite-initiated democratization a fragile process in which the possibilities for retrenchment, retreat, and return of repression remain real, as the events in many developing countries in recent years have so vividly demonstrated.

Thus the end of the Cold War and the ascendance of the new world order may not usher in a new dawn of prosperity for the South; quite to the contrary, with the emergence of trading blocs globally, as each nation or bloc seeks to maximize its domination and exploitation of preferred sectors of the periphery, such relationships may render some parts of the Third World even more dependent, marginalized, and impoverished.[13] Those who point to the successful example of the NIEs in East Asia forget that the attributes that made their growth possible are for the most part absent in many parts of the Third World. The NIEs of East Asia developed in an era when protectionism and competition had much lower priority in the world market. Due to inadequate infrastructure and a poor educational system, the development of high technology is also problematic in many parts of the region.

Significant transformations of the past forty years have also diminished the strategic value of the Third World. The nuclear revolution, the emergence of information and service-oriented industries, and the decline of the Soviet power have all contributed to the declining political significance of the region. The massive nuclear arsenals of major powers have devalued conquered territory, including the Third World territory, in projection of power. With the ascendance of high technology and information-based industries as well as the environmental movement, it is likely that the Western reliance on raw materials (with the exception of oil) will decline in the near future.[14] Because the second Cold War was fought over the control of the Third World,[15] the disintegration of the Soviet Union also rendered the Third World strategically less significant. Since many developing countries that during the Cold War had adversarial relations with the United States (Cuba, Nicaragua, Angola, Ethiopia, Vietnam, and Cambodia, to name a few) were also the recipients of Soviet aid and arms, in the absense of Soviet assistance they have opted for a more accommodationist policy toward the United States. In due time the necessity of commercial ties with the North has rendered the ideological politics of the 1960s and 1970s irrelevant in the 1990s. So far a new sense of pragmatism seems to hold sway among many radical Third World states. Hence, the attempt to break away from the world market and chart a path of economic independence and self-sufficiency based on socialist or populist programs has not proven effective. A whole range of policies—such as nationalizing Western companies, setting up commodity exporting cartels such as the Organization of Petroleum Exporting Countries (OPEC), subsidizing indigenous manufacturing to promote import substitution, and calling for a new economic order based on redistribution of resources—have failed. The struggle against the "market" backed by developed economies has further weakened the Third World.[16] Therefore, it is not surprising that with the exception of East Asia, other regions of the Third World declined in terms of their average per capita gross domestic product (GDP) in the 1980s. Sub-Saharan Africa declined from 3.2 percent in the 1960s to -2.2 in the 1980s. Latin America and the Caribbean declined from 3.7 percent in the 1960s to -0.6 in the 1980s, the Middle East and North Africa declined from 5.5 percent in the 1960s to 0.8 in the 1980s. In contrast, East Asia improved from 5.1 percent in the 1960s to 6.7 in the 1980s.[17]

Similarly, the World Bank estimates that "as many as 950 million of the world's 5.2 billion people are chronically malnourished—more than twice as many as a decade ago. In Africa, per capita food production has declined every year for the past thirty years."[18] Hence, the average income in the 1980s fell by 10 percent in most of Latin America and by over 20 percent in Sub-Saharan Africa. In some urban areas, real minimum wages declined by as much as 50 percent.[19] A combination of decline in the price of raw materials, deteriorating trade with the North, diminishing South-South trade, declining foreign investment, the mounting debt crisis, the flight of capital, and the staggering population growth—all were responsible for the relative decline of the Third World economies in the 1980s.[20]

The problems of economic growth, political stability, equity, aid, gender, democracy, and environmental degradation will dominate Third World affairs in the coming decades. A crucial issue before the Third World is how it utilizes its limited resources to optimize development and growth. To achieve this goal, Third World nations must opt for a realistic development strategy. Thus an assessment of past history and present dynamics of the political economy of the Third World is a first step toward the development of any viable strategy of growth. This book is a modest attempt to grapple with some of the different issues of economic and political development. The book also delineates the regional disparities, thus explaining why there is no uniform strategy of growth. While the example of success in East Asia may provide some useful lessons for other countries, historical and cultural heritage also play a significant role in explaining success or failure. Therefore, what may work for one region may be totally inapplicable in another.

These issues are further expounded by the contributors to this volume. The first part of the book focuses on case studies of development in the different regions of the Third World. Drawing upon historical analysis and theoretical literature, the authors provide a comprehensive account of regional political economies. The chapters in Part Two discuss some of the most pressing problems facing the Third World political economies. In this section indepth study of such issues as financial aid, environmental degradation, and oppression of women are undertaken.

The diversity of regional case studies and theoretical approaches in this volume is intended to provide an account of the disparities of growth and development and the vexing dilemmas facing the Third World in the increasingly interdependent and competitive world of the twenty-first century. What follows is a brief description of each chapter.

[In Chapter Two Michael Foley investigates what he terms a "revolution" in Latin American political economy. The numerous military and civilian authoritarian regimes that pervaded the continent in the sixties and seventies have all been replaced by nonauthoritarian civilian governments. These civilian governments must now take up the task on which the military regimes, for the most part, failed to make much progress: economic growth sufficient to foster political stability. Foley shows the civilian, authoritarian, and military regimes to have been less successful in their penetration of civil society than is generally believed. Consequently, those regimes were unable to implement policies capable of solving the economic crises of the seventies and eighties, including the debt imbroglio. The new democratic regimes have been able to reduce the size of certain state institutions regulating the economy, while at the same time introducing neoliberal proposals for reform.⌐

[In several instances the authoritarian or military regimes were also inept at managing social protest, whether guerrilla movements in the countryside or urban demonstrations. Foley seeks to explain why the civilian governments that succeeded those regimes have survived despite the draconian austerity methods they have sometimes imposed. He appraises their prospects for the future, contending that the answer can be found in the reconstituted and resurgent civil society throughout Latin America. In this new civil society the elites have revised their attitudes toward the use of authoritarianism. There has also been an increase in the strength of autonomous groups capable of representing societal demands and of remaining independent of state control, particularly from the business sphere. Foley believes that the prospect for the future of democratization in many parts of Latin America would depend on the continued tolerance for economic austerity currently exhibited by their populations.⌐

In Chapter Three Margaretta DeMar provides a historical analysis of the Caribbean political economy and expounds on its present mode of integration. DeMar believes the internationalization of labor, of production, and particularly of finance capital has played a crucial role in the development of the Caribbean political economy. In her analysis, DeMar differentiates Caribbean history since the late fifteenth century into six periods, with a special emphasis on the period from 1970 to the present. She also delineates how the shift of the Caribbean islands from mercantilist to free trade relations with the metropole countries was integrated with the decolonization of the region. The absence of preferential trade arrangements such as the European Community's Lomé Convention and the relatively insignificant impact of the U.S.–Caribbean Basin Initiative are discussed as well.

DeMar explains how the internationalization of capital and decision-making concerning the dispensation of the capital has constrained the capacity of the Caribbean states to control the structure of their economies. She asserts that the Caribbean governments have become "agents" of the international political economy. Evidence for this belief is found in an examination of the state role in promoting the acceptance of internationally standardized technologies in local Caribbean national economies.

Further evidence is drawn from the ability of the International Monetary Fund to influence economic decisionmaking within Caribbean state structures. Finally, as is illustrated by the increasing presence of transnational corporation investments in the Caribbean states, DeMar tells us that the doctrine of internationalization of production, labor, and capital has been absorbed by Caribbean governments such as Antigua's Vere Bird and Jamaica's Michael Manley.

In Chapter Four Antony Gadzey examines the crisis of "statism" (extensive state domination of a nation's economy) in a number of African countries. Although several African governments (Angola, Mozambique) appear to be preparing for significant departure from statism, Gadzey points out why there is good reason to doubt the depth and duration of such changes. He believes the answer is to be found in African social and economic history. Gadzey asserts that one of the key issues in understanding the African political economy is to comprehend why surplus accumulation, particularly in agriculture, has yet to take place in many African countries.

Gadzey first divides African economic history into the precolonial, colonial, and postcolonial periods. He explores the critical shift from relative abundance to relative scarcity. Later he examines the inconsistency between the needs of the metropole with its commodity export policy and the development needs of the subjugated African populations. Finally, he analyzes postcolonial statist regimes and suggests policy reforms that might reverse their poor performances.

In his discussions Gadzey notes that the capitalist economies of Kenya and Ivory Coast, although successful in producing substantial agricultural and industrial surplus, have not been able to achieve this goal without extensive dependence on foreign capital. The wealth created has not been equally distributed, and Gadzey suggests this creates a strong possibility for future political tensions in both countries. Gadzey concludes, however, that capitalist transformation, but with a grassroots derivation, offers the greatest probability for a real solution to the stagnant development efforts of many African countries.

In Chapter Five Manochehr Dorraj analyzes the political economy of the Middle East and North Africa by studying three central factors instrumental in molding the political economy of the region: state and state formation, petroleum as both a financial and strategic asset, and the current drive toward democratization. Dorraj expounds on the historical development, obstacles to state formation, and the emergence of an authoritarian state in the twentieth century. He asserts that the influx of the petrodollar in the region since the 1960s has strengthened the autonomy of the state from the society.

Dorraj then focuses on the pivotal role of petroleum and OPEC as an example of regional and Third World economic cooperation and appraises the role of the organization in the development of the political economy of the region. He argues that the forecasts about the imminent fall of OPEC are premature and that the organization will continue to persist in the near future. He identifies two major factors as the primary source of continued OPEC viability. First, the symbiotic interdependence between OPEC and the oil market is too far-reaching to succumb to the temporary winds of shifting prices and market fluctuations. The global market needs OPEC as much as OPEC needs the global market. Second, overriding pragmatic considerations unite the political foes within the same organization. Despite internal divisions and even wars among its members, past experience has demonstrated to OPEC members that their power stems from collective bargaining and maintaining a united front. These two fundamental factors are the forces behind OPEC's resiliency. He then examines the limitations of a single commodity and mineral export-led growth.

The third central issue in the political economy of the region is democratization. Dorraj concludes that economic reform (privatization) has outstripped the process of political reform (political participation). The weaknesses of the incipient civil society has rendered elite-initiated democratization a highly manipulated process characterized by limited and controlled political openings followed by periods of retrenchment and return of political repression. The retrenchment policy, however, does not have long-term viability, and Middle Eastern societies can not insulate themselves from the impact of a global trend toward democratization.

In Chapter Six Richard Doner and Gary Hawes examine the politics of economic growth in two groups of Pacific Rim countries: The East Asian newly industrializing countries (NICS) comprised of Singapore, Hong Kong, Taiwan, and South Korea, and the ASEAN-Four, which includes Indonesia, Malaysia, the Philippines, and Thailand. The authors focus on the external as well as the internal sources of economic growth in the region. Critical external conditions include a Japanese-led product cycle, access to the U.S. market, and a particular structure of hegemonic power and interest in the region. In this context, the impact of the protectionist policies and the rapid diffusion of finance and technology, especially from Japan, are also analyzed. Turning to domestic factors, the authors address the significance of such issues as the state strength (in East Asia) in promoting economic growth, the constructive role of business groups, and associations and the private-public sector collaboration. The impact of economic and political liberalization is also analyzed.

Doner and Hawes contend that the development strategies and institutions common to Southeast Asian countries may bear some useful lessons for other less developed countries, most of which are resource rich and have little hope of developing autonomous and organizationally cohesive states typical of the East Asian NICs. The contribution of culture is addressed in this context. Using country and industry case studies, the authors conclude with some reflections on the consequences of these reforms for future growth and stability of the region, and theoretical approaches to the political economy of growth.

In Chapter Seven Robert Gamer presents a historical analysis of Chinese political economy. Gamer argues that rapid economic growth will continue in China but will not permeate the society unless accompanied by political change. Such change is unlikely to deviate fundamentally from traditional Chinese political culture. That culture, however, contained latitude for giving intellectuals more choice than they have today.

Gamer divides the evolution of Chinese political economy into four stages: first, the period immediately after the communist revolution; second, the period of collectivization and the Great Leap Forward; third, the great proletarian cultural revolution; fourth, the post-1978 period. He shows how economic growth demands and fosters change. The need for roads, airports, petroleum, telecommunications, convertible currency, banking, securities trading, and other infrastructural adjustments, for example, can put great strains on the Chinese financial and political system. Due to the attributes of Chinese history and culture, Gamer argues that future changes in China are unlikely to emulate Western democracy or its interaction with capitalism. Capitalism with a populist political program and regime is more in tune with Chinese Confuciusians as well as a communist heritage of hierarchy and egalitarianism.

In Chapter Eight John Newark discusses the changes in the nature of foreign aid in recent years. He argues that the donor community, with much success, has imposed a new conditionality on aid flows. Recipient nations must increasingly demonstrate a commitment to "market fundamentalism," which envisages a minimal role for the state in the promotion of development and widespread economic liberalization and privatization. The debt crisis has left many less developed countries with few options other than accepting the new proposals that represent a rather dramatic break with past practice.

After a brief examination of trends in aid flows, Newark turns to an assessment of both the theory and practice of market fundamentalism. It is argued that this approach has clearly failed to reduce the debt burden, to restart economic growth, or to provide a remedy for the increasing poverty. The evidence strongly suggests that there are important roles for the state to play in promoting economic development, which had been ignored by the advocates of the new strategy.

In Chapter Nine Marian Miller contends that while the global environment has risen on the agenda of world politics, global environmental politics are played out within the context of an inequitable economic system. Because of their role in the global economy, the Third World and developed nations often bring different interests to the bargaining table. An examination of the biodiversity regime is illustrative. As this regime has evolved, the developing countries have been particularly concerned about issues of sovereignty, technology transfer, and financial assistance.

While the 1992 biodiversity convention in Brazil addressed some of their concerns regarding the issue of sovereignty, asserts Miller, their interests regarding technology transfer and financial assistance were dealt with only in vague, noncommittal language. By adopting a common position, developing countries have been able to induce incremental changes in environmental politics; however, they are at a disadvantage because global environmental politics reflect the structure of the global economy, which is closely controlled by the developed countries.

In Chapter Ten Zehra Arat discusses the diversity of issues that face the women of developing nations. She asserts that women are among the poorest and the least powerful segment of the population throughout the world. The oppression of the Third World women, however, is more poignant due to the legacy of the Western imperialism—culminating in the form of economic dependency and crises. Moreover, the structural changes introduced by colonial powers, and later by international agencies, have further widened the gender gap in these countries.

Women have held subordinate positions since the beginning of civilizations and the formation of patriarchal states. However, as the state power increased and the country's integration into the capitalist world economy became strengthened, women's social and economic conditions deteriorated further. Both colonial and postcolonial state policies undermined women's social and economic value and marginalized their labor. Except for a few cases and short periods of reversals, the disassociation of women from the productive labor and formal economic sectors continued at an accelerated rate, and they were pushed toward reproductive tasks or allowed to participate mainly in the informal economy. Not recognized as full partners, either in the family or in the society, women are denied equal access to education, job training, employment, health care, and political power.

Development policies and projects, initiated either by national governments or international agencies, neglected women in planning and did not seek their participation at the stage of implementation, contends Arat. Consequently, women's lot was not improved even at times of economic growth. However, during the periods of economic stagnation and crisis—which have been the way of life in developing nations since the mid-1970s—women had to make adjustments, and they stretched their already long work days to make up for the lost family income. Partially as a reaction to the increasing levels of economic and political oppression, however, the same period was marked by the development of viable women's movements in several countries, as well as international cooperation and solidarity among women's groups. They researched and documented women's economic contributions, raised consciousness about the biases in the national and international systems, and pushed the policy agendas to include women's issues. Consequently, several international charters and agencies were created to improve women's prospects, and the existing development agencies made adjustments to incorporate women and their concerns into their programs. The full impact of these changes on the lives of the Third World women is yet to be seen.

In what follows these issues will be discussed in more depth and detail.

Notes

1. Anne O. Krueger, *Economic Policies at Cross-Purposes: The United States and Developing Countries* (Washington, D.C.: The Brookings Institution, 1993), p. 2.

2. Margaretta DeMar, "The 'New' Internationalization: Implications for Development and Welfare in the Third World," Cheryl R. Lehman and Russell M. Moore, eds., *Multinational Culture: Social Impacts of Global Economy* (Westport, Conn.: Greenwood Press, 1992), pp. 23–32. See also James A. Caporaso, *A Changing International Division of Labor* (Boulder: Lynne Rienner Publishers, 1987).

3. Ibid. See also Craig N. Murphy & Roger Tooze, eds., *The New International Political Economy* (Boulder: Lynne Rienner Publishers, 1991). Maurice Estabrooks, *Programmed Capitalism: A Computer-Mediated Global Society* (Armonk, N.Y.: M. E. Sharpe, Inc., 1988).

4. Paul Kennedy, "Preparing for 21st Century: Winners and Losers," *The New York Time Review of Books* (February 11, 1993), p. 33.

5. Ibid., p. 32.

6. Ibid., p. 35.

7. For studies on the rise of economic regionalism see Robert C. Hine, "Regionalism and the Integration of the World Economy," *Journal of Common Market Studies* 30, no. 2 (June 1922): pp. 115–123, and Rolf J. Langhammer, "The Developing Countries and Regionalism," *Journal of Common Market Studies* 30, no. 2 (June 1992): pp. 210–231.

8. Dennis Pirages, *Global Technopolitics: The International Politics of Technology and Resources* (Belmount, Calif: Wadsworth, Inc., 1989), pp. 144–156.

9. Kennedy, "Preparing for 21st Century: Winners and Losers," p. 43.

10. Donald Snow, *Distant Thunder: Third World Conflict and the New International Order* (New York: St. Martin's Press, 1993), p. 22.

11. Ibid., p. 203.

12. Zehra Arat, *Democracy and Human Rights in the Developing Countries* (Boulder: Lynne Rienner Publishers, 1991).

13. Dave Broad and Lori Foster, *The New World Order and The Third World* (Montreal: Black Rose Books, 1992), pp. 3–4.

14. Stephan Van Evera, "The United States and the Third World: When to Intervene?" Kenneth Oye, Robert Lieber, and Donald Rothchild, eds., *Eagle in the New World* (New York: Harper Collins, Inc., 1992), p. 115.

15. Fred Holiday, *The Making of the Second Cold War* (London: Verso Publishers, 1983).

16. Kennedy, "Preparing for 21st Century: Winners and Losers," p. 43.

17. Michael Dolan, "Global Economic Transformation and Less Developed Countries," Robert Slater, Barry Schutz, and Steven Dorr, eds., *Global Transformation and the Third World* (Boulder: Lynne Rienner Publishers, 1993), p. 265.

18. Gar Alperovitz and Kai Bird, "The Fading of the Cold War and the Demystification of Twentieth-Century Issues," Michael J. Hogan, ed., *The End of the Cold War: Its Meaning and Implications* (New York: Cambridge University Press, 1992), p. 212.

19. Ibid., p. 213.

20. Dolan, "Global Economic Transformation and Less Developed Countries," pp. 264–265.

Part 1

REGIONAL PERSPECTIVES
ON THIRD WORLD
POLITICAL ECONOMY

2

◆

Debt, Democracy, and Neoliberalism in Latin America: Losses and Gains of the "Lost Decade"

Michael W. Foley

A little over a decade ago, most of the Southern Cone of Latin America was in the grip of military dictatorships that, with apparent success, had seized power to stifle exploding social tensions and impose discipline on faltering economies. Central America, by contrast, was in the midst of revolutionary upheavals that threatened to bring the United States, and the region as a whole, into a conflagration unmatched since the Mexican Revolution. Mexico itself had built upon the ruins of that revolution a remarkably stable political system, dominated by the party of the revolutionary generals now firmly in civilian hands and experiencing, to all appearances, the fruits of thirty years of industrial expansion and the windfall of enormous oil holdings uncovered in 1976.

How different the picture today. The military regimes of the 1970s have all withdrawn, mostly in disgrace, their "economic miracles" shattered and their efforts to suppress social forces widely reviled. They have been replaced by civilian regimes capable in many cases of demanding far more sacrifice of their populations in pursuit of economic stability than military and civilian elites once thought possible. The conflicts in Central America have given way to remarkable, though still tenuous, settlements. In Mexico two successive adminstrations have had to deal with the deepest economic crisis of the twentieth century, and opposition forces came very close to wresting control of the political system from the ruling party in 1988. Throughout the region, finally, countries have faced a complex economic crisis that has turned back the clock for large segments of the population.

This revolution in the political economy of the region stems from the extreme inequality that has always characterized Latin American societies combined with questionable economic policies reaching back to the beginnings of import substitution industrialization in the 1940s; but the problems of the region were compounded by the neoliberal experiments of the military regimes, the remarkable financial somersaults of the 1970s and 1980s, the impact of the world recession of the early 1980s, and the explosion of repressed social tensions under a variety of more or less authoritarian regimes throughout the region. Paradoxically, the "strong" military and civilian authoritarian regimes appear in hindsight to have been quite weak in their penetration of civil society and their ability to implement policies capable of surmounting the crisis. In South America, at least, democratic regimes have been able to use a certain legitimacy to impose policies that would have been unsustainable in other circumstances. At the same time, civilian leaders have imposed their own versions of the neoliberal vision, scaling back both the size of governmental institutions and the scope of state action on the economy. Finally, the region has seen the emergence of autonomous forces in civil society at once committed to democracy and capable of confronting authoritarian and democratic regimes alike on a variety of fronts. The concluding section considers the implications of these changes.

The Flaws in the Authoritarian Heaven

Throughout Latin American, authoritarianism acquired a certain cachet in the 1970s, as elites attempted to deal with the strains of the rapid development that had characterized most of the region since 1940. Economic crisis accompanied by popular unrest, guerrilla movements, and, in some cases, the ascendancy of parties of the left brought military coups first in Brazil in 1964, then in Bolivia that same year, in Argentina in 1966 and again in 1976, and in Peru in 1968, followed by Chile and Uruguay in 1973. In Central America, demands for greater popular participation and the appearance of new political forces prompted repressive crackdowns in Nicaragua, Honduras, El Salvador, and Guatemala. Even in Mexico, where civilian control has been more or less assured since the mid-1930s and where the level of repression has always been relatively low, the government of José López Portillo moved to repress the independent peasant and labor mobilizations that had gathered steam during the previous administration.

In most cases, authoritarian regimes were justified by their supporters as essential to the establishment of economic discipline, and the new governments imposed harsh austerity measures followed by sometimes radical experiments in economic restructuring. The neoliberal experiments adopted after 1973 in Chile and Uruguay and in the wake of the 1976 coup in Argentina preceded by several years the similar measures undertaken in Britain by Margaret Thatcher and in the United States under the first Reagan administration. Brazil's military governors and Mexico's civilian administrations of the 1970s, by contrast, remained much more statist in orientation and much more committed than the governments of the Southern Cone to furthering industrial development. In most of these cases, supporters of authoritarian regimes and more sceptical outsiders alike noted what appeared to be "economic miracles" under authoritarian rule. The *New York Times* and the *Wall Street Journal* waxed eloquent about the recovery of the Chilean economy after 1976 (as they were to do again in the late 1980s, once the collapse of 1981 was forgotten). Brazil could point with pride to an enormous expansion of heavy industrial capacity in the early 1970s and to evidence of steadily rising incomes. Argentina experienced a consumer boom in the late 1970s, while Mexico was investing its newfound petroleum wealth in infrastructure development and social services. Even Bolivia under Hugo Banzer could attest to the economic advantages of authoritarian rule.

Most of these regimes employed repression generously in pursuit of their goals. Brazil and the countries of the Southern Cone were embarked on programs not only of economic but also of political restructuring. The military coups in these countries were intended not simply to block one or another party's ascent or to temporarily quell civilian unrest, but to replace the political system with another, more efficient form of public administration—justifying the label "bureaucratic-authoritarian," which the Argentine political scientist Guillermo O'Donnell was to give them.[1] The generals distrusted politics and politicians and moved quickly to suppress the politically active population, closing legislatures, outlawing or suspending party activities, removing party and labor leaders, jailing, torturing, and murdering thousands of activists and suspected activists.

Repression varied widely among regimes, from hundreds of torture victims and "disappeareds" in Mexico and Brazil to thousands in Argentina and Chile to tens of thousands in El Salvador and Guatemala. In Mexico, the wave of repression that followed the student massacre at Tlalteloco in 1968 abated under President Luis Echeverría, only to be renewed during the López Portillo administration. Repression in Mexico, however, has been largely random, concentrated in the countryside, and often carried out by more or less independent police units or local political bosses. In Brazil and the Southern Cone, it acquired a much more coherent character, coordinated by specialized security agencies like the Brazilian SNI (National Information Service) or the Chilean DINA (National Intelligence Directorate) or run through the military services themselves, as in Argentina. In Central America, the bulk of the state-sponsored terror was accomplished by networks linking military and police units with civilian organizations like El Salvador's ORDEN (National Democratic Organization), designed to mobilize significant portions of the population in a fight against "subversion," defined as any activity that challenged established economic and political arrangements.[2]

The suppression of politics and the widespread repression of dissent are only two expressions of the relative autonomy of authoritarian regimes from the societies they governed.[3] Equally striking in retrospect was the ability of these regimes to develop and implement economic policies at variance with the interests of important sectors of the elite. The neoliberal experiments of the Southern Cone are the most striking example. Here, military governments backed economic teams representing relatively pure versions of the monetarist orthodoxy then gaining strength throughout the West. While economic elites were generally willing to swallow the stabilization policies that these regimes initially imposed and, indeed, greeted with enthusiasm prescriptions for scaling back state spending and the privatization of state-run enterprises, other measures, such as tight credit policies, trade liberalization, and the subsequent influx of foreign investment, seriously threatened much of the industrial sector in Chile, Uruguay, and Argentina—so much so that observers have spoken of the de-industrialization of these economies during the late 1970s and early 1980s.[4]

In Brazil, similarly, heavy state investment in steel, petroleum, energy, and other lines of production, accompanied by the rapid growth of foreign investment in significant subsectors of the economy, eventually prompted complaints from Brazilian industrialists that they were being squeezed out of markets that should by rights belong to them and out of the process of decisionmaking that determined their chances.[5] In all these cases, however, the state was able, by and large, to impose its will on the business community for a considerable period of time, distributing the substantial gains from the "boom" years of the late 1970s to international capital, the largest enterprises of the industrial sector, and, in the cases where monetarist policy dominated, to financial interests.[6]

Eventually, of course, the piper had to be paid, but widespread pressure for change did not develop until these regimes proved themselves as vulnerable to economic failure as their more democratic counterparts. The change came precipitously, for most, in 1981 and 1982, but the roots of the crisis that engulfed the authoritarian regimes of Brazil, Mexico, and the Southern Cone reach back through the illusory boom of the 1970s to the consequences of the import-substitution industrialization (ISI) policies of the postwar period in societies characterized by extreme inequality. While these policies made possible the enormous industrial expansion of the more developed countries of the region, key elements in their design impeded the concomitant expansion of exports needed to finance development, while low-wage policies and inequality blocked the development of significant internal markets. As Jeffrey Sachs has shown, the fault lay not in heavy state investment, regulation, or taxation. Latin American countries are comparable to their more successful East Asian counterparts in most of these respects, and in regard to rate of taxation they actually lag considerably behind. The key to the slow growth in exports lay rather in exchange rate and trade policies that were prejudicial to the export sector throughout Latin America.[7]

Many Latin American countries did attempt to expand and diversify exports in the 1970s. Nevertheless, the more developed Latin American economies had not achieved either the level of exports or the security of markets that Taiwan, Korea, and other Asian exporters enjoyed by the time financial crisis engulfed the world economy in the early 1980s (see Table 2.1); and the industrial expansion that had begun in Central America in the late 1950s ran into serious difficulties by 1970. For various reasons, moreover, Latin American countries (like their Asian counterparts) had acquired considerable debt in the course of the 1970s. In Mexico and Brazil, debt financed not just capital spending but growing fiscal deficits. In the Southern Cone, where military governments had imposed monetarist formulas for economic restructuring, a combination of policies encouraged enormous inflows of foreign capital that financed short-lived commercial booms and disastrous speculative bubbles. The bubbles burst in 1981 in response to a downturn in terms of trade, rising international interest rates, and a slowdown in lending, but it was the fall of petroleum prices and Mexico's subsequent declaration of an inability to meet current interest payments in November of 1982 that brought the debt crisis into full view.

The economic collapse hit business hard. The World Bank reported in 1984 that "in Argentina bankruptcies and judicial interventions increased from fifty-two in 1977 to three hundred in 1981. In Chile several hundred bankruptcies were reported in 1982." Unemployment increased precipitously, and consumption fell by 2 to 10 percent during 1981–1982 in countries that had seen both rising employment levels and rising real wages during the 1970s.[8] By 1983, the authoritarian regimes in these countries were in disarray. To one degree or another all had had to make concessions to both aggrieved businesspeople and the larger populace while struggling to meet international obligations. Argentina's military government resorted to a catastrophic military adventure in the Malvinas War in an attempt to divert public attention from the crisis. Chile's General Pinochet replaced the hardline monetarists (the so-called Chicago Boys) with economists more willing to use state powers to shore up crumbling financial institutions and to cushion the blow of the recession on incomes.[9] Brazil and Uruguay's military leaders struggled to maintain their control of the process of democratization. And Mexico's new administration

Table 2.1   Share of Exports in GDP for Selected Latin American and East Asian
            Countries

	1965	1983	1987	1991
Mexico	9	20	7	16
Brazil	8	8	9	10
Argentina	8	13	10	11
Chile	14	24	34	36
Peru	16	21	9	9
Colombia	11	10	19	21
Indonesia	5	25	26	27
Republic of Korea	9	37	45	29
Malaysia	44	54	64	81
Thailand	18	22	30	38

Source: World Development Reports, 1985, 1989, and 1993, Tables 5 and 9 (Washington,
D.C.: IBRD/World Bank).

attempted to regain the confidence of the business community, badly shaken
by the nationalization of the banks in late 1982, while applying harsh austerity measures in the face of growing popular challenges. At the same time,
Mexico led the way in extracting new terms from its creditors and from the
International Monetary Fund (IMF), without, however, gaining significant relief in a badly deteriorated international economic environment.

In each of these cases, civilian opposition could claim that it was the
nature of authoritarian rule itself that had contributed to the crisis. The
very autonomy that had attracted business elites to authoritarian solutions
in an earlier period worked to exclude those same elites from consultation
and influence on economic policy making.[10] If "the flaw in the pluralist
heaven," as E. E. Schattschneider put it, is that "the heavenly chorus sings
with a strong upper class accent," at least one important flaw in the authoritarian heaven appears to have been the failure of military governors to
listen to even so restricted a "heavenly chorus."[11]

Representatives of the popular sector, for their part, could argue that
the foreign debt for which the population was being forced to endure such
sacrifices was illegitimately imposed on their societies and ought to be re-
pudiated along with the governments that had acquired it. Popular protests
multiplied throughout the region, in some cases forcing cancellation of
policies imposed in an effort to manage the debt.[12] Authoritarian regimes,
it appeared, were no more adept at managing either economies or popular
protest than their democratic predecessors.[13] Societal pressures, finally,
contributed to considerable concern within authoritarian establishments
themselves about the costs of continued authoritarian rule. Military establishments in particular found themselves increasingly divided over the
question as factions, and in some cases whole branches of the armed

services became convinced that authoritarian rule threatened the integrity of the military institution itself.[14] What had appeared to be autonomous states backed by powerful repressive apparatuses came apart, in some cases suddenly, under pressures from within and from the larger society.

The restoration of democratic regimes in the Andean countries, by contrast, pursued a more clearly political logic. As Conaghan, Malloy, and Abugattas put it, "Democracy resurfaced as the political formula to cure the severe representation crisis induced by military authoritarianism."[15] In Peru and Ecuador in particular, business opposition to the reformist tendencies of the military governments were exacerbated by the military's efforts to marginalize business leaders from decisionmaking. Interest groups representing business gained in strength and professional acumen in the effort to counter governmental policy and were instrumental in furthering neoliberal discourse against what was seen as the heavily statist orientation of the military governments. The transition to democracy took place, therefore, not in the context of the generalized economic crisis of the 1980s but in the late 1970s, before the crisis broke. Although we might expect the democratic regimes that emerged to be much more fragile than their counterparts elsewhere on the continent because they replaced less onerous military regimes and could be saddled with the blame for the ensuing crisis, they persisted throughout the troubled decade of the 1980s with only rumors of military opposition.

Each of these regimes, moreover, saw important experiments in neoliberal economics, this time under civilian administrations but no less oblivious to political pressures than similar efforts in the Southern Cone. In Bolivia in particular, under the Paz Estenssoro government, neoliberal policy was seen as part of a battle to reconstitute state authority in the face of widespread corruption and bureaucratic overextension. As Paz's Minister of Planning Gonzalo Sánchez de Lozada put it, "The fundamental institutions of the state's productive apparatus have been feudalized, corruption has been generalized and is being institutionalized, and the mechanisms of control and oversight have stopped operating. In this context, the state is unarmed and lacks the capacity to execute and implement any economic policy that the government proposes to put into practice. Therefore, the first political goal consists of reestablishing the authority of the state over society."[16] As in the Southern Cone (and in Mexico today), the neoliberal project was associated with the ideal of a smaller, but, perhaps paradoxically, stronger state. As in the Southern Cone, its implementation depended heavily upon the concentration of power in the executive—a function, in the democratic cases, of the strengthened presidential powers bequeathed already strong presidential systems by outgoing military regimes.[17] And, as in the Southern Cone, business opposition eventually forced reconsideration of the neoliberal policies and, in Peru especially, a short-lived but disastrous return to essentially heterodox solutions under Alan Garcia.

The situation of the Central American countries in the late 1970s, by contrast, reflects lower levels of industrial development and unionization and, more tellingly, the failure of military reformism to take hold and alter power relations within these countries. The long personal dictatorship of the Somozas in Nicaragua and the increasingly repressive military governments of El Salvador and Guatemala faced growing unrest in the 1970s from elements of the business community and middle class and from an increasingly organized popular sector. Repression and unrest in fact fed upon one another in countries where control of political power had traditionally granted effective control of labor and control over labor provided elites with their only major hedge against the volatile and precarious international markets that dominated economic activity.

Economic developments after 1950, moreover, had served to exacerbate social tensions and provided the grounds for the political activation of urban and rural labor that elites found so threatening in the decades that followed. The modernization and expansion of export agriculture from the 1950s on and the creation of the Central American Common Market in 1960 together provoked increasing urbanization and the growth of an industrial workforce and urban middle class while contributing to increasing desperation in the countryside. The growing organization of urban workers and the middle class reverberated in the countryside, where repression provoked the radicalization of forces for reform.[18] The deepening of guerrilla conflicts in Nicaragua in 1978 and in El Salvador and Guatemala in 1979–1980 are directly correlated with the increasing desperation of popular sector leaders (and in the case of Nicaragua, of business and church leaders) under the repression of the late 1970s. The mild reformist military government of Honduras averted this outcome, though the military's support for the contra war and growing repression in the 1980s was followed by the first signs of guerrilla activity at the end of the decade.[19]

Democracy and Economic Reconstruction: Contradictory Imperatives?

The return to democratic forms that started in the Andean nations in the late 1970s continued, in Brazil and the Southern Cone, as both a return and a renewal of democratic institutions and practices. Mexico, likewise, has seen growing pressure for democratization, and all of Central America was, by 1990, in civilian hands, although most of these regimes could be described as democratic only in a restricted sense.[20]

At the same time, regimes throughout the region found themselves compelled to direct often painful processes of economic adjustment under circumstances that were by no means encouraging from an economic point of view. By 1985, when most of the region was under democratic forms of governance, foreign and domestic debt had risen to unprecedented levels, and most economies were scarcely in a position to restart, much less regain the considerable losses of the preceding few years. The situation changed little over the next several years. Though debt had increased enormously in the 1970s, as late as 1979 Brazil's external debt was just over $50 billion, and most of this was private sector obligations. By 1984, Brazil's external indebtedness had passed $100 billion, and the government had assumed the bulk of it. Brazil and Mexico had owed just over $3 billion in 1970, Argentina close to $2 billion.[21] Interest payments had spiraled as well. As a percentage of exports, interest payments for Argentina went from 7.0 percent in 1980 to 32.6 percent in 1985, for Brazil from 18.0 percent to 19.3 percent, and for Mexico from 15.8 percent to 25.3 percent.[22] Rising interest rates and a difficult international economic environment were reflected in increasingly onerous debt service ratios (interest plus amortization as a percent of export earnings—see Table 2.2 for comparative data).

Terms of trade turned decidedly against Latin American exporters in the 1980s, as the world economy entered a prolonged recession and First World countries adopted increasingly protectionist policies. (See Table 2.3.) Declines in terms of trade were more disastrous for primary commodity exporters like the countries of Central America and Bolivia (whose tin mining sector collapsed in the 1980s, driving many miners into the lowlands and coca production). It has been estimated, in fact, that, quite apart from the effects of the military conflicts in the region, the decline in terms of trade alone accounts for the trade deficits of El Salvador, Guatemala, Honduras, and Costa Rica in the early 1980s, and that without the impact of such price changes these countries would have registered surpluses.[23] Indeed, export volume, particularly in tropical and primary commodities, *grew* overall during the period, while incomes fell or remained stagnant.

The new democracies also faced a weakened industrial base. In some cases (Chile, Argentina, and Uruguay), this was the result of the neoliberal policies of military regimes, which subjected domestic industry to overwhelming foreign competition without compensating measures (see Table 2.4). In other cases (Mexico, Brazil, and Colombia), manufacturing continued strong into 1980 but declined thereafter in face of the recession that gripped all these economies. In Central America (with the exception of Costa Rica and Nicaragua), the spurt of industrial growth that began in the 1960s was largely spent by the 1970s, and war and the regional recession brought stagnation or declines in manufacturing activity.

Nevertheless, after the first shock of the crisis, the stronger economies of the Southern Cone, Mexico, Brazil, and Colombia show substantial

Table 2.2   Debt Service Ratios

	1975	1980	1983	1986	1991
Mexico	24.9	32.1	40.0	36.8	30.9
Brazil	17.9	34.6	28.6	33.2	30.0
Argentina	22.0	17.7	25.0	50.4	48.4
Chile	27.2	21.9	18.3	30.8	33.9
Uruguay	41.2	12.4	20.6	20.9	38.2
Bolivia	15.3	27.8	32.2	23.6	14.7
Ecuador	4.4	18.9	19.9	32.3	14.7
Peru	25.6	31.1	19.8	14.4	13.4
Costa Rica	10.7	16.8	51.6	26.3	18.4
El Salvador	9.0	3.3	16.9	18.0	5.8
Guatemala	1.8	2.4	12.1	23.3	6.7
Honduras	4.7	10.1	14.8	18.5	15.8
Nicaragua	12.0	16.0	17.6	13.0	62.4
Colombia	10.9	9.0	22.2	27.6	13.8
Venezuela	5.3	13.3	15.3	28.5	18.7

Source: 1975–1986: *World Debt Tables, 1987–88,* Vol. 2, Country Tables (Washington, D.C.: IBRD/World Bank, 1988); 1991: *World Development Report, 1993,* Table 24.

growth in export activity from the mid-1980s on, in both manufacturing and agriculture (though Argentine manufacturing activity was nearly stagnant). Costa Rica, Ecuador, and Venezuela, too, show substantial gains, though Venezuela in particular could scarcely recoup entirely from the loss of oil revenues as prices dropped during the decade. The hard hit primary commodity producers (Bolivia, Peru, and the Central American nations) won only uncertain advances (most notably, Guatemala) or saw actual declines in export earnings. But the relative success of some in expanding exports should not obscure the difficulty of the situation, which is clear in the overall stagnation of manufacturing activity (see Table 2.4). GDP growth has in fact been minimal or negative throughout the decade, as Table 2.5 shows, an effect as much of the enormous weight of the debt as of the world recession and the decline in the terms of trade Latin American nations face.

The new governments of the region have met the crisis with a variety of measures, but the majority have attempted to gain control of the inflation and balance of payments problems released by the international situation with a mixed bag of orthodox and heterodox policies while undertaking major economic restructuring along neoliberal lines. Argentina, Brazil, and most recently Mexico created new currencies (Brazil twice); Brazil's Collor de Mello froze private bank holdings upon taking office; and Mexico, Argentina, and Brazil have resorted to wage and price freezes in attempts to block inflation. Countries throughout the region, largely under urging from the IMF and World Bank, have cut government spending,

Table 2.3   Terms of Trade, 1970–1988 (index 1980 = 100)

	1970	1980	1985	1988
Mexico	108.2	100.0	97.7	66.8
Brazil	185.4	100.0	89.1	116.8
Argentina	138.4	100.0	89.8	86.2
Chile	238.3	100.0	79.3	94.2
Uruguay	197.3	100.0	87.2	99.4
Bolivia	68.9	100.0	84.4	57.0
Ecuador	129.8	100.0	93.7	50.1
Peru	130.5	100.0	80.8	79.8
Costa Rica	131.3	100.0	94.8	98.1
El Salvador	111.2	100.0	96.2	86.2
Guatemala	111.4	100.0	86.7	87.5
Honduras	122.9	100.0	93.1	101.9
Nicaragua	139.9	100.0	85.2	84.4
Colombia	76.5	100.0	98.3	70.0
Venezuela	14.6	100.0	93.4	41.5

Source: World Tables, 1989–90 Edition, (Washington, D.C.: IBRD/World Bank, 1990).

sold off state enterprises, and strengthened tax systems in efforts to slash government deficits. Such policies have met with varying degrees of success. Argentina and Brazil's earlier efforts were manifest failures. More recent initiatives await judgment. Bolivia's "shock treatment" under the Paz Estenssoro government blocked the continent's worst case of hyperinflation, and the Paz Zamora government appeared in 1990 dedicated to preserving the gains of that effort. Mexico's Economic Solidarity Pact of December 1988 continued into 1993 holding back inflation, without, however, achieving the announced goal of single-digit rates. Deficits proved harder to control, though Mexico enjoyed significant success with draconian cuts, in part because a significant portion of government budgets throughout the region continue to be consumed by debt payments.

The costs, both of short-term anti-inflationary measures and of the longer-term efforts to restructure Latin American economies (the so-called structural adjustment policies), have been enormous, with most of the weight falling on working and middle classes. In Mexico, where a dominant-party government with considerable political leverage over organized labor has been able to impose harsh austerity measures with some consistency through most of the decade, real industrial wages have fallen 45 percent since 1980.[24] Unemployment was a persistent effect of the recession throughout the region. Mexico, for example, lost some three hundred thousand jobs in an economy that needs to create a million new jobs a year just to keep up with population growth, and jobs continue to evaporate despite significant new investment, most of which, it appears, has gone into the

Table 2.4 Growth in Manufacturing and Exports, 1970–1988 (millions of 1980 U.S. dollars)

	Manufacturing as % of GDP				Manufacturing Exports				Non-Fuel Primary Commodity Exports			
	1970	1980	1985	1988	1970	1980	1985	1988	1970	1980	1985	1988
Mexico	22.1	24.1	24.0	24.0	1,279	2,234	5,200	14,256	2,532	2,767	3,190	3,475
Brazil	28.8	31.4	28.8	29.0[a]	1,123	7,770	14,469	17,093	6,746	11,973	15,793	17,200
Argentina	27.5	25.0	23.1	23.1	682	1,861	2,171	2,377	4,204	5,883	7,233	6,704
Chile	27.4	24.4	21.9[b]	22.3[b]	95	448	453	954	2,069	4,196	4,791	5,346
Uruguay	30.1[c]	25.9	22.6	23.9	142	405	384	658	553	655	699	738
Bolivia	13.4[b]	18.8	12.8	13.7	25	28	5	26	783	692	312	377
Ecuador	19.5	19.3	19.3	16.9[b]	10	74	106	222	591	843	1,003	1,709
Peru	22.6	22.4	20.9	20.8	41	666	858	607	2,642	2,455	2,280	2,039
Costa Rica	21.9[d]	28.3[d]	27.7[d]	27.9[d]	126	354	377	515	511	671	725	748
El Salvador	16.7	16.2	15.0[b]	15.6[b]	198	255	198	199	515	799	557	479
Guatemala	16.2[b]	16.9[b]	16.1[b]	16.0[a,b]	240	359	381	439	617	1,111	928	713
Honduras	13.8	15.1	15.3	15.0[a]	51	102	96	103	517	708	779	793
Nicaragua	22.3	26.7[b]	28.6[b]	32.0[b]	83	57	43	25	430	346	334	249
Columbia	24.2	25.9	24.5	24.6[a]	233	804	728	1,353	2,385	3,034	2,567	3,453
Venezuela	13.3	16.4	20.0	19.9	104	330	717	1,755	517	715	1,126	2,593

Notes: a. 1987
b. As % of GNP
c. Industry as % of GDP
d. Industry as % of GNP
Source: Calculated from *World Tables: 1989–90 Edition* (Washington, D.C.: IBRD/World Bank, 1990).

Table 2.5   Growth of Production, 1965–1980 and 1980–1987

	Average Annual Growth Rates					
	GDP		Agriculture		Manufacturing	
	1965–1980	1980–1987	1965–1980	1980–1987	1965–1980	1980–1987
Mexico	6.5	0.5	3.2	1.4	7.4	0.0
Brazil	9.0	3.3	3.8	2.6	9.6	1.2
Argentina	3.5	–0.3	1.4	1.6	2.7	0.0
Chile	1.9	1.0	1.6	3.6	0.6	0.9
Uruguay	2.4	–1.3	1.0	0.2	3.1[a]	–3.2[a]
Bolivia	4.5	–2.1	3.8	2.5	5.4	–6.9
Ecuador	8.7	1.5	3.4	3.6	11.5	0.2
Peru	3.9	1.2	1.0	3.0	3.8	1.5
Costa Rica	6.2	1.8	4.2	1.7	8.7[a]	2.0[a]
El Salvador	4.3	–0.4	3.6	–1.6	4.6	–0.3
Guatemala	5.9	–0.7	—	—	—	—
Honduras	5.0	1.3	2.0	1.7	7.5	1.9
Nicaragua	2.6	–0.3	3.3	–0.2	5.2	0.6
Colombia	5.6	2.9	4.3	2.1	6.2	3.2
Venezuela	3.7	0.2	3.9	3.5	5.8	3.0

Note: a. Industry (growth in manufacturing, as the most dynamic aspect of industrial production, is the preferred statistic).
Source: World Development Report, 1989 (Washington, D.C.: IBRD/World Bank, 1989).

stock market and government bonds.[25] Consumption declined in Mexico, Chile, Uruguay, El Salvador, Guatemala, and Nicaragua between 1980 and 1987. Government expenditures for education, health care, housing, and welfare fell throughout Latin America during the decade.[26]

Structural adjustment is broadly part of the turn toward the market that began to grip national economic planners throughout the world in the late 1970s. While it is important to note that the programs currently in vogue are a good bit more flexible than the dogmatic and simplistic monetarism of the experiments in the Southern Cone, structural adjustment programs, even in the hands of democratic governments, have generally demanded that working people bear the brunt of adjustment and have tended to favor financial interests and international capital over domestic industrialists. This is as true in the Mexico of Carlos Salinas de Gortari, where representatives of small and medium manufacturers have consistently if quietly opposed policies enthusiastically supported by the more powerful National Chamber of Industry, as it was in Margaret Thatcher's England in the early 1980s or in Augusto Pinochet's Chile in the late 1970s.[27] Restructuring involves chiefly an opening to international competition designed to weed out "inefficient" producers and stimulate exports. The program also calls for the scaling back of government intervention in the economy, chiefly through cutbacks in government spending and the privatization of parastatals, but also through streamlining government regulation of business. By 1990, major efforts in this respect had been undertaken in Mexico, Argentina, Chile, Bolivia, Ecuador, and Costa Rica; and the conservative governments that dominated most of the region were either continuing similar policies bequeathed them by their predecessors or moving to adopt at least some elements of the package.

Such policies, and the austerity measures that accompany them, are often extremely unpopular. Government cutbacks mean extensive layoffs; the sale, and in some cases dismemberment, of parastatals can result in layoffs or harsher labor-management relations; reduced government spending often entails the withdrawal of subsidies on basic goods and services, from public transportation to housing to bread and tortillas; foreign competition means bankruptcy and unemployment for some and the prospect of increased foreign presence in the national economy. All of these measures have provoked protests throughout the region, in some cases confronting democratic governments with the very forces that once played an important role in overthrowing their authoritarian predecessors. In some cases, such protests have won important concessions not only from governments but from the IMF and foreign creditors.[28]

It is remarkable that, despite their economic difficulties and the unpopularity of the measures they have taken, civilian governments have survived as well as they have. Whether or not this is an indication that the cycle of dictatorship and democracy that has characterized much of the region is at an end is the question we will consider in the next section.

Authoritarianism in Retreat: Prospects for Democracy

Authoritarian governments throughout Latin America retreated during the 1980s before the onslaught of a newly activated civil society. In some cases, no doubt, liberalization or even withdrawal was dictated by forces within the authoritarian coalition and in other cases, under pressure from foreign allies.[29] Nevertheless, throughout the region a reorganized or newly organized civil society has actively confronted authoritarian regimes and their democratic successors, demanding to be heard and asserting its right to be heard. Independent labor movements sprang up and grew in Brazil and Mexico, contesting the government's hold on older unions and insisting on democratic procedures in union affairs. In situations as diverse as those of Chile, Guatemala, and El Salvador, unions decimated by years of repression rebuilt themselves in the mid-1980s to contest government economic policy and challenge the regime. In Brazil,

Chile, and El Salvador, the Church made itself a shelter for dissent and played a strong independent role in documenting human rights abuses and demanding an end to the repression; and throughout the region, grassroots religious organizations (the so-called base Christian community movement) promoted participation and activism by the poor, generating a new leadership for local and regional organizations of all kinds.[30] Neighborhood associations, peasants' organizations, women's groups, professional associations, and business chambers asserted their independence and struggled to build effective, and in many cases, democratic organizations in the 1980s. Even in Colombia, Venezuela, and Costa Rica, where elite accommodation had achieved more or less stable, if in some respects limited, democratic rule throughout the 1960s and 1970s, new groups formed and entered the political arena during this period.[31]

The resurgence of civil society is widely thought to contribute to the democratization of the region in two ways: First, by providing autonomous channels of interest representation, such organizations have challenged attempts by authoritarian states to either silence or coopt societal demands. Second, arising as many of these organizations have in opposition to the antidemocratic practices of government controlled groups, new and reconstituted interest groups have devoted considerable efforts to developing and consolidating democratic practices, both internally and among themselves. In the process of furthering their own claims against the state, moreover, such groups have been impelled to challenge the undemocratic practices with which they have been met and, in many cases, to join large movements for democratization.

The ability of a renewed civil society to challenge authoritarian states, however, is not without its limits. While regimes such as the military government of Brazil in the 1970s or the dominant-party Mexican state today, which pursue liberalization for their own reasons, may find it difficult to contain a newly empowered civil society, in other settings brutal repression or simple intransigence may set back the organization of such groups or silence them, at least temporarily, as in El Salvador in the 1970s and early 1980s or in Chile under General Pinochet. Broad popular opposition to a regime, moreover, does not automatically effect a transition to democracy, nor need such a transition, once started, necessarily satisfy the concrete demands of opposition groups.[32]

Regimes, moreover, need someone with whom to negotiate the specifically political terms of a transition, as Alfred Stepan has argued; this means that forces in civil society must submit to the mediating efforts of parties and politicians. Civil society is apt to distrust politics and politicians, however, on at least two grounds: the unsatisfactory performance of politicians before or during the military regime and the necessity, imposed by the political process, of compromising the central demands of at least portions of civil society. Indeed, insofar as any transition from authoritarianism requires a certain class compromise to satisfy the fears of the antidemocratic right, popular organizations of various kinds are apt to find their substantive demands frustrated.[33] In this respect, a strengthened civil society may contribute to the complexity and difficulty of any easy democratic settlement.

One of the remarkable features of the current situation is that the new democracies have held, generally speaking. While some writers have emphasized the importance of political pacts among major actors in muting destabilizing pressures on new democracies, the recent experience of Latin American countries suggests that larger economic and political factors are at work in the relative success of civilian regimes in managing pressures from below and staving off intervention from the military representatives of the right.[34] On the economic side, while the crisis and the policies intended to surmount it have struck hardest at the livelihoods of working people, organized opposition to those policies has been muted or unsuccessful in many cases precisely because of the magnitude of the crisis. Organized labor, in particular, has lost considerable leverage in the face of increasing unemployment and continuing recession. In Bolivia, the militant Bolivian Workers Confederation (COB) failed to carry through a general strike in April of 1990 against the Paz Zamora government in large part because the traditional mainstay of the movement, Bolivian miners, had been decimated by mine closings in the early 1980s. In Argentina, the Peronist government of Carlos Menem faced down rebellious unions through 1989 and early 1990, and Mexico's PRI (Institutional Revolutionary Party) maintained continued, if sometimes shaky, control over the labor movement throughout the austerity program of the later De la Madrid and Salinas administrations.[35] Though John Walton finds a "modal pattern" among countries in the form of protest undertaken, with strikes more common where unionization is well developed and demonstrations where opposition parties have some strength, it is noteworthy that food riots and relatively anomic demonstrations run through all the countries affected by austerity measures.[36] Riots in Venezuela in March 1989 (claiming some three hundred lives) and in Argentina in May of the same year, while they forced democratic governments to attempt to meet popular demands (and provoked careful attempts on the part of the Menem government to sidestep future outbreaks as new austerity measures were imposed), did not seriously threaten either regime.

The lack of significant, organized antidemocratic activity on either the right or the left in the new democracies of the early 1990s must be attributed as well to changes in both elite and popular attitudes. It is important not to overstate the argument. While some have made a great deal of the supposedly authoritarian political culture of the Ibero-American heritage, others have noted the long pedigree of liberalism in Latin America and the peculiar resistance of even military authoritarians to dispensing with democratic forms and rationalizations.[37] Even if, as many have argued, social actors in Argentina tended to treat democracy from a largely instrumentalist perspective up through the 1970s, it is not at all clear that this was the effect of an inbred political culture and not merely a rational response to the existing rules of the game after the fall of Perón.[38]

Whether or not Latin America has witnessed a retreat from a long-standing political culture of authoritarianism, however, most observers agree that the authoritarian interlude contributed to a revaluation of democracy on the part of significant portions of both the right and the left. There is little doubt that this trend has been reinforced by the collapse of communism in Eastern Europe in the fall of 1989. From the peaceful withdrawal of the Sandinistas in the face of a crushing electoral defeat, to the return to civilian life of two of the most important Colombian guerilla groups in 1983 and 1990, to the turn toward electoral politics on the part of El Salvador's FLMN (Faribundo Martí National Liberation Front), the revolutionary fervors of the 1960s and 1970s have abated. The participation of large sectors of the business communities of Brazil, the Southern Cone, and the Andean nations in the drive toward democratization likewise suggests a reduced propensity on the right to go knocking on the door of the military.

Again, it would be well not to exaggerate the change in attitudes. Much of the Latin American military apparently remains committed to a notion of internal subversion that lumps human rights organizations, parties of the left, and the handful of armed opposition groups still left in the region in one bag.[39] And elements of the militaries of Argentina, Brazil, and Chile are eager to defend their role in their respective "dirty wars on terrorism," even in the face of exposures of severe human rights abuses.[40]

The limits of the wave of democratization are apparent everywhere in fact. The peace accords that ended the civil war in El Salvador failed to grant civilians effective control over the military budget, just as Colombia's popular Constituent Assembly refused to find new constitutional means to curb military abuses. Though Guatemala averted a presidential coup de main, the interim president, Ramiro de León Carpio, despite a distinguished career in defense of human rights, could not curb increasing human rights abuses or effectively challenge military prerogatives. The double hostage crisis of the summer of 1993, in which competing bands of former contras and ex-Sandinista militiamen held prominent Nicaraguans captive over political issues, was resolved peacefully, only to issue in a new stalemate between the major political forces of the country. The Colombian government was engaged throughout 1989 and 1990 in a protracted battle with drug interests, complicated by links between police, military, and the drug cartels battling both guerrillas and the civilian left, hundreds of whose militants have been assassinated since 1985. Despite the new constitution and political opening, by 1993 a new counterinsurgency campaign was in full swing, bringing with it complaints of repression of grassroots and left political activists.

Constitutional crises, moreover, wracked Brazil, Venezuela, and Guatemala, where presidents were removed for malfeasance and, in the Guatemalan case, an attempted coup de main. Alberto Fujimori's presidential coup was apparently highly popular in Peru, but his extraconstitutional government had not succeeded by late 1993 in winning over other political actors or rebuilding a competitive electoral system. The Fujimori government's battle against the Sendero Luminoso insurgency has experienced increasing success since the capture of Abimael Guzmán in 1992, but has cost thousands of lives, with police and military implicated in severe human rights abuses, including the massacre of prisoners in the prison rebellion of 1986. The government has refused to recognize Interamerican Commission of Human Rights charges in most of the cases.[41] Human rights groups have also singled out Mexico and Brazil for censure on human rights abuses, while the Mexican opposition claims that political repression had increased considerably under the Salinas de Gortari government, despite the rhetoric of democratization. Recent electoral reforms were carried out without the support of the major opposition parties, who continue to claim that the government is preparing for massive electoral fraud in the 1994 presidential elections.[42] Argentina's Carlos Menem began his career by making peace with a military still unwilling to repent for the "dirty war" on civilians in the late 1970s. The success of his economic program has brought both the president and his Perónist Party considerable popular support. But Menem's efforts to win constitutional revisions to allow him a second term in office and the government's apparent involvement in efforts to intimidate and silence opposition in the media call into question once again the Perónists' democratic convictions.

Democracy, moreover, has not significantly altered the determination of governments throughout the region to continue to ask the working classes to bear the costs of adjustment. Though Brazil and Mexico both experienced some easing of the debt burden, recessionary policy and political upheaval in Brazil and the radicalization of the neoliberal program in Mexico seem to portend continuing unemployment and falling incomes for many in the lower and middle sectors.[43] The economic initiative announced by the five Central American presidents in June 1990 involved efforts to revitalize the Central American Common Market, link renegotiation of the countries' debt, and rebuild infrastructure—but no provisions to right the severe maldistribution of resources that has prevented previous such efforts from reaching the working classes.[44]

Conclusion

The 1980s thus brought tremendous changes in the political economy of Latin America—but without fundamentally altering the distribution of political and economic power. Indeed, the combination of neoliberal policies and economic crisis resulted in a considerable redistribution of wealth upwards—just as in the United States during the same period. The resurgence of democracy, moreover, has been accompanied by the renewed power of business groups, especially those oriented to the international trade and financial markets. But whether with business cooperation or in relative isolation from interest group pressures, the virtually continent-wide adoption of neoliberal and market-oriented policies has meant a significant change in development policy and, with it, the structure of Latin American economies.

Though export diversification and promotion policies had been introduced in the early 1970s in most of the countries of Latin America, the neoliberal governments of the late 1970s and 1980s broke definitively with the import substitution industrialization model of the post–World War II period. In Chile and Argentina under the military and in Mexico under the Salinas de Gortari administration, that break has been sharp and painful, with domestically oriented and small and medium manufacturing concerns and their workers bearing the brunt of the adjustment.[45] In Colombia, recent announcement of a step-by-step reduction of tariffs over the next five years indicates that the break will be gradual, like the largely successful export diversification drive of the 1960s and 1970s.[46] Costa Rica's Rafael Calderón seemed to be offering a characteristically Costa Rican "neoliberalism with a human face," in combining renewed austerity with promises of governmental efforts to provide better housing and medical care to the poor. Whatever the temper of the change, however, Latin American economies are decidedly trimmer, decidedly more open to international trade and foreign investment, and decidedly more export oriented than they were ten or fifteen years ago. That some of the weight loss may have included important industrial muscle, and that the exercise has not attracted significant new investment and indeed may have crippled the government's ability to deliver needed stimulus to these economies, remain major worries throughout the region.

Both the renewal of democracy in Latin America and the move to more open market economies find considerable support, rhetorical if not material, in the current international environment. Indeed, in the wake of events in Eastern Europe, it is often difficult to remember that the worldwide trends that seemed to peak there began in Latin America. It may also be difficult to remember that the human rights policies of the Carter administration did much to focus attention on human rights issues and gave considerable aid and comfort to democratic forces within Latin America, or that the accession of Ronald Reagan to the presidency of the United States temporarily set back efforts to force repressive governments from power. Apart from the ideological currents, however, the wrenching changes in the world economy in the 1980s played a tremendous role in shaking authoritarian claims to special powers of economic management, as they have contributed to the crisis that Latin American governments continue to struggle with. The policy choices with which civilian governments have confronted this crisis, however, while certainly conditioned by the economic situation and by prevailing notions in the international financial community, also reflect domestic configurations of power and influence and the ideological hegemony, perhaps temporary, of a new class of technocrats, many of them trained in the United States.

Finally, in no small part due to the efforts of these groups, the period has seen the shrinking of governments in much of the region, accompanied by the growth of an autonomous and combative civil society. Efforts to meet debt obligations and halt inflation have included vigorous attacks on fiscal deficits, including in some cases tax reforms, but demanding in all cases cutbacks in government services, trimming government employment rolls, and scaling back or eliminating subsidies to consumers and producers alike. Brazil, Argentina, Chile, Mexico, Bolivia, Ecuador, and Venezuela have all undertaken to sell off state-run enterprises in an effort to acquire cash or eliminate parastatals that had become a drain on national treasuries. Often these measures have been accompanied by rhetorical attacks on the inefficiency and corruption of big government and, at times, by more or less self-conscious efforts to strengthen government by reducing its size and scope. Whether the states that are emerging from this experience are more or less "autonomous" than they were in the past remains open to question. What is clear is that they are confronted today by a larger number of interest groups, better organized and more firmly committed to maintaining their autonomy vis-à-vis the state than ever before. While the "flaw in the pluralist heaven," in Latin America as in the United States, is that some interest groups have proven more equal than others, there remains considerable hope that the efflorescence of civil society will remain a permanent force for democracy, and for economic justice, in Latin America, whatever the current proclivities of its elites.

Notes

1. See Guillermo O'Donnell, *Modernization and Bureaucratic-Authoritarianism* (Berkeley: Institute of International Studies, University of California, 1973, 1979).

2. On the development of paramilitary "death squads" in El Salvador and Guatemala, see the two volumes by Michael McClintock, *The American Connection* (London: Zed Books, 1985). The intelligence agencies of the military regimes of South America have not been extensively studied; but see Chapter 2 of Alfred Stepan's *Rethinking Military Politics: Brazil and the Southern Cone* (Princeton, N.J.: Princeton University Press, 1988).

3. It may be no accident that the notion of the "relative autonomy of the state" achieved considerable scholarly circulation in the late 1970s and early 1980s as these states demonstrated their capacity to operate in isolation not only from the mass of their citizens but in many cases from elements of the very coalitions that encouraged military intervention in the first place.

4. On the neoconservative military regimes, the best economic analysis is José Ramos, *Neoconservative Economics in the Southern Cone of Latin America, 1973–1983* (Baltimore: Johns Hopkins University Press, 1986). See also Alejandro Foxley, *Latin American Experiments in Neoconservative Economics* (Berkeley: University of California Press, 1983).

5. See Fernando H. Cardoso, "Entrepreneurs and the Transition Process: The Brazilian Case," in *Transitions from Authoritarian Rule: Comparative Perspectives*, Guillermo O'Donnell, Philippe C. Schmitter, and Laurence Whitehead, eds., (Baltimore: Johns Hopkins University Press, 1988), pp. 137–153.

6. The "autonomy" of the state with regard to business is less clear in Mexico, where the oil surplus enabled the government to lavish benefits on nearly all sectors up through 1981. With the onset of crisis and the appearance of widespread capital flight, however, President López Portillo nationalized the banks, prompting a break with the business community that is only just now on the mend.. The storm of business protest that followed the nationalization arguably had a great deal to do with the neoconservative and probusiness thrust of subsequent administrations. See Sylvia Maxfield and Ricardo Anzaldúa, eds., *Government and Private Sector in Contemporary Mexico*, Monograph Series, Vol. 20 (La Jolla, Calif:. Center for U.S.–Mexican Studies, University of California, San Diego, 1988).

7. For detailed economic analysis, see Jeffery D. Sachs, "External Debt and Macroeconomic Performance in Latin America and East Asia," *Brookings Papers on Economic Activity* 2 (1985). On the implications of significant "undertaxation" in Latin America, see E. V. K. FitzGerald, "The Fiscal Crisis of the Latin American State," in *Taxation and Economic Development*, J. F. J. Toye, ed., (London: Frank Cass, n.d.), pp. 125–160.

8. *World Development Report, 1984* (Washington, D.C.: IBRD/World Bank, 1984), pp. 33–34.

9. Barbara Stallings's account is particularly helpful. See "Political Economy of Democratic Transition: Chile in the 1980s," in *Debt and Democracy in Latin America*, Barbara Stallings and Robert Kaufman, eds., (Boulder: Westview Press, 1989), pp. 181–200.

10. Barbara Stallings, for instance, reports that the appointment of Hernán Büchi as head of the Chilean Finance Ministry in early 1984 did a great deal to regain business support. "Whereas [Sergio] de Castro [Finance Minister and leader

of the Chicago Boys team up to 1982] refused even to receive Chilean business leaders and appeared to hold them in complete disdain, Büchi listens to them and tries to obtain their backing for government policies." Stallings, "Political Economy of Democratic Transition," p.191. Büchi was later to run (and lose) as the "Pinochet candidate" in the presidential elections of 1989.

11. Elmor Eric Schattschneider, *The Semi-Soverign People: A Realist's View of Democracy in America* (New York: Holt, Rienhart and Winston, 1960), p. 35.

12. See John Walton, "Debt, Protest, and the State in Latin America," in *Power and Popular Protest: Latin American Social Movements*, Susan Eckstein, ed., (Berkeley: University of California Press, 1989), pp. 299–328.

13. On the equivocal record of the authoritarian regimes, see Jonathan Hartlyn and Samuel A. Morley, "Political Regimes and Economic Performance in Latin America," in *Latin American Political Economy: Financial Crisis and Political Change*, Jonathan Hartlyn and Samuel A. Morley, eds., (Boulder: Westview Press, 1986), pp. 15–37; John W. Sloan, "The Policy Capabilities of Democratic Regimes in Latin America," *Latin American Research Review* 24, no. 2 (1989): pp. 113–126. In regard to the relative success of Chile's economy since 1983, it is important to note that

(1) the overall record of the military regime was considerably worse than that of previous democratic administrations and of comparable democratic countries during the same time period (see Hartlyn and Morley);

(2) policies since 1983, while continuing the general "liberalization" undertaken by the Chicago Boys, have been considerably more pragmatic, especially in the willingness to employ government to provide government, protect agriculture, and shore up the financial sector; and

(3) orthodox monetarist expectations about the inverse relationship between unemployment and rising real wages were contradicted not only by the experience under the Chicago Boys but by recent developments under the Alywin government, as well, which have seen both rising wages and declining unemployment.

See "Inter-American Development Bank," in *Economic and Social Progess in Latin America: 1989 Report* (Washington, D.C.: IDB, 1989), p. 291; for the monetarist experience and theoretical arguments, see Ramos, "Neoconservative Economics," pp. 61–64.

14. Alfred Stepan distinguishes a number of routes by which military dissatisfaction might grow. See Alfred Stepan, "Paths Toward Redemocratization: Theoretical and Comparative Considerations," in *Transitions from Authoritarian Rule: Comparative Perspectives*, pp. 64–84, and *Rethinking Military Politics*, especially Chapter 3.

15. Catherine M. Conaghan, James M. Malloy, and Luis A. Abugattas, "Business and the 'Boys': The Politics of Neoliberalism in the Central Andes," *Latin American Research Review* 25, no. 2 (1990): pp. 3–30.

16. Quoted in Conaghan, Malloy, and Abugattas, "Business and the 'Boys,'" p. 18.

17. See Conaghan, Malloy, and Abugattas, "Business and the 'Boys,'" pp. 20–26; on the dubious role of presidential systems in Latin American politics, see Scott Mainwaring, "Presidentialism in Latin America," *Latin American Research Review* 25, no. 1 (1990): pp. 157–179.

18. The connection between urban and rural organization in Central America has been little remarked, but see Jenny Pearce's account of the development and radicalization of a peasant organization in El Salvador in *Promised Land: Peasant Rebellion in Chalatenango El Salvador* (London: Latin American Bureau, 1986.) On the impact of agricultural modernization in the area, see Robert G. Williams, *Export Agriculture and the Crisis in Central America* (Chapel Hill: University of North Carolina Press, 1986), and Charles D. Brockett, *Land, Power, and Poverty: Agrarian Transformation and Political Conflict in Central America* (Boston: Unwin Hyman, 1988). For concise country studies in the context of a synthetic discussion of U.S. policy in the region, see Morris Blachman, William M. LeoGrande, and Kenneth Sharpe, eds., *Confronting Revolution: Security Through Diplomacy in Central America* (New York: Pantheon, 1986).

19. On the complex causes of guerrilla war in Latin America, see Timothy P. Wickham-Crowley, "Winners, Losers, and Also-Rans: Toward a Comparative Sociology of Latin American Guerrilla Movements," in *Power and Popular Protest*, pp. 132–181.

20. If we take "democracy" to include at a minimum the three essential conditions of

(1) meaningful and effective competition for the key positions of political power;

(2) a highly inclusive level of political participation, excluding no major adult social group; and

(3) the civil and political liberties necessary to insure the effective exercise of the above,

then it would be hard indeed to credit either Guatemala, where high levels of repression have severely restricted political competition, or El Salvador, where, until the Peace Accords of 1992, the repression had the added effect of barring a significant sector of organized opposition from normal political processes. The peace accords and consequent reincorporation of the FLMN into public life have altered the picture considerably, though serious questions persist about the willingness of powerful groups to concede political space to the left. In the Honduran case, increased repression in the late 1980s and the considerable de facto governmental power exercised by the Honduran military likewise call into question the democratic credentials of that regime. On the difficulties of definition, see John Booth's excellent discussion in "Elections and Democracy in Central America: A Framework for Analysis," in *Elections and Democracy in Central America*, John A. Booth and Mitchell A. Seligson, eds., (Chapel Hill: University of North Carolina Press, 1989). See also Larry Diamond, Juan J. Linz, and Seymour Martin Lipset, eds., "Introduction: Comparing Experiences with Democracy," in *Politics in Developing Countries: Comparing Experiences with Democracy* (Boulder: Lynne Rienner Publishers, 1990), pp. 1–38.

21. Inter-American Development Bank, *Economic and Social Progress in Latin America: 1989 Report,* Tables E-1 and E-5. Total Latin American and Caribbean debt went from $67,991.4 million in 1975 to $172,423.4 million in 1980 to $356,665.3 million in 1986. While privately held debt merely doubled, public and publicly guaranteed debt increased six times over; *World Debt Tables, 1987–1988,* Supplement 1 (Washington, D.C.: IBRD/World Bank, 1988).

22. World Bank, *World Debt Tables 2,* 1988–1989 (Washington, D.C.: World Bank, 1989).

23. Richard S. Newfarmer, "The Economics of Strife," in *Confronting Revolution*, p. 216. "By 1982 one dollar of the region's exports at 1976 values was worth only seventy-eight cents. Said differently, the region had to produce 28 percent more in export volume just to buy the same amount of imports." "The 1982 trade deficit was $1,259 million. Without the shift in terms of trade the region would have had a trade surplus of $334 million."

24. According to International Labour Office statistics. See Ian Roxborough, "Organized Labor: A Major Victim of the Crisis," in *Debt and Democracy in Latin America*, edited by Barbara Stallings and Robert Kaufman (Boulder: Westview Press, 1989), pp. 91–108. José Luis Calva, citing Mexican government statistics, puts the drop at over 50 percent since 1977—see his *Crisis agrícola y alimentaria en México, 1982–1988* (Agricultural and food crisis in Mexico, 1982–1988) (Mexico City: Fontamara, 1988), Tables XX (Appendix) and 26.

25. *La Jornada* (1993).

26. *World Development Report 1989*, Table 9; *World Development Report 1993*, Table 11. There is some debate over the effects of cutbacks on mortality rates, with some demographers finding continued declines through the period in rates of infant mortality, while the World Health Organization claims that government cutbacks have cost some 500,000 additional lives during the period. See Ralph Hakkert and Franklin W. Goza, "The Demographic Consequences of Austerity in Latin America," in *Lost Promises: Debt, Austerity, and Development in Latin America*, William L. Canak, ed., (Boulder: Westview Press, 1989), pp. 69–97.

27. On the politics of adjustment, see especially Joan M. Nelson, ed., *Economic Crisis and Policy Choice: The Politics of Adjustment in the Third World* (Princeton: Princeton University Press, 1990).

28. See John Walton, "Debt, Protest, and the State in Latin America," and John Walton and Charles Ragin, "Austerity and Dissent: Social Bases of Popular Struggle in Latin America," in *Lost Promises: Debt, Austerity, and Development in Latin America*, William L. Canak, ed., (Boulder: Westview Press, 1989), pp. 216–232. See also Edward C. Epstein, "Austerity and Trade Unions in Latin America," in *Lost Promises*, pp. 169–189.

29. Alfred Stepan has made a strong case that Brazil follows the former pattern; Chile and Uruguay also may be included. See *Rethinking Military Politics*. The Central American countries, particularly El Salvador and Nicaragua, fit the latter characterization.

30. A carefully nuanced, up-close account is Daniel H. Levine's *Popular Voices in Latin American Catholicism* (Princeton, N.J.: Princeton University Press, 1992).

31. On the role of such organizations, including the new unionism, the popular church, and neighborhood and women's organizations in Brazil, see Alfred Stepan, ed., *Democratizing Brazil: Problems of Transition and Consolidation* (New York: Oxford University Press, 1989) and Maria Helena Moreira Alves, *State and Opposition in Military Brazil* (Austin: University of Texas Press, 1986). On the role of civil society in Chile, see Manuel Barrera and J. Samuel Valenzuela, "The Development of Labor Movement Opposition to the Military Regime," in *Military Rule in Chile: Dictatorship and Oppositions* (Baltimore: Johns Hopkins University Press, 1986), pp. 230–269; see also J. Samuel Valenzuela, Arturo Valenzuela, and Manuel Antonio Garretón, "Popular Mobilization and the Military Regime in Chile: The Complexities of the Invisible Transition," in *Power and Popular Protest*, pp. 259–277. On new social movements in Mexico, see Joseph Foweraker and Ann L. Craig, eds., *Popular Movements and Political Change in Mexico*

(Boulder: Lynne Rienner Publishers, 1990), and Carlos Monsiváis, *Entrada libre: Crónicas de la sociedad que se organiza* (Free entry: Chronicles of a society organizing itself) (Mexico City: Biblioteca ERA, 1987). On the development of the Mexican peasant movement, see Michael W. Foley, "Agenda for Mobilization: The Agrarian Question and Popular Mobilization in Contemporary Mexico," *Latin American Research Review* 26, no. 2 (spring 1991). On the role of the Church in Brazil and Chile, see Thomas Bruneau, *The Church in Brazil: The Politics of Religion* (Austin: University of Texas Press, 1982); Scott Mainwaring, *The Catholic Church and Politics in Brazil, 1916–1985* (Stanford: Stanford University Press, 1986); Brian H. Smith, *The Church and Politics in Chile: Challenges to Modern Catholicism* (Princeton, N.J.: Princeton University Press, 1982). On the rise of liberation theology and the popular church, see Christian Smith, *The Emergence of Liberation Theology: Radical Religion and Social Movement Theory* (Chicago: University Press, 1991); Philip Berryman, *Roots of Rebellion: Christians in the Central American Revolutions* (Maryknoll, N.Y.: Orbis, 1984); Daniel Levine, ed., *Religion and Political Conflict in Latin America* (Chapel Hill: University of North Carolina Press, 1986); Daniel H. Levine and Scott Mainwaring, "Religion and Popular Protest in Latin America: Contrasting Experiences," in *Power and Popular Protest*, pp. 203–240; Alexander Wilde and Scott Mainwaring, *Voice of the Voiceless: The Progressive Church in Latin America* (Notre Dame: University of Notre Dame Press, forthcoming). On women's organizations, see Jane S. Jaquette, ed., *The Women's Movement in Latin America: Feminism and the Transition to Democracy* (Boulder: Westview Press, 1991). An important recent collection of analyses and case studies is Arturo Escobar and Sonia Alvarez, *The Making of Social Movements in Latin America: Identity Strategy and Democracy* (Boulder: Westview Press, 1992).

32. See the pessimistic assessment of Maria Helena Moreira Alves, "Interclass Alliances in the Opposition to the Military in Brazil: Consequences for the Transition Period," in *Power and Popular Protest*, pp. 278–298.

33. See Alfred Stepan, *Rethinking Military Politics*, Chapter 1. On the necessity of class compromise, see Adam Przeworski, "Some Problems in the Study of the Transition to Democracy," in *Transitions from Authoritarian Rule: Comparative Perspectives*, pp. 47–63; and Adam Przeworski and Michael Wallerstein, "The Structure of Class Conflict in Democratic Capitalist Societies," *American Political Science Review* 76, no. 76 (1982): pp. 215–238. The concrete reality of such a compromise is brought home, if rather too glibly, in Daniel Levine's study of an earlier transition, that of Venezuela in 1958, in "Venezuela Since 1958: The Consolidation of Democratic Politics," in *The Breakdown of Democratic Regimes: Latin America*, Juan J. Linz and Alfred Stepan, eds., (Baltimore: Johns Hopkins University Press, 1978), pp. 82–109.

34. On the concept and practice of "pacted democracy," see Guillermo O'-Donnell and Philippe C. Schmitter, *Transitions from Authoritarian Rule: Tentative Conclusions about Uncertain Democracies*, pp. 37–47, and Terry Karl, "Petroleum and Political Pacts: The Transition to Democracy in Venezuela," in *Transitions from Authoritarian Rule: Latin America*, Guillermo O'Donnell, Philippe C. Schmitter, and Laurence Whitehead, eds., (Baltimore: Johns Hopkins University Press, 1986), pp. 196–220.

35. On the difficulty of assessing trade union response to economic change, see Epstein, "Austerity and Trade Unions in Latin America."

36. See John Walton, "Debt, Protest, and the State in Latin America," p. 316 and Table 10.2.

37. The first argument has long been identified with Howard Wiarda. See especially his *Politics and Social Change: The Distinct Tradition* (Amherst: University of Massachusetts Press, 1974; 2nd ed., 1982). Alain Rouquié argues the last point from numerous examples in his article, "Demilitarization and the Institutionalization of Military-dominated Polities in Latin America," in *Transitions from Authoritarian Rule: Comparative Perspectives,* pp. 110–114.

38. See Guillermo O'Donnell, "Tensions in the Bureaucratic-Authoritarian State and the Question of Democracy," in *The New Authoritarianism in Latin America,* David Collier, ed., (Princeton: Princeton University Press, 1979), pp. 285–318, and *Modernization and Bureaucratic-Authoritarianism* (Berkeley: Institute of International Studies, University of California, 1979).

39. In a meeting of military chiefs in Mar del Plata, Argentina, in November 1987, the Chilean representative argued that "without doubt, all the scourges that afflict humanity and Latin America in particular, such as narcotics trafficking, subversion, homosexuality, promiscuity and disinformation, are tactics that form part of a strategy of world domination" on the part of what he and other participants freely labeled the "International Communist Movement," in Alan Riding's "Latin Military Still Seems to Emphasize Role in Fighting Communism," *New York Times,* November 3, 1988. A year into the formal end of hostilities in El Salvador, moreover, President Cristiani and members of his ARENA Party continue to speak of the FLMN as former terrorists and to question their commitment to peaceful resolution of conflict.

40. The Chilean military's self-defense, on the discovery of mass graves in the north of the country in late May 1990, was measured; military leaders said they acted appropriately at the time but that they were willing to cooperate in investigations "to strengthen national unity and consolidate democracy." *Latin American Weekly Report,* WR-90–24 (June 28, 1990). Nevertheless, as controversy grew both military leaders and members of parties of the right vehemently defended military conduct in the coup of 1973, and that stance had not significantly abated in the debates surrounding the commemoration of the coup in 1993.

41. On the early history of the counterinsurgency effort in Peru and human rights abuses, see Cynthia McClintock, "Peru's Sendero Luminoso Rebellion: Origins and Trajectory," in *Power and Popular Protest,* pp. 89–91. Sendero Luminoso's fortunes had declined so much by the summer of 1993 that they announced a temporary suspension of their popular war. On the recent situation in Peru, see Human Rights Watch, *Human Rights in Peru: One Year After Fujimori's Coup and Untold Terror: Violence Against Women in Peru's Armed Conflict* (New York: Human Rights Watch, 1993 and 1992).

42. See, for instance, the report by Larry Rohter, "Government Critics Harassed in Mexico, Setting Off a Storm," *New York Times,* June 21, 1990. Salinas established a National Commission on Human Rights in June 1990, with a distinguished panel, in response to pressure from human rights groups and the opposition Democratic Revolutionary Party, but the record of the commission has been mixed. See Human Rights Watch, *Unceasing Abuses: Human Rights in Mexico One Year After the Introduction of Reform* (New York: Human Rights Watch, 1991).

43. In Mexico the appointment of Carlos "Hank" Gonzalez as secretary of agriculture in January 1990 signaled the consolidation of the hold of the neoliberal team under Finance Minister Pedro Aspe. Salinas de Gortari's successful overtures to Washington to negotiate a free trade agreement (NAFTA), accompanied by wide-ranging constitutional and statutory changes, including the first steps toward

privatization of the *ejido* (the Mexican land reform community) indicate how far the administration is willing to go in pursuing the modernization of the Mexican economy. See Michael W. Foley, "Privatizing the Countryside: The Mexican Peasant Movement and Neoliberal Reform in Contemporary Mexico," *Latin American Perspectives* (forthcoming). The costs of trade liberalization, initiated in 1986 with Mexico's entry into General Agreement on Tariffs and Trade (GATT) have already been considerable, with thousands of bankruptcies and continuing unemployment. In the summer of 1993, much of Mexican agriculture, large and small, faced bankruptcy, thanks to high interest rates and foreign competition, and the banks' handling of billions of dollars of bad debt became a subject of public controversy. Mexico's debt by late 1993 was in fact higher in nominal terms than at the height of the debt crisis, fueled primarily by private bank borrowing in the low-interest rate markets of the United States. With a growing trade deficit and devaluation a strong probability in the near future, Mexico could again face a debt crisis.

44. See Lindsey Gruson, "Can Central America Win a War on Poverty?" *New York Times,* June 24, 1990.

45. On the political fallout of these moves, see Sylvia Maxfield, "International Economic Opening and Government-Business Relations," in Wayne A. Cornelius, Judith Gentleman, and Peter H. Smith, eds., *Mexico's Alternative Political Futures*, Monograph Series, vol. 30 (LaJolla, Calif.: Center for U.S.–Mexican Studies, University of California, San Diego, 1989), pp. 215–236.

46. *Latin American Weekly Report,* WR-90-09 (March 8, 1990).

3

The Changing Political Economy
of the Caribbean

Margaretta DeMar

Any effective discussion of the changing political economy of the Caribbean must address three basic questions at the outset. First, since little consistency is attached to the term Caribbean, how is the Caribbean to be delimited? This chapter confines its discussion to the independent island members of the Caribbean Community.[1]

Second, what is the appropriate conceptualization of political economy? This study conceptualizes the political economy as the interaction of sociopolitical processes, including state processes, class processes, international relations, and transnational relations, as they combine to organize patterns of production and exchange activities that in turn distribute goods and services internationally and intranationally.[2]

Third, since change is a relative concept and may exist within broader continuities, where does one look for it and how does one know one has found it? The framework used here to define and highlight change focuses on the most recent phase of the internationalization of capital, as interpreted in the works of Steven E. Sanderson,[3] David Barkin,[4] and Robert W. Cox.[5] This new phase, beginning in approximately 1945 but accelerating and more apparent since the 1970s, involves an integration of production on an increasingly global and rationalized basis and has generated a new international division of labor such that less developed countries are no longer limited to being primary product and raw material exporters, as under the classical international division of labor, but rather may also produce manufactures and other nontraditional goods. Neither transnational participation in equity nor even trade is required for manifestation of the internationalization of production; instead, the process is reflected through the standardization of production processes, goods, and consumer tastes across national borders and through the "system's growing ability to reproduce the most advanced labor processes throughout the world."[6] Reinforcing the development of this increasingly global productive structure, and emerging parallel to it, is an incipient international political structure that involves "hierarchical consensus formation" among certain multilateral forums and institutions, the central agencies of advanced capitalist countries, and a force of "ideologically conditioned agents in key positions within Third World countries" that "enforces conformity through its control of the preponderance of international finance."[7] Indicators of the internationalization of production's manifestation—and examples of change —in a particular country or region include: a transformation of the labor process associated with an expansion of the capitalist organization of production; use of technologies that are standardized on an increasingly global basis; direct investment by transnational corporations into, or out of, the area as a reflection of the mobility of capital; integration into the international system at the level of production rather than through commodity trade alone; participation in the mutual structural adjustment of advanced and underdeveloped economies; and a reorientation of state power such that the state often becomes the authorized agent of the international system.[8]

Using this framework to reveal the changing nature of the political economy of the Caribbean, this chapter divides itself into four sections. The first provides a brief overview of the elements of the Caribbean political economy from early British colonialism[9] to the 1970s, a time period that overarches two phases in the international political economy: (1) internationalization through commodity trade and the operation of the classical international division of labor, ending in approximately 1945; and (2) beginning in approximately 1945, the initial stages of the internationalization of production and the onset of the new international division of labor. The second section provides a more detailed discussion of the elements of the Caribbean political economy from the 1970s to the present, a time period that coincides with the acceleration of the internationalization of production in the international political economy and the greater visibility of the new international division of labor. Next comes an evaluation of the continuities and changes in the Caribbean political economy, focusing on the indicators of the internationalization of production as they have manifested in the region. Finally, the fourth section presents concluding remarks.

Early Colonialism to the 1970s

Soon after the onset of British rule, the Caribbean was articulated into the emerging international capitalist system through commodity trade. After World War II, the region remained largely a primary product exporter, articulated into the international capitalist system through commodity trade but now also to a limited extent through production, especially with the gradual inclusion of import-substitution manufacturing in most regional economies.

Sociopolitical Processes

State Processes[10]

Beginning with early colonialism, Great Britain dominated colonial "state" structures in the Caribbean, but allowed limited local participation on some islands until the 1860s in the form of elected assemblies.[11] Following World War II, Britain gradually transferred power to local hands, filling Westminster-style parliamentary structures with native personnel and broadening the scope of decisionmaking step-by-step, until the process was complete with the granting of independence, beginning in 1962 with Jamaica and Trinidad and Tobago (hereafter, Trinidad).[12]

Social Processes

The white planter class constituted the region's political elite from the 1600s to the early 1900s. In the 1930s, though, when Britain reintroduced elected assemblies and removed substantial property requirements for election, the newly self-conscious, mostly brown or black, petty bourgeoisie and on some islands the more privileged within the unionized working class began developing into a political elite, a position they consolidated with independence. After independence, competing parties, which had emerged largely out of these single bases of support, began to reflect social divisions, appealing to one class or another, or one race or another.

The planter class also dominated economically throughout the first three centuries of colonialism. Toward the end of the nineteenth century, though, a national urban bourgeoisie evolved from the old planter and merchant classes and was increasingly dominant following World War II. Its relative economic power declined in the 1950s, however, as new foreign economic elites moved to the islands in response to "industrialization-by-invitation" programs and as middle-class politicians began to use the state to promote the weaker classes.[13]

International Relations

With independence, the emphasis in Caribbean international relations shifted gradually from Britain toward North America, although Britain remained important, especially to the smaller Eastern Caribbean states.

Organization of Production and Exchange

Sectoral Distribution

From the early days of British colonialism, Caribbean production focused primarily on estate-based export agriculture, especially sugar, a focus that continued to a large degree throughout the era. Below the surface of this continuity, however, numerous modifications were taking place, with the addition of a peasant sector following slave emancipation in the 1830s; light manufacturing, mineral extraction, and peasant-produced exports[14] in the late nineteenth century; and state-promoted import-substitution industrialization in the late 1950s.[15] By the 1960s, despite continuing dependence on agriculture, Caribbean economies had achieved a certain diversification. In countries where a mineral sector existed, it dominated, while manufacturing, tourism, and in a few countries, offshore banking, were contributing an increasing share of the gross domestic product (GDP). Simultaneously, an unorganized and unregulated informal sector of street vendors, petty traders, and family-owned enterprises began to evolve in urban areas in response to the encroachment by mineral companies and others on the small-farm sector.[16]

Patterns of Ownership and Control

Beginning soon after British rule, control in the Caribbean over the productive assets associated with determining the overall economy's production and exchange priorities was highly concentrated, increasingly concentrated, and often subject to substantial foreign input. This pattern began with land ownership in the early slave-based plantation system and continued through an increase in foreign absentee ownership of estates after 1750 as sugar profits declined, through Emancipation as many landowners fell into ruin, and through the later nineteenth and early twentieth centuries as foreign corporations took over many of the estates left functioning and promoted the "factories-in-the-field" approach to sugar production that led to larger, but fewer, estates.[17] After World War II, land ownership lost its primacy and became only one of several types of control that could shape each Caribbean society's economic decisions and activities.[18] Nevertheless, the distribution of land, capital, and other assets continued to be highly uneven,[19] and foreign ownership and control increased, especially in the "commanding heights" of the economy.

Relations of Production

Until Emancipation, relations of production in the Caribbean took the form of landed master and slave, within the broader context of the international capitalist system.[20] After Emancipation, productive relations were increasingly differentiated; former slaves became agricultural proletarians, self-provisioning peasants, or a combination of the two, while newly arrived indentured laborers, primarily from South Asia, operated under productive relations that resembled the former master-slave relationship. Relations of production took an increasingly capitalist-proletarian form from the late nineteenth century on, especially in the light manufacturing and mineral sectors, and especially as foreign capital began organizing production to some degree. Even the agricultural sector had an increasingly capitalist theme, although relations of production remained mixed and food production for the local market was generally outside the capitalist organization of production.

Extent of Capitalization and Modernization

Prior to Emancipation, the level of capitalization in Caribbean production was quite low since the coercive form of labor exploitation reduced the relative cost of labor. Even after slave emancipation, the influx of indentured labor dampened the planters' enthusiasm for increasing production's capital intensity. Nevertheless, over the next century, capitalization did increase substantially, if unevenly, especially on islands newer to sugar production, and especially as foreign corporations moved into the sugar industry. From the 1950s on, the capital intensity of production accelerated significantly, particularly in conjunction with foreign ownership, mainly British and American, and particularly in the mineral and manufacturing sectors.

Level Responded To

Caribbean decisions regarding production began responding to external factors from the early days of plantation production under British rule, an orientation that continued as indentured labor and wage-workers replaced slaves, as corporations replaced planters, and as mineral exports were added to agricultural exports. The one overall exception to this tendency was during World War II, when Caribbean production took on an unusual and brief internal orientation since the Great Depression had contracted foreign demand for the region's exports while the war had restricted the availability of imports.[21] Sectorally specific exceptions include the internal orientation of peasant production following Emancipation[22] and that of the manufacturing sector in the later 1950s and 1960s as it responded to government incentives promoting import-substitution industrialization.[23]

Distribution of Economic Product

International

The 1600s to 1750 was the golden era for the Caribbean's claim on global economic product, as a result of the enormous profits accrued from sugar

production.[24] After 1750, though, the American Revolution, the emancipation of slaves, and the loss in 1846 of British preferential treatment of
colonial sugar dealt a triple blow to the region's international position.
This decline deepened in the latter part of the nineteenth century as an increasing share of Caribbean-produced profits was repatriated into foreign
corporate hands for reinvestment outside the region. Only in the mid-
twentieth century did the downward trend reverse itself, as the changing
structure of Caribbean economies converged with international-system priorities to create a boom period, especially in the early 1960s, that increased the region's claim on world economic product.[25]

Intranational

Prior to Emancipation, the highly skewed intranational distribution of economic claims followed class lines, with large estate owners at the top and
slaves at the bottom. Emancipation did lead to a slightly more egalitarian
distribution, since those former slaves who acquired land gained some
control over, and claim on, economic product, but the high level of black
emigration during the same era draws into question how significant this
improvement was overall.[26] Generally, the intranational distribution continued to be highly polarized and increasingly concentrated throughout the
colonial era and on into independence.[27] Even in the boom period of the
early 1960s, the fruits of growth stayed in only a few hands (see Tables
3.1 and 3.2), tending especially to bypass those who worked in the agricultural sector. Furthermore, the expanding industrial sector's expected
contribution to improving unemployment never materialized,[28] and the relative gap between the haves and have-nots widened.[29] As a result of such
trends, economically motivated emigration continued apace between
World War II and the 1970s.[30]

The 1970s to the Present

In the 1970s, the collapse of the Bretton Woods international monetary
system, combined with two successive "oil shocks," had devastating balance-of-payments effects on most Caribbean economies. In addition,
petrodollar recycling made new foreign development loans[31] increasingly
available to the more developed of these economies. Together, these
events created the basis for the region's current debt problem. They also
laid the foundation for the Caribbean's increasing, though uneven, integration into the international capitalist system at the level of production
in the 1970s and 1980s, even as commodity trade remained extremely important. In the early 1980s, the particular manifestation of the Cold War
at the time created a brief surge in the region's perceived strategic importance

Table 3.1 Energy Intake Requirement Ratios and Percentage of Households
Deficient in Intake, Barbados and Trinidad and Tobago, 1969

	Energy Intake/ Requirement (%)	Households Deficient (%)	Protein Intake/ Requirement (%)	Households Deficient (%)
Barbados	94	65	111	39
Trinidad	119	39	127	31

Source: P. N. Sen Gupta, "Comparative Studies on Food Consumption and Nutrition in Three Caribbean Countries: Barbados, Trinidad and Tobago, and Guyana," *Ecology of Food and Nutrition* XI, no. 3 (1981): pp. 184, 186–187.

Table 3.2 Jamaican Income Distribution, 1958

Proportion of the Population	Share of National Income
Bottom 20%	2%
Bottom 60%	19%
Top 10%	43%
Top 5%	30%

Source: Owen Jefferson, "Some Aspects of the Post-War Economic Development of Jamaica," in Norman Girvan and Owen Jefferson, eds., *Readings in the Political Economy of the Caribbean* (Kingston: New World Group Ltd., 1971), p. 110.

to the West, which then ebbed in the late 1980s. In the 1990s, dramatic changes in the world's interstate structure and international economy have heightened Caribbean fears of even further marginalization from the global political economy. Not only have the fall of communism in Eastern Europe, the demise of the Soviet Union, and the end of the Cold War decreased the region's importance to the West, they have also added numerous new supplicants for foreign assistance, potentially threatening the Caribbean's already minimal share. On the economic front, the creation of a single market in the European Community and the formation of the North American Free Trade Agreement have increased Caribbean concern regarding its preferred status in those two regions. Such anxieties have precipitated internal moves toward greater regional economic and political integration and greater integration of the region into the international capitalist system at whatever level possible, commodity trade or production.

Sociopolitical Processes

State Processes

The Westminster-style constitutional structure of state processes has continued to prevail in the region, but during the early part of the period a number of deviations from that structure, some radical and some conservative, also occurred. The obvious example is the New Jewel Movement experiment in Grenada from 1979–1983, but others include the sometimes doubtful nature of two-party politics in Trinidad under Eric Williams and in Antigua and Barbuda (hereafter, Antigua) under Vere Bird, the 1972–1980 Jamaican experiment with expanded community participation, and the increasingly authoritarian systems with restricted rights and expanded obligations developing in the late 1970s and 1980s in Trinidad and over the past decade in Antigua and Dominica.

The failure of the Jamaican and Grenadian experiments with more radical options appears to confirm the necessity of maintaining the state's coalition with local capital—or at least of maintaining the bourgeoisie's confidence in the state—along with maintaining an eye to the potentially negative impact of allowing ideological rhetoric to outstrip changes in practice, particularly if such rhetoric proves offensive to a powerful neighbor.[32]

The fallout from these experiments, combined with trends in the international capitalist system and in Caribbean insertion into that system, generated a greater political conservatism in the region in the 1980s, particularly noticeable after the electoral victory in Jamaica of Edward Seaga and the Jamaica Labour Party (JLP) in 1980 and the United States' invasion of Grenada in 1983. By the mid-1980s, the constitutional structure for all the countries studied here had reverted to either a parliamentary or parliamentary/authoritarian form. In the 1990s, there has been some loosening of this political conservatism in some countries, as reflected in the return to power of the People's National Party (PNP) and Michael Manley in Jamaica in 1989 and of the People's National Movement (PNM), now under Patrick Manning, in Trinidad in 1991. Yet, this loosening may be more apparent than real, at least on the economic front, where the policies of these leaders and of Manley's successor, PNP leader Percival J. Patterson, look decidedly similar to those espoused by their opposition predecessors.

Two other political developments in the 1990s deserve mention. First is the decline of the old guard in the top political positions. Lynden Pindling's twenty-five-year reign over the Bahamas ended with the Progressive Liberal Party's electoral defeat in 1992 and his resignation as party leader soon after. Vere Bird of Antigua has announced his retirement from politics at the end of his term in 1994. In Jamaica, ill health forced Michael Manley to step down as party leader of the PNP and prime minister of the government in 1992, and in the 1993 election, veteran JLP member and former Prime Minister Hugh Shearer lost his seat in Parliament and subsequently announced his retirement from political life. Second is the Windward Islands' consideration of political union. A regional constituent assembly, created by Dominica, Grenada, St. Lucia, and St. Vincent and the Grenadines, has concluded that there is "overwhelming support for a union along federal lines."[33] The assembly's recommendations, however, are only consultative and progress toward the actual implementation of political union does not appear imminent.

Social Processes

The political elite of the region has continued to consist generally of the petty bourgeoisie or on some islands the top trade union echelon. The narrow class or ethnic appeal of parties appears to be blurring, however. On one hand, in a number of countries, platforms of competing parties look increasingly similar; on the other, some parties in the region appear to be attempting "catch-all" status.[34]

The commercial bourgeoisie continues to dominate as the local economic elite. Local productive capitalists have also developed on some of the larger islands, but they tend to be subordinate to commercial interests. In addition, the foreign economic elite continues to be active and powerful in all sectors, but now represents a broader range of national origins, notably Japanese and Israeli.

Although the local bourgeoisie is influential, it is not necessarily the hegemonic power in the political and economic systems that it has been in most advanced countries. Rather, as Carl Stone notes, it is "simply one class within a wider group of elite interests competing to influence the state."[35] It "tends to remain either a dependent appendage of foreign interests, a basically small business formation lacking effective control of local economic forces, or grows as a client of state promotion through import-substitution policies."[36] In Barbados, commercial capital and the "petty bourgeoisie in the state and professions constitute the ruling power bloc"[37] while in Antigua, the functioning "coalition" that formed between the state and the foreign economic elite allowed the black petty and middle-class elite essentially to vanquish the remainder of white planter class power in the system in the 1970s and 1980s.[38] Less successful was the attempt in the 1970s by Michael Manley's PNP in Jamaica to combine a certain amount of local capitalist support with weaker-class support in forming a power base. Bourgeois support evaporated rapidly, and the numbers of the weaker classes did not provide a sufficient counterbalance to the power exerted by other interests.

The weaker classes have not regained effective influence in the region's state-society coalitions since 1983. In the 1980s, the parties that weaker classes supported were generally out of power, and weaker-class causes could be championed only to the extent that parties in opposition can champion causes. The 1990s brought the return of these parties to power in some countries, but the policies the parties now advocate offer members of the weaker classes little positive choice at the polls. In Trinidad,

PNM leader and Prime Minister Patrick Manning is pursuing exchange liberalization and privatization of state assets even though the PNM was the major critic of privatization during the rule of the National Alliance for Reconstruction (NAR) in the 1980s. In the 1993 Jamaican elections, both the PNP and JLP were running on platforms advocating market-oriented policies, trade and exchange liberalization, and privatization. As these policies continue to erode weaker-class standards of living, labor unrest has become more prominent. In 1992 and 1993, flour, sugar, banana, and air traffic control workers in Jamaica and sugar, water and sewage, sanitation, and public sector workers in Trinidad took part in strikes or work stoppages to protest their economic and political status.[39] One union leader expressed the general mood, saying, "I'm certainly not prepared to make any sacrifice that will ensure the further enrichment of those who already have more than they need."[40]

Conversely, the state-bourgeois coalition appears to have been reestablished throughout the region. For example, there has been ample evidence of bourgeois support for, and willingness to work with, the Jamaican state under the PNP, based on perceptions of mutual interest, the most dramatic example being the intervention in April 1992 of Gordon "Butch" Stewart, chair of the Sandals hotel chain, to halt the precipitous slide of the Jamaican dollar by selling the banks U.S.$1 million each week at a rate of U.S.$1.00 = J$25.00 (about J$4.00 below market rate at the time) on the understanding that the U.S. dollar would be resold at no more than a 0.5 percent markup.[41] Other companies followed suit, and within two weeks the value of the Jamaican dollar was relatively stable.

Regarding the distribution of foreign and domestic influences within the society, the balance of power has shifted back and forth a bit over the past two decades. During the more nationalistically inclined years of the 1970s, foreign capital's relative economic position declined, although this was often by its own choice. In the 1980s, though, with political ideology's reaffirmation of the need for foreign investment-driven development, the potential influence of foreign economic elites rose once again. This relative influence has become all the greater now that foreign capital no longer finds the region particularly attractive relative to other areas of the world. The shortage of investors relative to the perceived need has pushed Caribbean states to provide incentives for foreign investment to an unprecedented degree and in new forms, such as the export processing zone.

International Relations

In the past two decades, bilateral-type agreements, regional agreements and organizations, and metaregional global multilateral agreements and organizations have all combined to influence the Caribbean's political economy.

Bilateral. Bilateral-type preferential arrangements, involving trade, investment, and/or debt reduction, such as the European Community's (EC) Lomé Convention; Canada's Caribcan; and the United States' Caribbean Basin Initiative (CBI), 807 program,[42] and Enterprise for the Americas Initiative (EAI), all work to condition, and thus constrain, Caribbean structural adjustment within the new international division of labor. Preferential trade, financing, and investment programs developed in the 1970s and 1980s encourage the production of specified goods. For instance, the EC's compensatory financing of certain primary exports from the African, Caribbean, and Pacific (ACP) countries helps to ensure that these countries will continue to produce such goods for EC markets, while without the financing it appeared possible that such production might cease.[43] Even more determining in Caribbean decisions about what to produce is the list of goods that such treaties *exclude* from preferential treatment. For example, Caribcan and the CBI offer one-way duty-free access to imports from the Caribbean, but Caribcan excludes from duty-free access textiles and apparel, footwear, and leather products, while the CBI excludes textiles and apparel, footwear, leather products, canned tuna, flat goods, watches and watch parts, and petroleum and petroleum products, all goods in which the region has a comparative advantage. Thus, in pursuit of U.S. and Canadian national interest, the agreements potentially condition production away from regional efficiency.[44] Certain goods excluded from duty-free access to the U.S. market can still gain preferential access through the 807 program if they contain U.S. components, the exporter paying duty only on the Caribbean value added. Caribbean economies have found this program particularly important in the form of the "Super 807" program applicable to garment items assembled in the region that are cut in the United States from U.S.-formed fabric.[45] Such policies shape Caribbean production toward the use of U.S.-made components.

The more recent Enterprise for the Americas Initiative intends to constrain Caribbean policy in the direction of hemispheric free trade, open investment regimes, and further development of the private sector. In return for access to a proposed multilateral investment facility, access to markets, and possible opportunities for debt reduction through debt-for-equity, debt-for-nature, and debt-for-development programs, participating Caribbean countries are to commit themselves to an open investment regime, commercial debt reduction, and "strong reform programs in conjunction with the International Monetary Fund."[46]

Also influential in the Caribbean's political economy have been United States and European Community moves in the last two years to create or deepen regional integration schemes that do not include the Caribbean, at least initially. The EC's creation of a single market in 1992 has been of particular concern to Caribbean banana producers, especially the Windward Islands, where bananas provide approximately half the export earnings. Preferential access, considered a requirement for the Caribbean's relatively high-cost bananas, had previously been granted by specific EC countries to those ACP countries that had been former colonies. As a result, virtually all Caribbean bananas had gone to the United Kingdom. Fear grew that with the single market and consequent changes in the preferential scheme Caribbean bananas would have to compete—unsuccessfully—with the much less expensive "dollar bananas" from Central and South America that were already providing 60 to 70 percent of the EC market.[47] Instead, the EC's decision strengthened the relative position of ACP producers.[48] The decision has not been popular outside ACP countries, however. Both the World Bank and the United States have lambasted the EC's decision while Germany, the largest EC banana importer, has formally questioned the decision in the EC's legal system. Dollar banana exporting countries have brought the issue before the General Agreement on Trade and Tariffs (GATT) and have won against the EC in the initial GATT inquiry. Regardless of its final outcome, the EC banana question demonstrates how changes in the outside world can reverberate on a gigantic scale within the Caribbean region.

In a similar vein, Caribbean fears that Mexico's accession to the North American Free Trade Agreement (NAFTA) will erode the benefits of the 807 programs for non-CBI-eligible goods has led to the introduction of the "Caribbean Free Trade Agreements Act" in the U.S. House of Representatives. If approved, the bill would temporarily provide each CBI country with NAFTA parity in tariff and quota treatment of U.S. imports excluded from duty-free treatment.[49] At the end of three years, though, the preference would end unless the country had entered into two-way free trade with the United States, either through accession to the NAFTA or through a bilateral trade agreement. U.S. policy's constraining influence toward two-way hemispheric free trade is apparent here as in the EAI; the bait is just different.

Regional. Regional organizations, including the Caribbean Community (Caricom) and its associated financial institution, the Caribbean Development Bank (CDB), have also been important in defining the Caribbean political economy over the past two decades.[50] The Caribbean Development Bank has been instrumental in focusing its members' development policies toward cutting government expenditures on nonproductive services and stimulating economic growth, especially since the 1980s.[51] Thus, it has reinforced many of the attitudes multilateral lending institutions deem appropriate. More recently, though, CDB statements have increasingly emphasized poverty alleviation and positive environmental impacts. Furthermore, the bank began a basic needs program four years ago to fund small-scale, labor-intensive projects in the poorer borrower countries. In its loan evaluations, however, the CDB continues to promote the multilateral lending institutions' "party line" of growth, private sector emphasis, and "sound macroeconomic frameworks."[52]

Increased intraregional trade and, since the 1980s, export-led growth and encouragement of the private sector have been the policy emphases of the Caribbean Community.[53] Developing out of the Caribbean Free Trade Agreement of 1965, Caricom officially became a customs union in 1973. Over the years, Caricom has been successful in generating a noticeable growth in intraregional trade; for instance, the ratio of exports to the region to total exports grew from 11 percent to 40 percent for Eastern Caribbean countries as a result of Caricom membership. Moreover, much of this increase took the form of manufactured goods and nontraditional agricultural exports. The system underwent a marked decline, though, in the 1980s, when economic crisis limited the ability of key participants to follow the rules.[54] Intraregional trade consequently declined by over 47 percent between 1981 and 1986. Although the situation began to improve somewhat in the late 1980s, observers note a continuing propensity for the organization not to follow through on its cooperative agreements, calling implementation Caricom's Achilles' heel.[55]

The acceleration of outside regional integration schemes in the 1990s has propelled Caricom into seeking to deepen its own integration, focusing particularly on questions of a common external tariff (CET), monetary union, and creation of a regional authority. In 1992, after failing to implement a previously agreed-upon 0–35 percent CET, the organization agreed to a CET with a beginning range of 0–45 percent that would decrease gradually over a five-year period to a range of 0–20 percent by the end of 1997.[56] Regarding monetary union, agreement-in-principle is widespread among Caricom member governments, but action to create a proposed regional body to coordinate members' monetary policy as a first step toward that goal has been lacking.[57] Similar hedging on the surrender of sovereignty is apparent in the rejection by Caricom heads of government of a high-level recommendation to create a Caricom Commission that would have the authority to execute decisions to which Caricom members had already committed themselves. Instead, the government leaders created the Caricom Bureau, made up of three heads of government and Caricom's secretary-general, thus maintaining national primacy within the regional organization.

Changing global economic structures have also generated new momentum in Caricom attempts to broaden economic cooperation with Latin American countries. First, Caricom has proposed the creation of an Association of Caribbean States, open to states bordering, or in, the Caribbean. Second, in the discussion stages are a free trade agreement with Colombia, a trade agreement with the Central American Economic Integration Treaty (Sieca), and development of a common strategy with Sieca in multilateral and "third country" regional bloc negotiations. Third, Caricom and Venezuela have recently joined in an agreement providing for one-way Caribbean duty-free access to the Venezuelan market for thirteen hundred items by 1996. Reciprocal duty-free access to Caricom markets for Venezuelan goods will come into force after an initial five-year, one-way, period.[58]

Global. In the 1970s, and especially in the 1980s and 1990s, global multilateral organizations, notably the International Monetary Fund (IMF) and the World Bank, have been particularly, and increasingly, influential in shaping a number of Caribbean political economies. This is especially the case for IMF loan recipients, Barbados, Dominica, Grenada, Jamaica, and Trinidad. Jamaica is the largest per capita debtor in the region and has been continuously involved with the IMF, and often with the World Bank as well, since 1977, while Trinidad and Barbados have joined the ranks of Caribbean countries subject to conditional loans for balance-of-payments difficulties more recently.

Conditions attached to IMF and World Bank stabilization loans[59] generally include currency devaluation, reduction or elimination of subsidies, trade and exchange liberalization, reduction of government expenditures, and privatization of state assets, with each new round of loans signaling a new round of these activities. In recent years, though, there has been a slight shift in thinking at these institutions, moving away from strictly monetary economic models to more real economy models that allow for some growth and, most recently, occasionally including references in public statements to cushioning the social impact of adjustment. Indicative of such changes is the recent IMF prescription against further devaluation of the Barbados dollar and advising instead that Barbados "go up-market and compete on the basis of quality."[60] Nonetheless, overall, the IMF and the World Bank encourage the increased integration of Caribbean economies into the global political economy and expansion of the capitalist organization of production within the region.[61] To these ends, their policies encourage, on the one hand, a dismantling of any barriers to international integration, and on the other, business expansion, promotion of the private sector, industrial restructuring, and improvement of infrastructure.

The impact of IMF and World Bank structural adjustment programs in the region has been well documented elsewhere;[62] suffice it to say that their constraining influence has generally reduced state autonomy in economic decisionmaking, the state's ability to respond to the demands of the weaker classes for social responsibility, and eventually even the state's ability to respond to the middle classes and local capital. In the 1990s,

Jamaica's economic deregulation, Trinidad's privatizations and exchange liberalization, and Barbados's privatizations and attempts at a wage freeze and price decontrol are all of dubious social consequence and are all directly attributable to the countries' applications to the IMF for balance-of-payments loans. Another example of these narrowed Caribbean policy parameters is the attempt in 1992 of the IMF and the World Bank to use loan negotiations with Caricom member states to pressure Caricom to lower its proposed CET levels.[63]

Moreover, some Caribbean officials have internalized the ideology and approach to development that these multilateral institutions espouse.[64] For instance, Grenada is undergoing a self-imposed three-year structural adjustment program running through September 1994 to "help solve the country's chronic budgetary imbalances."[65] Thus, the International Monetary Fund and the World Bank narrow the degree of freedom the state has in directing the national political economy, sometimes even when they themselves are not directly involved. Furthermore, the state becomes the authorized executor of international system policies, as illustrated in Jamaican deregulation, Trinidadian exchange liberalization, and Barbadian privatization.[66] These policies, in turn, affect the economic decisions of other actors in Caribbean societies.

On the other hand, the flow of influence is not always from the international system to the Caribbean. State policies in the region have also affected the international system. For instance, many Caribbean state policies in the 1970s and 1980s increased foreign debt at the global level. The Jamaican government of the 1970s used much of its foreign borrowings for development projects and to finance social programs that did not generate foreign exchange with which to repay the loans and interest.[67] Windfall oil profits spared Trinidad some of this difficulty. Yet, Trinidad did not escape unscathed since the profits were spent in ways that increased popular expectations without generating the ability to respond to them on a continuing basis.[68] Such regional actions increased future dependence on international financial institutions and foreign public and private creditors, which in turn contributed to a change in the role of international financial institutions in the 1980s.

On other occasions, even after foreign financial intervention was required and conditions made for such intervention, some independent Caribbean state action contradicting international system dictates has been apparent. For instance, in the late 1980s, even IMF supporter Edward Seaga intervened to maintain the value of the Jamaican dollar at U.S.\$1.00 = J\$5.50 after the rate had fallen well below the J\$6.00 mark, contrary to IMF demands for continuing realignment of Jamaican currency value to the market rate. More recently, Jamaica has stretched, if not contradicted, IMF conditions by lowering the personal income tax rate, raising the tax-exempt threshold, and granting large pay increases to public sector workers.[69] Similar independent actions taken by Caribbean policymakers contrary to IMF and World Bank conditions include the maintenance or reimposition of tariffs, import controls, and foreign investment limits. Such activity, though, is a small and declining countertrend to the reorientation of state power in the region such that the state becomes an agent of the international system. For the most part, conditional loans present narrowing parameters to state policies and encourage deeper integration into the international division of labor.

Transnational Relations

Transnational relations have also been increasingly important in shaping the Caribbean political economy as they interact with other sociopolitical processes. Although the lack of state regulatory power over capital has been an element in Caribbean state decisionmaking for some time, the internationalization of production and its associated indicators have further narrowed the capacity of Caribbean states to control the shape of their economies, influencing decisions to adopt more relaxed safety or environmental standards or to provide incentives for investment in the form of infrastructure, tax holidays, free trade zones, export processing zones or wage restraints.

Organization of Production and Exchange

Sectoral Distribution

In the 1970s, government policy favored manufacturing on an import-substitution basis, with a continuing emphasis on the mineral sector as well. In the 1980s and 1990s, as global parameters have shifted, the emphasis in Caribbean policy, or at least policy rhetoric, has favored export-led growth, with an emphasis on nontraditional goods, especially manufactures. In reality, however, "anything and everything" has been the basic guideline to government sectoral policy priorities. Minerals and tourism are resurgent one year and receive favor while another year nontraditional agriculture and manufactured exports are the goal. Similarly, at the same time that export-led growth ostensibly prevails, domestically oriented production, especially of foodstuffs, is also extolled.

  Such policy orientations have led to a sectoral distribution of production and exchange in Caribbean economies that essentially continues past patterns but with some new twists. Although traditional agricultural exports, especially sugar, are declining in importance, they still remain important foreign exchange earners in many countries.[70] Nontraditional exports, both processed and primary, contribute an increasing share of GDP, but mining continues to be relied on to the extent that it is able to provide. For instance, Jamaica's bauxite and alumina earnings gained ground as that market shifted in 1989 and 1990. On the other hand, petroleum earnings in Trinidad slumped tremendously in the second half of the 1980s. They experienced a brief miniresurgence in 1990 as a result of the Persian Gulf conflict, but in 1992, the hydrocarbons sector as a whole declined 4 percent over 1991.[71]

A renewed emphasis on agriculture has also occurred as countries scramble to find new foreign exchange earners and to substitute domestic production for imports. For most countries, export agriculture has a growing nontraditional bias, usually in the form of winter vegetables, horticultural products, or ethnic foods.

Generally speaking, manufactures have been a growth sector for extraregional exports but have been weakening in their overall contribution to GDP.[72] For instance, St. Vincent and the Grenadines has increased exports of electronics and clothing and Jamaica has experienced growth in export processing.[73] If domestically oriented production is added to the overall picture though, Dominica, Jamaica, Trinidad, and Barbados have all experienced declines in the manufacturing sector in the past two years, records that are indicative of the region as a whole.

Also in the running for sectoral favorite is tourism. In Antigua, the collapse of sugar in the early 1970s led to its replacement by tourism. In Jamaica, tourism climbed to become the number one foreign exchange earner in the late 1980s. In 1990, Dominica, Grenada, and St. Vincent and the Grenadines joined Jamaica in double-digit growth in tourism earnings. Even Barbados is expecting tourism to be the power behind its recovery despite a decline in that sector's earnings in 1992. On the other side, Bahamian tourist revenues have decreased in their contribution to GDP in recent years, with tourism down 10 percent in 1992 over previous years.[74]

In the commercial sector, the local bourgeoisie continues to predominate, but the informal sector is increasingly important as greater, if unofficial, reliance is put on it for reproduction of much of the population.

Thus, in some ways, the current sectoral distribution of production and exchange in the Caribbean reflects the French proverb that the more things change, the more they stay the same. Because of the relatively negative position of Caribbean countries in attracting foreign capital and generating domestic capitalists who would set up manufacturing production, Caribbean economies, for the most part, have not risen above their former status as primary product exporters, even though their economic structure is considerably more diversified. Even those who no longer find their major export earnings coming from traditional exports, such as sugar and bananas, generally rely on unprocessed or minimally processed minerals or on tourism for the bulk of their export earnings despite the rising contribution of manufactured exports. In each case, demand for these goods is determined outside the control of local decisionmakers, and, in each case, there is little domestic demand to absorb any shortfalls in foreign demand.[75]

Patterns of Ownership and Control

In the 1970s, a combination of world events and state ideology increased the state's role in most Caribbean economies, often to the point where the state was directly involved in ownership of a large part of the economy. In most cases, the government wished to gain greater local, especially state, control over economic decisionmaking and thus to gain greater autonomy and freedom in its pursuit of what it had determined to be national economic goals, the most critical being social programs to benefit the masses of voters from the weaker classes. As a result, foreign ownership declined somewhat as nationalizations began to occur, often by "default" in the sense that the state bought operations that foreign capital was about to abandon anyway. Also, world economic events, combined with concerns about political risk, slowed down foreign direct investment linked to the state's continuing import-substitution orientation. Although moves toward state ownership fit the increasingly nationalist, or state nationalist, ideology advocated by some dependency theorists and adopted by most states of the region, in practice the state found itself operating often inefficient production units with dubious structural, and especially foreign exchange, impacts. Moreover, in many cases, despite official state ownership of an enterprise, foreign management often remained under contract and thus decisionmaking was still subject to outside influence.

In the 1980s, multilateral lending institutions advocated divestment of state enterprises for those regional economies undergoing stabilization. In that decade, a significant amount of divestment did occur but seldom with much sense of government enthusiasm or even acceptance. In the 1990s, however, no longer is this the case. The Grenadian state is giving up controlling interest in the National Commercial Bank and has targeted the Grenada Electric Company, the Central Garage Corporation, and the Grenada Model Farms Corporation for sale as soon as feasible.[76] Barbados has targeted the state-owned Arawak Cement Company, Barbados Dairy Industries, Barbados National Oil Company, National Petroleum Corporation, and Heywoods Hotel for sale, after earning U.S.$30.8 million in its divestment program's first year.[77] Trinidad and Jamaica are also deep into privatization programs, and interestingly both under leaders whose parties had criticized such schemes until only a few years ago.[78] Even economies not subject to externally imposed stabilization have jumped on the privatization bandwagon. For instance, the Bahamian government intends to divest itself of its broadcasting corporation, ZNS, and its state-owned hotels.[79]

What effect this shift in the balance between state and private ownership will have on the balance between foreign and domestic ownership is unclear at this point. On one hand, divesting governments generally espouse the principle that the companies should stay in local hands as much as possible. For instance, the Grenadian government planned to offer 39 percent of the National Commercial Bank to the Grenadian public. On the other hand, foreign investors appear quite active in taking over former state corporations. For example, the U.S.-based Enron Oil and Gas Company is the likely electricity provider in the divestment of the Trinidad and Tobago Electric Commission, while a Finnish company is interested in the planned privatization of the Grenada Electric Company.[80]

In some other areas of the economy, the local bourgeoisie has retained significant influence. Ownership and control in the local capitalist sector tend to be highly concentrated. For instance, twenty-one families basically control the locally owned segments of the Jamaican productive and commercial sectors,[81] while the local Barbadian bourgeoisie funnels itself, for the most part, into four corporations.[82] The continuing commercial bias of domestic capital in most of the region has left it with little inclination, or capacity, to generate significant influence over the productive structure of Caribbean economies, however, even in response to CBI incentives to establish locally owned manufacturing production or Caricom's intent to create a larger, regional market though the formation of a common market.[83] Instead, domestic capital has focused on opportunities to expand the circulation of capital rather than to deepen production.[84]

Relations of Production

Since the 1970s, increasing numbers of Caribbean people have been incorporated into capitalist relations of production, especially within the traditional sector. Peasant-based production is on the decline, at least on the larger islands. For example, Michael Kaufman[85] notes a 30 percent drop in the number of small farms in Jamaica between 1968 and 1978, reflected in a massive rural-urban migration. At least some of those arriving in the city have become part of the proletariat. In other cases, the shift in relations of production is more subtle, reflecting an informal proletarianization, as in the case of banana-producing peasants in Dominica. Michel-Rolph Trouillot argues that in Dominica, "the conditions with which [the peasant] deals make him more like a proletarian selling his labor power than a peasant selling a product."[86] By law, Dominican bananas intended for export must be delivered to the Dominican Banana Growers Association (DBGA). In

turn, Geest Industries Limited, a British-based subsidiary, is the monop-
sony buying from, or more accurately, through, the DBGA at a market price
that Geest virtually sets.[87] Finally, the Dominican peasant is not generally
producing bananas as an addition to self-provisioning sufficient for subsistence, but rather as a way of supplementing self-provisioning to achieve
subsistence.[88] Thus, the appellation "peasant" may hide as much as it un-
covers in its description of these relations of production.

More generally, peasants of the region increasingly produce agroindustrial inputs and exportable goods, especially nontraditional crops. Others, harkening back to post-Emancipation days, are semiproletarians, combining wage work with self-provisioning. In some countries, though,
opportunities for wage work in the countryside are extremely limited. In
this case, a split in the family is likely, the man going to the city to work
and the woman remaining behind to farm.[89] Thus, in a subtle way, capitalist relations are extending to include more and more of the people who
have previously been outside that realm. Ironically, the proletarianization
of Caribbean societies has also been increasing from the other direction in
that as the state and middle-class sectors decline in response to economic
restructuring and austerity programs, many of their former members have
entered the proletariat.[90]

A countertrend to increasingly capitalist relations is also noticeable,
though, as people who are able to are increasingly growing as much of
their own food as possible to supplement the declining purchasing power
of their wages. More obvious is the burgeoning of the informal sector in
the cities as the formal sector's ability to absorb the population moving
from the countryside declines. Even as early as 1981, analysts estimated
that 33 percent of the labor force in Kingston, Jamaica, was employed in
the informal sector.[91] Since then, the number of plant layoffs and closures
has risen with the economic crisis, increasing unemployment in the formal
sector and increasing the number of people the informal sector is absorbing.[92]

Extent of Capitalization and Modernization

Another indicator of change in the region reflecting the internationalization of production is the increasing use of globally standardized technologies in both foreign-owned and nationally owned industries to produce
goods that meet international standards. In the Caribbean, this generally
involves increased mechanization and capitalization, but seldom the use of
state-of-the-art high technology. Still, a number of modern products are
produced at home, sometimes by local capital, rather than imported. In
Trinidad, the local corporation, Calypso Chicken, is the counterpart of the
transnational corporation, Kentucky Fried Chicken, in Jamaica. Similarly,
the Caribbean uses modern technologies to produce modern products or

services for export. Data processing, semiconductor production, and electronic equipment are common exports from the region. In other cases, such modern production is not destined for specifically internal or external markets but rather for the world market, essentially the market created by both domestic and foreign consumers with substantial purchasing power.

Level Responded To

Caribbean production and exchange decisions in the 1980s and 1990s have been increasingly responding to factors at the global level, from the decisions of the banana-growing informal proletarians in Dominica, to their corporate overseers, to transnational corporations looking to the Caribbean's potential to serve as a global platform. Yet, other decisions, such as that of most local capital not to pursue productive opportunities afforded by the internationalization of production generally, and the CBI and Caricom specifically, reflect not-so-global concerns.

Distribution of Economic Product

International

In the 1970s, the growth experienced in the previous era reversed itself, worsening the position of the Caribbean in the international distribution of claims on the goods and services produced in the world.[93] Especially detrimental were developments in the monetary sector. Drastically increased energy costs, based on OPEC price hikes and the increasing energy dependence of the economies that had been constructed during the previous two decades, combined with foreign exchange leakages from the mineral, industrial, and tourist sectors, began to show up in chronic balance-of-payments deficits, large borrowings of foreign exchange to cover the difference, and large debt-service payments waiting a few years in the future.

The downward slide continued through much of the following decade. In the late 1980s, though, the Caribbean had some success with export-led growth at the same time that commodity prices were rising on the world market. Nonetheless, the modest economic growth experienced was eclipsed by the huge growth of international debt for many countries in the region.

The 1990s have brought mixed results for Caribbean economies (see Table 3.3). Jamaica, and perhaps Trinidad, appear to have hit bottom in implementing their stabilization programs and experienced modest rises in GDP growth and declines in inflation and external debt in the first two years of the decade.[94] Barbados, on the other hand, is still experiencing a downward slide, with negative growth in GDP and real output, combined with rising inflation.[95] Antigua expects growth in its GDP this year following five years of decline, while other countries, including Dominica, are experiencing positive but declining growth rates.[96]

Even with Jamaica's and Trinidad's slight improvement, the fallout from the past decade's increasing debt continues as the overriding issue in the region today and has become increasingly relevant to the welfare of all Caribbean classes.[97] Not only is "luxury" consumption dependent on imports, as in the days of internationalization through commodity trade alone, but now production itself is also often dependent on imports of inputs and machinery.[98] Foreign exchange shortages or an increased relative cost of foreign exchange can thus have devastating consequences for production and employment levels, which, in turn, affect the distribution of claims on economic product both internationally and intranationally. Moreover, the prospects for continued growth under the new international division of labor appear less glowing since the region is not generally in a position to take advantage of the opportunities presented by the internationalization of production.[99] The commercial bourgeoisie's predominance in the economy militates against accelerated growth in locally owned manufacturing production while the comparative advantage the region may have as a global platform for transnational corporations is small and likely to erode since most countries' labor costs are relatively high compared to the rest of the Third World, the level of skills is not that high, and even proximity to the United States market is outdone by Mexico.[100] Thus, the restructuring of Caribbean economies that has occurred under the new international division of labor has had uneven results concerning the region's position in the international distribution of economic product.

Intranational

The impact of restructuring on the intranational distribution has been much more consistent; it has polarized that distribution even further (see Table 3.4 for the general Caribbean case and Tables 3.5-3.7 for illustrations from Jamaica). In addition to facing the international bias, the weaker classes of the Caribbean also confront the disproportionate influence of domestic elites, whose interest more often than not differs from their own.[101] The position of the weaker classes has generally deteriorated in the 1980s and 1990s after a brief, small improvement in some countries in the 1970s. Rural areas, particularly the small-farm sectors, are declining at an accelerating rate.[102] The working class also generally finds its position eroding as incentives for foreign investment, conditions for foreign loans, and attempts to achieve international competitiveness have all cut into the legitimacy of its members' claims for more of the economic product. In

Table 3.3   Per Capita Income and Growth in Selected Caribbean Countries

Country	Per Capita Income, 1992 (U.S.$)	Growth in Per Capita Income, 1980–1991 (%)
Antigua and Barbuda	4430	3.8
Bahamas	11750	1.3
Barbados	6630	1.3
Dominica	2440	4.7
Grenada	2180	5.3
Jamaica	1160	–0.3
St. Kitts–Nevis	3960	5.8
St. Lucia	2490	2.9
St. Vincent and the Grenadines	1730	5.2
Trinidad and Tobago	3670	–5.2
(United States)	(22240)	

Source: Latin American Weekly Report (May 20, 1993): p. 225.

Antigua, the Antigua Trades and Labour Union (Atlu) complains of an "ever-widening gap between the wages of managers and the wages of workers."[103] In Jamaica, the elimination of subsidies, lifting of price controls, and de facto currency devaluation resulting from exchange liberalization that were part of a deregulation program launched in late 1990 have all combined to reduce purchasing power even further, especially for poor Jamaicans. For instance, the Jamaican dollar fell from J$9.00 = U.S.$1.00 in May 1991 to nearly J$30.00 = U.S.$1.00 less than a year later, while inflation ran at 80 percent[104] in 1991 and even reached 105 percent during the 1991/92 financial year.[105] Exchange and inflation rates have improved substantially since then but continue to eat away at buying power.

Unemployment rates in the region also remain staggeringly high, with a "normal" range of 20 to 25 percent. St. Vincent and the Grenadines suffers from 40 to 45 percent unemployment, even as the value of electronics exports soars.[106] Furthermore, little relief is in sight. Trinidad's rate increased 85 percent in the decade between 1981 and 1991[107] while Barbados's jumped 30 percent in one year.[108]

The number of malnourished also reflects the position of the weaker classes in the intranational distribution of claims on the economic product. Evidence of increased malnutrition has been mounting over the last decade in Jamaica[109] and indications are that malnutrition is a growing problem elsewhere in the region as well.[110]

Regional Perspectives in Political Economies

Table 3.4 UNDP **Human Development Index and World Rank**

	HDI Index			HDI World Rank		
Country	1990	1992	Change	1990	1991	Change
Antigua and Barbuda	.832	.785	-.047	46	60	-14
Bahamas	.920	.875	-.045	28	32	-4
Barbados	.945	.928	-.017	22	20	+ 2
Dominica	.800	.819	+.019	53	51	+ 2
Grenada	.751	.787	+.036	64	59	+ 5
Jamaica	.761	.736	-.025	59	69	-10
St. Kitts–Nevis	.719	.697	-.022	65	79	-14
St. Lucia	.699	.720	+.021	68	72	-4
St. Vincent and the Grenadines	.636	.709	+.073	79	76	+ 3
Trinidad and Tobago	.876	.877	+.001	39	31	+ 8

Source: Latin American Weekly Report (June 24, 1993): pp. 284–285.

Table 3.5   **Land Distribution in Jamaica, 1968 and 1978**

		Farms				Land in Farms		
	Number		Percent		Acreage		Percent	
	1968	1978	1968	1978	1968	1978	1968	1978
Under 1 acre	57737	39733	29.9	26.5	22736	14830	1.5	1.3
1–4.9 acres	93961	70980	48.6	47.3	206480	156160	13.9	14.2
5–24.9 acres	37607	36875	19.4	24.6	340757	387360	22.9	35.2
25–49.5 acres	2280	1868	1.2	1.2	74718	72440	5.0	6.6
50+ acres	1767	544	0.9	0.4	844497	470570	56.7	42.7
Total	193352	150000	100.0	100.0	1489188	1101360	100.0	100.0

Sources: 1968: Evelyne Huber Stephens and John D. Stephens, *Democratic Socialism in Jamaica* (Princeton, N.J.: Princeton University Press, 1986), p. 29. 1978: Michael Kaufman, *Jamaica Under Manley,* (London: Zed Press, 1985), p. 14.

Moreover, because profit-oriented production priorities in these societies naturally follow purchasing power, and because upper-strata and overseas consumers have the necessary purchasing power to drive the higher profit rates capital requires, the wants and needs of those consumers tend to override those of low-income consumers in determining what

Table 3.6   Jamaican Class Distribution, 1973

Class	Percentage
Capitalist	less than 0.5
Upper middle	4–5
Urban middle strata	
salariat	8–9
petty bourgeoisie	4–6
Middle and large farmers	3–4
Urban working class	22–24
Small farmers	17–20
Agricultural working class	4–7
Marginals	
marginally employed	12–15
unemployed	22

Source: Evelyne Huber Stephens and John D. Stephens, *Democratic Socialism in Jamaica* (Princeton, N.J.: Princeton University Press, 1986), p. 36.

Table 3.7   Share of Labor Income Accruing to Top 20 Percent in Jamaica

1972	53%
1974	57%
1976	58%
1977	58%
1978	58%
1980	67%
1981	75%

Source: Carl Stone, "Running Out of Options," *Caribbean Review* XV, no. 3, (1987): p. 41.

Caribbean societies will produce and import, as evidenced in Jamaica in the mid-1980s by the "proliferation of satellite dishes and new Mercedes automobiles" at the same time that austerity measures cut deeply into the consumption of the poor.[111] Consumers with little purchasing power do not have sufficient clout to orient productive and commercial priorities into providing for their needs and find that they must meet their needs in the domestic basic goods market, for the most part supplied by the dwindling traditional sector, or in the high-cost formal commercial sector. In the first case, more and more people are chasing fewer and fewer goods. In the second, low-income consumers have insufficient purchasing power to purchase adequate quantities to meet their needs. Either way, the intranational distribution of claims on economic product has become even more concentrated than in previous eras.

Very recently, a few government policies have addressed themselves toward mitigating the gap between haves and have-nots. For example, the Trinidadian government has enhanced food programs, lowered customs duties on certain prescription drugs, and provided tax relief to those earning less than TT$16,000 (U.S.$3,720).[112] The Jamaican government has also decreased its personal income tax rate, from 33.3 percent to 25 percent, and raised its tax-exempt threshold from J$14,322 (U.S.$589) to J$18,480 (U.S.$760). Along similar lines, Jamaica approved large salary increases for civil servants.[113]

Important as such measures are, it is primarily the middle class that will benefit. Moreover, in Jamaica, in order to finance income tax relief, the general consumption tax (GCT) is rising from 10 percent to 12.5 percent, and the list of consumer items exempted from the GCT is shrinking,[114] a move that is likely to affect the Jamaican poor negatively. As the *Sunday Gleaner* editorializes, "The minister of finance has a problem in financing the budget, but the vast majority of Jamaicans are going to have an even greater problem surviving at subsistence levels."[115] Many in other Caribbean countries will likely face the same dilemma.[116]

Discussion

The purpose of this chapter has been to discuss the political economy of the Caribbean in terms of the internationalization of production and the new international division of labor in order to separate change from continuity. The particular pattern of Caribbean insertion into the global political economy and the uneven penetration of the internationalization of production into the Caribbean political economy make this separation difficult in that, in some ways, the region's insertion into the new international division of labor is incomplete, and certainly behind the rate of Latin America or East Asia, while in others, it appears to have been ahead of its time. The existence of peasants, informal proletarians, and semiproletarians indicates incomplete integration, as do outmigration and the increasing importance of the informal sector. Compared to that of the First World, the local Caribbean bourgeoisie is more commercial than productive in nature, indicating that many of the old distortions of the periphery remain. Similarly, the continuing dependence on primary product and raw material exports is in keeping with the region's place under the classical international division of labor. On the other hand, two trends associated with the internationalization of production were apparent in the region well before the post–World War II era. Multinational investment has existed in the region since the mid- to late-1800s and wage labor since slave emancipation in the 1830s. Whether indicative of late or early integration into the internationalization of production, these trends would seem to imply continuity rather than change. And, in some instances, notably the continuous commercial nature of much of the Caribbean bourgeoisie, this does appear to be the case. In other instances, though, there are qualitative changes indicative of the most recent phase of the internationalization of capital within these seeming continuities. For example, pre-war multinational investment in the Caribbean generally focused on a particular agricultural or mineral resource specific to the region and oriented itself toward the export of primary products and raw materials so much associated with the classical international division of labor. Much postwar multinational and transnational investment continues along these lines. Significantly, though, much of it has also focused on manufactures, first, primarily for the domestic market in the form of import-substitution industrialization, but more recently, as part of the export-led growth programs underway in most of the countries of the region. Moreover, both local state and local private capital have also been involved in the production of processed goods, with or without an affiliation with transnational capital.

Similarly, although wage labor has been common in the region for over 150 years, it has undergone both an expansion to include increasing numbers of people and a qualitative change. First, up until the 1930s most wage work in the region, that is, agricultural wage work, was on a piece-rate basis rather than a daily- or hourly-rate basis. Second, wage labor is an indicator of the internationalization of production because it is taken to be an indicator of the increasing generalization of the capitalist organization of production. As new sectors have been added to the productive and commercial profiles of regional economies, wage labor relations have expanded in proportion to total production. Even in sectors where noncapitalist relations may still exist, such as among some peasants and some artisans, many have a work process that is increasingly outside their control and increasingly determined by either transnational or local productive or commercial capital. Moreover, just as Alain de Janvry[117] has argued in the Latin American case, the incomplete quality of the Caribbean's capitalist integration into the international system appears to capital's advantage in this region and may actually contribute to the internationalization process, in the sense that remaining peasant production in the agricultural sector, artisan production in the informal sector, and commercial transactions in the informal sector are "safety valves," taking over in reproducing the labor force where capitalism fails to provide the means. Profit levels based on low wage rates can thus continue, where under other circumstances they might be unable to do so.

Other changes in keeping with the expected influences of the internationalization of production and the new international division of labor are also apparent in the region. Although subtle and sometimes difficult to trace, a transformation of the labor process has occurred for a broadening segment of the regional population. With the emergence of an informal proletariat, more of the production of the traditional sector is influenced by internationalized capital, whether under domestic or foreign ownership. Also, more nontraditional goods, both manufactures and primary products, are being produced. Furthermore, they are being produced according to international quality standards and according to the standardized technologies most familiar to First World industry but increasingly available worldwide. Moreover, much of what is being produced is oriented not so much to the export market or to the domestic market, but to the world market, which does little to distinguish upper-strata domestic consumers from overseas consumers.

The mutual structural adjustment of national economies and reorientation of state power associated with the internationalization of production and the new international division of labor are also apparent in the region. Government interventions increasing the state's regulatory reach into the local population, such as wage restraints, new and/or increased taxes, and attempts at greater enforcement of tax regulations, are reflections of the state's role as the authorized agent of the international system. Along these lines, Hilbourne Watson notes the lack of autonomous decisionmaking in economic restructuring, claiming that "Caribbean development strategies are, historically speaking, forms of adjustment to the needs of international capital."[118]

> Terms such as import-substitution or export-led growth strategies are far less illuminating than they appear. They are little more than the public policy devices of Third World regimes as they respond to the dynamic rhythm of the internationalization of capital in different periods.[119]

This lack of autonomy has increased with the prevalence and permeation of international debt as the overriding issue in the region in the 1980s and 1990s. Caribbean economies find themselves increasingly subject to the dictates of the incipient international political structure through its control of financial adjustment procedures in return for balance-of-payments loans. Probably the clearest regional example of this is the moderate and accommodating stance of the most recent Manley Administration of Jamaica (1989–1992)[120] with respect to the International Monetary Fund, international capital, and the United States government as contrasted with its much more antagonistic relationships in its previous terms (1972–1980). Most recently, the implementation of the Single Europe Act and the emergence of NAFTA have done little to add to decisionmaking autonomy in Caribbean countries and indeed are likely to constrain it further as pressures to join the free trade movement rise and one-way preferences erode away.

This brings us to the shift in the relationship of the Caribbean political economy to the outside. For the most part, the decisionmaking deck has been stacked against autonomous, unconstrained action in the Caribbean's dealings with the external world since the region was first colonized. The dependence on, domination of, or simply reliance on forces outside the region continues today, probably to an even greater degree than before, but the nature of that outside to which the region relates has changed considerably, with consequences in turn for the Caribbean political economy. The internationalization of capital and the emerging international political structure have changed the centers of external power, but the centers of external power are no less critical in determining the outcomes of cross-pressures on state and societal decisions in the Caribbean. Most of the region's countries have shifted their outward focus from the United Kingdom to the United States or, more broadly, to North America. Some authors view this as a metamorphosis from British colonies to American satellites. Yet, with the blurring of distinctions between internal and external, or national and transnational, brought on by the internationalization of capital, such a characterization misleads as much as it clarifies. Caribbean countries are instead perhaps satellites of international capital centered in the United States. Or, perhaps they are satellites of the incipient international political structure developing parallel to internationalized production, part of which is incorporated in the central agencies of the United States government; part of which is found in other First World governments, the International Monetary Fund, the World Bank, and other international institutions; and part of which resides in the Caribbean governments and financial structures themselves as the ideology of internationalization is absorbed by numerous Caribbean officials, including, for instance, Vere Bird of Antigua, Eugenia Charles of Dominica, Edward Seaga, and more recently, P. J. Patterson of Jamaica, and Patrick Manning of Trinidad. Thus, continuing to refer to the United States as an "imperial," or even a "neoimperial," power is a somewhat dubious notion, despite appearances and activities to the contrary. This is not to deny the continuing domination of the Caribbean region by foreign states, as illustrated by attempts to condition the mutual structural adjustment of Caribbean and "conditioning" countries in the new international division of labor through preferential trade agreements and the like. For the most part, though, there is a new imperialist force operating over the region in the form of the emerging international political structure combined with the decisionmaking power of internationalized capital.

The blurring of internal and external influences into global influences is apparent in the more specifically economic realm as well. This is important in that it implies that mere local or state ownership of a productive mechanism is insufficient to create much of a change in production priorities or in intranational distributions of economic product in the region. Furthermore, the balance of foreign versus domestic ownership is becoming moot with respect to orienting production and exchange toward the state's development goals, should those goals differ from what would occur through the internationalization of production as it is manifested in that country. If either domestic or foreign capital is to survive, it must respond to factors at the global level, an action that may not be conducive to given national development goals. There is, however, likely to be a distinction between domestic and foreign, especially transnational, ownership in the sense of ease of mobility and sensitivity to potentially favorable or unfavorable conditions within the Caribbean and outside. Also, because most transnational corporations are horizontally integrated, the question may not be whether the company will produce a particular product in a Caribbean location or in another location but rather whether the company will continue to produce the product at all or instead shift to other types of products or endeavors, in the Caribbean or elsewhere. Transnational decisions are made on the basis of what is good for the transnational corporation, not the host state nor the host population. There may be a coincidence of interest; there may not. Even nationally controlled corporations, though, if they are in actual or potential competition with transnational or foreign capital in their domestic or export markets, are increasingly restricted to making decisions on the basis of the same logic as transnational capital. They cannot be tied much more than transnational capital to national development goals if they are to be successful. And, even state-owned enterprises may confront similar parameters. If they require export markets or global economies of scale, as in the case of proposed Trinidadian steel production or proposed Trinidadian-Jamaican aluminum production, they become just as dependent on outside or global factors in their decision-making as transnational capital and all the previous historical actors in Caribbean political economies have been. Now, though, those outside factors are less under the control of any national state.

Conclusion

The political economy of the Caribbean is the result of a complex set of tensions between commercial and productive emphases, domestic and foreign influences, peasant and capitalist forces, formal and informal sectors, and overarching all of these, continuity and change. Threads of continuity in the Caribbean political economy from the days of pre-war colonialism include the commercial emphasis of most local capital; the export orientation of much production; and the importance of traditional primary product and, more recently, raw material, exports. Others include the continuing existence of a peasant sector, foreign ownership or control of a sizable part of national economies, and, especially, externally based limits on local decisionmaking.

Six categories of change are also apparent in the region's political economy. First is a change in sectoral emphasis from agriculture to mining, manufacturing, offshore banking, or tourism, depending on the country, and from there, to whatever works at a given moment combined with nontraditional exports of all types, both processed and unprocessed. Second, there has been a change in the destination of production, broadening from the export market to the world market, one reflection of which is the increasing volume of Caribbean production destined for the domestic market in the form of industrial inputs or processed goods.

Third, the national origin of producers is changing. Ownership of manufacturing production has broadened to include some state capital and local private capital, at least on the larger islands. Moreover, even within foreign-controlled production, the number of nations of origin is broadening. A fourth change is the differentiation of the peasantry into self-provisioners, producers of food staples for the local market, producers of agricultural exports, producers of agroindustrial inputs for the world market, informal proletarians, semiproletarians, and any combination of the above.

Fifth, the level to which economic decisionmakers are responding is altering. Whether made by transnational capital, local private capital, state capital, or even noncapitalist peasants, many decisions respond to global factors at the level of production in the sense that they respond to global markets or actual or potential competition from imports or transnationally based production at home. Finally, there is the changing nature of the "outside" to which the Caribbean political economy continuously relates. External influences, whether political or economic, have become global, meaning that the lines between external and internal are blurring, sometimes to the point of disappearing. This has resulted in a shift of the dominating influences over the Caribbean from a foreign state or states and the corporations therein to the international or global system in the form of internationalized capital and the nascent international political structure emerging parallel to the internationalization of production. The possible emergence of major trading blocs in the form of an expanded NAFTA, a pan-European single market, and a Japanese-led Asian group would shift the form of the "outside" still further. For the most part, though, the motivation for forming or deepening such blocs appears to be to facilitate the trends associated with the internationalization of production and the globalization of the economy and to accelerate their momentum within a region rather than to erect barriers to these trends and decelerate their momentum between regions. For the Caribbean, what this process of regionalization will likely mean, especially if it becomes part of a hemispheric bloc, is an additional layer of constraining influence to which its political and economic decisionmakers will be subject.

Therefore, the Caribbean political economy has changed and continues to change despite the underlying continuity of its reliance on, and insertion into, the international capitalist system. Unfortunately for the people of the region, such changes show no promise of improving the region's ability to capture a growing share of the global economic product. Nor do they appear any more likely to change the seemingly immovable pattern of the weaker Caribbean classes' failing to capture a share of the benefits during boom times or to avoid bearing the brunt of the detrimental impact of downturns in the region's relative economic fortunes.

Notes

1. The countries falling into this category are: Antigua and Barbuda, the Bahamas, Barbados, Dominica, Grenada, Jamaica, St. Kitts–Nevis, St. Lucia, St. Vincent and the Grenadines, and Trinidad and Tobago. Guyana and Belize have been omitted since they are on the mainland, although they do share many of the characteristics to be described here. Monserrat continues its colonial status.

2. This conceptualization borrows from Susan Strange, "International Political Economy: The Story So Far and the Way Ahead," in W. Ladd Hollist and F. LaMond Tullis, eds., *An International Political Economy* (Boulder: Westview Press, 1985), pp. 1–12; and W. Ladd Hollist and James A. Caporaso, "International Political Economy Research: What Is It and Where Do We Turn For Theory?" in W. Ladd Hollist and F. LaMond Tullis, eds., *An International Political Economy* (Boulder: Westview Press, 1985), pp. 27–52.

3. See Steven E. Sanderson, "Florida Tomatoes, U.S.–Mexican Relations and the International Division of Labor," in *Inter-American Economic Affairs* 35, no. 3 (1981): pp. 23–52; Steven E. Sanderson, "A Critical Approach to the Americas in the New International Division of Labor," in Steven E. Sanderson, ed., *The Americas in the New International Division of Labor* (New York: Holmes and Meier, 1985), pp. 3–25; and Steven E. Sanderson, *The Transformation of Mexican Agriculture* (Princeton, N.J.: Princeton University Press, 1986).

4. See David Barkin, "Internationalization of Capital: An Alternative Approach," in *Latin American Perspectives* 8, nos. 3, 4 (1981): pp. 156–161; Carlos Rozo and David Barkin, "La Produccion de Alimentos en el Proceso de Internacionalizacion del Capital," (The Production of Food in the Process of Internationalization of Capital) *Trimestre Economico* 50, no. 3 (1983): pp. 1603–1626; and David Barkin, "Global Proletarianization," in Steven E. Sanderson, ed., *The Americas in the New International Division of Labor* (New York: Holmes and Meier, 1985), pp. 26–45.

5. See Robert W. Cox, *Production, Power, and World Order: Social Forces in the Making* (New York: Columbia University Press, 1987).

6. Sanderson, *The Transformation of Mexican Agriculture*, p. 5.

7. Cox, *Production, Power and World Order*, p. 260.

8. Adapted from Sanderson, *The Transformation of Mexican Agriculture*, p. 18.

9. This chapter's historical discussion will limit itself to the British colonial experience, not addressing these islands' earlier experiences under Spanish and/or French rule.

10. The analytical separation of state processes and social processes is somewhat artificial for several of the processes described since they may involve the interaction of state and social aspects, and it is that interaction that is contributing to a particular organization of production and exchange activities in the economy.

11. Britain allowed elected assemblies until the 1860s in colonies brought under its rule before the nineteenth century and in all its colonies in the 1930s, following major social unrest.

12. Occurring simultaneously with the transfer of power was a short-lived experiment in regional political integration, the West Indian Federation, which disbanded in 1962.

13. Carl Stone, "Democracy and Socialism in Jamaica: 1972–1979," in Paget Henry and Carl Stone, eds., *The Newer Caribbean: Decolonization, Democracy, and Development* (Philadelphia: Institute for the Study of Human Issues, 1983), pp. 235–255. "Weaker classes" comprise the working class, the agricultural proletariat, peasants, those in the informal sector, the underemployed, the unemployed, and any other marginalized groups.

14. Michael Kaufman, *Jamaica Under Manley: Dilemmas of Socialism and Democracy* (London: Zed Press, 1985), p. 9.

15. Unlike Latin America, the Caribbean did not implement any major program of import-substitution industrialization during World War II, due, at least in part, to resistance by the ruling British government. See Richard Bernal, "The Great Depression, Colonial Policy and Industrialization in Jamaica," *Social and Economic Studies* 37, nos. 1, 2 (1988): p. 34. By the 1950s, though, increasingly autonomous local policymakers doubted the agricultural sector's ability to cure the burgeoning unemployment problem and advocated expanding other sectors, particularly manufacturing. Furthermore, they believed that such expansion would require foreign input to make up the small size of domestic markets and shortages of capital and entrepreneurial ability. To this end, they provided legislative incentives for domestic and foreign investment, especially in import-substitution industrialization. Owen Jefferson, "Some Aspects of the Post-War Economic Development of Jamaica," in Norman Girvan and Owen Jefferson, eds., *Readings in the Political Economy of the Caribbean* (Kingston, Jamacia: New World Group, Ltd., 1971), p. 112.

16. See Michael G. Salmon, "Land Utilization Within Jamaica's Bauxite Land Economy," *Social and Economic Studies* 36, no. 1 (March 1987): pp. 77–78 and 85–87; and Michael P. Todaro, *Economic Development in the Third World*, 4th ed. (New York: Longman, Inc., 1989), p. 268–270. This sector developed alongside the already-existing informal domestic food market.

17. See Jeb Mays and Phillip Wheaton, *Jamaica: Caribbean Challenge* (Washington, D.C.: EPICA Task Force, 1979), pp. 17–34. See also W. K. Marshall, "St. Lucia in the Economic History of the Windward Islands: The 19th Century Experience," *Caribbean Quarterly* 35, no. 3 (September 1989): pp. 30–31.

18. For instance, control or ownership of capital or commercial assets.

19. For instance, in Jamaica in 1961/62, 71 percent of all farms were under five acres and together accounted for 12 percent of Jamaica's farm acreage. Conversely, O.2 percent of farms were over five hundred acres and accounted for 45 percent of total farm acreage. See Jefferson, "Some Aspects of the Post-War," p. 110. See also Table 3.5, this chapter.

20. Planters generally sold their crop on consignment to metropolitan merchants and bankers and in return were directly supplied or provided with credit to buy supplies elsewhere. Thus, foreign capital was very much involved in facilitating production but not in directly organizing production.

21. Clive Y. Thomas, *The Poor and the Powerless: Economic Policy and Change in the Caribbean* (New York: Monthly Review Press, 1987), p. 49.

22. Even this small, internally oriented component shrank, however, in the latter part of the nineteenth century as supplemental wage-work became less available and peasants began producing exports in addition to provisions for themselves and the local market.

23. In the instance of import-substitution industrialization, there appears to be a qualitative difference to the internal orientation in that at least those decision-makers linked to multinational corporations were making decisions increasingly on the basis of global market strategies, even if the intended market was internal.

24. Mays and Wheaton, *Jamaica*, p. 17.

25. For instance, in Jamaica, growth in GDP averaged 7 percent per year. See Jefferson, "Some Aspects of the Post-War," p. 109; and John S. Gafar, "Economic Growth and Economic Policy: Employment and Unemployment in Jamaica, 1972–84," *The Journal of Developing Areas* 23 (October 1988): p. 64.

26. At the same time that a supposed labor shortage led to a program of importing indentured labor until approximately 1917, emigration levels, motivated by a lack of adequate livelihood opportunities at home, especially for former slaves and their descendants, were not far short of indentured East Indian immigration levels. Computed from Thomas, *The Poor and the Powerless*, pp. 35, 42.

27. For instance, peasant land ownership began declining on the larger islands in the mid-1950s. Kaufman, *Jamaica Under Manley*, p. 14. On some other islands, though, notably Dominica, it was the estate sector that declined. Michel-Rolph Trouillot, *Peasants and Capital: Dominica in the World Economy* (Baltimore: Johns Hopkins University Press, 1988), p. 135.

28. For example, in the Jamaican case, which may be generalized to a large degree, the reverse occurred. From 1955–1966, the total employment created by incentive-driven investment was 9,000 jobs, while over the same period, mechanization removed 10,000 jobs from the sugar industry alone; meanwhile, the labor force was expanding by 20,000 annually. Jefferson, "Some Aspects of the Post-War," p. 112. Similarly, the Jamaican unemployment rate rose from 12 percent to 23 percent between 1962 and 1972, with similar or sometimes even higher rates in other countries. Gafar, "Economic Growth," p. 64.

29. For instance, analysts estimate that the relative and absolute income of the bottom 30 percent of the Jamaican population fell by 30 percent between 1962 and 1972. Gafar, "Economic Growth," p. 64.

30. The destination, however, shifted toward the United States and Canada as their immigration restrictions relaxed while Britain's tightened.

31. These loans increasingly came from commercial banks.

32. See Evelyne Huber Stephens and John D. Stephens, *Democratic Socialism in Jamaica: The Political Movement and Social Transformation in Dependent Capitalism* (Princeton, N.J.: Princeton University Press, 1986).

33. "Regional Assembly Issues Final Report," *Latin American Regional Reports—Caribbean (LARR—C)*, (October 1, 1992): p. 5.

34. For instance, Trinidad's primarily Afro-Trinidadian-based PNM is attempting to appeal to "people of all classes, all races, [and] from all walks of life." See "Manning Passes Local Polls Test," *LARR—C*, (November 5, 1992): p. 6.

35. Carl Stone, "Decolonization and the Caribbean State System," in Paget Henry and Carl Stone, eds., *The Newer Caribbean, Decolonization, Democracy, and Development* (Philadelphia: Institute for the Study of Human Issues, 1983), p. 42.

36. Stone, "Decolonization and the Caribbean," p. 42.

37. Hilbourne Watson, "Recent Attempts at Industrial Restructuring in Barbados," *Latin American Perspectives* 17, no. 1 (1990): p. 16.

38. Paget Henry, "Decolonization and the Authoritarian Context of Democracy in Antigua," in Paget Henry and Carl Stone, eds., *The New Caribbean, Decolonization, Democracy, and Development* (Philadelphia: Institute for the Study of Human Issues, 1983), p. 301.

39. Moreover, the working class is the top level of the weaker classes. Those at lower levels are feeling even less benefit from the current state-society coalitions.

40. "Unions Assert Themselves in 1993," *Latin American Regional Reports— Caribbean and Central America (LARR—C&CA)*, (January 21, 1993): p. 2.

41. Supporting the notion of state-bourgeois perceptions of mutual interest, Stewart explained his action, saying that his objective was to "prevent the social unrest that would accompany soaring inflation and the effect this would have on his hotel business." "Hotelier Halts Slide of Local Currency," *LARR—C*, (June 18, 1992): p. 6.

42. This actually refers to sections 806.30, 807, and 807A of the U.S. tariff code.

43. See John Ravenhill, "What Is To Be Done for Third World Commodity Exporters?: An Evaluation of the STABEX Scheme," *International Organization* 38, no. 3 (Summer 1984): pp. 537–574.

44. Such attempts at conditioning have not been entirely successful, however, in that a number of excluded goods provide the growth market in U.S. imports from the Caribbean. Nonetheless, production levels of these goods are likely to be lower than if they were eligible for duty-free access.

45. Carmen Diana Deere, coord., *In the Shadow of the Sun: Caribbean Development Alternatives and U.S. Policy* (Boulder: Westview Press, 1990), p. 167.

46. U.S. House Subcommittee on International Development, Finance, Trade, and Monetary Policy of the Committee on Banking, Finance, and Urban Affairs, Hearing on The President's Enterprise for the Americas Initiative, 102nd Cong., 1st sess., May 15, 1991, p. 2.

47. "Producer Challenge To EC Banana Rules," *Latin American Weekly Report (LAWR)*, (June 20, 1993), p. 281.

48. The agreement guarantees a market of 857,000 tons duty free, with a duty of 750 ECUs (U.S.$945) per ton beyond that while imposing a quota on dollar bananas of two million tons with a customs duty of 100 ECUs (U.S.$126) per ton and a customs duty of 850 ECUs (U.S.$1,071) per ton beyond that, virtually guaranteeing a decline in the share of dollar bananas in the overall EC market. See "Producer Challenge," p. 281.

49. U.S. House Subcommittee on Trade of the Committee on Ways and Means, *The Caribbean Basin Free Trade Agreements Act,* 103rd Cong., 1st sess., written comments on H.R. 1403, June 7, 1993.

50. The Inter-American Development Bank is another regional institution, but at the hemispheric level. Its policy thrust since the 1980s has been to promote sound macroeconomic policies, although it is generally considered more flexible in its requirements than the IMF and the World Bank. See *IDB Report*, various issues.

51. Peggy Antrobus, "Crisis, Challenge and the Experiences of Caribbean Women," *Caribbean Quarterly* 35, nos. 1 and 2 (March/June 1989): p. 19.

52. See "CDB Focus on Environment and Poverty," *LARR—C*, (December 10, 1992): pp. 4–5.

53. "Barbados Wants Caricom Review," *LARR—C*, (December 7, 1989): p. 7.

54. Particularly devastating was the breakdown of the Caribbean Multilateral Clearing Facility, which had allowed participants to avoid using hard currencies in regional trade.

55. "Ramphal's Team Issues Final Report," *LARR—C*, (July 23, 1992): p. 3.

56. "At Last an Agreement on External Tariff," *LAWR*, (November 12, 1992): pp. 8–9.

57. "Monetary Union Now Irrelevant," *LARR—C&CA*, (July 22, 1993): p. 5.

58. "Venezuela Certain Candidate for ACS," *LARR—C*, (July 23, 1992): p. 4.

59. The conditions for World Bank Structural Adjustment Loans are similar in form and only slightly more lenient than those of the IMF.

60. Bernard Fritz-Krochow, head of the IMF mission to Barbados in 1993, said, "the economic risks of devaluation outweigh the possible benefits" and that Barbados could never devalue its dollar enough "to compete on cost with countries such as the Dominican Republic—how far would you want your dollar to drop?—comments very uncharacteristic of earlier IMF stabilization ideology. See "Devaluation Not the Answer for Barbados," *LARR—C&CA*, (July 22, 1993): p. 5.

61. Albeit, their policies sometimes simultaneously expand the informal sector of the economy.

62. See for example, Antrobus, "Crisis, Challenge," pp. 17–28; Giovanni Andrea Cornia, Richard Jolly, and Frances Stewart, eds., *Adjustment with a Human Face*, Vols. I and II (Oxford: Clarendon Press, 1987); Deere, *In the Shadow of the Sun*, Chapters 2 and 3; and Susan George, *A Fate Worse than Debt* (New York: Grove Press, 1988).

63. "Multilateral Lenders Using Muscle on CET," *LARR—C*, (November 5, 1992): pp. 4–5. The United States also decried the "high" CET rate and used its influence to obtain a reduction. Whether this action reflects a bilateral constraint between the United States and the countries of the Caribbean region or a metaregional, "global" constraint with key agencies of the government acting as part of the incipient international political structure is difficult to judge.

64. Antrobus, "Crisis, Challenge," pp. 18–19; and Cox, *Production, Power and World Order*, p. 260. These leaders include, among others, Edward Seaga, P. J. Patterson, and Patrick Manning, and could even possibly include Michael Manley in his most recent term as prime minister. In most of these cases, internalization is difficult to distinguish from response to outside forces.

65. "IMF Mission," *LARR—C*, (October 1, 1992): p. 5.

66. Grenada's self-imposed structural adjustment program may fit this category since the IMF was reviewing the program at the end of its first year and the result of the review would then determine whether Grenada's credit rating would "[look] any better to donor agencies and whether the island will succeed in raising much-needed developmental capital." See "IMF Mission," p. 5.

67. Omar Davies, "An Analysis of the Management of the Jamaican Economy: 1972–1985," *Social and Economic Studies* 35, no. 1 (1986): p. 80.

68. See Richard Auty and Alan Gelb, "Oil Windfalls in a Small Parliamentary Democracy: Their Impact on Trinidad and Tobago," *World Development* 14, no. 9 (1986): pp. 1165–1169.

69. Nonetheless, the Jamaican government has increased other, often more regressive, taxes and still preaches the gospel of wage restraint as "part of the goals set under the Extended Fund Facility with the IMF." See "Cut in Income Tax; Lower Import Duties," *LARR—C&CA*, (February 25, 1993): p. 7.

70. For instance, Jamaica's exports of sugar in 1991 earned U.S.$92 million. One of the major reasons that sugar exports from the region are declining is that the U.S. sugar quota has declined precipitously—56 percent from 1989/90 to 1992/93—and promises to continue in that direction. "Yet Another Cut in U.S. Sugar Quota," *LAWR*, (September 10, 1992): p. 8.

71. "Caribbean Hard Hit by Global Slump," *LARR—C*, (December 10, 1992): p. 4.

72. There are exceptions in some countries in some years. For instance, manufacturing output in Trinidad rose by 13 percent between 1991 and 1992. "Caribbean Hard Hit," p. 4.

73. Much of this growth has been due to the U.S. 807 program.

74. "Caribbean Hard Hit," p. 4.

75. See, for example, Trevor Harker, "Caribbean Economic Performance—An Overview," *Social and Economic Studies* 12, no. 3 (1992): pp. 101–143.

76. "Brathwaite Defends Divestment Policy," *LARR—C*, (August 27, 1992): p. 7.

77. "Profitable Privatizations," *LARR—C*, (October 1, 1992): p. 4.

78. See "Power Utility May Be Sold Off," *LAWR*, (August 13, 1992): p. 9; and "'State Capitalism' a Thing of the Past," *LARR—C*, (February 25, 1992): p. 3.

79. "Ingraham Planning Sweeping Changes," *LARR—C*, (October 1, 1992): pp. 2–3.

80. See "Divestments Will Go Ahead," *LARR—C&CA*, (July 22, 1993): p. 4; and "Brathwaite Defends Divestment Policy," *LARR—C*, (August 27, 1992): p. 7.

81. Stephens and Stephens, *Democratic Socialism*, p. 38.

82. Watson, "Recent Attempts at Industrial Restructuring," p. 16.

83. Moreover, many manufacturers have experienced difficulty surviving the competition with the onslaught of imports allowed through trade liberalization and deregulation in some countries, dampening whatever small incentive the CBI and Caricom might otherwise provide. See Winston H. Griffith, "Caricom Countries and the Caribbean Basin Initiative," *Latin American Perspectives* 17, no. 1 (1990): pp. 47–49.

84. See Watson, "Recent Attempts at Industrial Restructuring," p. 13; Winston H. Griffith, "Caricom Countries and the Caribbean," p. 36; and Hilbourne Watson, "The Internationalization of Capital, Development, and Labor Migration from the Caribbean," in Roy Glasgow and Winston Langley, eds., *The Troubled and Troubling Caribbean* (Lewiston, N.Y.: Edwin Mellen Press, 1989), pp. 177–179.

85. Michael Kaufman, *Jamaica Under Manley*, p. 14.

86. Trouillot, *Peasants and Capital*, p. 144.

87. There are indications that the EC banana decision may change this arrangement with Geest.

88. Trouillot, *Peasants and Capital*, p. 154.

89. Elsa Chaney, "Scenarios of Hunger in the Caribbean: Migration, Decline of Smallholder Agriculture, and the Feminization of Farming," *International Studies Notes* 14, no. 3 (Fall 1989): p. 68.

90. See Evelyne Huber Stephens and John D. Stephens, "Manley Prepares to Return: PNP Options in Today's Jamaica," *Caribbean Review* 16, no. 2 (Winter 1988): p. 18; and Watson, "Recent Attempts at Industrial Restructuring," p. 27.

91. Todaro, *Economic Development*, p. 269.

92. Peter B. Doeringer, "Market Structure, Jobs, and Productivity: Observations from Jamaica," *World Development* 16, no. 4 (1988): p. 466.

93. For example, Jamaica experienced a 3 percent average annual decline in real GDP from 1972–1980. Gafar, "Economic Growth," p. 64.

94. See "Michael Manley Calls it Quits," *LAWR*, (March 26, 1992): p. 7; and "Manning to Launch Adjustment Effort," *LAWR*, (June 11, 1992): p. 9.

95. See "Barbadian Setback," *LAWR*, (August 13, 1992): p. 9; "Economic Upswing," *LARR—C*, (February 25, 1993): p. 5; and "'Mini-Reshuffle' of Sandiford's Cabinet," *LARR—C*, (May 14, 1992): p. 7.

96. See "Growth After Five Years of Decline," *LARR—C&CA* (April 1, 1993): p. 5; and "Economic Slowdown," *LARR—C*, (April 2, 1992): p. 4.

97. As CDB president, Neville Nichols, notes, "to the people, the concept of adjustment now means long queues for the purchase of staple food, including even those we produce for ourselves; health services that have run out of essential medicines and other basic items; schools, especially those serving the rural poor, that sometimes have teachers but no teaching supplies; families unable to send their children to school because they can afford neither lunch nor bus fares." "CDB President Warns of Looming 'Threats' to the Caribbean Well-Being," *LARR—C*, (June 18, 1992): p. 1.

98. Barkin, "Global Proletarianization," p. 41, makes this observation regarding underdeveloped countries, generally, as they undergo integration into the new international division of labor.

99. See Dennis A. Pantin, "Prospects For the FDI Export Model in Jamaica and the Caribbean," *Latin American Perspectives* 17, no. 1 (1990): pp. 55–72; Watson, "Recent Attempts at Industrial Restructuring," pp. 17–27; and Griffith, "Caricom Countries and the Caribbean," pp. 35–50.

100. See Griffith, "Caricom Countries and the Caribbean," pp. 46–47; and Watson, "Recent Attempts At Industrial Restructuring," pp. 17–18 and 22.

101. Weaker classes also must confront any interaction of external and domestic elites' coinciding interest. Furthermore, often it is external influence that contributes to the relative power of the current local political elite.

102. Chaney, "Scenarios of Hunger," p. 68.

103. "Growth After Years of Decline," *LARR—C&CA*, (July 22, 1993): p. 5.

104. "Liberalization To Be Accelerated," *LARR—C&CA*, (May 13, 1993): p. 3.

105. "Largest-Ever Tax Package Unveiled," *LARR—C&CA*, (May 13, 1993): p. 6.

106. Economic Intelligence Unit, Country Report: Trinidad and the Eastern Caribbean, No. 1, (London: Economic Intelligence Unit, 1990), p. 43.

107. The 1991 figure of 18.5 percent was down substantially from the peak of 22.3 percent in 1987. See "PNM Government 'Dragging Its Feet,'" *LARR—C*, (May 14, 1992): pp. 6–7.

108. Barbadian unemployment rose from 17.7 percent in September 1990 to 23.1 percent in September 1991. "Minister Defends Privatization," *LARR—C&CA*, (April 1, 1993): p. 5.

109. Wilma Bailey, "Child Morbidity in the Kingston Metropolitan Area," *Social Science and Medicine* 26, no. 11 (1988): pp. 1117–1124.

110. A number of Caribbean ministers of agriculture at a global conference on malnutrition in 1992 urged international lending institutions to allow some flexibility in structural adjustment programs so that "in dealing with the widespread problem of malnutrition, we can cater to the needs of our people as we see fit." See "'Flexibility' To Deal With Malnutrition," *LARR—C&CA*, (January 21, 1993): p. 4.

111. Stephens and Stephens, "Manley Prepares To Return," p. 18.

112. "Softening the Impact," *LAWR*, (May 20, 1993): p. 222.

113. Most dramatic was the raise approved for teachers of 60 percent in the first year and 30 percent in the second year of a two-year contract. "Largest-Ever Tax Package," p. 6.

114. "Largest-Ever Tax Package," p. 9.

115. "Largest-Ever Tax Package," p. 6.

116. Emigration, temporary or permanent, is still a prominent response to conditions in the region but has become more difficult as receiving countries erect more and more barriers to entry.

117. Alain de Janvry, *The Agrarian Question and Reformism in Latin America* (Baltimore: Johns Hopkins University Press, 1981), p. 173.

118. Watson, "The Internationalization of Capital," p. 169.

119. Watson, "Recent Attempts at Industrial Restructuring in Barbados," p. 15.

120. A stance deepened by Manley's successor, P. J. Patterson.

4

◆

The Political Economy of Centralization and Delayed Capitalism in Sub-Saharan Africa

Antony T. K. Gadzey

Shortly after independence, many sub-Saharan African[1] countries abandoned the vestiges of the open colonial economies fashioned more or less after Western capitalism and embraced, in various degrees, socialism and centralization.[2] Centralization is indicated by a combination of different variables that collectively confine the authoritative allocation of political and economic values to a relatively small number of state actors. In extreme cases, overcentralization has fostered personalized rule and dictatorships. Details of these differences are presented later. But three and a half decades later, African economies are in a crisis, most still unable to transform the subsistence economies they inherited or reverse their commodity trade asymmetries with the West.

This chapter argues that centralization, especially in its manifest tendency of extending state control over every aspect of economic activity, contributes enormously to sub-Saharan Africa's economic paralysis and political disarray. This is so not only because of the many negative patterns scholars have associated with the centralized strategy: the difficulty of administering effectively from one command center the administrative details of a whole country,[3] severe errors in planning and implementing development plans and projects,[4] the tendency toward autocratic and corrupt governments,[5] and finally, the denial of effective local government authority.[6] In addition to illustrating the centralized strategy's tendency to choke on its own internal dynamics, this chapter emphasizes its basic incapability to reflect and resolve the overwhelming development challenge faced by the newly independent African countries, namely, bringing to fruition the seeds of capitalism so improperly and inadequately seeded during the last few decades of colonialism.

The chapter will attempt to demonstrate a fundamental inconsistency between the overcentralization tendencies of African leaders and Africa's socioeconomic realities and general aspirations at the time of independence in the early 1960s. Africa's development requirements at independence—conditions that for the most part remain unchanged into the 1990s—revolved around the discovery of basic forms of accelerating capital accumulation, for which grassroots capitalism, with all its shortcomings, remains the most suitable system. Development, defined as an incremental improvement in the productive and consumptive capacity of a large segment of a society, is unlikely to occur in Africa as long as the objectives of those who exercise allocation power diverge from the socioeconomic realities and objectives of their people.

The good news is that three recent developments suggest the beginnings of a fundamental rethinking of Africa's socialist and centralization policies that might bring the old policies back in line with the socioeconomic challenges socialism and centralization could not solve.

First, change is inevitable for many countries in the region, which for all pragmatic purposes are now dysfunctional. After three decades of self-rule, most countries in the region are still characterized by low production and consumption, repeated food crises, large external debts, and a basic inability to use needed foreign technology. Economic stagnation has created so much political disarray that many governments in the region no longer meet the empirical definition of a state based on its ability to exercise control by defining, implementing, and enforcing laws, policies, and regulations.[7] Corrupt and inefficient administrations and increasingly repressive and extractive tendencies have eroded the legitimacy of many African governments.

Second, there is some similarity between the reactions to socialist paralysis in Eastern Europe and the growing disenchantment with socialism and centralization in Africa. Both have produced serious reevaluation of the appropriateness of socialism and centralization as development strategies, even though reevaluations in Africa have not produced similar revolutionary changes as in Eastern Europe.

In Africa the reevaluation is noticeable in three important developments. First, beginning with the Lomé Agreement, the Third World's approach to the so-called capitalist North has graduated from the anticapitalist rhetoric of the 1960s. By the late 1980s, one sensed an emerging concerted thought in certain African leadership and academic circles in support of greater openness toward the Western capitalist countries.

Readiness for greater openness to the West could not have been possible without a second development—a toning down of anti-Western rhetoric. The new consensus appears to have first blossomed at the September 1989 Nonaligned Nations' Conference in Belgrade, Yugoslavia. Commenting on the significance of the change, Flora Lewis wrote,

> It is another sign of changing times. The Yugoslav hosts have made an intensive effort to deradicalize, lower the pitch—in short, what they call "modernize" the triennial meeting. Revolutionary exhortations and diatribes against "imperialists" no longer win stormy applause. . . . The nonaligned are facing an identity problem now that they don't really have anybody to be nonaligned with, and the enemy is more likely to be the neighbor than a superpower. Most of the leaders here are more concerned about economics than ostentatious Third-world politics. . . . It is a striking change from the founding summit session here in 1961.[8]

Because much of the phenomenon of "Third Worldism"—an enduring idea during the 1960s that some third and neutral alternative was possible—was for many African leaders captured in nothing more than rhetorical symbolism, giving up that rhetoric said something significant about their dying faith in the Third World as an economically self-sufficient and politically independent and neutral entity.

Finally, and most relevantly important, pro-Western rhetoric has been underscored since 1982 by extensive International Monetary Fund (IMF) and World Bank–sponsored market reforms, which by early 1994 have involved as many as forty sub-Saharan states. Many of the reform measures are far-reaching, going beyond the traditional IMF interest in stabilization to include a broader program of policy change. The shutting down or significant reductions in the number of state corporations, the freezing of state hiring, the privatization of agricultural production and pricing, and the disbanding of state marketing boards that could give producers greater control over export commodity earnings have had the collective effect of substantially surrendering state autonomy and government power to the private sector—in effect, ending economic centralization.

At face value, the coincidence of these ostensible changes in Third Worldism and IMF/World Bank reforms in practically all sub-Saharan African states suggests a fundamental change in African development thinking and strategy. What is not so clear is how one might interpret this new consensus on two levels: in the short term, the extent of African leaders' commitment to these market reforms, and in the long term the implications of IMF/World Bank market reforms for the evolution of African economies to full capitalism.

Evaluating African leaders' commitment to market reforms is made particularly difficult by the mixed signals coming from their varied reactions. Although there has been some well-documented pockets of resistance, in a majority of the forty African countries undertaking the reforms, the imposed IMF/World Bank austerity has not yet induced any of the much-feared massive political opposition.[9] Opposing governments see the reforms as imposing a no-win tradeoff between very uncertain economic gains if the reforms are successful and the certain painful surrendering of much of the control and power that comes with centralization and socialism. For the cooperating states, it is still unclear whether their cooperation is born out of genuine conviction that centralization imposes severe social and economic costs completely unjustifiable by whatever short-term political gains they might bring.

That brings us to the longer-term implications of the reforms for development in the region. In contrast to the openly procapitalist and pro-Western stance of the East European revolutionary governments, there is no open commitment to capitalism on the part of African leaders, particularly those who seem to accept the IMF/World Bank market-oriented austerity as unavoidable. This makes one wonder whether the reforms are a step toward the realization of full capitalization and democracy in the only region of the world where these two fundamentals of the modern nation state have never been firmly established.

These lingering doubts on the part of African leaders about the new direction in Third Worldism in general, and about the long-term implications of the IMF/World Bank reforms in particular, provide strong incentives to examine why African leaders hold so tenaciously to the political gains from centralization even while its costs in terms of economic failure are so obvious. If centralization and its supporting ideological rhetoric provide African leaders any gains at all, they come in the form of political coalitions so vital to regime survival. Why did African leaders have to rely upon ideologically founded coalitions to sustain their rule? Why did they choose centralization and ideology over a more open economic system and democratic processes that are more adaptable to the main task of achieving full capitalization of the African economies? And have the conditions forcing that choice on African leaders changed sufficiently to give way to fundamentally new thinking in development philosophy?

This chapter discusses African regimes' ideological approaches to the challenge posed by the condition of incomplete capitalization that they inherited despite the fact that the commitment to ideology seems to have been neither very strong nor protracted. Ironically, even at the height of African leaders' strong ideological orientation during the early 1970s, ideology never became for most of them a consuming passion or a strong belief system that formed and implemented policy. And as these new trends in Third Worldism indicate, in the 1990s, ideology no longer plays as significant a role in determining the policy. But the ideological roots of the current development crisis in the region are deep and resilient.

They are particularly important for analysis because they provided rallying points around which African leaders built various political coalitions and alignments to support their weak regimes. What is here discussed as ideology, for lack of a better term, was more a pragmatic, one might even say convenient, instrument for building political coalitions where a politically weak colonial inheritance,[10] lack of development, and tribally fragmented politics[11] made the building of political coalitions through formal political structures such as party politics, socialization, and corporatist strategies practically impossible. As Crawford Young puts it,

> New rulers quickly become aware of the insecurity of their hold on power. . . . But in reasserting the hegemony of the state, they could not fall back upon the formulas which had served so well as colonial ideology: trusteeship, good government. They were thus driven to weave together radical and populist political language and exclusionary political institutions. . . . Thus, the new states were not simply bureaucratic autocracies, alien to boot, like their colonial predecessors. They were political monopolies legitimated by frequently radical nationalist ideology, ritually consecrated by periodic electoral ceremonies.[12]

And as long as the problem of regime insecurity persists, leaders will cling to the ideas and coalitions built on these ideologies even if, for pragmatic reasons, many of them are today more savvy and diplomatic and less ideological in their pronouncements.

We begin by identifying the main challenge to independence as the discovery of the right mix of policies to reverse "semicapitalism"—a condition of capitalism insufficiently introduced into Africa rather than the reverse condition of overexploitation as argued in radical theory. Semicapitalism exists in most parts of Africa not only because the colonial commodity export trade—the first potential capitalist process—lacked many of the features of a full capitalist process, but more particularly because its total external focus deprived it of the normal forward and backward linkages necessary to make commodity trade an adequate lead-off sector for the complete capitalization of the larger subsistence economy. So the challenge to African leaders has been to reverse the noncapitalist features of both the commodity trade and the subsistence sectors, a daunting challenge for which independence nonetheless provided African leaders a great opportunity to resolve. Yet, the strategies they chose—centralization and ideological coalitions—were so inappropriate for dealing with the conditions of semicapitalism that a severe tension has developed and continues between the socioeconomic realities and the choice of political strategy. That in turn has made reliance on centralization ideology and regime security indispensable, generating a vicious circle that makes the current apparent change in development philosophy the more doubtful.

Commodity Trade as a Semicapitalist Process

Commodity trade exports of former European colonies in Africa and the Third World generally are often described in the radical literature as "capitalist" to suggest that they were the beginning of capitalism in Africa. But how capitalist is Africa? The temptation to describe Africa's commodity trade as capitalist and to equate its historical manifestations within colonial Africa with the introduction of full capitalism may be excused on two grounds. Commodity production—the highest form of capitalism in colonial Africa—was essentially intended for an external exchange market where the driving motivation was the maximization of profits and only secondarily the satisfaction of basic needs. It also opened for the ordinary peasant farmer the first reliable access to the foreign capitalist market and to hard currency, enabling him to participate in international trade. Beyond these features, however, that characterization is fundamentally flawed.

Western capitalist manifestations in Africa, and for that matter in most other parts of the Third World, are perhaps better described as "indeliberate semicapitalism" for three reasons. First, it is semicapitalist because African commodity exports never developed the elements of a full capitalist process: a self-sustaining capability, forward and backward linkage possibilities, and a sufficient competitive spirit. Second, it is indeliberate because the trajectories of factors toward the end of the colonial period when commodity trade was first introduced into Africa do not amount to our understanding of exploitation. And last, many of the current manifestations of semicapitalism could be reversed through establishing full-fledged capitalism.

Defining Capitalism

The particular historical capitalist conjuncture in Africa, characterized by its several trade asymmetries, does not constitute the essence and potential of capitalism as a development process for so-called peripheral states. Bill Warren[13] demonstrated why the main attraction of the capitalist system is its self-sustaining capability by which it autonomously generates increasing use-value within the domestic economy, including even precapitalist economies with low purchasing power. This self-sustaining dynamic starts whenever, in response to various pressures or profit incentives, a subsistence economy is pushed into generating more than its sustaining or consumption value. The creation of surplus begins the permanent transformation of subsistence production as it encourages further accumulation of use-value through direct and indirect investments and forward, backward, and horizontal linkages. Soon, such sufficient use-value is generated that it exceeds the efficient management of the original producers and so encourages specialization and the reproduction of capital.

The interrelated processes of use-value generation and specialization explain the self-sustaining dynamism of capitalism. Its presence generates a new class whose self-sustaining mechanism and contribution to the general welfare do not derive from direct production but from commercialization and other services related to the surpluses others produce. Heilbroner emphasizes that capitalism is not the simple quantitative production of goods or money:

> What is capital, then, if it is not just production goods or money? The initial answer, familiar to students of Marx but usually strange to others, is that capital is either of these things when it is used to set into motion a process of continuous transformation of capital-as-money into capital-as-commodities, followed by a retransformation of capital-as-commodities into capital-as-more-money. This is the famous M-C-M formula by which Marx schematized the repetitive, expansive metamorphosis through which "capital" manifests itself.[14]

The capability of this autonomous system to revolutionize subsistence economies makes it especially appropriate for the development needs of predominantly precapitalist economies such as those of Africa. Says Warren, "There is no reason why the continuously expanding productive power of the system should find itself more than temporarily restrained by the limits of existing purchasing power."[15]

Indeliberate Asymmetries

The essential capability of capitalism to transform feudal economies reshapes the relevant theories on how Western capitalism impacted Africa. Failed capitalism can no longer be explained in terms of its inappropriateness under African feudal conditions. Because commodity trade was driven by the same capitalist profit maximizing drive, and because it linked Africa effectively with the outside capitalist system, commodity trade was potentially capable of pulling the rest of the African economy into full-fledged capitalism. That is, it had at least the minimum requirement of a capitalist system: a reliable market, a capability of converting commodity into money, and, by enabling African commodity producers and governments that lived off commodity export tax revenues the purchasing power to acquire manufactured imports, the capability of converting money into commodities. That completes the M-C-M process at least in principle; export commodities are intended to generate money, and these revenues provide the ability to purchase goods and accumulate investment capital. Yet this did not happen. Why?

What factors inhibited the full potential of the capitalist dynamic in Africa? Why did African commodity trade lack the forward and backward linkages by which initial development in one sector induces improvements in others? If capitalism could thrive even in areas with low purchasing power such as Africa, why did the precolonial economies of Africa, already rather sophisticated in terms of local and long distance trade,[16] fail to find in the introduction of commodity exports the necessary catalyst for a complete capitalist transformation?

The obvious answer points to the lack of forward and backward linkages between this modern sector and the traditional subsistence sector. While commodity trade was potentially capable of igniting the capitalist M-C-M process, it could do so only if producers generated surplus. Yet the production of many export commodities did not constitute the production of surplus understood technically as production over consumption, as many of these crops like cocoa, coffee, sisal, and so on were not being consumed locally but were valued only in external markets. So not much of the revenue they generated went into investment either to improve the commodity export sector itself or to improve the subsistence sector.

The argument of insufficient surplus capacity within the commodity trade sector is to be distinguished from radicals' familiar claim of insufficiency of domestic resource, the result of colonial drainage of resources from Africa (and elsewhere in the Third World), and the destruction of whatever was valuable in Africa.[17] Radicals explain the failure of capitalism in Africa in terms of a grand conspiracy theory. Radical theory argues that the expansion of European capitalism to Africa was designed to produce "peripheral capitalism"—a condition of permanent dependency. African countries, which exist in the periphery of the European and American capitalist structure, are bound to specialize as commodity exporters, while the more dynamic aspects of the commodity export industry like marketing (shipping), raw material processing, and manufacturing with their related innovations, technologies, and jobs are located in Europe. Thus, African economies would remain basically underdeveloped or, at best, be secondary and dependent on the industrialized countries. Consequently, the disruptions in African economies that made possible these capitalist manifestations are equally condemned as capitalist ploys to force underdeveloped countries into commodity specialization to guarantee commodity supplies for manufacturing at the core.

While dependency literature makes important contributions that enhance our understanding of the historical effects of capitalist development outside its originating core, the tendency to exaggerate the external sources of Africa's problems may divert attention from such important internal factors as leaders' ignorance and greed, which affect policy formation and implementation equally, if not more. The resource drainage theory in particular is not very persuasive because it has not been sufficiently demonstrated how development in the core depended on resources from the periphery.[18]

Nor is it accurate to assume commodity trade's disruptive effects on African subsistence economies are the permanent manifestations of capitalism whenever capitalism exists in its core countries. Such a position is not sufficiently cognitive of the fact that similar disruptions elsewhere resulted in more development than in Africa. Karl Marx went to great lengths in pointing out the necessary tradeoff between shorter-term costs and the tremendous longer-term benefits of a capitalist transformation:

> England, it is true, in causing a social revolution in Hindostan (India), was actuated only by the vilest interests, and was stupid in her manner of enforcing them. But that is not the question. The question is, can mankind fulfill its destiny without a fundamental revolution in the social state of Asia? If not, whatever may have been the crimes of England, she was the unconscious tool of history in bringing about the revolution.[19]

According to John Roemer,[20] the diversion of existing trade patterns or the alienation of resources from one location for manufacturing to another does not necessarily amount to exploitation as long as, at the historical time, the best alternative opportunities for utilization in the producers' country and for the local trading of the exported commodities were either inferior or nonexistent. There is no question that in the interwar period, when most of today's specialized exports from sub-Saharan Africa were developed, there were no African domestic markets for these goods. Even today, the very negligible domestic consumption of most of these exports diminishes substantially producers' influence over prices.

In addition to these economic factors, the failure to evolve effective, timely policies by both colonial and indigenous governments contributed enormously to perpetuating the conditions of semicapitalism. For the colonialist government, the problem was a lack of incentive and hence delay in formulating and implementing a self-sustaining economic policy for the African colonies. The British colonial policy is very illustrative of this first trend:

> At its thirteenth meeting in March 1947, the British Colonial Economic Development Council (CEDC) discussed a memorandum prepared by the Chairman, Viscount Portal. The note recommended the institution by Act of Parliament of a Colonial Development Corporation (CDC) to promote increased Colonial production on an *economic and self-sustaining basis,* with particular reference to the production of foodstuffs and raw materials where supply to the United Kingdom, or overseas, would assist the British balance of payments. At the same time, *that is as a secondary motive* by increasing their outputs, the Colonies themselves would become more prosperous and so there would be mutual advantage.[21]

In other words, even though the British had colonized Africa for more than a hundred years prior to World War II, it was not until after the war that budgetary pressures forced the British to establish a plan on agricultural policy for its African colonies. Additionally, the delay itself was not as damaging as the fact that commodity trade was introduced as a tax-gathering mechanism and not as the beginning of a comprehensive development program. Its aim, as clearly stated in the quotation above, was to enable the territories to become administratively self-financing; more than 60 percent of the export earnings was earmarked as a colonial tax. Because the colonial state siphoned off most of its earnings, commodity trade lacked the savings and investment for increased production and efficiency capacity—the essence of a capitalist process. Therefore, the culpability of the Western capitalism for African underdevelopment is not that it came to Africa but that it was insufficiently introduced. As Cooper pointedly states,

> The laments of international organizations and development economists about the intractable backwardness of Africa is not a conspiratorial attempt to conceal the pillage of Africa, but a reflection of the fact—although they would not put it this way—that Africa is an underexploited continent.[22]

However, colonial policy is ultimately insufficient to explain the reluctance to alter subsistence farming in Africa during this time. As Ralph A. Austen[23] accurately argued, the existing social environment of insufficient labor laws and competing new occupations made intensive farming unattractive. Africa's economic problems started in the long period of power transition from colonialism, which lasted anywhere from the mid-1940s till the early 1960s. It was a time when decolonization politics overshadowed looming economic problems. Subsistence food production decreased as the attraction of city white-collar jobs pulled potential farm labor away from the rural areas. Paradoxically, this worsening economic condition was not approached with a sense of crisis. Neither the departing colonial state nor the incoming native administrations sought seriously to redefine property rights and establish state policies to accommodate the emerging economic scarcity. And without well-defined and protected property rights, wealthy individuals could not impose new wage laws and labor discipline whereby the increasing influx of labor in the cities would be forced to work for stable wages.

Reversing the Symptoms of Semicapitalism: The Challenge to African Leaders

Ultimately, then, delayed capitalism before independence has to do with a number of inadvertent factors: colonial policy neglect, labor diversion effects on food production, and a social environment nonconducive to change. That historical evidence supports the realization that the essentially expansionist and revolutionary nature of capitalism can stagnate when its basic dynamics are impaired. In other words, failed capitalist evolution in Africa has very little to do with either the capitalist essence or immutable structures. This conclusion does not support political resistance to further capitalism, or a continuation of the colonial state-dominated structures that fostered the conditions of semicapitalism in the first place. Presenting a nonstructuralist interpretation of capitalist evolution in Africa is not intended to dismiss the cost of its several asymmetries. Rather, it points to the great potential for reversing many of its negative symptoms through carefully coordinated policies once independence was attained. Our plan in the next section is to outline three broad African regime responses to colonial semicapitalism and to evaluate their consequences.

Semicapitalism and African Regime Responses

From the evolving African development literature, three broad African regime types have been identified: statist-socialist, statist-mercantilist, and political-capitalist.[24] *Statism* indicates a highly centralized economic and political authoritarian state. Statist regimes are characterized by either total state domination and/or mediation of all major economic activity; even where some private enterprise survives, the extensive state regulation of prices and planning of production reduce private autonomous decision-making. So defined, most African regimes would qualify as statist regimes. However, there are important distinctions on the basis of the differing objectives of power that centralization is supposed to serve.

Some regimes use statism as a mechanism for an ideologically socialist restructuring of the semicapitalist colonial economy and are here referred to as *statist-socialist* regimes. Then there are the *statist-mercantilist* regimes, for whom statism represents nothing more than a mercantilist instrument for the creation of national wealth and ruler power. These two are still to be distinguished from the *political-capitalist* regimes in which significant centralization of political power coexists with, and is often used to promote, both state and private capitalism. The difference shows up in several important ways, and we discuss three: attitude toward foreign capital, basic development strategy, and tolerance of political opposition as they relate to our objective of explaining the delayed onset of autonomous capitalism in Africa.

Statist-Socialist Regimes

For the statist-socialist regimes, the very expansion of Western influence and power into Africa constitutes the exploitation of one nationality

(African) by another (European). African development can only come through some form of struggle with the international capital and capitalists who, as the argument goes, would do everything, including the alienation of the domestic bourgeoisie, to perpetuate Africa's dependency. Regimes that evoked this kind of ideology include, among the first generation of independent states, Ghana under Kwame Nkrumah and Tanzania under Julius Nyerere (two countries whose socialism is exceptionally well documented), Guinea under Sekou Torre, Mali under Modibo Keita, and in more recent times, Somalia under Mohamed Siad Barre, Madagascar under Didier Ratsiraka, Guinea-Bissau under Amilcar Cabral, Mozambique under Samora Machel, Angola under Agostinho Neto and Jose Eduardo dos Santos, Zimbabwe under Robert Mugabe, and Congo-Brazzaville under Alphonse Massemba-Debat and Marien Ngouabi. Chazan included many of these regimes in what she called "African neo-Marxists" in order to emphasize their strong socialist orientations.

While it lasted, much of this strong anti-Western and anticapitalist critique, however, was nothing more than rhetoric—most of these regimes continued to deal with foreign capitalists even as they denounced them and nationalized their enterprises. And as indicated in the introduction, much of this ideology has disappeared. However, the claim to an ideologically neutral Africa provided motivation for the strong authoritarian state system that still dominates the region. Because the socialist regimes see development as a struggle between different nationalities within the international system, they clamor for statism as a coalition-building strategy—all the people in solidarity against domination by another.

Continuing influences of this ideology can be seen in the promotion of various economic autarkic policies as inclusionary coalition strategies. Indeed, most of these regime leaders preferred the label "African-socialists," to emphasize their objective of discovering uniquely African paths to development that are neither (Western) capitalist nor (orthodox) socialist (e.g., Ujamah in Tanzania). The goal, of course, is to solidify the people behind their leader as a distinct politically independent and neutral entity. But the coalition's ostensible objective of partnership between the people and their leader often conceals the regime's intent and ability to deny society any meaningful power and participation as the ideologically founded coalition quickly turns into a strategy of regime power consolidation. Often, therefore, the socialist world view tends to centralize political power. Most of these regime leaders tolerate no opposition whatsoever to their regimes. The state must have a dominant role in or even absolute control of the economy, and the private entrepreneurial classes must be discouraged or even suppressed to stamp out foreign capitalist encroachment as the only way to guarantee an equitable distribution of development benefits to what they fondly termed the "disfranchised." Shaw describes how under many such African regimes, the neocolonial struggle has turned into a systematic corporatist strategy of suppressing dissenting groups and classes:

> In the African case, transnational elements of the bourgeoisie are coming under increasing pressure from more national factions, particularly in those countries that have already exhausted the import-substitution bonanza. Hence the need to go beyond simplistic formulations of neo-colonialism as well as of dependence, and to refine different variants with the corporatist mold for Africa.[25]

Statist-Mercantilist Regimes

"Statist-mercantilism" accurately describes the second group of African regimes mainly because, as Thomas M. Callaghy argued, "In the basic mercantilist equation of African state formation the key element in the search for sovereignty and unification is power, the basis of power is wealth, and the foundations of wealth are foreign exchange and economic development."[26] Such regimes express no hostility toward external capital and capitalists. On the contrary, their ruling classes seek increased foreign investment by encouraging regulated investment, particularly where such regulation would direct foreign investment into projects that would maximize the interests of the state, which is often synonymous with ruling class or even ruler's interests—a reason most foreign investors's shy away from these states. Society's interests do not feature importantly in such regime/ foreign capitalist nexus.

The most notable African mercantilist regimes include Zaire under Mobutu Sese Seko, Uganda under Idi Amin, the Central African Republic under Colonel Jean-Bedel Bokassa, Liberia under Samuel Kenyon Doe, and Ethiopia under Mengistu Haile Mariam. Besides their visibly personalized rule, these African regimes are noted for their brutal suppression of opposition groups and social classes. Unlike in the socialist regimes where class confrontation reflected ideological differences, in the mercantilist states class wars are usually over declining state wealth. Nyang'oro expresses this view when he says,

> The African state which seems to be an inadequate representative or reflection of class confrontation in society consequently becomes a non-dynamic entity in society. Its primary role thus becomes that of maintaining "order" for its own sake, with the state's longevity (or survival) largely depending on nothing happening to precipitate any kind of crisis, be it political or economic.[27]

Political-Capitalist Regimes

In contrast to the socialist and mercantilist objective of the previous regime groups, the intent or thrust of the political-capitalist African regimes is state-sponsored capitalist transformation. Their world view excludes much of the anticapitalist critique of the socialists, and they deal openly (as opposed to cunningly) with international capital by providing the most attractive domestic conditions for foreign investment. In contrast to mercantilist regimes' personalized designs on the state, the political capitalist regimes use state mediation to promote state and private capitalism, particularly when state intervention is necessary to provide the conditions favored by foreign capital. State mediation of private industrialization includes the regulation of exports, imports, and foreign exchange, the subsidization of selective private industries, and the promotion of package technology transfers.

Regimes of this kind emphasize no particular ideology nor are their coalition strategies, if any, very clear. They seem to have concluded that Africa is part of one world capitalist system, without focusing particularly on the place of Africa in that hierarchically structured system. They do not hesitate therefore to open their countries to Western capitalist influence.

Only a handful of African regimes have promoted private capitalist transformation or made the important shift from state-dominated economy to large-scale privatization. Often associated with state-sponsored capitalism are Kenya under both Jomo Kenyatta and Daniel arap Moi, Côte d'Ivoire under Felix Houphouet-Boigny, Botswana under Quett K. J. Masire, probably Malawi under H. Kamuzu Banda, and Cameroon under both the Ahmadou Ahijo and Paul Biya regimes. Popularly called "the showcase of capitalism in Africa," Kenya best illustrates the political-capitalist regime model. Kenya has developed the largest private business entrepreneurial class in sub-Sahara Africa. The successful transformation from an economy dominated by European plantation farming began with two major policy changes by the Kenyatta administration. As soon as Kenyatta emerged as the strong man from the Mau Mau civil war, he established a major land reform program that provided plots to 1.5 million former plantation peasants. His Africanization policy also opened businesses to Kenyan entrepreneurs. Until recently, President Daniel arap Moi's regime has followed Kenyatta's private capitalist programs with much success.

Another Anglophone African country often mentioned in connection with the political capitalist model is Nigeria, before its discovery of oil. According to one assessment by Sara Berry, Nigeria has achieved a significant shift from family-based labor to relatively large-scale capitalist labor farming in which the labor is often supplied by migrants from the neighboring states, particularly to the north.[28] But even more spectacular than the much-publicized cases of Kenya and Côte d'Ivoire has been the quiet and exceptionally successful capitalist transformation in Botswana. Botswana emerged from eighty years of British colonial domination and unconcealed neglect in 1966 as a drought-stricken, underdeveloped back-water, surrounded by a hostile South Africa and given little chance of surviving as an independent nation. After two decades of state active involvement in promoting private and state capitalism, Botswana has emerged as one of Africa's rare showcases of successful autonomous development, transforming its less-than-auspicious beginning into a healthy economy with a 13 percent average annual growth rate. It is not only one of the world's fastest growing economies, but it spreads this wealth to its population, which in 1987 had a per capita income of $1,050 as compared to $69 in 1966.

Likewise, a number of Francophone African countries like Côte d'Ivoire and Cameroon have also achieved sustained capitalist growth, though since the early 1980s these economies have run into some of the political problems associated with state-sponsored capitalist development. In Cameroon, state-sponsored experimentation with large-scale, capitalist rice farming in its Yagoua region has been a technical success that led to a spectacular increase in its peasant workers' income. The project's impressive performance legitimated both the Ahmadou Ahijo and Paul Biya regimes because, as Claude reports, it enabled Cameroon to achieve substantial self-sufficiency in food whereas before it had exported cotton and imported food.[29]

Unlike the state domination of Cameroon's capitalist agriculture, capitalist transformation in Côte d'Ivoire is dominated by direct foreign (mainly French) capital.[30] It has been accurately argued by many observers that the Ivorian capitalist model and its pre-1982 success were due to this massive infusion of foreign capital. At its peak performance in 1980 (that is, before the economic crisis that resulted in a dramatic loss of confidence by foreign capital) Côte d'Ivoire received more than double the foreign capital ($1,141 million) of any African country other than Nigeria.[31] Comparable figures for Cameroon and Kenya, the other capitalist states heavily dependent on foreign capital, were $573 million and $538 million, respectively.

Evaluating African Regime Responses

In this section, the three distinctive regime responses will be evaluated in terms of how well they tackled the main constraints on autonomous capitalist development in Africa. This review of the constraints perpetuating semicapitalism in Africa suggests three important criteria for evaluating regime performance. First, it was necessary to dismantle the overbearing colonial state structure and reverse state-centered capital accumulation. Second, foreign control of the manufacturing aspects of African commodity exports had to be brought under domestic control, and production and trade eventually had to be diverted from current patterns of dependence. Finally, an open political environment that promotes the free expression of conflicting ideas and interests had to be created.

Dismantling the Colonial Statist Structure

Producers' capacity to generate and control their surpluses is crucial to their ability to recycle these surpluses in generating the self-sustaining M-C-M capitalist process. Grassroots accumulation should be preferred to state-centered accumulation not only because it is more adaptable to capitalist competition but also because it captures more adequately the overall objective of development, which involves the incremental improvement in the skills and technological capacities of *a majority of producers* of a country. The presence of a few state capitalist projects, however well intended, is not synonymous with this concept of development. To the extent that the overbearing colonial state prevented the unfolding of this process, the success of African regime performance has to be judged in terms of how successfully each regime reduced colonial state domination over producers and promoted private enterprise. Of particular interest is the extent to which colonial commodity and food export taxes have been reduced so as to channel a greater portion of foreign earnings directly to producers.

Robert Bates presents a detailed study of various commodity marketing boards in a number of African countries.[32] These boards were established shortly before independence, and their aim was to stabilize the producers' earnings against the backdrop of widely fluctuating world market prices. Over time, they had become an easy tax-gathering device for the colonial state. According to Bates, most African regimes failed to abandon this colonial practice. Indeed, Bates's figures from Ghana, Nigeria, Senegal, and Uganda show that the marketing boards abandoned their original role of stabilizing producer prices, becoming instead instruments for increased state-centered accumulation. In several of these countries, not only did the state board regulation of commodity exports intensify, but domestic food crops also came under similar control by state marketing boards. Bates quotes estimates from other sources indicating that official marketing costs took between 10 to 35 percent of the differential between the world price and the price paid to domestic producers.[33] As a result, in countries like Ghana, cocoa producers were receiving less than 20 percent of the foreign price of cocoa. Many of these commodity marketing boards have been kept in place until, forced by the IMF, they were finally abandoned in the 1980s. Apart from Kenya, the last countries to abandon these boards belong to the statist-socialist and statist-mercantilist regime types. In other words, the rapid growth in the parastatal sector that characterizes these two regime types has been accomplished through an unrelenting exploitation of the very commodity producers whom independence supposedly freed from colonial exploitation.

Relative to the other two regime types, the political-capitalist regimes have had some success in reversing colonial state/society relations. While these regimes also held on to these marketing boards, often the revenues were used to provide capital for investment by private individuals, as in the case of the Western Nigeria Development Corporation and the Western Regional Finance Corporation.[34] State sponsorship of individual private enterprises in Kenya and Côte d'Ivoire further suggests that those regimes dedicated to capitalist transformation did use state resources to promote state and private capitalism.

Using the state political process to promote private individual accumulation, as in Cameroon, Kenya, and Côte d'Ivoire, has produced mixed results. On the positive side, the early success of these countries in using their market-oriented states to promote private capitalism reversed a long tradition in Africa of state exploitation of its own citizens for colonial or indigenous power rule. More importantly, it followed a growing practice that has produced development for both industrial countries and a number of newly industrializing countries (NICs). Since Keynesian times, a positive involvement of the state has been crucial in sustaining and advancing development whenever the economy lingers in recession. Government supply-side economics has been usefully applied in even so-called free-market economies of the western industrialized countries. Contrary to earlier reports attributing the success stories of the Far Eastern Gang of Four to their open market policies, later accounts show their achievement as dependent upon constructive, some would even say mercantilist, state involvement with their private sector economies.[35]

Successful cooperation between a market-conforming state and the private capitalist sector casts some doubt on the overall message of the minimalist government role emphasized in the current IMF/World Bank-induced reforms. These reforms could be misleading to the extent that the reduction in the size of government called for by the IMF and the World Bank follows from, or is seen to reflect, the neoclassical economists' doctrine that capitalist development is maximized when the economic role of the state is reduced to a minimum, giving the private sector maximum freedom. Certainly, many of the huge but inefficient bureaucracies need to reduce their responsibilities to a level commensurate with their limited capacities. And it may be politically insensitive to keep in power incumbents who have come to represent government as a source of personal aggrandizement and so are delegitimized before the people.

Yet shrinking the state in pursuit of the minimalist government model per se may not work for Africa. Certainly, it is not enough for the state under IMF intervention to legislate macropolicy changes and expect the in-experienced market forces in African countries to respond perfectly—a typical neoclassical fallacy. The issue of state involvement in economic planning is not the size but the quality and development sophistication of state personnel. Elsewhere,[36] a detailed description of the proper role a so-phisticated state dedicated to promoting grassroots capitalism could play in guiding Africa to sustainable development may be found. Given the in-sufficiency of African domestic capital, expertise, and technology, the state becomes a necessary catalyst in development, linking its own, as well as foreign financial and technological resources and marketing expertise into direct contact with private producers. Under such circumstances, cap-italist development can occur only if, in addition to market-oriented policy changes, various state personnel are actively involved in coordinating and encouraging capitalist transformation. Says Richard Sandbrook,

> This analysis can be extended to the economic challenge facing develop-ing countries today. Those societies with state institutions able and will-ing to play an active economic role of *the right sort* . . . will be at a com-petitive advantage. The tasks of this developmental state extend far beyond the mere creation of an "enabling environment" for private en-terprise, the position adopted by the World Bank and others.[37]

The objective of an enlightened state elite intent on promoting grass-roots capitalist development would be to bring together all three func-tionaries of the M-C-M productive process: the financier, the producer, and the trader. The complete severance of commodity production from its marketing and manufacturing function would rob the producing African economies of the mutually reinforcing benefits to be gained when the three functions are integrated. When integrated, those in marketing and manu-facturing would pass on to producers the benefits of modern technologies, quality control, and reliable prices, which are crucial to their own suc-cessful operations. In turn, they will be able to sign productive contracts directly with small holders and can accordingly better plan their invento-ries. That all three have a stake in the producer's success is the greater rea-son the producer would not be left to the fate of his current inefficient technologies and market uncertainties. At the same time, the likelihood of producers' defaulting on loans is reduced if they realize further financing depends on their payment of existing loans.

Government personnel with access to external capital, domestic banks, and marketing agencies are optimally positioned to carry out this coordi-nation. Such coordination should not be impossible because it stands to benefit from various local and nongovernmental organizations already in existence in almost all African countries—religious organizations, village associations, cooperatives, credit unions, farmer groups, professional associations, chambers of commerce, and industry. Government could build upon this solid base. A Scandinavian Institute of African Studies Report on cooperative schemes in Africa has identified a variety of thriving grassroots, nongovernmental cooperatives in almost all sub-Saharan African countries. Most of these organizations are built around a common ownership of land and other resources that could be harnessed for qualitative improvement.[38] What they often lack is capital, which could be supplied from both a more liberal tax policy and the direct action by state elites in linking such groups to domestic and foreign financial sources. For rural areas, where poor infrastructure may act as a deincentive to potential investors, only some guarantees by the government would promote the establishment of private enterprises.

The potential of useful state intervention in the economy is great, but there is potential danger. While state-sponsored capitalist experiments in Kenya, Nigeria, Cameroon, and Côte d'Ivoire seem to lean in this direction, there is danger of state domination or dependence of private producers on the state if the state fails to transfer total ownership and responsibility of these projects to the private individuals who work on them. For example, while the IMF and both governments of Ahijo and Biya hail the impressive technical success of the Yagoua capitalist rice project, these impressive aggregates, according to one estimate by Claude, hide the deteriorating conditions of the peasants who are tenant farmers on state land. The Nigerian case illustrates another potential danger of state-sponsored capitalism.[39] Where the state maintains virtual control of these projects, project performance would tend to fluctuate directly and severely with the political fate of its initiating regime. In Nigeria, the transition from small-scale family-labor farming to large-scale migrant-labor farming has suffered two setbacks. The discovery of oil shifted attention away from agriculture and provided the necessary condition for the formation of what Callaghy calls a form of "pirate capitalism"—a process dominated and corrupted by a corrupt patrimonial administration.[40] And as will be explained later in the discussion of class struggle in Africa, this lurking danger has already caught up with the Ivorian state-sponsored capitalism, not because of its extreme dependence on external capital but because of Houphouet-Boigny's strategy to use foreign capital to bribe the opposition.

Reversing Commodity Export Specialization

Obviously, modern development in Africa is impossible as long as African countries continue their current commodity export specialization. However, because foreign domination was the consequence of sharply differentiated production and consumption capacities between Africans and their European colonizers, only a fundamental change in African productive and consumption capacity would begin to alter foreign economic domination. This is not to deny the need for a fundamental restructuring of colonial trade, foreign-dominated manufacturing, and other industrial aspects of African commodity exports. Rather it is to argue that overcoming foreign domination could occur only through fundamental change in the productive and consumption capacities between the two peoples and through policy intervention, such as nationalization of foreign enterprise. The so-called radical states that engaged in extensive nationalization in the 1970s have paid a heavy price.

Because foreign investment interests conflict with the goal of these mercantilist states to maximize state power, foreign investment to these countries quickly dried up,[41] making the 1970s through the early 1980s the period with the highest rate of capitalist flight from Africa in recent years. The countries that at one time or the other nationalized foreign enterprise, such as Tanzania, Zaire, Uganda, Congo, Somalia, Ghana,[42] and Mali, have been virtually abandoned by foreign investors. The radical nationalization of foreign enterprise produced such a negative outcome in Zaire that foreign industries nationalized in the early 1970s were later invited to return. And lack of foreign investment contributed significantly in placing these countries among African countries with the worst economic records in the 1970s and early 1980s—a reason that all of them had to accept the harsh conditionalities of borrowing from the IMF and the World Bank.

Without new national and continental markets to absorb African commodities, exports to the same European markets as before independence would have to continue. The successful establishment of an autonomously expanding grassroots capitalism will solve the problem of foreign control over the trade and manufacturing aspects of African exports more efficiently and faster than will policy instruments. In the longer term, both trade diversion and export diversification would result from the autonomously expanding economies in these countries rather than from nationalization and other radical interventionist policies. A successful recapturing of the foreign-dominated aspects of current African exports is not necessarily synonymous with the forceful relocation of European industries using African raw materials in Africa. Rather, trade diversification concerns the relocation of trade according to the dictates of new and expanding country and continental production possibilities and demands. As the self-sustaining process gathers its own momentum at the grassroots level, forward and backward linkages would develop. That is, increasing local and regional demands and productive efficiency would shape new products as well as trade routes.

Frederick Cooper argues this was the method used by the landless class of Kenya to gain substantial control over the foreign-dominated aspects of their cash crop industry. "As this class extended its control over agriculture," comments Cooper, "it began to move into manufacturing as well, both cooperating with and pushing away multinationals."[43] The Kenya case underscores the reality of the international capitalist market and Africa's inescapable place in that market, as the landless class works closely with foreign capital, technology, and technical know-how in a mutual learning process to increase growth.

Regime Response and Domestic Class Struggle

To distinguish African socialism from orthodox Marxist-Leninism, Africanists deny the existence of class distinctions and class struggle[44] in Africa. However, the private ownership of land in most African countries started the momentum toward class stratification even before the colonials came. Differences in the degree of land possession meant different responses to the same social problems and constraints on the land that were driving the precolonial economies toward capitalism and that produced the "classless" population described earlier. Class formation further accelerated during colonialism as the chiefs, who, for a bribe, signed off their people into colonialism and joined local personnel who worked for the colonial administration in using their access to the colonialist wealth to distinguish themselves from the ordinary folks. But social class formations along income differentials really took off with the institution of socialist command economics in postcolonial Africa. The centralization of wealth in the hands of a few government and bureaucratic elite provided an irresistible magnet of much corruption and personal aggrandizement. The result is a wealthy elitist class, distinct above all social classes regardless of tribe, education, or occupation—a state-sponsored class whose destruction is a major target of the current democratic movement.

To the extent that the socialist state is a breeder of class distinctions in Africa, one can expect greater intolerance of class struggle mainly but not exclusively in the statist-socialist and mercantilist-socialist regimes. These regimes oppose class struggle and stifle all class-promoting activity, they smother formal opposition parties, deny press freedom, detain without trial the leaders of opposition parties, suppress such class interest articulation as workers' strikes, and go to extremes in their attempt to nullify the current liberalization movement.

Even though regime orientations as defined here make a difference in the level of class struggle allowed in a particular country, African class struggle is further complicated by the differing impact of colonial patterns. Unlike the French, who for love of empire never went home from Africa, the British undertook a rapid decolonization. Succumbing to the general antidomination mood after the war and having lost the capacity to administer their colonies—the British economic infrastructure having been severely damaged from bombardment during the war—the British simply packed their colonial bags and went home. They left behind an economic, political, and bureaucratic vacuum, since British indirect rule meant that very little of the British economic and political institutional machinery and maturity was transmitted to its former colonies.

Filling that vacuum resulted in immediate internal class struggle in most former British colonies. The struggle to define the sharing of governmental power and its peaceful transition among the various governmental elites meant a greater level of class infighting and political instability in the former British colonies—a development that kept much needed foreign investment away. Nonetheless, this struggle was a very healthy exercise, since it is not clear how African development, completely neglected during more than a century of colonialism, could take off again without the discovery of political and economic processes that yield the highest level of class consensus. If, prior to building this class consensus, the state becomes the channel for a stupendous flow of foreign capital, it risks becoming a target for private rent-seeking activity, and the state is easily corrupted.

In that sense, political-capitalist regimes like Liberia under President William R. Tolbert, Jr., Gabon under both Presidents Leon M'Ba and Albert Omar Bongo, Côte d'Ivoire under President Felix Houphouet-Boigny, Togo under President Gnassingbe Eyadema, and Kenya under President Daniel arap Moi, who use their huge inflows of foreign capital to bribe their opposition, are no better off than state-mercantilist states like Zaire under President Mobutu Sese Seko, where socialism was introduced not for ideological reasons but because it centralized wealth and enabled incumbents to bypass or weaken their opposition and fend off class struggle. In the short term, the problem for such regimes is that they are seen as the privileged site for private enrichment. However, the problem of classes struggling to control an illusory wealthy state pales before the longer-term problem of suppressing internal class struggle. They might have secured their regimes in the short term, but at the considerable cost of delayed class struggle that is bound to explode sooner or later.

France's direct and massive involvement in its former African territories has been part of its strategy of unilateralism in global affairs aimed to promote French nationalism and independence from American and other European countries. However, as that unilateralism is superseded and circumvented by France's membership in the European Community (EC), which seeks increasingly to project a common European image, we can expect a sharp decline in France's effort to sustain its puppet regimes in its former African territories. Already, France has been forced to give up its unilateral trade arrangement with these former states and deal with them indirectly through the EC's trade arrangement under the expanded Lomé

Convention. Further curtailment of French unilateralism can be expected in the financial and diplomatic areas as European unification intensifies toward the Maastricht objective. And when that happens, the French-dependent African regimes will be forced to deal with the harsh realities of suppressed internal class divisions and the problems of regime legitimacy, problems they have so far evaded because of their dependence on France. Without France's abundant supplies of funds to bribe authorities or troops to suppress internal opposition, we can expect these Francophone states to undergo the same internal class struggles that have accompanied the nation-building process in the Anglophone countries. On a more positive note, reduction in French involvement may pave the way for a serious approach to various proposed subregional economic integration schemes in central and West Africa.

Conclusion: Taking A Broader Perspective

A dominant theme in these discussions has been the inconsistency between Africa's precolonial and colonial socioeconomic experiences and the adoption of statism in the postcolonial period. The tendency to expand state control of the economy and the building of large and impressive state and social infrastructures that have come to characterize the statist approach to development in the region have no natural roots in African history, culture, and economy. Consequently, a big psychological gap exists between the people's development aspirations and the regimes' objectives and strategies. Thus, ultimately, the objective has been to emphasize this inconsistency as more accountable for the current economic crisis than the trajectory of any external factors. And considerable evidence supports that observation.

The external nexus explanation of the left blames the current economic crisis on neocolonial forms of exploitation: the domination of Third World economies by multinational corporations based in industrial countries, the declining terms of trade for African commodity exports, and their large debt service to income ratios. However, differentials in the economic performance of African countries and between them as a group and other low-income countries can be better explained in terms of the difference in the intensity of state domination than by reference to such external factors. The evidence often used to support the argument of the continuing drainage of resources through the "debt trap" is not particularly persuasive in the African case. Without doubt, some sub-Saharan countries have been hard hit by their debt burden. As Table 4.1 indicates, in 1987 São Tomé and Príncipe and Côte d'Ivoire paid over 15 percent of their GNP in total long-term debt service obligations. Other comparably high figures for

Table 4.1   Basic Economic Indicators for Sub-Saharan States

	Average annual growth rate (%)			Taxes on international trade and transactions			Total long-term debt service as a percentage of GNP		
	1965–1973	1973–1980	1980–1987	1972	1980	1987	1970	1980	1987
Ethiopia	1.1	0.0	–1.6	30.4	35.7	—	1.2	0.8	3.4
Chad	–1.3	–3.5	2.4	45.2	—	46.2	0.9	0.4	0.7
Zaire	0.3	–4.7	–2.5	57.9	38.4	33.4	1.1	3.6	4.7
Guinea-Bissau	—	–4.2	0.8	—	—	39.8	—	3.8	7.2
Malawi	4.3	1.4	0.0	20.0	22.0	16.8	2.3	5.9	6.0
Mozambique	—	—	–8.2	21.7	17.3	—	—	—	—
Tanzania	1.2	–0.9	–1.7	21.7	17.3	8.6	—	—	—
Burkina Faso	1.2	2.5	2.5	51.8	43.7	39.4	0.7	1.2	1.7
Madagascar	1.1	–1.5	–3.7	33.6	27.6	—	0.8	1.8	7.7
Mali	—	4.3	0.7	—	17.9	28.1	0.2	0.6	1.7
Gambia, The	1.7	0.2	0.8	70.7	65.3	66.4	0.2	0.3	8.2
Burundi	3.2	1.9	–0.2	40.3	40.4	—	0.3	0.7	3.6
Zambia	–0.5	–2.2	–5.6	14.3	8.3	32.9	—	—	—
Niger	–3.7	2.6	–4.9	—	36.4	—	—	4.9	7.2
Uganda	0.7	–6.2	–2.4	36.3	44.3	75.3	0.5	1.3	1.9
São Tomé and Príncipe	—	7.2	–6.0	—	—	—	—	2.2	15.3
Somalia	0.1	4.6	–2.5	45.3	52.5	—	0.3	1.4	0.9
Togo	2.0	1.5	–3.9	—	32.0	32.3	1.0	4.2	5.5
Rwanda	3.2	2.2	–1.0	41.7	42.4	—	0.1	0.4	1.0
Sierra Leone	2.3	–0.8	–2.0	42.4	49.6	40.4	3.1	3.8	0.5
Benin	0.0	–.3	–0.6	—	56.0	—	0.6	0.8	2.0
Central African Republic	1.5	–0.5	–0.7	—	—	—	1.7	0.2	2.1
Kenya	4.7	1.3	–0.9	24.3	18.5	19.2	3.0	5.5	7.6
Sudan	–1.7	3.5	–4.3	40.5	42.6	—	—	—	—
Lesotho	4.2	6.6	–0.9	73.7	—	67.8	0.5	0.7	2.3
Nigeria	5.3	1.2	–4.8	17.5	22.4	6.6	0.7	0.8	3.9
Ghana	1.0	–2.1	–2.0	40.6	44.2	42.5	1.2	2.3	3.7
Mauritania	1.2	–0.6	–1.6	—	30.1	—	1.8	4.5	9.9
Liberia	2.4	–0.7	–5.2	31.6	33.6	26.9	4.3	3.5	1.0
Senegal	–0.8	–0.5	0.1	30.9	34.2	—	1.1	6.4	6.4
Zimbabwe	2.6	–2.0	–1.3	—	4.4	15.6	—	—	—
Swaziland	5.8	0.3	1.2	49.7	67.4	42.2	3.1	2.3	5.2
Côte d'Ivoire	4.5	1.2	–3.0	—	42.8	—	3.1	9.5	15.6
Congo, People's Republic of	4.2	1.1	7.1	26.5	13.0	—	3.4	5.7	10.3
Cameroon	–0.4	5.7	4.5	—	38.4	18.7	1.0	3.4	4.8
Botswana	9.3	7.3	8.0	47.2	39.1	13.4	0.7	1.5	5.2
Mauritius	0.8	3.9	4.4	40.2	51.6	50.5	1.4	3.6	4.6
Gabon	4.9	–1.2	–3.5	44.9	19.7	16.2	3.8	10.8	2.3
Seychelles	2.6	4.5	1.3	53.2	—	—	—	0.2	4.2

Note: The following sub-Saharan states have been omitted for lack of adequate data: Djibouti, Angola, Equitorial Guinea, and Comoros.
Source: Selected from *World Bank Data* (World Bank: n.p., 1989, pp. 221–298). We defer to this source for all measurement criteria.

Madagascar, Mauritania, Gambia, Burkina Faso, Kenya, and the People's Republic of the Congo range from 6 to 11 percent. However, considering all the African countries as a whole, the debt burden is not that decisive. Excluding the Congo, Côte d'Ivoire, and São Tomé and Príncipe, the average debt service to GNP ratio of about 4 percent does not amount to a "debt trap." Additionally, the causes for debt accumulation by states in the region go back far beyond the more recent hikes in petroleum prices, which are often blamed for the debt crisis. Serious debt accumulation in the region began with the failed import-substitution development strategy embraced particularly by the statist-socialist regimes. The steadily falling rate of production since 1970 coincides with the peak in centralization in most African states (see total long-term debt service column in Table 4.1). As a recent World Bank study reports, since the early 1970s the sub-Saharan states would not have placed so much burden on their GNP and export earnings by 1987 if they had maintained their 1970s rate of agricultural production.[45] At the 1970 rate, the region could have earned an additional $9 to $10 billion—an increase approximately equal to the region's total debt service payments in this period (1986–1987).

The evidence on Africa's declining terms of trade is even less persuasive. As Figure 4.1 indicates, notwithstanding some fluctuations, the export prices for four major sub-Saharan African export commodities have generally remained above their 1961 levels for the entire period of African independence. The general downturn that occurred around 1986 has already bottomed out. The sharp drop in the terms of trade since 1980 is a correction for the historically sharp increases from 1975 to 1980. Contrary to the external nexus argument, Africa's imports would have shrunk far more substantially had this historically high peak in the prices of cocoa, coffee, and copper not occurred in the post-1970 period, when their domestic production declined steadily. The average annual growth rate of exports from sub-Saharan Africa (including oil from Nigeria) fell from a healthy 6.6 percent in 1965–1980 to -0.8 for the same period in 1980–1987.[46]

Commodity producers' failure to increase production in order to take advantage of these historically high commodity prices has two probable explanations. Some would blame inelasticity in commodity production and trade. But that explanation is less credible, considering the rather lengthy period of price hikes. Besides, Togo and Côte d'Ivoire were able to take advantage of the increased high prices for cocoa, not by increasing their own output but by outbidding Ghana's producer prices consistently and thereby providing incentives for cocoa smuggling to their countries from neighboring Ghana—the largest cocoa producer in the region. Thus, the more plausible reason is that high taxation of commodity exports under a statist system (such as in Ghana as compared with both Togo and Côte

Figure 4.1   Export Prices for Four Major Sub-Saharan African Commodity
Exports, 1961–1987

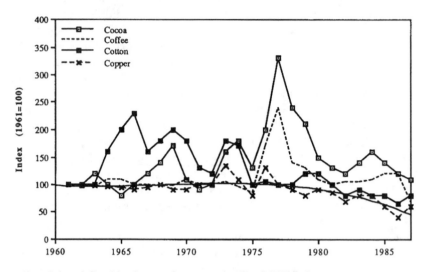

Note: Prices deflated by the manufacturers unit value (MUV) index.
Source: Extracted from *World Bank Data* (World Bank: n.p., 1989), p. 32.

d'Ivoire) prevented the benefits and incentives of increased world market
prices from reaching producers. Thus, declining production at a time of a
historical peak in world commodity prices is further evidence of the strong
disincentive to produce that centralized systems generate. The overall effects of export prices on their consumption of imports (the terms of trade)
averaged over the entire period of 1961–1985 remains largely unchanged
over the 1961 level (See Figure 4.2) and remains more positive than the
comparative terms of trade averaged for all low-income countries together.

While not discounting completely the negative effects of external market factors, the politics of overcentralization has the greater blame for
Africa's economic paralysis. Berry's study is among a growing number of
studies that demonstrate the seriousness of government pricing disincentive effects on sub-Saharan productivity.[47] Price regulation shifts incentives away from production and toward exchange and rent-seeking activities. The increased extraction of agricultural surplus without an increase in
the productivity of peasant agriculture as a whole only made an already
poor peasantry poorer and further distanced them from their respective
regimes. In addition, the peasantry was very frustrated by the cajoling and
ordering around that came with centralization of power.

Figure 4.2 Comparative Terms of Trade Between Sub-Saharan Africa and All
Low-Income Countries

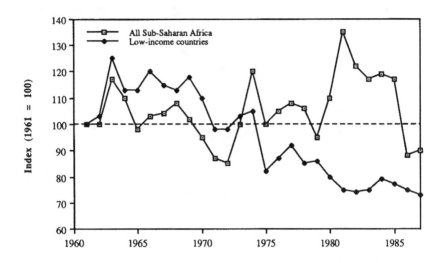

Source: Extracted from *World Bank Data* (World Bank: n.p., 1989), p. 24.

The tendency of command economies to overexploit the surplus from
production is, however, just one of the many fundamental flaws of socialist praxis and the utopianism of its theory of production. In various degrees, these other flaws of socialist praxis showed up under all socialist
regimes of Africa: disregard of the standards of efficiency and rationality
in planning production; reliance on excessive manpower in the absence of
the high technology used in Western industrial production; enormous resource waste that comes from the allocation of production quotas and artificial prices that paid no attention to supply and demand; a wage scale
that aspired more to the political needs of largely delegitimized leaders
than to incentives of a competitive reward system; the priority allocation
of resources for military and industrial expansion at the expense of agriculture and consumer-goods production; and a single hierarchical decisionmaking structure that was completely overwhelmed. Thus, as a development theory, socialism is utopian because, unlike capitalism, it is not
self-executing; that is, it does not interpret itself automatically and is not
based on verifiable images of reality. Rather, it is based upon the authoritative interpretation of changing realities by each African socialist leader,
each of whom defined his own criteria of verification.

Further evidence of the ineffectiveness of state-centered development is the sharp difference in economic performance between the highly

Figure 4.3   Gross National Income per Capita in Sub-Saharan Africa and
Other Developing Countries

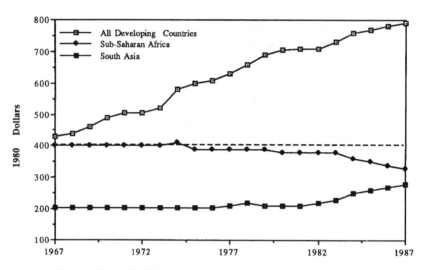

Source: Extracted from *World Bank Data* (World Bank: n.p., 1989), p. 20.

centralized states and those that have retained relatively free markets. With
the exception of Nigeria (whose current problems are mainly due to the mis-
management of its oil boom), the other five African countries—Equatorial
Guinea, Ghana, Liberia, São Tomé and Príncipe, and Zambia—that have
slipped from middle-income to the low-income ranking (as classified in the
World Development Report) have been noted for their extensive state-
dominated economies at one time or the other (see average annual growth
rate in Table 4.1). In contrast, countries where the private sector has been left
to operate largely unhindered, such as Cameroon, Kenya, Botswana, Mauri-
tius, and Côte d'Ivoire (before the 1980s), have remained relatively efficient.
In terms of overall GDP growth rate over the period 1961–1985, Ghana and
Equatorial Guinea, which until the recent reforms were noted for their highly
centralized systems, contrast very sharply with the free economies of Côte
d'Ivoire and Cameroon, even though these two sets of countries share common geographic borders and export the same cash products.

The tendency to excuse African performance because of deplorable
Third World conditions hides important differences. The seriousness of the
effects of centralization on the region's economic growth becomes even
clearer when its economic performance is compared with that of other developing regional groups such as South Asia. Since the early 1970s,
Africa's economic performance has been the worst among developing
country regions. As Figure 4.3 indicates, the region's average annual per
capita growth rate has gone down steadily from 2 percent for the period

Figure 4.4 Rate of Return on Investment in Sub-Saharan Africa and South Asia

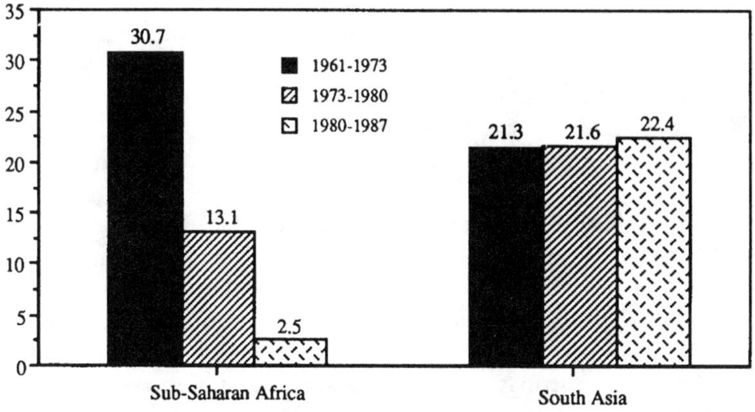

Source: Extracted from *World Bank Data* (World Bank: n.p., 1989), p. 20.

1961–1973, to -0.1 percent for 1973–1980, and to -2.6 percent for 1980–1988.[48] Important country-to-country differences notwithstanding,[49] economic decline is general for the entire region. African economic performance contrasts sharply with the steady growth of the more open economies of the South Asian LDCs (less developed countries)—Bangladesh, Bhutan, Burma, India, Maldives, Nepal, Pakistan, and Sri Lanka—considered among the poorest of the poor. Comparative economic growth figures for the Asian LDCs rise from 1.2 percent, to 2.0 percent, and 2.8 percent, for the same period. Even though the average per capita national income of the sub-Saharan states remains higher in absolute terms than that of the South Asian LDCs, the latter are maintaining the same positive upward trend as all LDCs combined. In contrast, the centralized economies in sub-Saharan Africa show a declining growth trend. These sharply contrasting trends are also reflected in their levels of economic efficiency, measured in terms of rates of return on investment. Figure 4.4 shows a sharp drop in economic efficiency for the African countries from a healthy 30.7 percent before 1973 to a mere 2.5 percent by the end of 1987. In contrast, the South Asian countries have maintained a slight growth rate over their 1973 performance.

To conclude, the aim is not to deny external constraints on development in Africa but to make it abundantly clear that internal economic, social, and particularly policy constraints are at least as important, if not more so, and that they are not necessarily the makings of a repressive colonial experience or of a current domineering external market. These trends are too significant to dismiss as reflections of common external market asymmetries that affect negatively all developing countries; they reflect systemic problems. Ultimately, of course, the objective is to point to the opportunities for African countries to shape their own capitalist systems autonomously by responding to the demands, challenges, and momentum of Africa's precolonial, market-oriented economies. The current crisis is largely the result of the inconsistency among African development needs, the challenges of independence, and the trajectory of regime responses. With all its weakness, grassroots capitalist transformation, as outlined in this chapter, offers better solutions.

It is also clear that the market reforms introduced by the IMF and the World Bank do not go far enough in addressing these fundamental problems. Some microstrategies for coordinating existing regimes and private producers that must accompany macromarket reforms have been suggested here. What is positive about the IMF intervention is that it may achieve a major shift in the distribution of accumulation power between the state and the society of private producers—a change that was necessary from day one of independence and yet for political reasons was never implemented by most African regimes. With the shifting of economic power from the state to grassroots producers, a new class-based production politics can be installed that holds potential for the economic revival and full capitalist transformation in Africa.

Notes

1. The term *sub-Saharan Africa* is used interchangeably with *Africa* to refer to the African countries south of the Sahara and north of the Republic of South Africa that have come to be regarded as a single socioeconomic region. This region possesses extensive similarities that constitute an optimal basis for a comparative study of this kind. Unlike their neighbors to the north and south, these countries had lived through generally similar forms of Western European colonialism. Their continuing attempts at postindependence nation building seem to have run into similar problems. The countries of the Mediterranean littoral (Morocco, Algeria, Tunisia, Libya, Egypt) and South Africa are explicitly excluded. Their religion, history, and socioeconomic culture disposes countries within this group to see themselves and to behave more as Middle East Arab countries than as African countries. South Africa's aggressive pursuit of apartheid until recently isolated it from the rest of the continent.

2. While, theoretically speaking, socialism is to be distinguished from centralization, they are here used interchangeably to make the point that in Africa, as indeed everywhere else socialism has been practiced, their fine distinctions have often been blurred. Later, an attempt is made to differentiate between African regimes in terms of whether centralization was seen as a practice of socialism.

3. Jon Moris, "The Transferability of the Western Management Tradition to the Non-Western Public Service Sectors," *Philippine Journal of Public Administration* 20, no. 4 (1976): pp. 401–427; David K. Leonard, "The Political Realities of African Management," in *Report of a Workshop on the Management of*

Agricultural Projects in Africa, (Washington, D.C.: USAID Special Evaluation Study No. 33, 1986), pp. 58–74. James S. Wunsch, "Centralization and Development in Post-Independence Africa," in James S. Wunsch and Dele Olowu, eds., *The Failure of the Centralized State: Institutions and Self-Governance in Africa* (Boulder: Westview Press, 1990), pp. 43–73.

4. Jon Moris, *Managing Induced Rural Development* (Bloomington, Ind.: Indiana University, International Development Institute, 1981); Dennis Rondinelli, *Development Projects as Policy Experiments* (London: Methuen, 1983); James S. Wunsch, "Administering Rural Development; Have Goals Outreached Organizational Capacity?" *Public Administration and Development* 6 (1986): pp. 287–308.

5. Dennis Austin, *Politics in Africa* (Hanover, N.H.: University Press of New England, 1984); Robert Jackson and Carl Rosberg, *Personal Rule in Black Africa: Prince, Autocrat, Prophet, Tyrant* (Berkeley: University of California Press, 1982).

6. Sheldon Gellar, "State Tutelage vs. Self-Governance: The Rhetoric and Reality of Decentralization in Senegal," in *The Failure of the Centralized State*, pp. 130–147.

7. Robert H. Jackson and Carl Rosberg, *Personal Rule in Black Africa: Prince, Autocrat, Prophet, Tyrant* (Berkeley: University of California Press, 1982), p. 6.

8. As quoted in *New York Times,* September 5, 1989, p. 15.

9. For documentation of bureaucratic opposition to IMF/World Bank austerity, see Jennifer Whitaker, *How Can Africa Survive?* (New York: Council on Foreign Relations Press, 1988); and Joan M. Nelson, "The Politics of Long-Haul Economic Reform," in Joan M. Nelson et al., eds., *Fragile Coalitions: The Politics of Economic Adjustment* (Washington, D.C.: Overseas Development Council, 1989), pp. 3–26.

10. For a well-balanced discussion of the politically weak foundations bequeathed to Africa as a result of inefficient and negligible colonial administrations, see James S. Wunsch, "Foundations of Centralization: The Colonial Experience and the African Context," in *The Failure of the Centralized State*, pp. 23–42.

11. Tribal politics is generally acknowledged as a problem affecting practically all the sub-Saharan countries, even though the problem is particularly acute in certain countries like Nigeria. See Donald Rothchild and V. A. Olorunsola, eds., *State versus Ethnic Claims* (Boulder: Westview Press, 1983).

12. Crawford Young, "The African Colonial State and Its Political Legacy," in Donald Rothchild and Naomi Chazan, eds., *The Precarious Balance: State & Society in Africa,* African Modernization and Development Series (Boulder: Westview Press, 1988), p. 57.

13. Bill Warren, *Imperialism: Pioneer of Capitalism* (London: NLB and Verso Editions, 1980).

14. Quoted in Robert L. Heilbroner, *The Nature and Logic of Capitalism* (New York: W. W. Norton & Company, 1985), p. 36.

15. Heilbroner, *The Nature and Logic of Capitalism*, pp. 13–14.

16. The view of preindependent African societies as undifferentiated rural societies of the typical precolonial subsistence period is naive and inconsistent with the realities of increasing economic scarcity and the management adjustments to scarcity that were emerging before independence. A number of authors emphasize the sophistication of indigenous African commerce at this time, including the emergence of middlemen and the development of various strategies for cushioning traders and farmers against environmental disasters. What is more, this evolution was hardly influenced by Western economic culture and politics. The combination of increasing commerce, the opening of roads, the growth of cities, and especially,

a rapidly increasing population relative to fixed amount of land yields and ineffi- cient manpower technology effectively ended pure communitarianism and con- tributed to a mass exodus of young people to cities in order to escape the difficult and nonlucrative subsistence agricultural life. For details, see, among others, Polly Hill, *The Migrant Cocoa Farmers of Southern Ghana: A Study in Rural Capitalism* (Cambridge, England: Cambridge University Press, 1963); William O. Jones, "Agricultural Trade Within Tropical Africa: Historical Background," in Robert H. Bates and Michael Lofchie, eds., *Agricultural Development in Africa: Issues of Public Policy* (New York: Praeger Special Studies, 1980); J. Carl Eicher and Doyle C. Baker, "Research on Agricultural Development in Sub-Saharan Africa," in L. R. Martin, ed., *A Survey of Agricultural Economics Literature* (St. Paul: University of Minnesota Press, 1981).

17. Only that part of the very extensive radical literature is cited that deals di- rectly with the subjection of the destruction of African values as a result of the in- troduction of Western capitalism. In *How Europe Underdeveloped Africa*, Walter Rodney comments, "Colonialism crushed, by force, the surviving feudal states of North Africa. . . . The French wiped out and the British eliminated Egypt, the Mahdist Sudan, Ashanti, Benin . . . as great states." Amilca Cabral comes to simi- lar conclusions in arguing that "the principal characteristic, common to every kind of imperialist domination, is the negation of the *historical process* of the domi- nated people by means of violently usurping the free operation of the process of development of the productive forces." And Andre Gunder Frank titles his exten- sively quoted work, "The Development of Underdevelopment."

18. An historically documented exception is the slave trade. Robert Anstey in his work, "The Volume and Profitability of the British Slave Trade, 1761–1807," in Stanley L. Eugerman and Eugene Genevese, eds., *Race and Slavery in Western Hemisphere: Quantitative Studies* (Princeton: Princeton University Press, 1975), presents detailed evaluation of the profitability of the slave trade. However, the slave trade has never been the focus of the drainage theory.

19. Karl Marx, "The British Role in India," *New York Daily Tribune* 25 (June: 1853): pp. 93–98, as quoted in Claude Meillassoux, ed., *The Development of In- digenous Trade and Markets in West Africa* (London: Oxford University Press, 1971), pp. 92–93.

20. See John Roemer, "Exploitation, Class, and Property Relations," in Ter- ence Ball and James Gar, eds., *After Marx* (London: Cambridge University Press, 1984).

21. As quoted in David John Morgan, *The Official History of Colonial Devel- opment. Vol. III. A Reassessment of British Aid Policy, 1951–65,* published by per- mission of the Controller of Her Majesty's Stationary Office (New Jersey: Hu- manities Press, Crown Copyright, 1972).

22. Frederick Cooper, "Africa and the World Economy," *African Studies Re- view* 24, nos. 2/3 (June-September 1981): p. 81.

23. Ralph A. Austen, *African Economic History: Internal Development and External Dependency* (London: James Curry Ltd., 1987).

24. See in particular, Naomi Chazan, "Myths and Realities in African Social- ism," in S. N. Eisenstadt and Yael Azmon, eds., *Socialism and Tradition* (New Jer- sey: Humanities Press, 1975).

25. Timothy Shaw, "Beyond Neo-Colonialism: Varieties of Corporatism in Africa," *Journal of Modern African Studies* 20, no. 2 (June 1982): p. 260.

26. Thomas M. Callaghy, "The State and the Development of Capitalism in Africa: Theoretical, Historical, and Comparative Reflections," in Donald

Rothchild, and Naomi Chazan, eds., *The Precarious Balance: State and Society in Africa* (New York: Cambridge University Press, 1988), p. 83. While Callaghy's mercantilist characterization of African regimes would seem to fit the many regimes whose sole objective is the amassing of the individual ruler's power and wealth, I do not think the term accurately represents all African regimes as his single categorization would suggest.

27. Julius E. Nyang'oro, "On the Concept of 'Corporatism' and the African State," *Studies in Comparative International Development* 21, no. 4 (1987): p. 50.

28. See Sear Berry, *Fathers Work for Their Sons: Accumulation, Mobility, and Class Formation in an Extended Yoruba Community* (Berkeley: The University of California Press, 1985).

29. As reported in Dominique Claude, "Production and Commercialization of Rice in Cameroon: The Semry Project," in *Structural Adjustment in Africa*, B. K. Campbell and J. Loxley, eds., (New York: St. Martin's Press, 1989).

30. Callaghy, "The State and the Development of Capitalism in Africa," in *The Precarious Balance*.

31. World Bank, *Sub-Saharan Africa: From Crisis to Sustainable Growth* (Washington, D. C.: The World Bank, 1989), Table 20. To put the comparative figures in perspective, it has to be recalled that much of Nigeria's heavy foreign capital inflow is directly related to its oil boom. Without a comparable oil exploration activity, it must be assumed that the heavy foreign investment in Côte d'Ivoire went mainly into its private and parastatal capitalist projects.

32. Robert Bates, *Markets and States in Tropical Africa: The Political Basis of Agricultural Policies* (Berkeley: The University of California Press, 1981), p. 26.

33. Ibid.

34. Ibid.

35. The state interventionist view can be found variously in Alice Amsten, "The State and Taiwan's Economic Development," in Peter B. Evans, Dietrich Rueschemeyer, and Theda Skocpol, eds., *Bringing the State Back In* (New York: Cambridge University Press, 1985); Bruce Cumings, "The Origins and Development of the Northeast Asian Political Economy," *International Organization* 38 (1984): pp. 1–40; and Frederick Deyo, ed. *The Political Economy of The New Asian Industrialism* (Ithaca, New York: Cornell University Press, 1987).

36. Anthony T. Gadzey, "The State and Capitalist Transformation in Sub-Saharan Africa: A Development Model," *Comparative Political Studies* 24, no. 4 (1992): pp. 471–473.

37. Richard Sandbrook, *The Politics of African Economic Recovery* (Cambridge: Cambridge University Press, 1993), p. 57.

38. Hans Holmen, *State Cooperatives and Development in Africa* (Uppsala: The Scandinavian Institute of African Studies, 1990).

39. Claude, "Production and Commercialization of Rice in Cameroon," in *Structural Adjustment in Africa*.

40. Callaghy, "The State and the Development of Capitalism in Africa," *The Precarious Balance*.

41. The exception until the late 1980s has been the corrupt regime of Mobutu Sese Seko of Zaire, which continued to attract U.S. government assistance as the frontline state for the U.S. strategy of containing the Soviet/Cuban Communist presence in Angola.

42. Ghana has made a significant recovery in attracting foreign investors following various compensations payments and on-schedule servicing of its foreign

debts, debts that its military leader, Colonel Kutu Acheampong, unilaterally rejected in 1971.

43. Frederick Cooper, "Africa and the World Economy," p. 48.

44. The notion of class struggle that appropriately describes the nature of class formation and struggle in Africa must be distinguished from the classical Marxist notions of class struggle as determined essentially by economic relations between workers and capitalists. Because both the colonial and postcolonial processes were integral parts of the process of class articulation in Africa, the notion of class struggle in Africa has a strong political component lacking in the Marxist definition of the term. As such, class struggle in Africa uses economic but mainly political instruments, becoming conceptually almost synonymous with what most people would consider as "democratization."

45. World Bank, *Sub-Saharan Africa: From Crisis to Sustainable Growth*, table 22, p. 258.

46. Ibid.

47. Berry, "Agrarian Crisis in Africa?" in *Fathers Work for Their Sons*.

48. Because of its large size relative to all other countries in the region, Nigeria's oil boom and bust has had extensive effects on the region's aggregates. Comparable growth rate figures for the region for the same periods but excluding Nigeria are 1.2, -0.7, and -1.2, respectively.

49. The 1987 figures range from a -2.2 percent for Uganda to 8.3 percent for Botswana.

5

State, Petroleum, and Democratization in the Middle East and North Africa

Manochehr Dorraj

A number of significant issues permeate the political economy of the Middle East and mold its dynamics and the pattern of its evolution. First is the nature of state and state formation and its relation to the society from which it evolves. Second, petroleum more than any other commodity in the modern Middle East plays a pivotal role in the economic growth of oil-producing nations. Countries such as Iran, Iraq, Saudi Arabia, and Kuwait, to mention a few, earn up to 90 percent of their foreign exchange from selling their oil. These single-commodity economies are at the mercy of fluctuations in the global oil market. The petrodollar in turn impacts states' capacities and resources, thus determining the choice of policy and political action. On the one hand it may provide the state with resources for public welfare and forge a base of support for the regime, as is the case with the sheikhdoms of the Persian Gulf (Saudi Arabia, Kuwait, Qatar, Bahrain, and the United Arab Emirates). If, however, it is distributed unevenly, it can exacerbate the existing social tensions and culminate a revolution, as was the case in Iran. Therefore, the petrodollar by itself may not buy legitimacy.

Realizing the limitations of financial rewards, many regimes have opted for a populist ideology and a corporatist strategy to forge a base of support and consolidate their power. The nuances of this ideology and its political manifestations reveal a delicate synthesis: the manipulation of historical memory and the collective mythology combined with a campaign of clientele politics and mass mobilization. Populism, however, does not connote popular sovereignty or democratic rule. Often mass mobilization from above replaces genuine political participation from below, and the clientele groups dominate popular organizations. Hence, the omnipresent repressive hands of the authoritarian populist state serve as a reminder to those who may contemplate active opposition to its policies and power.

This pattern of authoritarian rule has been challenged in the past decade. A number of international and domestic factors ushered in a wave of democratization, albeit manipulated and controlled from above. In some countries, such as Algeria, Egypt, Libya, and Iran, this process went hand in hand with privatization of state-owned enterprises. But for the most part, the Middle Eastern perestroika (economic reform and restructuring) has not been accompanied by a genuine glasnost (political opening). In countries such as Algeria, Tunisia, and Egypt, where democratization led to the ascendence of Muslim traditionalists and effectively challenged the existing power structure, the process came to an abrupt end by 1992. This reveals the limitations of an elite-initiated democratization and the weakness of the civil society and the intense insecurity of the ruling elite throughout the region.

The Iraqi invasion of Kuwait in August 1990 delivered yet another blow to the ideal of Pan-Arabism and forcefully accentuated the rise of regionalism. The challenge of Islamists in Algeria, Tunisia, and Egypt to their respective secular regimes, the creation of Islamic states in Iran, Afghanistan, and Sudan, and the continued confrontations between the Islamic Middle East and the West have revitalized populist Islam. Under the banner of cultural authenticity, Islam remains the most formidable ideological force in the region. Hence, the current trend toward liberalization in the region has been intertwined with the rise of Islamic revivalism. Muslim groups have actively mobilized to take advantage of political openings to push forward their Islamic agenda and enhance their political power. Islamic states may provide a short-term solution to the problem of identity crisis and legitimacy, but the twin challenges of economic reconstruction and political development amidst a growing population and depleting resources have created an endemic economic crisis for which no Islamic economic remedy has been found. Due to the pervasive role of Islam in cultural life, however, any genuine and enduring democratization of the region can not happen in defiance of Islam, but through its democratic reinterpretation. In what follows, some of these themes are propounded.

State and State Formation: State Without Civil Society

The state, more than any other entity, determines economic, social, and political life in the society. Through its policies, the state guides the process of economic growth and social and economic transformation. It provides security, executes laws, allocates resources, and metes out punishment. State policies also create and mold new classes and social groups, and in turn the state becomes susceptible to their pressures and political action. Due to the nonexistence or weaknesses of civil society, however, the domination of the interventionist state over political life remains pervasive.

In his contribution to the study of state in developing countries, Christopher Clapham has discerned several characteristics. He has identified the two salient attributes of the Third World states as power and fragility.[1] Many Third World states inherited the highly centralized colonial administration designed to subjugate an alien people. Hence, the monarchial tradition in much of the Third World that preceded the colonial era contributed to this tradition of highly centralized, arbitrary power.

This highly centralized and arbitrary rule induces insecurity not only in the public at large but also among the elite. Unsure of their own legitimacy—and often with good reasons—many Third World governments use their monopoly of power to extract as much from their subjects or "citizens" as they can. For the ruling elite, the state then becomes not only "a source of benefit in itself, but also a means to defend themselves against domestic discontent, and in some measures also against external penetration."[2] Therefore, by monopolizing the means of coercion, the state safeguards its privileges and continuity.

What distinguishes a Third World state from a totalitarian state is the former's permeation by the society in which it exists. The postcolonial state is vulnerable to public pressure. The state can be influenced and even subverted through popular action, but there is no "merging of state and society as the common expression of a set of shared values."[3] In other words, the state seldom tolerates development of an autonomous civil society and the contestation of its power by competing social groups. The illegitimacy of power and its concomitant insecurity and paranoia induce lawlessness and corruption. These attributes are reinforced by the lack of social consensus and a rift between the ruler and the ruled.

In the face of weak institutionalization, the power structure remains personalistic and clientelistic. In such circumstances, authority is often ascribed to individuals rather than institutions. Therefore, the rise of charismatic leaders is pervasive throughout the Third World.

These general characteristics of Third World states have their corollary in the Middle East. In the atmosphere of mistrust and lawlessness pervading Middle Eastern states, the political leaders often consider the government office as their personal property. Hence, elite recruitment and circulation is based primarily on kinship, ethnicity, and tribal, or personal ties. Saddam Hussein's Iraq and the power of his immediate family and the members of his Takriti tribe, Hafez Al Assad's Syria and his Alivi'te sect, and King Hussein of Jordan and his Hashemi'ite clan provide poignant examples. In such an atmosphere, nepotism and favoritism are rampant, and the creation of clientelistic groups through reward and punishment are the basis for mass mobilization and regime consolidation. These attributes, characterized by Weber as patrimonialism, a patriarchal political system based on a modern bureaucracy and administration, permeate the region.[4]

The formation of the modern state in the Middle East was due neither to the rise of an independent bourgeois class nor to the rise of secular nationalism. With the European encroachment on Muslim lands in the seventeenth and eighteenth centuries, many ruling elites in the Middle East further centralized their power and bureaucracy to defend themselves against the West as well as internal opposition. After the colonial conquests of the eighteenth, nineteenth, and twentieth centuries, the highly centralized colonial administration laid the foundation for the emergence of the future authoritarian state.[5]

Although deeply rooted in history and tradition, most Middle Eastern states have recent origins; many were created by European colonial powers after the First World War. The disintegration of the Ottoman Empire after 1918 left many territories under its rule (virtually the entire Middle East, with the exception of Iran) in the hands of the British, the French, and other European powers. For all practical purposes, the borders of Syria, Iraq, Jordan, Lebanon, Kuwait, and Palestine were drawn by the British and the French. Even the borders of Iran, Egypt, and the countries of the Arabian Peninsula were determined by imperial powers. The artificiality of the borders partially explains the pervasiveness of extraterritorial wars and conflicts in the contemporary Middle East.[6]

In order to entice Arabs to revolt against the Ottomans during World War I, the British had promised the Arabs that after the defeat of the Ottomans they would be granted a single nation of their own. But instead they divided the Arabs into separate sovereign nations, cultivating the inter-Arab rivalries they could divide and rule effectively. This colonial strategy, combined with the legacy of tribal feud among the Arabs, spurred an array of political conflict in the Fertile Crescent that was further exacerbated with the creation of the state of Israel in 1948.

The emergence of Pan-Arabic and Pan-Islamic ideologies was a response to divisions and rifts imposed by imperial powers. The unitarian thrust of these ideologies was designed to usher in the ideal of Arab and Islamic unity amidst the pervasive reality of sectarian, nationalist, and ethnic divisions in the Arab world. Imperialist powers manipulated these divisions, thus intensifying the endemic violence and contributing to the underdevelopment of the region.[7]

The Middle Eastern state, however, was not a mere creation of colonial powers; rather, it had deep roots in the patriarchal and patrimonial political culture of the region.

The overbearing dominance and the extractive nature of the Middle Eastern states rendered the system of private property and the bourgeois class associated with it very weak. Whereas the strength and the independence of bourgeois classes played a significant role in development of Western democracies, their financial and political weaknesses throughout the Middle East partially explains the failure of democracy in the region. Contrary to Adam Smith's edicts on the law of the market and the sanctity of the free enterprise system that played a significant role in development of Western capitalism and allowed a resourceful and self-confident bourgeoisie to develop its own autonomous institutions of power, there was no such parallel development in the Middle East. The lack of independent guilds in the Islamic Middle East and the financial and political domination of bourgeoisie organizations by the state partially explains why an independent and forward-looking bourgeoisie and civil society never emerged in the region. The despotism of the Ottoman sultans, Arab caliphs, and Persian kings who did not tolerate any alternative sources of power also suppressed the development of an independent bourgeoisie.[8]

Since capitalist development was introduced by the colonial powers, the bourgeois class lacked the ability to compete effectively with foreign capital and industry. Therefore, they either returned to investment in land or functioned as the middleman between foreign and domestic markets. To the extent the bourgeois class's inability to compete globally forced it to invest in land, it became tied to feudal interests and institutional and power structures associated with it. The extractive nature of the authoritarian state also led to the confiscation of private property and further weakened the bourgeoisie. The increasing integration of the Middle East into the global economy and its inability to compete after World War II further accentuated the weaknesses of the bourgeois class. Hence, an inadvertent consequence of Western influence and the concomitant cultural polarization (modern versus traditional) hindered achieving consensus and exacerbated social tensions.

Being a middleman and lacking the necessary financial strength or political autonomy, a large sector of the bourgeois class engaged in such nonproductive economic activities as construction, land speculation, usury, and import-export business. Whereas in East Asia the cooperation between the state and the industrial sector played a significant role in the economic success of the "four tigers" (Singapore, Taiwan, Hong Kong, and South Korea), in the Middle East such cooperation was either weak or nonexistent. In fact, the relation between the two may become predatory when the state completely devours or stifles a sector of the bourgeoisie through either extensive nationalization or expropriation. Such tactics are sometimes used to settle the inner-elite conflict.

The economically intrusive state, however, may not extensively engage in productive activity or creation of new resources; instead, it may opt for the exploitation of available natural resources. As Eberhard Kienle notes,

> This parasitic economic role of state may also explain the absence of nation states, since the lethargic and simple economies of Middle East (compared to nineteenth- and twentieth-century Europe) did not demand cultural and societal homogenization to function, nor did it need to facilitate complex communication and enhance popular mobilization in order to increase productivity.[9]

Therefore, the fragility of traditional monarchies in the region was due as much to the erosion of their legitimacy as to the paucity of their economic resources and the weaknesses of the bourgeoisie. The traditional monarchies were no match for nationalist and socialist groups who overthrew them in the 1950s and 1960s. Through nationalization, expropriation, and mass mobilization, the new regimes tightened their grip on society and further penetrated different aspects of social life.[10]

In single-commodity economies of oil-producing states such as Iran, Libya, Algeria, and Saudi Arabia, the petrodollar lends the state additional resources to assert its autonomy and repress its opponents. This has enhanced the petrostates' autonomy, allowing them to replace the mass organizations supportive of the regime for the civil society. The result is pacification and demoralization of the public at large and creation of clientelistic groups who function simultaneously as the executive arm of the state and pillar of support for its policies.[11] In varying degrees of control, revolutionary committees in Iran and Libya, the Ba'ath Party in Iraq and Syria, and the FLN (National Liberation Front) in Algeria perform this function.

Insofar as there are obstacles to nation building in the region, these obstacles also hinder state formation. In Lebanon, intense loyalties to religious sects have eroded the process of state formation. The existence of the Jordanian state, which is to a large extent based on loyalty to King Hussein and the royal family, is challenged by the commitment of its large Palestinian population to Palestinian nationalism. Hence, an endemic problem to nation building in the region is posed by the precarious loyalty of multiple ethnic groups who are fragmented in different territories divided by the colonial powers and suppressed by the dominant ethnic groups in possession of the state power. The Druze, for example, are divided among Syria, Lebanon, and Palestine. Kurds are scattered in Iran, Turkey, Iraq, and Syria. The autonomist drive of these ethnic minorities constantly challenges the centralized power of the authoritarian state. In countries with a long history and administrative tradition, such as Turkey, Egypt, and Iran, the task of state formation and nation building has been much less arduous.

The leaders in these countries have drawn on a long tradition of imperial and monarchial history as well as Islamic heritage to bind the nation and the state together.[12] Even in these countries, however, nation building has not proven to be free of problems. Turkey and Egypt, the two countries that in the twentieth century have struggled to forge an identity based on secular nationalism, are constantly challenged by Islamists. The Shah's ill-fated attempt to do the same in Iran backfired, engendering a theocracy. Hence, Pan-Islamism—the ideal of creating a single Islamic *umma* (the community of the faithful)—is yet another ideological obstacle to nation building and state formation. Unlike secular nationalism, which takes its ideological inspiration from loyalty to specific territory and state, Pan-Islamism supersedes such loyalties in favor of transnational Islamic solidarity and alliances. In this regard, Zionism, the nationalist ideology of the Jewish people based on loyalty to a specific territory, has been much more conducive to nation building. Equally foreboding are such transnational ideologies as Pan-Arabism, which propounds a single Arab nation and thus challenges the legitimacy of present nation-states in the Arab world.[13]

Among other problems is the tension between nation and state in the modern era. "Stateness" (achieving statehood), according to Gabriel Ben-Dor, has been a contradictory phenomenon. As he puts it:

> Through both direct rule and indirect cultural penetration, the European colonial powers exported to the Middle East the most advanced governmental technology available in the form of the state apparatus. This governmental technology has a logic of its own, which, however, is not easily exportable. The Europeans exported, instead, the logic of nationalism, taken from their own radical style of politics, which was soon to pass its peak (though not before it had created one of the greatest devastations in the history of humankind). Therefore, the people in the Middle East (chiefly Arabs) inherited the structure of the state and the idea of the nation. This is the heritage that generated the "dialectics of post-colonial stateness" and the grim struggle between the two poles. While the structure of the state was transferable, "stateness" was not. The contradiction between a centralized modern state and a revolutionary nationalism that engulfed the Middle East in 1950's and 1960's ushered in social revolutions throughout the region and since then violent clashes between state and its opponents had been the norm rather than exceptions.[14]

There is one major asset available to many Middle Eastern states to buy off the opposition and forge clientele groups: petroleum.

Petroleum and the Petrodollar

Three major revolutions have engulfed the Middle East in the post-independence era: first, the nationalist revolution that brought such leaders as Ataturk in Turkey, Mussadiq in Iran, and Nasser in Egypt to power, politicizing and capturing the imagination of popular masses; second, the Palestinian revolution, a drive for autonomy that elevated the Arab-Israeli dispute into one of the major sources of political radicalization in the region; third, the oil revolution that ushered in a new era of economic wealth, making unprecedented social and economic transformation possible.[15] As a politicized commodity responsible for the lion's share of foreign exchange in many oil-producing countries of the Middle East, petroleum plays a significant role in their economic and political development.[16] Much of the newly founded power of Middle Eastern oil-producing countries is due to their oil wealth. In the past decade Kuwait, a tiny monarchy in the Gulf, twice managed to bring the major global powers to the region to its defense; once during the Iran-Iraqi war and reflagging of the Kuwaiti tankers in 1987–1988 against Iran and a second time in 1990–1991 during the Gulf War against Saddam Hussein.

With about 60 percent of global oil reserves, the Middle East possesses significant financial and political powers. Some attribute the rise of oil wealth after the quadrupling of oil prices in 1973 to the emergence of an Islamic economic force.[17] Yet others link this economic power to the increased self-confidence of Muslims and their concomitant self-assertion and the rise of Islamic revivalism.[18]

Oil wealth, however, is a double-edged sword. While it has offered enough revenues and resources to the Arab states of the Gulf to create a social welfare system and buy off political acquiescence (namely Saudi Arabia, Kuwait, United Arab Emirates, Bahrain, Qatar, and Abu Dhabi), in other parts of the region oil wealth did not protect regimes from political turmoil and revolution. Oil wealth did not prevent revolutions in Iraq (1958), Algeria (1962), Libya (1969), and Iran (1979).

The quadrupling of oil prices after the oil price shock of 1973, however, was a double-edged sword of empowerment on the one hand and increased dependency and vulnerability on the other. The influx of petrodollars provided the necessary self-confidence and material means for many oil-producing states to assert themselves and allocate resources to spread their Islamic culture. However, the influx of the petrodollar also increased the oil-producing states' dependence on the West as they invested in Western banks, purchased capital goods, and their reliance on Western military supplies to protect their wealth increased.[19] There was a cost associated with this close alliance with the West, as the fate of the Shah of Iran and Anwar Al Sadat of Egypt attest. The erosion of nationalist legitimacy of these regimes ensued, and the leaders who embraced the West too closely did not survive the storm of Islamic wrath that swept throughout the region in the 1970s and 1980s.

Oil wealth has also been used by regimes to forge a national ideology by recreating the past history and mobilizing the masses around the new ideology. Ba'athism in Iraq, "socialism" in Algeria, and the "Third Universal Theory" in Libya fulfilled this ideological function.[20]

Yet, as the oil revenues plummeted after the oil price crash of 1986, foreign debt mounted and economic and political pressures on the regimes intensified. The Algerian regime chose retreat and political concession and opened up the political process to a multiparty system, albeit temporarily. The Iraqi regime opted for aggression, hoping that annexing oil-rich Kuwait would solve its growing economic woes.

While the control of oil wealth has been the source of much conflict in the region, the management of this strategic commodity also presented the region with one of the more successful examples of cooperation and collective action.

OPEC and the Political Economy of Oil

The oil power found an institutional outlet with the creation of the Organization of Petroleum Exporting Countries (OPEC) in 1960. Although encompassing several non-Middle Eastern countries, OPEC became the primary source of interest articulation and collective bargaining for the oil-producing nations of the Middle East and North Africa.

Four distinct stages can be discerned in the evolution of OPEC. First is the period between 1960–1967 known as the buyers' market, characterized by an overabundance of oil and thus depressed prices. The second period, which began with the Arab-Israeli war of 1967, is known as the sellers' market (1967–1978) and characterized by a quadrupling of prices after the Arab oil embargo of 1973. The price continued to surge until 1983, when a combination of an increased non-OPEC share of the oil market and the expansion of alternative sources of energy, such as nuclear power, induced a glut in the market. The subsequent third stage (1983–1990), known as the "soft market" era, is marked by the abundance of oil and plummeting prices, which reached a low of $9 per barrel during the oil price crash of 1986. This period ushered in a buyers' market.[21] The fourth stage began with the Iraqi invasion of Kuwait on August 2, 1990, a period that witnessed a sudden upward swing in the price of petroleum and brought back the sellers' market, only to be followed by a buyers market after the price dropped to $18 a barrel in 1992; by 1993 the price had stagnated in that range.

By 1985 the market share of OPEC had decreased significantly from its peak in 1973. OPEC's market share had dropped from a 65 percent high to a low of 41 percent in 1985.[22] The increase in the non-OPEC share of the market was due to three distinct factors. The spiraling prices of oil, which began with the Arab oil embargo of 1973 and reached its zenith in the aftermath of the Iranian revolution of 1979, made many Western nations look to non-OPEC sources of production. Hence, the higher prices for oil made non-OPEC producers more competitive and enlarged their market share. Since the cost of production of non-OPEC oil is much higher than OPEC oil, the non-OPEC producers can not compete effectively at the lower price level. For example, the average cost of OPEC oil per barrel is $2, whereas production cost for non-OPEC is typically five to fifteen times higher. The cost of production per barrel in the United Kingdom is $10, while in the new fields it is eight dollars more. In the North Sea producers face production costs as high as $30 per barrel.[23]

Also contributing to the non-OPEC share of the market was the discovery of many new oil reserves outside the organization. These new reserves included small-producing, less-developed countries such as Egypt, Brazil, India, and Malaysia. These less-developed countries alone produced an estimated five and a half million barrels a day in 1987, an increase of three million from 1970. Major new fields discovered in the late 1960s and 1970s also presented competition for OPEC. These new fields included fields in Alaska, Mexico, and the North Sea.[24]

At OPEC's seventy-sixth conference held in Geneva December 7–9, 1985, the Saudis (who are responsible for more than 35 percent of the output) decided to recapture market share at the expense of price. The Saudis also wanted to discourage conservation and investment in alternative sources of energy, drive the non-OPEC production out of the market, drain Iran and Iraq's financial resources to continue waging the war, and punish those who cheated on their quotas. Thus they flooded the market, which led to the oil price crash of 1986 and the plummeting of prices from $26 to $9 a barrel that year. In response to this Saudi strategy, three camps emerged within OPEC. First, Iran, Libya, and Algeria were opposed to the market share policy and wanted to see allotment of production quotas with fixed and higher prices. Second, the Gulf Cooperation Council countries (Saudi Arabia, Kuwait, the United Arab Emirates, Qatar, Bahrain, and Oman), which due to their surplus petroleum income could much better withstand the pressures of lower income, supported the Saudi strategy of increased share of market in the long term for short-term loss of income. Third, countries such as Venezuela and Indonesia sought a compromise that would prevent an all-out price war and guarantee higher production.[25] The compromise worked and OPEC held together despite internal factionalism.

The ensuing lower prices ultimately resulted in increased demand for oil. In 1986 world demand for OPEC oil increased to 18.3 million barrels a day from 15.4 million barrels the previous year.[26] Although production was increased among OPEC members, it was distributed unevenly and tended to benefit only nations with large reserves. Smaller oil-producing nations within OPEC, such as Libya, Qatar, and Algeria, were unable to increase production to counteract the losses that they were suffering as a result of the lowered prices. Algeria's income, for example, declined by 95 percent, while Saudi Arabia's income dropped by only 18 percent. Overall in 1986 OPEC revenues dropped 42 percent from 1985 levels.[27]

With the loss of income amounting to $55 million in July 1986, OPEC abandoned the strategy of market shares and returned to the quota system. After the oil price crash of 1986, many scholars depicted OPEC as a failing giant that would immediately collapse under the pressures of internal dissent.[28] OPEC, however, managed to prove the skeptics wrong. It survived an eight-year war between two of its members (Iran and Iraq), followed by the Iraqi-Kuwaiti-Saudi war (the Gulf War of 1991), as well as incessant conflict between the price hawks (Libya, Iran, and Algeria) and the price doves (Saudi Arabia, Kuwait, and United Arab Emirates).

The key to OPEC's resiliency lies in a number of structural factors in the global oil market, such as continued demand for OPEC crude and the realization among its members that they possess a monopoly on a rare and finite commodity that will bring optimal profit only through collective bargaining. So far such overriding economic considerations have acted as a catalyst to unite political foes in the same organization, and it should continue to do so in the near future.

Most analysts project a continued rise in demand for oil throughout this century and into the early twenty-first century. World gross domestic product outside the former Soviet bloc countries is projected to grow at an average annual rate of 2.7 percent. The industrialized nations will continue to dominate the demand. By one estimate, in the year 2000 they will account for 70 percent of projected world energy demand of 131 million barrels per day (mb/d) and 67 percent of world oil demand of 58 mb/d.[29] With this rise in demand, OPEC faces the dual task of increasing capacity and increasing market shares. While OPEC market shares have recovered since 1986 (surpassing 51 percent), its production has yet to reach the forecast supply requirement of 31.4 mb/d for the year 2000. Hence, OPEC refineries have to be modernized and expanded to meet demand and comply with new environmental regulations.[30]

The production in the former Soviet Union has fallen drastically since the mid-1980s. Compared to 1990, in 1991 the former Soviet Union's oil production declined by an estimate of more than 1 mb/d. Whereas in 1988 the output was 12 mb/d, by 1992 it plummeted to 9 mb/d. This decline forced many former customers of the Soviet oil producers, including Eastern Europe, to look for supplies elsewhere in the market.[31]

U.S. dependence on OPEC oil is also increasing. According to a study by the center for Global Energy Studies in London, U.S. dependence on

OPEC oil could increase by 43 percent of total imports by the year 2000 if the domestic production level remains the same.[32] Some findings indicate that since 1975 the crude oil reserves have declined in most of the world, while Middle East and OPEC reserves have increased. For example, a 1988 study by the Department of Energy indicates that reserves in Africa decreased from 65 to 55 billion barrels, in the Far East from 21 to 19 billion barrels, in Western Europe from 25.5 to under 22 billion barrels, and in the United States from 35 to below 27 billion barrels. In contrast, in the Middle East, an area that accounts for two-thirds of the noncommunist world total, the reserves rose from 368 to 402 billion barrels.[33] More recent data indicate that only 38 percent of the remaining recoverable oil is in the Western Hemisphere.[34] Hence, the non-OPEC supplies are projected to decline much faster than OPEC supplies.[35] A recent study concludes that outside OPEC "world oil production fell 2% as declines in the former Soviet Union and the U.S. more than offset gains elsewhere. Oil production is being concentrated more and more in the Middle East countries."[36]

The combination of these factors indicates that in the near future industrial growth in the West and burgeoning economies of East and Southeast Asia will have to rely heavily on OPEC oil for their energy supplies. The most recent statistics indicate that the demand for OPEC oil remains on an upward climb, and forecasters expect demand to increase 1.8–2.2 million barrels per day between the third and fourth quarter of 1993 with most members producing up to capacity.[37]

U.S. oil imports from OPEC, for example, have increased in recent years. In 1985 the United States imported 32 percent of its oil from OPEC members, while in 1990 this number jumped to nearly 45 percent. In addition, OPEC forecasters expect world gross product outside the former centrally planned economies to grow at an average annual rate of 2.7 percent from 1990–2000 and world oil demand to grow at 1.1 percent, raising world consumption by nearly 6 million barrels per day over the same period.[38] Such an increase in demand is not the characteristic of a dying entity.

Several additional factors may contribute to OPEC viability in the future. First, a dramatic decline in prices such as the one witnessed in 1986 would be harmful for some Western oil-producing countries with a high cost of oil production. For them a low oil price has a dual impact. While it may stimulate growth, lower inflation, and improved balance of payment, it also may induce increased demand, stifle conservation, and increase dependence on imports. Second, several non-OPEC oil-producing countries (e.g., Norway and Mexico) have shown an increasingly cooperative attitude, willing to cut production to help increase prices. Third, with coal and nuclear energy considered inferior to oil environmentally and the methane emission of gas now judged to be worse than carbon dioxide, a more cleanly refined oil may be looked at favorably.[39]

Even in the aftermath of the Iraqi invasion of Kuwait, when the outlook for OPEC unity seemed bleakest, some observers argued that, if the cartel were to dissolve, the major Gulf producers such as Saudi Arabia, Iran, and Iraq, and possibly Kuwait and United Arab Emirates would continue an informal dialogue that would prevent the oil market from entering the outright competition of a true free market. They reason that each of the countries has plenty in reserve and surely can not afford the price crash that would follow a free market situation. Iran and Iraq are in need of revenues to rebuild their war-torn and increasingly debt-ridden economies. Saudi Arabia, the richest OPEC member, could not afford a price crash. Its falling oil revenues and increasing spending have caused it to accrue a budget deficit of ninety billion dollars from 1983–1990.[40] If OPEC were to splinter, a partial free market similar to that of the price collapse of 1986 would ensue. The price hawks would band together and attempt to keep the prices high. As the collapse of 1986 showed, those countries simply do not have the resources to engage in a price war with the cash-rich members. Therefore, a major split within the organization or its downfall would not serve their interest.

While three OPEC members (Iraq, Kuwait, and Saudi Arabia) fought each other during the Gulf War of 1991, one of the inadvertent effects of the war was the strengthening of the organization. First, a new relationship among OPEC members was forged. With the defeat of Iraq, the position of price hawks in the organization was weakened and Saudi Arabia emerged as a more dominant player in the organization. With the Saudis firm in the saddle, the United States has increased its import of the OPEC oil since 1991. One estimate indicates that U.S. total import of foreign oil from Gulf states alone could increase to 43 percent of total imports by the year 2000. Saudi Arabia alone is responsible for 61 percent of U.S. oil imports from OPEC.[41] Second, realizing that their long-term interest is tied to discouraging investment in alternative sources of energy, OPEC nations have shown a greater interest in price moderation. Third, to ensure a better discipline, OPEC members have displayed an interest in stronger enforcement of output quotas. Fourth, OPEC members are more open to joint ventures with foreign oil companies than at any time in the last two decades. Several OPEC members that previously had closed their oil industry to foreign investment and joint ventures, such as Algeria, Iran, and Nigeria, now have changed course. Fifth, the renewed consumer/producer dialogue has brought in a new era of cooperation among oil-producing and oil-consuming nations. This new spirit was highlighted by the Isfahan conference of 1991 in Iran followed by the Paris conference of 1992.

While the short-term prospects for OPEC may not seem bleak, oil is a politicized commodity and remains most vulnerable to volatile politics of the region, which are external to the oil industry.[42] Since oil is a finite commodity and it is projected that with present levels of consumption much of the Middle East is going to run out of its oil within the next two to three generations, economic diversification of the region is of paramount significance. This, however, is a formidable task because very few alternatives can be produced to replenish the oil revenues. The region is primarily arid, resulting in poor potential for agriculture. Its population has historically been relatively uneducated and it lacks a skilled labor force. To make matters worse, the past sixty years have seen the population increase by a factor of twelve.[43]

Due to the harshness of terrains and inadequacy of water, agriculture has experienced only a limited success in the region. Since the agricultural sector had to compete with a burgeoning industrial infrastructure and it demands heavy state-subsidized investments, it has assumed the position of a stepchild in the development scheme of many oil-producing countries of the region. The result has been massive migration of peasants to the cities and further erosion of soil due to abandoning agriculture. The share of agriculture in economic output has also declined dramatically.[44] Therefore most Middle Eastern oil economies are now food importers and, with the exception of Gulf Cooperation Council countries, they are fighting an uphill struggle to provide for their people.[45] Other studies indicate a continued trade dependence and deepening of the debt burden in the region in the near future.

There are serious limitations to petroleum power. On the one hand, in petroeconomies the entire economy becomes dependent on a single commodity whose price is determined as much by economic as by political events that are outside the control of oil-producing nations. Oil consumption is not only dependent on the rate of growth and development in oil-importing nations but also dictated by the degree of conservation and their ability to develop alternative sources of energy. Moreover, non-OPEC production has also increasingly posed new competition for OPEC. For example, whereas in 1976 OPEC's share of the noncommunist world's total oil supply stood at 68 percent, by 1983 this amount plummeted to 46 percent.[46] Whereas OPEC supplied approximately 44 percent of total world oil consumption in 1979, its share declined to 26 percent by early 1985.[47] Although since 1986 the non-OPEC share of the market has declined and OPEC is regaining some of the lost shares, this trend can be reversed by certain unforseen political or economic factors. Therefore, diversification of these economies and development of a viable infrastructure is paramount for the future of development and growth in the region. No less significant is the development of a viable civil society and a participatory political system that would ensure sustained development and political stability.

Dilemmas of Democratization:
Perestroika Without Glasnost

Some scholars identify the prerequisites of a liberal democracy as dominance of rule of law, extensive civil liberties guaranteed by law, representative government that functions on the basis of free and frequent elections, a rational bureaucracy, and dispersion of economic power.[48] If we adhere to this definition, then no country in the Middle East region would qualify as a democracy. Although Israel and Turkey may come close, if one overlooks Israeli treatment of the Palestinians and Turkish treatment of the Kurds, for the most part the main features of democracy are lacking in the area. Despite the existence of parliamentary systems in much of the region, political authoritarianism is the norm rather than exception. As Hisham Sharabi, a leading Arab scholar, attests, while "China and India—two of the three largest literate cultures of the Third World—have succeeded in developing viable socialist or liberal systems, the Arab world—the third major literate culture in the underdeveloped world—has failed to achieve lasting development in either direction."[49] Sharabi identifies the Arab world as a neopatriarchal system. This system has four major characteristics. First, it is socially fragmented; that is, family, tribe, ethnicity, and religion (rather than nation or civil society) constitute the main basis of social relations. Second, it is based on authoritarian organization; that is, paternalism, domination, and coercion rather than cooperation and mutual recognition govern all social relations, institutions, and structures from family to state. Third, there is a prevalence of absolutist paradigms; that is, a closed, absolutist consciousness grounded in transcendence, metaphysics, revelation, and closure rather than in difference, plurality, diffusion, and openness. Fourth, there is a commonality of ritualistic practice; that is, behavior is primarily inspired by customs and rituals rather than creativity and spontaneity.[50] The characteristics Sharabi attributes to the Arab world can be extended to the Middle East in general. Therefore, it is appropriate to speak only about possibilities for democratization where power is more diffuse and less repressive and arbitrary. What has transpired in the region since 1987 has been a limited attempt at economic and political liberalization followed by periods of retrenchment and repression.

The democratization that had engulfed such South and Central European countries as Spain, Greece, and Portugal and parts of Latin America in the 1970s found a new momentum in the Third World in the 1980s. Several factors were responsible for these turns of events. First, the failure and inefficiency of state-owned enterprises by the 1980s became a luxury few governments could afford. The mounting debt crisis of the 1980s and the shortage of money also made many countries trim their budgets and sell their unprofitable nationalized industries. Second, the change in policy

of the International Monetary Fund and the World Bank, partially insti-
gated by the dictates of the increasingly integrative nature of international
capitalism in the 1980s, made their loans contingent upon reforms that actively promoted free trade and privatization. Since the economy in many
parts of the Middle East is highly politicized and centralized, decentralization of economic power often spills over to the political realm, diffus-
ing political power as well. The crash of oil prices in 1986 and the subsequent depletion of oil income have deprived the ruling elite of
oil-producing states of the ablity to buy off the opposition. Therefore, they
had to grant concessions and liberalize the political system. Third, the
meager economic achievements of the command economies of North
Korea, Angola, and Ethiopia stood in sharp contrast to the impressive success of such Southeast Asian countries as South Korea, Taiwan, and Singapore, which opted for the free enterprise system. Fourth, the democratic
revolution in the former Soviet Union and Eastern Europe has had a profound impact on many Middle Eastern and North African countries that
looked to the Eastern bloc as a model of economic development and an
ideological source of inspiration. Hence, the fate of such dictators as Nico-
lae Ceausescu, the former leader of Romania, has not gone unnoticed
among many authoritarian leaders; they must either reform and liberalize
or face mass revolt and destruction. The disengagement of the former Soviet Union from the Cold War also meant that many of the client states
that no longer could count on Soviet support had to moderate their policies
and liberalize their political systems to receive Western loans and investments. Therefore, in many parts of the region social compacts between the
elite and the society emerged, allowing a more inclusive and participatory
political system.[51]

These global trends had their impact on the Middle East and North
Africa as well. Two dominant features distinguish Middle Eastern attempts
at democratization. In much of the region, Algeria, Tunisia, Jordan, and
Egypt being the most notable examples, the democratization has been intertwined with Islamic revivalism, thus posing a dilemma before the secular elite. Should they let an experiment in democratization remove them
from power and transfer power to Islamists? All four governments have responded with an emphatic no, cracking down on Islamists, although in different degrees of harshness, and halting the democratic process. What lies
ahead for democratization in the region may be retrenchment followed by
a new outburst of democratic experimentations.

As noted earlier, there are many cultural obstacles to democratization
in the region. The most significant among them are the primacy of faith
over reason and tribal and ethnic loyalty over associational life and civil
society. Thus essential elements of civil society—political tolerance, ideological pluralism, and power sharing—lack deep roots in the political

culture of the region. Hence, the legacy of the colonial past and the prevalence of internal violence and extraterritorial wars have strengthened the grip of authoritarian regimes on political power. This is, however, only one side of the story. The Middle East is not immune to the global trend toward democracy and the logic of technological revolution and the postmodern society.

Paul Salem, an Arab scholar, contends that the age of ideology in the Middle East has come to an end. This has led to interest in democracy as the leaders search for a new basis of legitimacy.[52] To a great extent the ideological politics of the past have become irrelevant, and the logic of modernity and technological revolution is catching up with the Middle East as well.[53] In the face of one of the most rapid paces of change in human history, dogmatic embracement of ideologies of the past has proved to be undesirable if not impractical. Spurred on by the technological and computer revolutions, the dictates of survival in modern society demand flexibility, adaptability, and accommodation of change. Hence, the global communication revolution—faxes, computers, radios, televisions, and videos—no longer allow dictators to insulate their people and keep them ignorant about the rest of the world. Even seemingly immutable theocracies are not immune from the logic of postmodernity as the changes in Iran since 1988 attest. Constant reinterpretation of the faith and modernization of tradition is the Islamic Republic's way of coping with an ever changing world.

In the decades following World War II, countries such as Egypt, Algeria, Libya, and Iran after their respective revolutions opted for a populist course, nationalizing their industries and providing massive state subsidies for their citizens. By the late 1980s, as the limitations of the populist strategies of development were exposed, leaders looked to open up their sluggish economies to foreign trade, imports, and investment. As the pursuit of self-sufficiency and economic nationalism in an increasingly interdependent world proved to be an illusive dream, many leaders began to assess their economic policies. Thus, the increasing integrative thrust of international capitalism on the one hand and the collapse of the Soviet Union as a viable model of development on the other ushered in a wave of economic liberalization and privatization of state-owned enterprises. Economic liberalization requires rationalization, rule of law, free flow of information, and diffusion of economic power. Since economic and political power are linked, such economic diffusion of power has the potential to spill over into the political arena. But in the Middle East and North Africa liberalization has been primarily confined to the economic realm and has not been accompanied by an enduring attendant political democratization.[54] Insofar as democratization persists, it is controlled and manipulated, and it remains at the mercy of an insecure authoritarian elite that genuinely mistrusts democratic politics. Therefore, the first signs of serious challenge to a regime's monopoly of power are often suppressed brutally, and thus the liberalization is either halted or reversed, as has been the case in Egypt, Algeria, and Tunisia.

Salem identifies three possible paths toward democratization in the Middle East. First is the emergence of a Gorbachev-like leader who would take bold steps to initiate the process. Salem sees such a possibility as very remote, since the political landscape of the region is currently devoid of such bold visionary leaders. The second possibility would be outside intervention, as was the case after World War II in Germany, Italy, and Japan. Due to the legacy of colonialism and the intensity of nationalist sentiment in the region, any regime installed by the Western powers would lack legitimacy and credibility. The third path is youth rebellion. Salem sees youth as one of the major agents of social change in the region. Youth played an important role in democracy movements in South Korea, China, and Algeria. The fourth path may emerge from political action by a socioeconomic class, as was the case in the English, French, and American Revolutions.[55]

In the Middle East the steady growth of the middle class and the intelligentsia has increased their political strength, providing a social base for democracy that was nonexistent before. Members of middle classes are most likely to participate in political and social associations. They are also the primary producers and consumers of the cultural and intellectual life, and their ranks are prominently represented in the creation of civil society and the leadership of opposition movements.

In the past, many Middle Eastern regimes used the communist threat or the necessity to fight the Israeli foe as major excuses to put off the urgent task of democratization. As the communist threat has faded and the Palestinian-Israeli peace treaty has become a reality, in the absence of the old scapegoats the authoritarian regimes of the region are increasingly under pressure to deliver on the promise of democratization.

In countries such as Algeria, Jordan, Tunisia, and Morocco, by the late 1980s the acute financial crisis of the state put the politics of consensus and coalition building on the political agenda, albeit in limited and manipulated forms. In addition, the emergence and advance of civil society in some countries, most notably Turkey and Egypt, have politicized professional associations and enticed them to assert themselves and demand a larger voice in the political system.[56] Hence, increased corruption and the escalation of the crisis of legitimacy of the authoritarian state made the political cost of coercion something the elite could no longer afford. Fearing the diminishing returns of excessive repression, the ruling elites began to give some limited political concessions to their opponents.

One of the dilemmas of democratization, however, is that the process has been intertwined with the rise of Islamic revivalism. More than any other group, the Islamists have been able to take advantage of the political openings made possible by liberalization. The most dramatic example of this is the 1994 stunning electoral victories of Islamists in Turkey, one of the most secular states in the region. Faced with one of the most rapid paces of population growth, debt crisis, unemployment, and depleting resources, many governments in the Middle East and North Africa are no longer capable of providing adequately for the poor and the underclass. Due to the financial crisis of the state, Islamists have stepped in to fill the vacuum. By providing Islamic health centers, educational centers, banks, guilds, and associations, they are functioning as a de facto dual power, thus accumulating political capital and enlarging their base of support. They also use these organizations for political education, recruitment, and mass mobilization. The Muslim Brotherhood in Egypt is the primary example. As Saad-Eddin Ibrahim, an Arab scholar, has observed, "Islamists have used civil society organizations as proxy arenas for political discourse. Through them, they have been schooled in the arts of mobilization and articulation. They also have learned the imperatives of appealing to circles wider than their own if they are to win elections, perform well in office, and be reelected."[57] The necessity for such pragmatic appeals to the larger society may in turn break the sectarian mentality pervasive among Islamists and reveal the political value of tolerance, compromise, and coalition building.

Leonard Binder seems convincing in his assertion that democratization can not happen in defiance of Islam but through its reinterpretation and the emergence of Islamic liberalism.[58] Because of the pervasiveness of Islam in cultural life and due to the legacy of the past colonial domination of the region, democracy can not be exported to the region, it can only grow from its domestic soil. Since any genuine democratization requires popular participation, new interpretations of Islam that would accommodate democratic principles are indispensable to the development of democracy. Such liberal interpretations, though not pervasive, of Islam have emerged throughout the Muslim world, most notably in Egypt, Algeria, and Tunisia.[59] Such interpretations in turn have enhanced the popularity of Islam among the educated strata, putting the secular authoritarian regimes further on the defensive.

As Ibrahim has observed, the elite reaction to the increasing demand for democratization has led to the emergence of several survival tactics. First is the old familiar strategy of coercion, which has resulted in tragic disintegration in Iraq and Somalia and quasi-guerilla warfare in Algeria and parts of Egypt. While still pervasive, the political costs involved in excessive use of force renders it a strategy of last resort.

A second popular strategy is to take advantage of an existing crisis. The Libyan and Iraqi regimes are good examples. Discredited by their repressive rule and dismal performance, the two regimes portray themselves as being victimized by the United States and its Western allies. The lack of enforcement of a United Nation's resolution against Serbia or Israel and its resolute enforcement by the United States and its allies against Iraq and Lybia lends credence to the charges of these regimes. This allows them to distract attention from their own repressive policies and brand the democratic opposition as "the mouthpiece of imperialism."

The third major survival strategy is token power sharing with select opposition groups. Through a combination of coercion, intimidation, and accommodation, the regime attempts to isolate or coopt the major opposition parties. In countries such as Algeria, Tunisia, and Egypt, the ruling elite has employed the promise of power sharing to solicit the support of smaller secular or Islamic opposition groups against the major Islamic opposition. This strategy has effectively neutralized the FIS (Front for Islamic Salvation) in Algeria, Al-Nahda in Tunisia, and the Muslim Brotherhood in Egypt. This strategy holds the best promise of nonviolent democratization so far, as it has been practiced in Jordan with some limited success, whereas in Algeria, Egypt, and Tunisia there have been setbacks and retrenchment since 1992.

The fourth survival strategy involves symbolic participatory politics. One year after the Persian Gulf War, the ruling elites of Saudi Arabia, Oman, Bahrain, and the United Arab Emirates created appointed consultative councils. Although these councils have no legislative power, their creation bears symbolic significance as a step toward participatory politics.[60]

Democratization, however, will remain highly unstable if it is not accompanied with economic development, enhancement of social equality, and expansion of economic rights. In the absence of some measure of economic equity, the possibility of reversal and retreat is very likely.[61] In the volatile political atmosphere of the Middle East, democratization also requires political stablity, consensus building, and a legitimate framework for power sharing. The eruption of civil war in Yemen in May of 1994 is a dramatic example of the fragile political conditions and insecurities that pervade the region.

On the positive side, now that there is a peace settlement between Israelis and Palestinians, the diaspora of Palestinians—one of the central issues responsible for the radicalization of the politics of the region since 1948—may have been resolved. If the Palestinians are able to settle their internal power struggle and the peace process proves to be successful, then the polarized politics of hate and confrontation may end and a new era of peace, cooperation, and accommodation may begin. Such developments would have a positive impact on the forces of democratization throughout the region.

In fact, such optimistic political forecasts appeared even prior to the Palestinian-Israeli peace accords of 1993. In his appraisal of civil society in the Middle East, Augustus Richard Norton concludes that "the long-term prospects for successful democratization in Lebanon, Egypt, and Iran may be better than is commonly assumed." Meanwhile the prospects for Iraq, where "civil society has been systematically decimated," are bleak.[62]

Norton also argues that the prospect for democratization in some of the more traditional states could potentially be better than more modern states in the region. Since the state apparatus of control and repression is not well developed and its bureaucracy is not well entrenched, as the case of Yemen attested prior to its civil war, they may turn out to be surprising candidates for democratization.[63]

As the economic conditions deteriorate and the capability of the ruling elites to buy off a strengthened and emboldened opposition diminishes, Middle Eastern elites can no longer insulate their people from the impact of the global trend toward democratization. As Norton aptly notes, "The new language of politics in the Middle East speaks of participation, cultural authenticity, freedom, and even democracy. No doubt the defining concept of the 1990s is democracy."[64]

As the incipient civil society matures, the issues of democracy and democratization have become a part of the public discourse and consciousness. The barrier of fear has been broken, and the present retrenchments in Algeria, Egypt, and Tunisia could be followed by new and perhaps even more vibrant and mature movements of democratization.

Conclusion

The political economy of the Middle East is marked by an incomplete and problematic process of state formation in which the state dominates the civil society and maintains an absolutist posture, yet it also remains vulnerable to pressure and political action. Whereas in Southeast Asia, for example, a strong state and its partnership with the private sector culminated in protective policies and incentives that proved helpful to the process of economic growth, in the Middle East, the state's financial and institutional weaknesses and predatory character did not provide the supportive environment and policies necessary for development and growth. Hence, the preeminence of religious, ethnic, and tribal conflicts further hampered the task of state building and social consensus.

Although petroleum and the petrodollar may be a blessing insofar as they provide the necessary financial assets for investment and growth, they are also a curse insofar as the petroeconomies are among the least diversified economies of the region. Our study of evolution and viability of OPEC indicates that the organization will continue to persist in the near future and petroleum will remain the main source of income in petroeconomies into the year 2000. Petroleum is a blessing and a curse in yet another sense. While the influx of the petrodollar into the region since the 1960s has brought new wealth and progress, it has also emboldened the authoritarian regimes, supplying them with new and sophisticated means of coercion and control, thus rendering them (in many cases) more autonomous from their societies.

Under the influence of an increasingly integrative thrust of capitalism and the global trend toward democratization since the 1970s, many Middle Eastern elites also opted for elite-initiated social compacts in response to increasing popular demand for political participation. The most notable steps in the path of democratization have been taken in Egypt, Jordan, Algeria, and Tunisia. But as the democratic process strengthened and emboldened the Muslim parties and they in turn challenged the rule of secular elites, the democratic process came to an abrupt halt. But such retrenchment can not endure in the long run, because as the incipient civil society gains in maturity and sophistication, it is bound to have a more emphatic impact on democratization of the region.

The tasks of state formation, creating a stable, legitimate, and responsible state, economic cooperation as exemplified by OPEC, and the need for economic diversification and more equitable distribution of oil income as well as political democratization will continue to remain contentious issues dominating the political economy of the region into the year 2000.

Notes

1. Christopher Clapham, *Third World Politics: An Introduction* (Madison: University of Wisconsin Press, 1985), p. 39.
2. Ibid., p. 40.
3. Ibid., p. 42.
4. Max Weber, *The Theory of Social and Economic Organization* (New York: Oxford University Press, 1947), pp. 341–358.
5. Lisa Anderson, *The State and Social Transformation in Tunisia and Libya, 1830–1980* (Princeton, N.J.: Princeton University Press, 1986).
6. Arthur Goldschmidt, *A Concise History of Middle East* (Boulder: Westview Press, 1991), pp. 141–194.
7. George Antonius, *The Arab Awakening: The Story of the Arab National Movement* (Beirut: Khayyat's Publisher, 1955). See also Farah Tawfic, *Pan-Arabism and Arab Nationalism: The Continuing Debate* (Boulder: Westview Press, 1987). Haim Sylvia, ed., *Arab Nationalism: An Anthology* (Berkeley: University of California Press, 1962). Albert Hourani, *Arabic Thought in the Liberal Age, 1798–1939* (London: Oxford University Press, 1962).
8. James A. Bill and Robert Springborg, *Politics in the Middle East* (New York: Harper Collins, 1990), pp. 67–69.
9. Eberhard Kienle, *Ba'th Vs. Ba'th: The Conflict between Syria and Iraq* (London: I. B. Tauris and Coltd, 1990), p. 22.
10. Ibid.
11. Eric Davis, "Theorizing Statecraft and Social Change in Arab Oil-producing Countries" in Eric Davis and Nicolas Gavrielides, eds., *Statecraft in the Middle East: Oil, Historical Memory and Political Culture* (Gainesville: University of

Florida Press, 1991), pp.1–35. See also Jacques Delacriox, "The Distributive State in the World System," *Studies in Comparative International Development* 15, (1980): pp. 3–21. Hazem Belawi and Giacomo Luciani, eds., *The Rentire State* (London: Croom Helm, 1987). Peter Evans, Dietrich Rueschemeyer, and Theda Skocpol, eds., *Bringing the State Back In* (Cambridge: Cambridge University Press, 1985).

12. James Bill and Robert Springborg, *Politics in the Middle East,* pp. 40–41.

13. Ibid., pp. 47–49.

14. Ibid., p. 86.

15. Hisham Sharabi, ed., *The Next Arab Decade: Alternative Futures* (Boulder: Westview Press, 1988), p. 2.

16. Peter M. Oppenheimer, "Arab Oil Power: Permanent Eclipse? Or Temporary Fading?" *Middle East Review,* (spring 1988): pp. 9–16.

17. Sheikh R. Ali, *Oil and Power: Political Dynamics in the Middle East* (London: Printer Publishers, 1987), pp. 22–23.

18. Daniel Pipe, *In the Path of God: Islam and Political Power* (New York: Basic Books, 1983).

19. Eric Davis, "The Political Economy of the Arab Oil-producing Nations: Convergence with Western Interest," *Studies in Comparative International Development* 19, no. 2 (1979): pp. 75–94.

20. Eric Davis, "Theorizing Statecraft and Social Change in Arab Oil-producing Countries," Eric Davis and Nicolas Gavrielides, eds., *Statecraft in the Middle East: Oil, Historical Memory and Political Culture* (Gainesville: University of Florida Press, 1991), pp. 10–11.

21. Morris A. Adelman, *The International Oil Industry: An Interdisciplinary Perspective* (New York: St. Martin's Press, 1987).

22. Fadhil Al-Chalabi, OPEC *at the Crossroads* (New York: Pergamon Press, 1989), p. 80.

23. Ibid., p. 161.

24. David Hawdon, ed., *Oil Prices in the 1990s* (Great Britain: St. Martin's Press, 1989), p.55.

25. Ian Skeet, OPEC: *Twenty-five Years of Prices and Politics* (Cambridge: Cambridge University Press, 1988), p. 215.

26. Wilfred L. Kohl, *After the Oil Price Collapse:* OPEC, *The United States, and the World Oil Market* (Baltimore: The Johns Hopkins Press,1991), p.14.

27. Ibid., p. 16.

28. Mohammad W. Ahrari, OPEC: *The Failing Giant* (Lexington: The University of Kentucky Press, 1986).

29. Subroto, "The Role of OPEC in the 1990's" OPEC *Review* 16, no. 4 (winter 1992): p. 3.

30. Ibid.

31. Ibid., p. 7.

32. Ibid.

33. *Petroleum Economist* 4, no. 1 (January 1988): p. 2.

34. Joseph P. Reva Jr., "Dominant Middle Eastern Oil Reserves Critically Important to World Supply," *Oil and Gas Journal* 89, no. 38 (September 23, 1991): pp. 62–68.

35. Roger Vielroye, "Middle East Oil Producers Getting Set for Demand Surge in Mid 1990's," *Oil and Gas Journal* 9 (April 1990): pp. 21–27.

36. Scott Pendleton, "Oil Industry Shrinks in U.S. But Gets No Federal Help," *Christian Science Monitor* (February 11, 1993): p. 9.

37. Robert J. Beck, "World Oil Flow Steady in 1992: Stable Market Ahead. . . . ," *Oil and Gas Journal* 91, no. 10 (March 1993): p. 18.

38. Jahangir Amuzegar, "OPEC and a New Oil Order," *Finance and Development* 29, no. 1 (September 1992): p. 32.

39. Ibid.

40. "The End of OPEC," *The Economist* 360, no. 7668 (August 18, 1990): pp. 55–56.

41. Subroto, "The Role of OPEC in 1990's." *OPEC Review* 16, no. 4 (winter 1992): p. 7.

42. Kohl, *After the Oil Price Collapse: OPEC, the United States, and the World Oil Market*, p. 211.

43. Alan Richards and John Waterburry, *A Political Economy of the Middle East: State, Class, and Economic Development* (Boulder: Westview Press, 1990), p. 53.

44. Ibid., p. 70.

45. For example, one study concludes that "Arab imports of agricultural commodities such as wheat and sugar soared from $6.6 billion in 1974 to $21.2 billion in 1981." And at this level of dependency, the so-called rich Arab states are not spared. The oil states' food imports grew by an annual average of 27 percent with the growth rate highest in Saudi Arabia at 37 percent. Arab countries now import 10 percent of all food grain on the international market, and if present trends continue the figure could easily rise to 50 percent. See Bahgat Korany, "Unwelcome Guests: The Political Economy of Arab Relations with the Superpowers," in Hisham Sharabi, ed., *The Next Arab Decade: Alternative Futures* (Boulder: Westview Press, 1988), p. 71.

46. Ibid., pp. 72–76.

47. George Abed, "The Lean Years: The Political Economy of Arab Oil," in Hisham Sharabi, ed., *The Next Arab Decade: Alternative Futures*, p. 96.

48. Tamara J. Resler and Roger E. Kanet, "Democratization: The National-Subnational Linkage," *In Depth* (winter 1993): p. 12.

49. Hisham Sharabi, *The Next Arab Decade: Alternative Futures* (Boulder: Westview Press, 1988), p.2.

50. Ibid., pp. 2–3.

51. Manochehr Dorraj, "Privatization, Democratization and Development in the Third World: Lessons of a Turbulent Decade," *Journal of Developing Societies* 10, no. 2 (spring 1994): pp. 173–185.

52. Steven R. Dorr, "Democratization in the Middle East" in R. Slater, B. Schutz, and S. Dorr, *Global Transformation and the Third World* (Boulder: Lynne Rienner Publishers, 1993), p. 144.

53. The Persian Gulf War of 1991 and the humiliating defeat of Saddam Hussein accentuated this fact by revealing the emptiness of his nationalist rhetorics.

54. David Pool, "The Links between Economic and Political Liberalization," in Tim Niblock and Emma Murphy, eds., *Economic and Political Liberalization in the Middle East* (London: British Academic Press, 1993), pp. 40–54.

55. Steven R. Dorr, "Privatization, Democratization and Development in the Third World: Lessons of a Turbulent Decade," pp. 144–145.

56. Ibid., p. 150.

57. Saad Eddin Ibrahim, "Crises, Elites, and Democratization in the Arab World," *Middle East Journal* 47, no. 2 (spring 1993): p. 304.

58. Leonard Binder, *Islamic Liberalism: A Critique of Development Ideologies* (Chicago: University of Chicago Press, 1990).

59. John Esposito and James Piscatori, "Democratization and Islam," *Middle East Journal* 45, no. 3 (summer 1991): pp. 427–440.

60. Ibrahim, "Crisis, Elites, and Democratization in the Arab World," pp. 302–304.

61. Zehra F. Arat, *Democracy and Human Rights in Developing Countries* (Boulder: Lynne Rienner Publishers, 1991).

62. Augustus Richard Norton, "The Future of Civil Society in the Middle East," *Middle East Journal* 47, no. 2 (spring 1993): p. 216.

63. Ibid.

64. Ibid., p. 206.

6

◆

The Political Economy of Growth in Southeast and Northeast Asia

Richard F. Doner and Gary Hawes

This chapter explores the sociopolitical sources and implications of economic growth in the developing market economies of Asia. It focuses
specifically on two groups of countries in what has become the most
rapidly developing region in the world—the Western Pacific Rim. One
group, the East Asian newly industrialized countries (NICs), comprises Singapore, Hong Kong, the Republic of China (Taiwan), and South Korea.
The second group, the ASEAN-Four, includes Indonesia, Malaysia, the
Philippines, and Thailand. These four, along with Singapore and Brunei,
comprise the Association of Southeast Asian Nations (ASEAN).

These countries merit examination in part because of their impressive
economic growth. From 1965 to 1980 the NICs grew at an average annual
rate of 8.8 percent while the ASEAN-Four expanded at 7.1 percent. These
rates compare with a 3.7 percent average rate for all industrial market
economies and a 2.9 percent rate for the U.S. economy.[1] Despite a global
economic slump in the early 1980s, this growth has continued. Indeed, as
Table 6.1 shows, the 1988–1991 GDP growth rates remain very impressive
overall, while Malaysia and Thailand show signs of consistent growth at
rates even higher than the NICs.

Both groups have also experienced significant structural changes as
reflected in expanding shares of industry and declining shares of agriculture in GDP (see Table 6.2). Exports have also expanded markedly for both
groups (see Table 6.3), and manufactured goods have grown as a percentage of exports in both groups (see Table 6.4).

These two groups also exhibit some important differences. Specialization in manufactures has occurred later and to a lesser extent in the more

Table 6.1   Average Annual Percentage GDP Growth

	1965–1980	1980–1988	1988–1991
South Korea	9.6	9.9	7.4
Taiwan	9.7[a]	6.8[b]	5.7
Hong Kong	8.6	7.3	2.7
Singapore	10.1	5.7	7.9
Thailand	7.2	6.0	9.8
Indonesia	8.0	5.1	6.7
Malaysia	7.3	4.6	9.0
Philippines	5.9	0.1	3.8

Notes: a. 1970–1980
b. 1980–1986
Sources: World Bank, *World Development Report, 1990* (New York: Oxford University Press, 1990) Table 2. For Taiwan: Seiji Naya, Miguel Urrutia, Shelly Mark, and Alfredo Fuentes, *Lessons in Development: A Comparative Study of Asia and Latin America* (San Francisco: International Center for Economic Growth, 1989), Table A.2.

resource-rich ASEAN-Four than the East Asian NICS (see Tables 6.2 and 6.4). Income growth rates have been more rapid and income distribution more equal in the NICS than in the ASEAN-Four. Large agricultural sectors and weak productivity gains in agriculture in the ASEAN-Four have slowed income growth relative to the NICS.[2] Finally, the NICS have outperformed the ASEAN-Four with regard to the development of human capital as measured by literacy rates and relative numbers of scientists and engineers (see Table 6.5).

We are thus interested in explaining both the impressive performances and the differences between the two.[3] We make two sets of arguments. In the first we explore attempts to explain the economic success of both the NICS and the ASEAN-Four. The literature on this issue revolves around debates over the relative contribution of: (1) the neoclassical economists' prescriptions for limiting government intervention in the market and "getting the prices right," (2) sector- or industry-specific state intervention, and (3) non-state institutions. Although we agree that avoiding certain price distortions is important, we question the power of neoclassical explanations for the East and Southeast Asian successes.

We find that efficient, activist states make important differences. It is impossible to explain the NICS' rapid and impressive industrialization without considering the ways in which state officials have gone beyond neoclassical prescriptions such as free trade regimes and realistic exchange rates to adopt sector-specific measures. In so doing, they have often reconciled the interests of diverse economic agents with the broader needs of national economic growth. Conversely, the frequent absence of such

Table 6.2   Structure of Production (percentage of GDP)

	Agriculture			Industry			Services		
	1960	1970	1985	1960	1970	1985	1960	1970	1985
NICS									
Hong Kong[a]	4	2	1	38	37	30	55	56	68
Korea	37	27	14	20	30	41	43	44	45
Singapore	4	2	1	18	30	38	79	68	61
Taiwan	29	16	6	29	41	50	43	45	44
ASEAN-Four									
Indonesia	54	47	25	14	18	36	32	35	39
Malaysia	36	31	20	18	25	37	46	44	43
Philippines	26	28	27	28	30	33	46	43	40
Thailand	40	28	17	19	25	30	42	46	53
South Asia									
Bangladesh	58	55	48	7	9	15	36	37	37
Burma	33	38	48	12	14	13	55	48	39
India[a]	47	43	35	19	20	27	28	28	38
Nepal[b]	NA	68	58	NA	11	14	NA	21	27
Pakistan	44	33	25	15	20	28	36	37	47
Sri Lanka	32	27	24	20	23	27	48	46	50
Industrial Market Economies									
Australia[c]	12	6	6	40	41	35	48	54	59
Canada	6	4	3	34	32	24	60	65	72
Japan[a]	13	6	3	45	47	41	43	47	56
United States[b]	4	3	2	38	35	32	58	62	66

Notes: NA = not available.
a. 1984
b. 1983
c. 1982
Source: James, Naya, and Meier, *Asian Development: Economic Success and Policy Lessons* (Madison: University of Wisconsin Press, 1989), Table 1.5.

examples of government intervention in the ASEAN-Four helps to account for their relatively inferior performance relative to the NICS.

However, state-sponsored measures alone do not constitute a sufficient explanation of developmental success. Most critically, sectoral studies suggest that NIC successes are often a function of states responding to, learning from, and strengthening private sector interests and institutions such as business groups and business associations. Such institutions have begun to make important contributions to economic growth and diversification in the ASEAN-Four. Our emphasis, in short, is on the development of an institutional explanation of economic performance that builds upon but

Table 6.3   Export Growth Rates

Country	Average annual percentage growth in exports	Global rank in percentage growth of exports	Ratio of exports to GDP, various years		
	1970–1987	1970–1987	1970	1978	1986
South Korea	26.8	1	14.0	30.3	40.9
Taiwan	23.5	2	29.7	52.4	60.4
Hong Kong	19.0	3	92.9	84.6	111.3
Singapore	18.7	4	81.9[a]	128.9[a]	129.8[a]
Thailand	17.9	7	16.7	21.5	28.2
Indonesia	17.2	8	12.8	21.7	20.8
Malaysia	14.9	16	46.1	49.1	56.8
Philippines	10.4	49	19.1	18.2	24.7

Note: a. Merchandise trade only.
Sources: For export growth rates: GATT, *International Trade, 1987–88,* Vol. 1, Table 13, p. 21; for exports as a share of GDP: Naya et al., *Lessons in Development: A Comparative Study of Asia and Latin America* (San Francisco: International Center for Economic Growth, 1989), Table A.10, p. 301.

Table 6.4   Product Composition of Pacific Basin Developing-Country Exports, 1963 and 1988 (percentages)

Country	1963				1988			
	Fuel	Nonfuel	Manufacturing	Other	Fuel	Nonfuel	Manufacturing	Other
Hong Kong	0.0	7.8	72.5	19.7	0.2	3.2	95.0	1.5
Singapore	16.7	52.0	26.7	4.6	12.5	13.2	70.2	4.1
Taiwan	0.9	61.1	18.1	19.9	0.6	7.4	91.9	0.1
Korea[a]	3.4	50.0	46.6	0.0	1.5	6.1	91.0	0.4
Malaysia[a]	4.1	90.3	2.9	2.7	19.2	39.1	41.4	0.3
Thailand[a]	0.0	96.5	1.8	1.7	0.7	46.8	51.3	1.2
Philippines	0.4	94.7	4.0	0.9	2.1	36.1	35.8	26.0
Indonesia[a]	38.5	61.2	0.3	0.0	48.9	26.0	25.1	0.0

Note: a. Latest data refer to 1987.
Source: Marcus Noland, *Pacific Basin Developing Countries: Prospects for the Future* (Washington, D.C.: Institute for International Economics, 1990), Table 1.2, p. 4.

also relaxes some of the more rigid assumptions of statism and more actively incorporates political interests.

A second and subsidiary set of arguments we will make has to do with the factors underlying the political and institutional variations between and within the NICS and ASEAN-Four. The emphasis here is on broader factors such as natural resource endowments, external constraints, and ethnicity.

We address these issues in general and through short textile industry case studies for the NICS and the ASEAN-Four in regional discussions below.

Table 6.5 Human Capital Indicators

Country	Literacy rates (percent)			Psacharopoulous Index[a]		Scientists and Engineers (per million population)
	1960	1970	1980	1968	1986	
Hong Kong	71	77	90	1172	2010	NA
Singapore	50	72	84	1024	2179	1939 (1984)
Taiwan	54	85	90	1097	1966	1426 (1986)
Korea	71	88	96	1013	2261	2123 (1986)
Malaysia	23	58	60	563	1210	182 (1983)
Thailand	68	79	86	213	930	150 (1975)
Philippines	72	83	75	1030	1921	213 (1982)
Indonesia	47	57	62	296	842	228 (1984)

Notes: NA = not available
a. The Psacharopoulos index measures the per capita educational capital embodied in the labor force.
Sources: Literacy data are from James, Naya, and Meier, *Asian Development: Economic Success and Policy Lessons* (Madison: University of Wisconsin Press, 1989), Table 6.8, p. 195; all other data are from Noland, *Pacific Basin Developing Countries: Prospects for the Future* (Washington, D.C.: Institute for International Economics, 1990), Table 1.5, p. 10.

The case studies are designed not to represent an ideal typical model of how two regions have developed, but rather to illustrate the importance of subnational variables and the subtle differences between two regions of the Third World that share a record of rapid economic growth.

Models of Southeast and Northeast Asian Development

Two contending schools of thought or models purport to explain the success of Northeast Asia. One model is offered by the market-oriented, neo-classical economists; the second model, more eclectic in nature, emphasizes a variety of international, state, institutional, and societal factors but generally goes under the rubric of the state-centered approach.

Market-Oriented Explanations

Within the market-oriented approach it is only fair to stress that neoclassical economists are not in complete agreement about how to conceptualize their model. However, without doing great violence to the discipline it can be argued that the economists generally emphasize five common economic characteristics or factors: (1) the outward-looking development strategies of Northeast Asia involve a market- or private sector-oriented approach, (2) that price distortions in the national economy were reduced to correspond to conditions in the world economy, (3) that the open Northeast Asian economies required cautious financial management, (4) the

Asian NICs have given priority to economic growth over social welfare spending, and (5) the combination of outward-looking, market-oriented policies and cautious macroeconomic management gave the NICs a great deal of flexibility.[4] In sum, the Northeast Asian NICs have allegedly succeeded by choosing a neutral or outward-looking policy regime (one not biased in favor of import-substitution), and by limiting the role of public enterprises. Entrepreneurs were thus freed to innovate, to pursue their natural comparative advantage, and to follow the dictates of the market, not the whims of policymakers nor their politically generated prices. This pattern of limited government intervention in the market, coupled with cheap labor and an open economy, have guaranteed the private sector stability and predictability, the means to achieve competitiveness on a global scale, and access to the international market so that the entrepreneurs could actually discover areas where they have a comparative advantage. In shorthand, the model is often reduced to "getting the prices right" and letting market-based prices determine resource allocation. Doing so results in export growth that is in turn positively correlated with broader economic growth.

This approach suffers from several important weaknesses. As discussed below, there are problems of generalizability and relevance. Due to the impact of Japanese colonialism and (in the case of Taiwan) capital and entrepreneurial resources from mainland China, South Korea and Taiwan began the postwar period with strong supplies of physical and human capital. This meant that policy reforms were more likely to succeed here than in most developing countries.[5]

Even more serious are questions about the central tenets of the free market position. The links between an outward-oriented trade regime and low price distortions on the one hand, and growth and technical efficiency on the other are significantly looser than neoliberal economists have asserted. Getting the prices right is not so much in doubt here.[6] What is to be questioned is the number and kind of prices the NIC governments decided to get right. Import liberalization, for example, was much more selective than assumed by the neoclassical school. The South Korean trade regime had a modest proexport bias but also a "substantial industry-bias in favor of the promoted infant industries." Empirical studies also do not bear out neoclassical assumptions as to the absence of credit rationing.[7] All of this adds up to what Pack and Westphal term a "dual policy structure" in the NICs: Market forces and neutral incentives prevail in industries where the country has a static comparative advantage, while positive incentives and direct government intervention are used in sectors where the country is weak but wishes to be strong.[8]

Neoclassical neglect of these tendencies may stem from ideological predilictions. But the more important culprit has to do with levels of analysis;

neoclassical studies that seek to explain overall national growth tend to rest on macro- and cross-national measures while ignoring sectoral analyses. Such neglect, argues the state-centered school, disguises a great deal of government intervention in the market.[9] The NICs may have, on average, relatively low rates of protection for industry, but they also have targeted certain sectors or industries that are protected by high tariff rates, by quantitative restrictions, by subsidies, or by all three.[10] Likewise, negative, coercive state powers have been used to force corporate mergers, the development of new products, and the penetration of new markets. Indeed, the degree to which NIC state officials view growth through the lens of specific industries and clusters of industries is sharply at odds with the macrofocus of neoliberal analyses.[11] Finally, if one looks at the preferential allocation of credit in the NICs, one sees a level of financial repression significantly at odds with neoliberal descriptions and prescriptions.[12]

In short, careful analyses at the sectoral and subnational level undercut many of the positions taken by neoclassical scholars.

State-Centered Approach

We can disaggregate the statist explanation of NIC economic growth into several layers of causality. First, whereas neoliberals stress the virtues of allowing domestic prices to fall in line with international prices, which allows industries with a comparative advantage to flourish, the state-centric school emphasizes what might be termed "structured" capital accumulation, or government encouragement and incentives for investment in key industries and in ways designed to yield the rapid transfer of new technology into production.[13] As practiced by the NICs, structured capital accumulation has meant that the state helps to: (1) create an entrepreneurial class, (2) identify critical economic areas for investment, (3) expose these industrialists to the pressures of international competition, and (4) supply local entrepreneurs with advice and occasional strategically applied help.[14]

Second, each step is an example of how state policies alter incentives. That is, they reduce and spread the risk of productive investment for otherwise hesitant entrepreneurs. These state policies are necessary because of the assumption that market failure is more prevalent in developing than developed countries and that the market itself, like the political sphere, can generate problems that require government intervention. Stated differently, state policies proceed from a strain of thought linking Weber, Gerschenkron, and Hirschman in focusing on the solutions to collective action problems of the development process. In late-developing countries, individual firms have neither the long-term perspective nor the resources to undertake projects necessary for national growth.[15] State policies can thus help to bring returns to individual activities in line with broader goals of sectoral or national growth; they help capital as a whole to attain long-term perspectives and solutions that would be hard to attain otherwise.[16] Such policies include many of those noted earlier: selective credit allocation and interest rate distortions, direct subsidies, foreign investment guidelines, foreign exchange allocation, and selective trade controls. An important result of these measures has been to lower the cost of investment goods, thereby stimulating the demand and supply of such goods and spurring "capital accumulation, industrialization, and structural change."[17] Supplementing these distorting measures have been state policies to expose local firms to international competition.

In addition to structured capital accumulation where the state supports investment in key industries, and state intervention to consciously manipulate or replace normal market outcomes, a third aspect of the state-centered model is its emphasis on a particular set of institutional features of states that affect the ability of social groups and political elites to realize their objectives. Most critically, the Taiwan and South Korean states have been relatively independent and, to a degree, insulated, from social forces opposed to economic reforms. This insulation allegedly allows state technocrats to pursue the rational planning and efficient implementation of development policy. But we believe even the autonomy and insulation of the state from societal pressure groups and organized political interests are insufficient to explain the decision to support the kinds of policies described above. After all, there has been no shortage of strong leaders who were free of or destroyed independent opposition groups. Marcos made great progress in this direction in the Philippines, General Zia was strong in Pakistan, and there is no lack of other examples from Asia, Africa, and Latin America.[18] Thus, in addition to autonomy and insulation, the NIC states have been unique in the cohesiveness of their decisionmaking structures, in the expertise and instruments available to them, and in the purposes to which they deployed these instruments.[19] This last point merits special attention: Many countries have utilized the policy instruments seen in the NICs. Few have done so with such selectivity and with such an emphasis on achieving dynamic efficiency measured by international competitiveness.

Thus at a fourth level of causality, these institutional characteristics themselves require explanation. Explaining the unique institutions of Northeast Asia has led to the identification of several features of the international context that were important, including geopolitics, the regional product cycle, and open markets. Natural resource constraints also played a role, although their actual impact is much less clear.

Geopolitical arrangements promoted the emergence of strong states in part by encouraging new forces while suppressing societal interests potentially opposed to economic reform and industrial growth. In pre-World

War II Taiwan, Japanese colonialism not only encouraged the diffusion of industrial and managerial skills, it also replaced the traditional oligarchy with a new elite including Japanese and collaborating Taiwanese businessmen. This was, Gold notes, "a revolutionary move in a formally anticommercial society."[20] After the war, under the guidance of U.S. advisors, both Taiwan and South Korea implemented thoroughgoing land reform in the early 1950s, thus eliminating the conservative land-holding elite that might have been a hindrance to the implementation of policies favoring industry. The anticommunist ideology of the day made union organization doubly difficult.[21] The United States also provided these two countries with high levels of economic assistance after independence—levels that allowed the governments to subsidize industrialization and consumption while at the same time investing in physical and human capital without recourse to international indebtedness. For example, in the early 1950s U.S. civilian aid of some $90 million a year financed about 40 percent of Taiwan's goods and services imports,[22] and it was even higher for Korea—accounting for five-sixths of all Republic of Korea imports during the 1950s.[23] This aid not only legitimized the new regimes; it financed an initial but short import-substitution phase in the 1950s that constituted "a rare breathing space, an incubation period allowed to few other peoples in the world."[24] Later, through the U.S. manipulation of disbursement and stated intention to withdraw the financial support over time, aid provided the United States with leverage to press for reforms and to provide incentives for the two countries to move toward export promotion. As Haggard notes, "In both cases the reforms were ultimately sold to the political leadership as leading to a degree of political independence."[25] Immediate security threats from the People's Republic of China (PRC) and North Korea further legitimized military rule, empowered the leadership, especially in the Korean case, to crack down on "political capitalists," and helped "to concentrate the rulers' minds on performance-enhancing measures as a means of their own survival."[26]

Spillover from Japan's postwar industrial evolution provided important economic opportunities that Korea and Taiwan, led by newly strengthened states, were quick to grasp. In the late 1960s, U.S. economic advisers resisted industrialization efforts by Korea and Taiwan on the grounds that such plans violated the law of comparative advantage. But both countries obtained Japanese technology and financing in part because "the new programs provided the structure necessary to receive declining Japanese heavy industry."[27] Finally, Korea and Taiwan benefited from a broader free trade environment. Both made the transition to export-oriented industrialization at a time when the markets of Western Europe and especially North America were open and receptive to imports of low-wage manufactures, and when transport costs fell. It can be argued that each of the factors just enumerated meant that the international environment was conducive to rapid industrialization in Northeast Asia in ways that will not be replicated for other developing nations.

Statist analyses have been extraordinarily helpful in moving our understanding of development beyond the value and structural-functionalist emphasis of modernization theory and the external determinism of dependency theory. Yet the statist school requires further elaboration. One area of weakness has to do with the specific ways in which natural resource endowments influence state structure and policy choice. Statist authors have generally agreed with the argument that Korea and Taiwan's lack of comparative advantage in natural resources encouraged a transition to export-led growth. The broad logic is the following: Korea and Taiwan did not have the option of drawing on commodity export revenues to finance the protection and subsidies necessary for an extended stage of import-substituting industrialization (ISI). When balance of payments problems resulting from ISI appeared, the NICs' tendency was to devalue and promote, whereas resource-rich Latin America and Southeast Asia could continue to finance imports with revenues from natural resource exports.

But the statist literature has not gone much beyond understanding natural resource endowments as a background or boundary condition influencing the length of the ISI stage.[28] This is not a significant problem for explaining the broad policies common to the two East Asian NICs and the outstanding differences between the poorly endowed NICs on the one hand and the richly endowed ASEAN-Four on the other. This level of causation is, however, insufficient for explaining differences among similarly endowed countries, as between South Korea and Taiwan, and among the ASEAN-Four. We need an understanding of the ways in which resource constraints interact with other domestic factors to promote or limit entrepreneurial pursuit of special privilege and government protection and to influence institutional developments within the state and private sector. This requires a better understanding of the links between industrial policy and political struggles among a wide variety of political actors and economic sectors.[29]

A second shortcoming of the statist literature is its tendency to paint the strong state NICs as homogeneous. Although both Korean and Taiwan states exhibit significant cohesion, case studies reveal variations on state structures and policy preferences. We can thus distinguish between "South Korea's growth-first policy, its promotion of large industrial combines, and its heavy use of sector specific, discretionary industrial policy," and Taiwan's policy of growth only with stability, its reliance on small and medium enterprises, and its more general industrial policy."[30] These differences can be traced in turn to the initial conditions found at independence and the cumulative impact on social coalitions of different approaches to ISI and export-oriented industrialization (EOI).

A third and more serious weakness in the state-centered school has to do with private sector preferences. The statist school attributes major policy shifts to state officials with long-term perspectives, limiting the private sector role to one of information and implementation. Entrepreneurs are generally assumed to prefer short-term, rent-seeking, "distributional" type objectives. This leads to the conclusions that in the NICs, "there is no evidence that local industry was the driving force behind export-oriented policies, even though it was to profit from them enormously."[31] Encouraging longer-term, "productive" behavior requires the political control, or even elimination, of previously privileged groups.[32]

This approach fails to capture situations in which private entrepeneurs, while not the driving force for export policies, provide support and ideas for such major policy shifts. If, even in strong state Korea, "political leaders and planners relied heavily on the ideas of and cooperation from the entrepreneurial sector," then the statist approach may obscure more nuanced processes in which state officials rely on, negotiate with, and learn from private business.[33]

The failure to recognize and explore such interactions leads to an important gap in much of the statist literature—a relatively undeveloped sense of politics. The assumption of state autonomy, expertise, and cohesion can blur the need to explore how rulers try to secure legitimacy and political support by making deals and creating coalitions. Similarly, it can obfuscate the particularities of societal coalitions and groups. Many of these problems are evident in the case of the Korean auto industry and, as we shall see, in the Taiwan textile case.[34]

This more complex process of state-societal interaction is captured by Peter Evans's concept of "embedded autonomy . . . an apparently contradictory combination of Weberian bureaucratic insulation with intense immersion in the surrounding social structure."[35] Evans is thus drawing our attention to both the ways in which technocrats are insulated from some kinds of social pressure and the ways in which the technocrats (as members of a regime intensely committed to rapid industrialization) must also work with and respond to the private sector. Such an embedded autonomy has two further components—collective business representation (associations) and public-private sector networks—both of which are underplayed in statist accounts. The contribution of centralized private sectors to economic adjustment in developing countries has long been recognized, and as Evans notes, developmental states require "appropriate private interlocutors."[36] But with rare exceptions, little attention has been devoted to business associations in developing countries in general and in the NICs in particular.[37]

Organized business interacts with state officials through networks. The state-centric model has recognized the existence of such linkages, but it has done little systematic investigation of them. To some degree, this neglect is justified by the need to contrast the highly active and effective role of the state in the East Asian NICs with other regions, especially in creating productive entrepreneurs. But we suspect that neglect of linkages also reflects conceptual and methodological problems. The pluralist versus corporatist and social versus state corporatist dichotomies may be too broad to capture the shifting and sector-specific relations between state agencies and organized private sector interests.[38] Further, these relations are often informal and may be empirically difficult to measure.

Despite these difficulties, public-private sector linkages merit greater attention because of their critical information and implementation functions. From the statist perspective, "A concrete network of external ties allows the state to assess, monitor and shape private responses to policy initiatives, prospectively and after the fact. It extends the state's intelligence and enlarges the prospect that policies will be implemented."[39] These networks may, in addition, be the arenas in which state officials negotiate with and learn from entrepreneurs.

Whatever the direction of influence, the form and success with which a country undertakes economic adjustments are a function of at least two network dimensions: density and institutionalization. Density refers to the number of access points between public and private actors and is a function of the level of government and business concentration and the degree of differentiation between the two. Taiwan's networks are less dense than those of Japan and South Korea because of relatively low levels of business concentration in Taiwan and a high level of social differentiation between mainlander state officials and Taiwanese entrepreneurs. Density contributes to efficient policy formulation and implementation. Thus, the mutliplicity of access points in Japan extends the range of policy instruments available to the government, whereas the thinner linkages in Taiwan may help to explain weak planning capacity relative to Japan and South Korea.[40]

But even dense networks are likely to be inefficient in promoting economic adjustment if they are highly personalized or clientelist. Seen comparatively, the East Asian cases highlight the value of institutionalized, function-based networks in providing dependability for the private sector and consistency in terms of outcomes.[41] We believe the value and variety of networks can best be demonstrated by the discussion of two brief case studies of textiles in Taiwan and Thailand. The Taiwan case follows below and the Thai case will be discussed later when we seek to explain the ASEAN-Four record of rapid growth and diversification.

Textiles in Taiwan. The evolution of Taiwan's textile industry illustrates some of the statist approach's strengths and weaknesses. Textiles were Taiwan's leading foreign exchange earner throughout the 1960s and 1970s and constituted the core of almost a third of the country's top 106 business groups by the mid-1970s.[42] During the 1950s, the industry was largely of an ISI nature, devoted to the domestic market with an eye to saving foreign exchange. By the late 1950s, the industry (and the country at large) faced typical ISI problems: a balance of payments crisis and saturation of the domestic market. In response, textile firms moved to earn rather than save foreign exchange through an impressive series of export promotion measures. These measures included a Contract of Cooperation through which cotton spinners agreed to reduce capacity, to purchase cotton and to set prices collectively; a Responsibility Export Scheme under which producers agreed to sell only 40 percent of output domestically and export the rest; and an Export Encouragement Fund drawn from levies on cotton purchases. Successful agreements to coordinate production cuts among firms continued into the 1970s.[43]

These and other measures were supplemented by a series of low-interest state loans and tax rebates, as well as by the establishment of a textile technical college and a textile industry research center in the 1970s. Perhaps most important were successful efforts to reconcile the interests of various producers. In the 1960s and 1970s, weavers and spinners reached a compromise whereby the spinners agreed to lower prices and stabilize supply in exchange for an end to pressure for liberalization of yarn imports. Agreements were also reached among (1) the upstream, state-owned producer of petrochemical feedstock, which attempted to raise its prices in light of global oil price rises; (2) producers of petrochemical intermediates who wanted to pass on these price increases to downstream consumers such as synthetic fiber firms; and (3) the downstream firms who wanted to import cheaper intermediates in order to keep costs down and remain competitive.[44]

The statist approach is helpful in illuminating at least four important aspects of this evolution, beginning with the initiation of major policy shifts in the industry. There is no doubt as to the state's leadership during the 1950s. With sectoral plans for the textile industry developed as early as 1950, the government provided protection and financial support for a domestic-oriented industry. Underlying this effort were state officials' desire to reduce dependence on the United States and develop a self-sustaining economy.[45]

Under the pressure of foreign exchange shortages, the state also played a major role in promoting the critical shift toward exports in the late 1950s. As argued by the state-centered model, the private sector responded to the ISI crisis by advocating cartelization of the domestic market and higher levels of state protection for import substitution. The move toward exports thus *had* to be initiated by a state operating in isolation from these private sector interests.[46]

Institutional changes within the state, moreover, reflected consolidation around a more export-led strategy. These changes allowed the state to act as a "big leader"—its initiatives made "a real difference to investment and production patterns in an industry."[47]

Second, state officials fulfilled the important collective goods functions of spreading or socializing risks. This involved making low-interest loans and agreeing to reduce import controls if producers agreed to procure new machinery and expand exports. It also involved undertaking investments exceeding the capacity or desire of the private sector but necessary for the industry as a whole.[48] For example, the government developed the state-owned China Petroleum Corporation to ensure that upstream production "not become the captive of one or two private interests."[49] In addition, the government imported power looms from Japan with help from a U.S. engineering firm and promoted midstream operations by helping to draw private sector capital into a major rayon producer, the China Man-Made Fiber Corporation. Risks were also reduced by an "entrusted spinning and weaving scheme," which assured both markets and raw materials. Working through industry associations, the state allocated cotton to spinners who sold yarn back to the government for a small profit. The state then provided the weavers with yarn in return for fabrics.

Third, as implied above, state officials helped to reconcile the interests of different firms. Within segments of the textile industry, they promoted agreements to reduce output in the face of overcapacity. Among segments, they facilitated cooperation between spinners and weavers in imposing the "entrusted spinning and weaving scheme" and the agreements between downstream firms and their monopolistic petrochemical suppliers.[50] These measures helped to ensure that positive externalities (beneficial spin-offs and contributions to national competitiveness) of each segment could be captured by the industry as a whole and that "neither the country's efforts at backward integration into intermediary products nor the export competitiveness of its textile products is threatened by unresolved private conflicts."[51] Thus no one segment of the industry could pursue international profits and competitiveness at the expense of other segments and the nation as a whole.

A fourth important state contribution lay in strengthening the collective organizational capacity of private firms. Although textile associations played important roles in implementing many interfirm agreements, the associations' ability to draw members and enforce agreements required state legitimation and support.[52] This supports Evans's suggestion that state actors in Northeast Asia facilitated the emergence of appropriate private interlocutors necessary for effective state measures.[53]

But the Taiwan textile case also highlights statist shortcomings. Consider first the need for an insulated state to counter "backward" private sector preferences in initiating the export shift of the early 1960s. A recent study by Kuo suggests that the textile firms themselves recognized the limits of import-substitution industrialization and organized rapidly for exports. Although largely ISI, there had been some export activity based on state export subsidies initiated in 1954.[54] In the late 1950s, local firms did push for price cartels, but they also drew on South Korean experience to propose government provision of low-interest loans and special input procurement for exporters.[55] In this view, the government responded to these proposals only after the bureaucracy consolidated around a more general export-oriented strategy. And that consolidation itself did not reflect a conscious move toward liberalization by a rational state. It was instead more of a defensive measure to reduce external vulnerability taken under transnational persuasion and a consequence of the decision to emphasize economic growth, not conquest of the mainland.[56] Further formulation and implementation of export-promoting measures involved regular consultations between state officials and local firms or associations.[57] The crisis, in this view, brought the government and firms together to search for new solutions.

This softer statist perspective suggests that the state acted less as a "big leader" and more as a "big follower"; that is, it facilitated private sector investments rather than pointing investors in directions contrary to their original preferences. This does not deny the need for an activist state. Textile firms probably lacked sufficient cohesion to agree on a policy change. And they certainly lacked political influence to press for a new policy had they agreed on one. The state's most important function here was one of resolving collective action problems among organizationally and politically weak firms. The state identified correct policy directions emerging in part from the private sector and strengthened those interests favoring such a direction through organizational and risk reduction measures.

The softer statist school also places greater emphasis on the contribution of textile associations. Wade characterizes Taiwan trade associations in general as useful and busy, but only as "the government's hand-maidens."[58] This certainly was the case in the 1950s when the government's Textile Committee included a few textile producers acting simply as "transmission belts" for government policies.[59] But some evidence suggests that by the 1960s the textile associations were playing more important roles. Kuo argues that a number of state initiatives were responses to associational suggestions ranging from proposals for low-interest loans to overcapacity reduction cartels and arrangements for raw materials procurement.[60] Wade himself notes that the Taiwan Textile Federation has drawn the government's attention to problems in the production structure by showing the weakness of the island's dyeing and finishing facilities and by helping "to find firms willing to invest in the gap."[61] A fuller list of such activities remains to be compiled. But such an inventory, when considered with the high level of membership in textile associations by big Taiwan business groups and the close linkages between different associations, might well suggest a private sector more organized and aggressive than anything suggested by the "handmaiden" category.[62]

Information on state-private textile networks is scanty. What little evidence there is suggests linkages that, although thin, have been increasingly dense and function- rather than clientelist-based. Access points include official visits to firms or small groups of firms, official participation in negotiations among associations, and formal, regular meetings between the Ministry of Economic Affairs and producer groups. By and large, these linkages have been fairly opaque, with officials avoiding open contacts, doing things "as though behind a screen," and preferring decisions to come from the private sector parties themselves.[63] Yet the shift to export promotion involved more frequent and openly acknowledged meetings between officials and producers.[64]

Ties between firms and officials also became less personalized over the years. In the 1950s, allocation of loans, cotton, and other privileges from the state occurred through clientelist channels. As exports became more important, however, state assistance was directed toward sectors rather than particular firms. Negotiations with the private sector focused on associations or other groups of firms. This process was not, moreover, driven by the state alone. Firms found their new sources of export incomes larger than the protection and privileges they received through clientelistic ties. Pursuing exports required new policies and regularization of bureaucratic procedures achievable through associational activity and negotiations with technocrats rather than patrons.[65]

Our treatment of the Taiwan textile industry has certainly not undermined the argument that autonomous, coherent states are critical to economic policy change. But the case does suggest that private sector preferences may be less backward and that business associations and public-private sector networks more active than stipulated by the statist school. What seems in retrospect to have been a conscious process of state leadership may in fact be one of learning through incremental adaptation. This indicates the importance of nonstate institutions not simply as implementing handmaidens, but as sources of initiative and negotiating partners for state officials. In this model, the state's primary functions involve choosing the best policy from among contending proposals and improving the chances of that policy's implementation by reducing risk, reconciling divergent interests, and otherwise strengthening the policy's supporters. The state is less an all-knowing creator than a force for overcoming barriers, a "central agent mediating among market agents, forcing and facilitating information interchange and insuring the implementation of the decisions reached."[66]

We have provided evidence from only one case in support of a softer statist or nonstate institutionalist model. There are certainly other cases in which policy changes were and could only have been a function of isolated states countering opposing private sector preferences. But some evidence suggests that the softer state argument can accurately describe other policy shifts, even in South Korea where the state is usually assumed to have been more dominant than in Taiwan. Thus, Pack and Westphal argue that "some highly successful, selectively promoted industries were identified by the government on the basis of—thus only after—their initial and profitable inception by private market agents." And a recent study of the Korean auto industry during the 1980s concludes that "*it is not the state but local capital that determined the path, speed, and result of automobile industrialization.*"[67] Moreover, nonstate institutions may prove even more important in Southeast Asian countries whose states lack the autonomy and coherence of the NICs. It is to Southeast Asia that we now turn.

Explaining Development in the ASEAN-Four

ASEAN performance has been quite strong relative to the majority of developing countries but clearly inferior to the NICs. To account for this record and differences among the four, we draw on a combination of market-based, statist, and nonstatist institutional explanations. We argue that since much of the region's growth has been a function of commodity export revenues and market-conforming policy liberalization, neoclassical approaches do explain part of the economic story. The free market view is strengthened by evidence of extensive state intervention that did not yield the benefits seen in the NICs. This does not, however, mean that the neoclassical explanation of Southeast Asian success is complete. Nor does it mean that thoroughly following neoclassical prescriptions would have yielded optimal outcomes. Below we identify cases of useful institutional activity and areas of market failure where such activity would have been useful.

Market-Oriented Explanations

The ASEAN countries have gotten prices right (at least for their commodity exports) more often than most developing countries. And of the four, those that have conformed most closely to the neoclassical ideal, Thailand and Malaysia, have generally performed the best.[68] This combination of overall market-conforming policies and correlation between policy and national economic performance suggests stronger support for the neoclassical approach in the ASEAN-Four than in the East Asian NICs.

In general terms, the ASEAN-Four have, over the last century, evolved as open, market-oriented producers of raw materials for the international economy. Primary commodities accounted for roughly 90 percent of export revenues in each of the four in 1970 and remained significant into the 1980s, ranging from 50 percent of export revenues (Thailand) to 89 percent (Indonesia) in the late 1980s.[69]

These exports generated sufficient foreign exchange to finance extensive protection and government intervention. Country-specific political factors, especially the influence of Chinese business interests, have shaped the relationship of commodity exports with overall trade regimes and levels of state intervention and help to explain intraregional variation. As of 1992, Malaysia's overall tariff level was the lowest of the four (15.64 percent), reflecting the weakness of Chinese political strength and government fears that high tariffs would benefit ethnic Chinese. (On the other hand, nontariff barriers in Malaysia have been extensive.) A similar explanation helps to explain Indonesia's overall average tariff rate of 21.68 percent, whereas Thailand's tariffs average (and the relative strength of its business class) is the highest of the four at 43.83 percent.[70] In other words, when the political elite fears the strength of the business class or when the business class is dominated by an ethnic minority, business is less likely to win tariff protection.

On the other hand, in both Malaysia and Indonesia where suspicion of a Chinese-dominated business class is highest, export revenues have financed extensive state intervention. Efforts to promote the ethnic (Malay) majority have resulted in Malaysia's state enterprise share of industry and manufacturing exceeding those of its three neighbors. For different reasons (discussed below), state ownership in the Philippines rose sharply to over 25 percent of nonfinancial corporations between 1965 and 1980.[71] The four countries have also violated free trade precepts with regard to financial policy. The governments of the Philippines, Indonesia, and Malaysia (especially after 1969 ethnic riots) have all engaged in extensive selective credit allocation. Even in Thailand, where selective credit policies have been minimal, the financial sector is far from free.[72]

Yet the process of import substitution and other policy biases did not completely isolate these economies. Although the ISI process was of longer duration in Southeast Asia than in the NICs, the ASEAN-Four did not engage in a wholesale deepening of the ISI process as happened in the larger nations of Latin America. Thailand, the Philippines, and Malaysia took some very partial steps toward export promotion as import substitution encountered the usual domestic market limitations in the late 1960s and early 1970s. But more important changes took place in the late 1970s and 1980s in response to a combination of commodity price declines (see Table 6.6) and shortages of external finance. Each of the four undertook varying de-

Table 6.6   Export Price Index Numbers of Primary Commodities

	1980 = 100							
ITEMS	1982	1983	1984	1985	1986	1987	1988	1989
Rice	71	71	69	66	61	60	82	81
Oilseed cake	92	105	83	65	79	87	114	107
Sugar	30	30	20	15	22	25	37	46
Copra	69	109	158	85	44	69	88	77
Palm oil	77	85	127	86	44	59	75	60
Coconut oil	66	107	182	103	43	63	81	74
Lumber	70	76	72	62	79	88	100	103
Logs	77	74	68	67	89	107	110	102
National rubber	58	75	67	53	57	69	83	66
Tin	76	75	69	68	44	47	52	61
Crude petroleum	109	96	93	91	54	56	56	59

Source: United Nations, Department of International Economic and Social Affairs, Statistical Office, *1989 International Trade Statistics Yearbook* (New York: United Nations, 1991), Vol. 1, pp. S–118 to S–119.

grees of cutbacks in state expenditures, reductions in barriers to trade, monetary austerity, and exchange rate adjustments. These reforms clearly helped to stimulate the region's recent manufactured export growth.[73]

The region also took advantage of fortuitous external circumstances. U.S. security interests after World War II allowed Thailand to escape British financial sanctions for the kingdom's quasi-support for Japan. The Korean War expanded commodity export revenues to (then) Malaya and Thailand. During the Vietnam War, extensive U.S. spending helped Thailand to expand its infrastructure, to strengthen its consumer goods sector, and to finance its military.[74] The countries have also had access to significant sums of foreign investment, with foreign direct investment (FDI) from Japan and the NICs expanding significantly in the latter 1980s (Tables 6.7 and 6.8). These flows reflected a shifting division of labor that increased ASEAN opportunities for export of low-technology goods formerly produced in the NICs.[75]

However, the market explanation for ASEAN performance requires qualification. There are, first of all, serious questions as to the depth of manufactured export growth. In the Philippines exports have been concentrated in garments, electronic components, and handicrafts. The garment and electronics industries have remained foreign-dominated export enclaves operating on a consignment basis. There are few domestic inputs, and spin-offs, such as technological advances and entrepreneurial developments, have been minimal. A similar problem exists in Malaysia where manufacturing export growth has been based largely on footloose production of multinationals in free trade zones.[76]

Table 6.7   Foreign Direct Investment Inflows, 1975–1985
(millions of dollars)

	Average 1975–1980	Average 1981–1985
Korea, Republic of	60.7	116.3
China, Republic of	91.3	189.0
Hong Kong	241.1	561.7
Singapore	502.0	1130.5
Thailand	85.2	280.3
Indonesia	289.9	229.4
Malaysia	524.3	1083.0
Philippines	73.6	58.1

Source: United Nations Centre on Transnational Corporations, *Transnational Corporations in World Development: Trends and Prospects* (New York: United Nations, 1988), Annex Table A.1.

Table 6.8   Foreign Direct Investment as Share of Total Investment

Countries	Period	FDI in millions of U.S. dollars	Percentage of total investment
Hong Kong	1965–1970	195.4	16.8
	1975–1985	227.3	22.1
Korea	1966–1976	50.0	1.55
	1977–1985	89.8	0.45
Singapore	1966–1976	274.5	22.53
	1977–1985	982.6	17.34
Taiwan	1966–1976	46.1	1.82
	1977–1985	155.8	1.41
Indonesia	1966–1976	108.4	4.23
	1977–1985	227.8	1.30
Malaysia	1966–1976	193.5	13.94
	1977–1985	868.9	10.93
Philippines	1966–1976	20.7	0.83
	1977–1985	55.8	0.65
Thailand	1966–1976	63.6	2.19
	1977–1985	201.2	1.69

Source: James, Naya, and Meier, *Asian Development: Economic Success and Policy Lessons* (Madison: University of Wisconsin Press, 1989), Table 4.11, p. 123.

In addition, the market approach may exaggerate the impact of policy reforms. Trade liberalization was more discussed than implemented during the 1980s and thus accounts for little of the manufactured export growth. The case of Thailand, the most successful exporter of the four, stands out in this regard: Although Thai manufactured exports grew rapidly in the second half of the 1980s, the trade regime had become *increasingly* import-substitution oriented during much of the same period.[77] The most important liberalization measure involved exchange rate adjustments, which occurred in Thailand, Indonesia, and the Philippines. Where these devaluations were supported by deflationary fiscal and monetary policies, as in Thailand and Indonesia, they facilitated the growth of manufactured exports. Where they were overwhelmed by domestic expansionary policies and inflation, as in the Philippines, they had minimal impact.[78]

The third major weakness of the neoclassical explanation is its failure to account for the actual and potentially positive impact of nonmarket institutions. A focus on this issue can help to explain both the region's weaknesses relative to the NICs and some of its successes relative to other LDCs (less developed countries).

The Relative Weakness of Southeast Asian Institutions

Until recently academic studies labeled most Southeast Asian states "bureaucratic polities." These were allegedly closed systems of military and administrative privilege devoted not to developmental policy but to the proliferation of benefits for a small elite of office holders. Officials were indifferent or opposed to the promotion of broader economic development through private sector growth. Indeed, government officials presumably "sought to keep local capitalists as social and political outsiders . . . who depended on the bureaucrats for political protection and who were in turn parasitized economically by the officials."[79] In the bureaucratic polity schema, Southeast Asian entrepreneurs functioned to avoid government extractions, not to promote broader growth.

As we shall see, this was an overly static picture, but it does highlight important contrasts between Southeast and Northeast Asia. In the NICs, states became legitimate in part through economic performance; strong states rewarded chosen capitalists, but in return the governments extracted costly new investments and forced the pursuit of risky endeavors that enhanced national exports and comparative advantage. Economic performance has traditionally been either less important as a source of legitimacy in Southeast Asia or, as in the case of Indonesia, relatively easy to achieve due to natural resource exports. In the ASEAN-Four, legitimacy has depended on a combination of political stability and selective benefits. Toward opponents, especially lower-class opponents, governments have tended toward authoritarian rule. Toward business, on the other hand, political elites have stressed patron-client ties, patrimonialism, and, in a few cases, state-sponsored corporatism. Under conditions of limited political participation, individual regime supporters have vied for access and proximity to inner circles of power.

As noted below, this patrimonial pattern has probably been most marked in the Philippines. But corporate empires have been built by those politically close to or related to President Suharto in Indonesia. In Malaysia, a multiethnic economic elite has used its control of the ruling National Front to advance its political and economic fortunes. And in Thailand, links to the monarchy and to the military (which exerted authoritarian rule into the early 1970s) have been important sources of economic growth.[80] The ASEAN-Four have thus not had the autonomous and cohesive states, the highly organized private sectors, nor the dense and function-based linkages between state and private sector seen in Northeast Asia. Put in earlier terms, states in the ASEAN-Four enjoyed neither the autonomy nor the embeddedness in highly organized private sectors seen in the NICs. In the following paragraphs we address the origins and costs of these features.

Natural resource endowments, external influences, and ethnic features help to explain why states in Southeast Asia intervene in markets in ways that are different than in Northeast Asia and why Southeast Asia's institutions are weak relative to the NICs. Access to commodity export revenues allowed impressive economic growth without centralized and capable state agencies oriented toward performance-based manufacturing. Pockets of strength do exist in these states, but they tend to occur in areas of finance and trade, that being the highly efficient and relatively independent Thai Central Bank and Finance Ministry. Commodity export revenues have also influenced the links between capital and state in Southeast Asia. Yoshihara Kunio argues that access to oil or other mineral resources helps to explain the proliferation of particularistic, rent-seeking ties between entrepreneurs and states. This factor also accounts for variation within the region; Thailand's lack of mineral resources relative to the other three countries accounts for government-private sector linkages in Thailand that are fairly institutionalized relative to other Southeast Asian countries and even on a par with Japan a few decades ago.[81]

External factors reinforced the institutional impact of the region's resource endowments. Consider the contrast with the East Asian NICs: In Northeast Asia, Japanese colonialism promoted industry and administrative infrastructures. U.S. interests tended to emphasize the geopolitical and helped to strengthen the position of state officials in response to external threats. In Southeast Asia, Japan stressed raw materials exploitation. Western interests, dominated by private rather than security concerns prior to World War II, also stressed raw materials exploitation and the commercialization of agriculture. In Thailand and Indonesia, this process reinforced "bureaucratic-aristocratic" elites who felt little pressure to undertake industrial projects. In the Philippines the process generated a new class of landowners separate from the bureaucracy. Subsequent U.S. investment in the Philippines helped spawn ISI-based entrepreneurs. The result was "coalitional immobilism," in which private forces with crosscutting interests were well entrenched *prior* to economic reform efforts initiated in the Marcos regime. The Philippines highlights the problems that can result from the insufficient development of a state apparatus.[82]

The United States did have security objectives in Southeast Asia, but they tended not to engender sharp shifts in existing political economies and institutional arrangements. After World War II, U.S. views of Southeast Asia were shaped by "indirect interests"—the economic needs of Japan. Despite Southeast Asian pressure to initiate industrialization, concern with Japanese economic and political stability led Washington to promote Southeast Asia as a source of raw materials and markets for Japan rather than as a nascent source of manufactured goods.[83] Nor did the Vietnam War lead to any appreciable expansion of state leverage and cohesion. In the case of Thailand, the war helped to enlarge the infrastructure, expand the private sector, and finance an already powerful but decidedly nondevelopmental military. In the Philippines and Indonesia, war-inspired external support strengthened the hands of Marcos and Suharto against domestic opponents. But it neither destroyed the latter's interests nor imposed rigor on the state. Indeed, authoritarianism grew in the Philippines but served only to streamline "earlier patterns of patrimonial plunder."[84] In sum, Southeast Asia did not experience the powerful organizing and motiviating effects of direct external threats seen in South Korea and Taiwan. Conversely, longer import-substitution periods led to the emergence of politically stronger bourgeoisies in Southeast Asia than in the NICs. These factors resulted in political arrangements under which technocrats have not enjoyed the protection from short-term pressures seen in South Korea or Taiwan. The problem has been most acute in the Philippines; martial law under Marcos led not to a regularization of rules but to easier circumvention of bureaucratic decisions by Marcos cronies.

Finally, the region's institutional weaknesses are a function of externally influenced ethnic heterogeneity. When small-scale trade and processing activities related to the export of raw materials developed in response to the European industrial revolution, those sectors of the economy that were not under the direct ownership of the colonial elites often fell under the control of ethnic minorities—usually the Chinese. These ethnic minorities had generally arrived in Southeast Asia to work in the mines and plantations, but quickly moved to take advantage of commercial opportunities. The colonial retreat opened up new vistas for the Chinese who, while often viewed as pariahs rather than as partners in development, replaced Western interests in plantations, mining, and banking. As a result, unlike homogeneous Northeast Asia, key sectors of the Southeast Asian economies have long been controlled by the Chinese. In the Malaysian case, Indians have also been important.

Business dominance by an ethnic minority has had several institutional consequences. Unlike South Korea but similar to Taiwan, it has meant high levels of social differentiation between business and government. It has impeded the inflow of ethnic Chinese talent into governments and obstructed the growth of the dense, function-based, public-private sector links more typical of Northeast Asia. In addition, because the Chinese were politically dependent and could not trust the state for protection, they tended to avoid exposure to state enforcement. "This made it easier to avoid government exactions, and it also helped to transform Chinese-dominated sectors of the economy into closed shops. . . ."[85] On the other hand, state officials relied on Chinese-generated wealth and thus tended to leave these networks alone.

Southeast Asia's ethnic features have also led to more fragmented business communities in Southeast Asia than the NICs. Intra- and inter-industry divisions have mirrored divisions among different Chinese dialect groups, as well as between Chinese and non-Chinese. These divisions and the political weaknesses of ethnic Chinese have limited the growth of peak business associations that could speak for entire industrial sectors. This is especially the case in ethnically tense Indonesia. But clear limits on business associations were traditionally the case in Thailand as well.[86] These limits on associational growth have in turn undermined the growth of institutionalized links between states and private sectors.

These institutional weaknesses have had costs. Government intervention has had an industry bias in favor of infant industries, but it has lacked the selective proexport bias and the dynamic performance requirements seen in the NICs.[87] Unlike the NICs, the ASEAN-Four have, until recently, not developed agencies capable of screening foreign investment on the basis of potential technology benefits.[88] The level of public-private sector cooperation on issues requiring collective action such as overcapacity, human capital, investment in research and development, and technology transfer has also been generally low.

The Relative Strength of Southeast Asian Institutions

Southeast Asia's economic performance may be inferior to that of the NICs, but it is strong relative to most LDCs. While the ASEAN-Four are fortuitous in their resource endowments and proximity to the dynamic Northeast Asian region, our contention is that this performance has also been in part a function of efficient nonmarket, but largely private sector institutions. We also argue that recent economic and political developments have encouraged the growth of such institutions and their ties to the state. This has led toward a more functional embeddedness of state agencies in the private sector.

Contrary to the bureaucratic polity assumption that Southeast Asian private sectors were largely pariah in nature, the region's most impressive institutional growth is found in the private sector in the form of business networks, groups, and banks. This growth is in part a simple reflection of private institutions emerging to resolve market failures common to developing countries.[89] It is also an organizational consequence of private rather than public sector management of raw material exploitation, finance, and trade.[90] And finally, it is a function of the state characteristics noted earlier that weakened state-private sector linkages: In response to state policies toward business ranging from indifference to predatoriness, ethnically linked entrepreneurs forged ties based on "trust and enforcement which depended on group identity."[91]

The Thai case illustrates both these origins and the important functions of private sector institutions. Sino-Thai firms, business associations, and firm networks emerged in the nineteenth century to dominate not only rice milling but also shipping and finance. After World War II, several large banks, drawing on extensive personal and trade networks with other Asian port cities, emerged to organize and finance commodity exports. One of these, the Bangkok Bank, subsequently helped to build Thailand's large textile and apparel industry. Indeed, commercial banks became a core of postwar business groups and have provided critical support for more recent, independent conglomerates.[92]

Thai institutions are probably the region's best developed, with the Philippines at the weak end of the continuum. Owing partly to Marcos's reliance on a select group of cronies, business associations in the Philippines have been "notoriously weak and poorly institutionalized. . . ."[93] Yet private sector groupings of various kinds are generally common throughout the region. They include, among others, business conglomerates, such as Astra in Indonesia and UMW in Malaysia; social networks, such as merchant groups in the Philippines, and (largely sector-based) trade associations, such as textile and pharmaceutical groups in Indonesia and Malaysia.[94] It is likely that these networks have been responsible for much of the region's success and relative flexibility in commodity exports.

But if Southeast Asian private sectors have been better organized for economic development than assumed by the early bureaucratic polity literature, business has not, with the exception of cooperative ties in commodity exports, had similarly organized public sector counterparts or the linkages through which to negotiate with state officials.[95] This state of affairs helps to explain the region's relatively high dependence on raw materials and cheap labor.

During the mid-late 1980s, however, a more constraining external context and greater domestic demands on political leadership have created pressure for further institutional development. Declines in external funds and commodity export prices (see Table 6.6) have led to a greater emphasis on manufactured goods and/or commodities with greater domestic processing as sources of export earnings. Moreover, with rising wage levels in the region relative to countries such as China and Pakistan, the ASEAN-Four have been forced away from reliance on cheap labor and toward higher value-added exports. Reinforcing these developments has been the cumulative social and political impact of two decades of economic growth. The diversification of the region's elites, the broadening of its middle classes, and the growing sophistication of its producers have meant that particularistic benefits are less effective in buying off key members of the elite.

A general move toward regularization of state administrative procedures has been one consequence of these pressures. In Indonesia, for example, President Suharto moved to facilitate exports by reforming the country's notoriously corrupt Customs Department. Anek Laothamatas has documented similar developments in Thailand under pressure from domestic business interests looking to foreign sales to supplement saturated domestic markets.[96] Increasing privatization of state enterprises throughout the region is also part of this move toward greater administrative efficiency.[97] As governments are moving to liberalize and privatize, it becomes more difficult simply to issue orders to the managers of state-owned enterprises or regulators of particular sectors of the economy. Having lost these tools that previously allowed for tight, top-down management of the economy, the state finds itself in a position where it must negotiate and cooperate with elements of the private sector. Also, privatization of formerly state-owned segments of the economy can lead to a more diverse and dynamic private sector. This, then, contributes to the denseness of ties between the state and the private sector. In fact, it might be argued more generally that pressures arising out of a more constraining international environment in the late 1980s and a dynamic process of growth have led to a second consequence. In this case the consequence is greater state support for and negotiations with private sector peak associations. This has been strongest in Thailand, where, beginning in the early 1980s, state technocrats strengthened the country's peak business associations through the establishment of Joint Public-Private Sector Consultative Committees.[98] More recently, Thailand floated the idea of a corporatist-type National Agricultural Council. The Thai Board of Investments has also created a BOI Unit for Industrial Linkage Development (BUILD), in which the government, as a trusted third party, hopes to introduce buyers and sellers to each other. Similar, if less publicized, moves have occurred in Malaysia, where much of the 1991 plan came from proposals by private sector associations, especially the Federation of Malaysian Manufacturers.[99]

However, political and institutional factors have limited the degree to which the ASEAN-Four have been able or willing to reform state agencies, to promote business organization, and, perhaps most importantly, to rework ties between state officials and local entrepreneurs. During the early 1990s, a fragmented party system and uncertainty surrounding the military's role has generated considerable regime instability in Thailand. This has led to fluctuation in support for liberalization, administrative reform, and overall coordination.[100] Recent Malaysian politics has been marked by splits within the United Malay Nationalist Organization (UMNO), the dominant Malay organization, as well as within UMNO's two major coalition partners, the Malaysian Chinese Association and the Malaysian Indian Congress. By intensifying intraelite competition, these divisions have accentuated an existing tendency toward the use of state development policies to benefit politicians and their cronies.[101] In Indonesia, the very process of economic reform has raised fears of intensified patronage. Privatization has strengthened well-connected Chinese business groups and enriched family members of President Suharto. And while deregulation has empowered industry associations, observers fear that the result will be greater patron-client links rather than a "transparent and accountable working partnership."[102] In the Philippines, the Aquino administration was not able to do away with patrimonial features of governance. Indeed, there are fears that the country's more decentralized polity "simply gives more oligarchs a chance to claw for the booty of state."[103]

We have, in sum, simultaneous pressures for greater efficiency, organization, and coordination on the one hand, and for persistent particularism on the other. The tension between these factors can be seen in what seems to be one of the more "successful" instances of institutional change—the Thai textile and apparel industry.

Textiles in Thailand. The Thai textile industry is weak relative to that of Taiwan, but strong compared to most other LDCs, including its ASEAN neighbors.[104] Thailand clearly lacks Taiwan's capacity to produce fibers, yarns, and finished fabrics that are competitive in the markets of the industrialized world. These weaknesses, in our view, reflect a state unable to encourage the provision of collective goods and reconcile the interests of the various components within the textile complex. On the other hand, Thailand has large yarn and fabric subsectors and expanding capacity in fiber production. The country now ranks among the world's top fifteen garment-exporting countries, one of a handful of less-developed countries capable of breaking into the ranks of the world's major clothing exporters.

These strengths partly reflect the benefits of nonstate institutions such as banks, business conglomerates and groups, and business associations. But they are also a function of the Thai state's hands-off approach allowing for strong competition among producers. In one subsector where the state has been heavily involved—dyestuff production—its intervention has been politicized and clientelist in nature. As discussed below, this has led to heavy protectionism, inefficiency, and a lack of linkages between fabricmakers on the one hand and garment producers on the other. Thailand thus faces a dilemma common to many LDCs: Economic growth generates problems that require greater provision of collective goods and reconciliation of diverse interests. States are often the principal agency capable of addressing these problems, but most LDC states are also vulnerable to capture by particular interests. The Thai textile industry thus offers a lens into the challenges of resolving industry-wide problems without a strong, NIC-like state.

Since its inception in the late 1960s, textile and apparel production has grown to become Thailand's largest source (13 percent) of manufactured exports. The industry accounts for over 27 percent of manufacturing value added and employs some 30 percent of the country's manufacturing workforce, the percentage having doubled between 1972 and 1987.

The contribution of state policy to this growth has been of a decidedly general nature. Most broadly, conservative macroeconomic policy encouraged investment through a stable monetary environment while exchange rate policy promoted stability and exports through realistic exchange rates. Since the late 1960s, the country's investment promotion agency, the Board of Investments, played a somewhat more specific role. The BOI has provided tax and tariff exemptions and encouraged the proliferation of textile and apparel firms. The latter measure was undertaken to promote exports, especially garment exports; a large number of firms were expected to exhaust Thailand's domestic market and be forced rapidly toward export markets. Other export-promoting measures include tax rebates on imported inputs, reimbursements of taxes on export sales, sales promotion activities by the Department of Export Promotion, and quota negotiation and allocation by the Ministry of Commerce.

Private sector institutions have also contributed to the industry's growth, albeit in a more direct fashion than the state. Banks, especially the Bangkok Bank, have been critical in this regard, sometimes going beyond normal financing activities. During the early 1970s, the Bangkok Bank established an in-house textile center whose activities included identifying and linking Thai engineering graduates with expanding textile firms. By 1976 this bank was financing some 70–80 percent of the country's textile activities. In the latter 1970s the bank funded the growth of the country's largest textile exporter, Saha Union, including support for the firm's buyout of joint venture contracts with Japanese firms that prohibited or limited exports. During a market downturn in the early 1980s, the Bangkok Bank also helped to organize a spinners' cartel and subsequently aided upstream and midstream firms contend with credit limits and devaluations.

Business groups or conglomerates have also strengthened the country's textile and apparel capacity through the internal provision of productive resources. Saha Union began as a maker of garment accessories and expanded into textiles, footwear, machinery, and petrochemicals in part through funds, technology, and managerial skills provided by the group's various firms. This group was an early export pioneer and currently holds some 25 percent of Thai garment export quotas.[105] Until the late 1980s, business associations' efforts have emphasized excess capacity problems and quota management. Spinners and weavers associations attempted, with limited success, to organize capacity reduction during periods of excess capacity. Garment association efforts to negotiate for and allocate export quotas, in conjunction with the Ministry of Commerce, have been fairly successful.

By the late 1980s, however, continued textile growth was threatened by increased labor costs, structural imbalances within the industry, and a shortage of skilled labor. As Thailand's industrial expansion led to rising wage rates, the country's garment exports began to face a substantial challenge from lower labor cost producers such as China and Indonesia. To sustain export expansion, Thailand had to begin moving into higher-quality and higher-value-added goods. But doing so has meant resolving a dualistic production structure and gaining access to increasingly skilled workers. As seen below, both of these problems are in large part the consequences of a state with little foresight or ability to reconcile diverse but ultimately mutually dependent interests.

The problem of a dualistic production structure refers to the lack of linkages between upstream and midstream producers of fiber, yarn, and fabric on the one hand and downstream producers of garments on the other. Upstream and midstream sectors expanded as relatively oligopolistic, import-competing activities plagued by at least three critical weaknesses: high costs, the use of old machinery, and a lack of dyeing and printing capacity. As a result, much of the fabric produced in Thailand is either used for garments sold domestically or exported as low quality "gray" cloth. The more competitive downstream garment sector, on the other hand, especially the larger firms, has expanded through exports requiring high-quality fabrics. But due to the upstream and midstream weaknesses noted above, Thai garment exports must use an increasing percentage of imported fabrics. As a result, Thailand loses significant amounts of value added to foreign textile makers, garment producers are unable to react quickly to changing market trends, and Thailand is hard pressed to meet low-wage competition by moving into higher-value-added goods. Finally, even if Thailand succeeds in resolving these structural imbalances, productivity improvement efforts will run up against a severe shortage of skilled workers, technicians, and engineers.

For our purposes, the critical aspect of these problems is their political and institutional origins. Not surprisingly, upstream and midstream weaknesses reflect high levels of protection that are in turn a function of rent-seeking, state revenue constraints, and state institutional capacities. Consider the problem of high textile costs: Until recently, the spinning and weaving sectors were dominated by large, politically influential firms able to raise the prices of their own goods and thus the costs of downstream garment firms. The lack of printing and dyeing capacity is partly the result of two inefficient domestic dyestuff producers whose political influence resulted in tariffs of over 50 percent and a shortage of dyestuffs for domestic firms. Also impeding the growth of printing and dyeing are environmental concerns: Because state officials have never provided (or encouraged the private sector to invest in) sufficient industrial water supplies and treatment facilities, officials have been reluctant to permit new dyeing plants in the Bangkok area due to their heavy use of industrial water and wastewater creation.

The use of old machinery is the result of protection—high tariffs on new imported machinery. These tariffs, however, are not the work of powerful domestic machinery producers, of which there are none. Despite the opposition of literally all sectors of the textile industry, the tariffs have been maintained at the insistence of the Ministry of Finance, which sees them as critical sources of revenue. And the shortage of skilled labor reflects supply factors as well as rapid growth in demand. The Thai government has simply not undertaken long-range manpower development efforts, even for this most important of industries.

These problems reflect the Thai state's inability to resolve the kinds of collective action problems effectively addressed by the Taiwan state: (1) promoting the supply of collective goods, such as trained personnel or shared water treatment facilities, and (2) structuring the trade regime and other incentives so as to promote the spillover of positive externalities among upstream, midstream, and downstream parts of the textile industry. This weakness is in some ways the flip side of the Thai state's strengths; Thailand's macroeconomic stability and its capacity to maintain a relatively competitive environment have been a function of fairly cohesive and expert state financial institutions (central bank and ministry of finance) operating largely isolated from fragmented private interests and line ministries. But this commitment to macroeconomic stability has discouraged proactive state efforts to resolve the collective action problems discussed here. And with the exception of export quota management, isolation of state officials has generally precluded the kinds of institutionalized networks between state and private sector necessary to address these problems.

Natural resources also enter into this picture. Unlike resource-poor Taiwan, Thailand's natural resource export revenues have provided it with an important foreign currency cushion during slumps in sales of manufactured goods. But the early 1980s slump in commodity prices, combined with Thailand's traditional emphasis on fiscal stability, have prompted some important changes. There is, first of all, greater concern with manufactured exports by macroeconomic policymakers. There has also been a political and organizational strengthening of export-oriented private interests within the industry. The need for greater exports has provided garment firms with greater leverage vis-à-vis upstream groups. The Thai Garment Manufacturers' Association has become a leader in efforts (1) to improve the quality of textile inputs through reduction of tariffs on imported machinery, (2) to expand dyeing and printing facilities and promote better communication through the creation of an association of dyers and printers, and (3) to expand industry training facilities financed in part through trade duties. The textile industry's peak association has also become more active as a forum for discussing environmental regulations and tariff reforms. All of these activities involve more systematic consultation between organized business interests and state agencies than previously.

The Thai case has illustrated both the obvious weaknesses and potential strengths of the ASEAN political and institutional arrangements. The shallowness of ASEAN-manufactured exports relative to the NICs stems from the lack of state capacity to reconcile the diverse interests within and among various industries. But nonstate institutions have addressed some of the market failure problems discussed throughout this paper. And backed by even a relatively weak state concerned with declining export revenues, these institutions have the potential to expand their range of productive activities in the years to come.

Conclusion

This chapter has briefly described and sought to explain the sources of rapid socioeconomic growth in two regions of the developing world—the Northeast Asian NICs and the ASEAN-Four. What we have found is that even though the two regions share a pattern of relative success in industrialization and export diversification, the reasons for this success are different both within the two regions and, even more so, across the two regions.

The pursuit of a more complete, and therefore more complex, set of explanations for the success of these two regions paradoxically limits our ability to generalize. What sets the two regions apart are differences in the timing of industrialization, in ethnic mixes, colonial histories, regional dynamics, regime types, resource endowments, and state-society linkages. While compared with the rest of the Third World these two regions have industrialized and diversified rapidly, they have done so in different fashions and at different times.

As a consequence, it is unlikely that any one model will adequately explain the experience of both regions. At a relatively high level of theoretical generality we find that the neoclassical explanations for industrial development and export diversification have little support in either Northeast or Southeast Asia. In Northeast Asia there is clear evidence of widespread government intervention to manipulate market outcomes or to provide collective goods in the case of market failures. These interventions come in a variety of forms, from credit rationing, to the repression of working class movements, to investment in research and development, and on to the direct coercion of the private sector to boost exports in selected sectors of the economy. In Southeast Asia, even though economies are, on average, more open, it is also clear that in broad terms the passage of these nations from raw materials exporters through extended periods of import substitution and on to industrial diversification and manufactured exports has been strongly influenced by government planning and policy choice. The state-centered approach, while not discussed in any great detail here, has been successful in documenting the extensive state efforts to support and develop a capitalist class of indigenous entrepreneurs.

However, in general theoretical terms and in the case studies, we also found that to differentiate among the experiences of individual countries it was necessary to move beyond the level of the state-centered models. This required a discussion of variations in institutions in each of the countries. And it was only at the subnational, sectoral level of analysis that it could be adequately documented that what at first impression appeared to be strong state leadership in a particular industry (such as textiles) actually involved intense patterns of public-private sector education, interaction, and collaboration. In this analysis it can be argued that neither the state nor the private sector has an exclusive lock on the right to provide leadership for an industry.

We believe, furthermore, that what has been documented in this chapter is the early phase of an ongoing trend. The demands for international competitiveness, the harsh rigors of penetrating an increasingly protectionist world economy, and the growing social diversity of these nations will likely lead to an increased reliance on institutions that allow for a pooling of resources between the public and private sectors.

If this is true, then, the finding has dramatic implications for the regimes of Southeast and Northeast Asia and the pursuit of legitimacy by individual political leaders. It implies a further diminution in the utility of patrimonial styles of leadership, and it implies a further rationalization of the political and economic systems of these regions. At a theoretical level this is an argument for a more active study and incorporation of politics, political leadership strategies, and patterns of coalition-building in our analysis of the political economy of industrialization. Rationalization of the political system will not eliminate political crises, class conflict, regional tensions, or bloodshed, but it will lead to the emergence of new styles of leaders, new strategies for winning legitimacy, and new patterns of state-society linkage. It will also guarantee that North and Southeast Asia will be fascinating case studies, not just because of their record of economic success, but also because they are the nations of the Third World most open to the corrosive and regenerative forces of change. For these reasons, the study of North and Southeast Asia will be a fertile field for those seeking insights on the future of the Third World.

Notes

1. Figures are unweighted averages from *World Development Report 1987* and *Taiwan Statistical Data Book 1987*, cited in Gary G. Hamilton, William Zeile, and Wan-Jan Kim, "The Network Structures of East Asian Economies," in Stewart R. Clegg and S. Gordon Redding, eds., *Capitalism in Contrasting Cultures* (New York: Walter de Gruyter, 1990), p. 105.

2. Marcus Noland, *Pacific Basin Developing Countries: Prospects for the Future* (Washington, D.C.: Institute for International Economics, 1990), p. 3.

3. There are also significant differences within both groups. We note these in passing but emphasize intragroup commonalities and intergroup differences.

4. William E. James, Seiji Naya, and Gerald M. Meier, *Asian Development: Economic Success and Policy Lessons* (Madison: University of Wisconsin Press, 1989), pp. 19–21; more generally, see Bela Balassa, *The Newly Industrializing Countries in the World Economy* (New York: Pergamon Press, 1981); Jagdish Bhagwati, *Anatomy and Consequences of Exchange Control Regimes* (Cambridge, Mass.: Ballinger, 1978); Anne Krueger, *Liberalization Attempts and Consequences* (New York: National Bureau of Economic Research, 1978); and Marcus Noland, *Pacific Basin Developing Countries: Prospects for the Future* (Washington, D.C.: Institute for International Economics, 1990).

5. H. Pack and L. E. Westphal, "Industrial Strategy and Technological Change: Theory Versus Reality," *Journal of Development Economics* 22 (1986): pp. 92–93.

6. Pack and Westphal, "Industrial Strategy," p. 125.

7. The quotation is from Pack and Westphal who argue that "the neoclassicals don't have all their facts straight" with regard to South Korea. H. Pack and L. E. Westphal, "Industrial Strategy," p. 90. See also Robert Wade, "East Asia's Economic Success: Conflicting Perspectives, Partial Insights, Shaky Evidence," *World Politics* 44, no. 3 (January 1992): p. 283; idem., *Governing the Market: Economic Theory and the Role of Government in East Asian Industrialization* (Princeton, N.J.: Princeton University Press, 1990), especially pp. 140–141; and Helen Shapiro and Lance Taylor, "The State and Industrial Strategy," *World Development* 18, no. 6 (1990): pp. 865–866.

8. Pack and Westphal, "Industrial Strategy," p. 102.

9. See for example, Colin I. Bradford, "Trade and Structural Change: NICs and Next Tier NICs as Transitional Economies," *World Development* 15 (1987): pp.

299–316; Wade, *Governing the Market*; and Richard Leudde-Neurath, "State Intervention and Export-oriented Development in South Korea," in Gordon White, ed., *Developmental States in East Asia* (London: Macmillan, 1988).

10. Robert Wade, "The Role of Government in Overcoming Market Failure: Taiwan, Republic of Korea and Japan," in Helen Hughes, ed., *Achieving Industrialization in East Asia* (Cambridge, Mass.: Cambridge University Press, 1988), pp. 129–163, especially pp. 139–144.

11. For example, Singapore's most recent development plan is explicitly premised on industrial clusters such as precision engineering, electronics, information technology, petroleum, and petrochemicals.

12. In addition to Wade, *Governing the Market*, see for example Chung H. Lee, "The Government, Financial System, and Large Private Enterprises in the Economic Development of Korea," *World Development* (February 1992); and Karl J. Fields, "Public Finance, Private Business: Financing of Business Groups in Taiwan," paper delivered at the 1990 Annual Meeting of the American Political Science Association.

13. Wade, *Governing the Market*, p. 26.

14. These are adopted in slightly modified form from Evans, "The State as Problem and Solution: Predation, Embedded Autonomy, and Structural Change," in Stephen Haggard and Robert Kaufman, eds., *The Politics of Economic Adjustment: International Constraints, Distributive Conflict and the State* (Princeton: Princeton University Press, 1992), p. 180.

15. For example, investment in a risky and costly steel mill may be beyond the means of any one entrepreneur or may be correctly judged to be poor strategy by the private sector. But the government, looking at the long term, may decide a steel industry is essential for further industrialization. In this light, government intervention to develop a steel industry would solve a collective action problem: what is in everyone's collective interest (building a steel industry to provide inputs for other already-established or new industries) is in no one's individual interest because steel mills are expensive and risky. Precisely this example is addressed in Alice Amsden, *Asia's Next Giant: South Korea and Late Industrialization* (New York: Oxford University Press, 1989), pp. 291–318.

16. Peter Evans, "The State as Problem and Solution: Predation," pp. 148, 154.

17. Colin I. Bradford, "Trade and Structural Change: NICs and Next Tier NICs as Transitional Economies," *World Development* 15 (1987): p. 309. See also Wade, *Governing the Market*, pp. 29, 334; and Stephan Haggard, *Pathways from the Periphery: The Politics of Growth in the Newly Industrializing Countries* (Ithaca: Cornell University Press, 1990).

18. As discussed below, however, Marcos was not as autonomous from societal forces as was, say, Park Chung Hee.

19. For example, merit-based civil service exams have been used to recruit incumbents into the Korean state since A.D. 788, whereas Mexico has not yet implemented exam-based civil service recruitment. Kim Byung Kook, "Bringing and Managing Socioeconomic Change: The State in Korea and Mexico," (Ph.D. diss., Harvard University, 1987), pp. 101–102, cited in Evans, "The State as Problem and Solution," p. 155.

20. Thomas B. Gold, "Colonial Origins of Taiwanese Capitalism," in Edwin A. Winckler and Susan Greenhalgh, eds., *Contending Approaches to the Political Economy of Taiwan* (Armonk, N.Y.: M. E. Sharpe, 1988), p. 116.

21. See Frederic Deyo, *Beneath the Miracle: Labor Subordination in the New Asian Industrialism* (Berkeley: University of California Press, 1989), especially Chapter 4, "The Political Demobilization of East Asian Labor."

22. Thomas G. Parry, "The Role of Foreign Capital in East Asian Industrialization, Growth and Development," in Hughes, ed., *Achieving Industrialization in East Asia*, p. 98.

23. Bruce Cumings, "The Origins of Development of the Northeast Asian Political Economy: Industrial Sectors, Product Cycles and Political Consequences," *International Organization* 38 (winter 1984), p. 24.

24. Ibid.

25. Haggard, *Pathways from the Periphery*, p. 98.

26. Wade, *Governing the Market*, p. 377. On the Korean military's suppression of rent-seeking entrepreneurs, see Kyong Dong Kim, "Political Factors in the Formation of the Entrepreneurial Elite in South Korea," *Asian Survey* 26, no., 5 (May 1976): pp. 465–477.

27. Cumings, "The Origins and Development," p. 33, and see Richard F. Doner, "Approaches to the Politics of Economic Growth in Southeast Asia," *Journal of Asian Studies* 50, no. 4 (November 1991): p. 825. Note also that both Korea and Taiwan looked to Japan for lessons as to both new industries and appropriate policies. See Wade, *Governing the Market*, p. 334.

28. Haggard, *Pathways from the Periphery*, p. 23, 35–37, 39–41. See also Robert Wade, "East Asia's Economic Success: Conflicting Perspectives, Partial Insights, Shaky Evidence," *World Politics* 44, no. 2 (January 1992): p. 311; and Shapiro and Taylor, "The State and Industrial Strategy," p. 871. The original argument along these lines is found in Gustav Ranis, "Challenges and Opportunities Posed by Asia's Superexporters: Implications for Manufactured Exports from Latin America," in Werner Baer and Malcom Gillis, eds., *Export Diversification and the New Protectionism: The Experiences of Latin America* (Champaign: Bureau of Economic and Business Research and College of Commerce and Business Administration, University of Illinois, 1981).

29. Preliminary work on these issues has been undertaken by T. J. Cheng and Lawrence Krause of the University of California, San Diego. We are grateful to Cheng for his thoughts. See also Haggard, *Pathways from the Periphery*, p. 35.

30. Tun-jen Cheng, "Political Regimes and Development Strategies: South Korea and Taiwan," pp. 139–178 in Gary Gereffi and Donald Wyman, eds., *Manufacturing Miracles: Paths of Industrialization in Latin America and East Asia* (Princeton: Princeton University Press, 1990), p. 171.

31. Haggard, *Pathways from the Periphery*, p. 39.

32. Stephan Haggard, "The Politics of Industrialization in the Republic of Korea and Taiwan," in Hughes, ed., *Achieving Industrialization in East Asia*, pp. 260–282. Haggard's reference to distributional type objectives draws on: Mancur Olsen, *The Rise and Decline of Nations* (New Haven, Conn.: Yale University Press, 1982).

33. The quote is from Kyong-Dong Kim, "Political Factors in the Formation of the Entrepreneurial Elite in South Korea," *Asian Survey* 16, no. 5 (May 1976): p. 471.

34. On the Korean auto case, see Richard F. Doner, "Limits of State Strength: Toward an Institutionalist View of Economic Development," *World Politics* 44, no. 3 (April 1992): pp. 398–431. On statism's "thin politics," see Wade, "East Asia's Economic Success," pp. 307–310.

35. Evans, "The State as Problem and Solution," p. 154.

36. Evans, "The State as Problem and Solution," p. 179. See also Peter Katzenstein, ed., *Between Power and Plenty: Foreign Economic Policies of Advanced Industrial States* (Madison: University of Wisconsin Press, 1978).

37. Tun-Jen Cheng, "Business Interest Associations in Export-Oriented Industrializing Economies: Theoretical Observations and a Korean Case Study," paper presented at the Annual Meeting of the American Political Science Association, Washington, D.C., 1988; and Richard Doner and Ernest J. Wilson, "Business Associations in Developing Countries," unpublished ms.

38. See for example, Wade, *Governing the Market*, pp. 375–377.

39. Evans, "The State as Problem and Solution," p. 179.

40. On public-private networks in general, see Katzenstein, *Between Power and Plenty;* on networks in Japan, see Daniel I. Okimoto, *Between MITI and the Market: Japanese Industrial Policy for High Technology* (Stanford: Stanford University Press, 1989), p. 151, 149–161. On networks in Taiwan, see Evans, "The State as Problem and Solution," p. 161. Differences in industrial concentration may be characterized as follows: whereas the Korean state has encouraged the growth of large businesss groups in the export sector, the Taiwanese export sector is dominated by small- and medium-sized export firms in part due to the state's antipathy to private sector power centers and in part due to inheritance patterns in Taiwan. Gary Hamilton and Nicole Woolsey Biggart, "Market Culture and Authority: A Comparative Analysis of Management and Organization in the Far East," *American Journal of Sociology* 94, Supplement (1988): S52–S94; Gary Hamilton, William Zeile, and Wan-Jin Kim, "The Network Structures of East Asian Economies," in Steward Clegg and S. Gordon Redding, eds., *Capitalism in Contrasting Cultures* (New York: Walter de Gruyter, 1990). Note also that different patterns of industrial organization can themselves influence performance. For example, Karl Fields has shown that although both Taiwan and South Korea encouraged the growth of trading companies patterned after the Japanese model, the Korean effort was much more successful thanks in part to support from the country's large business groups. Karl J. Fields, "Trading Companies in South Korea and Taiwan: Two Policy Approaches," *Asian Survey* 29, no. 1 (November 1989): pp. 1073–1089. On the other hand, networks of smaller family firms have provided crucial corporate financing and flexibility in Taiwan. Susan Greenhalgh, "Families and Networks in Economic Development," in Edwin A. Winckler and Susan Greenhalgh, eds., *Contending Approaches to the Political Economy of Taiwan* (Armonk, N.Y.: M. E. Sharpe, 1988).

41. Evans, "The State as Problem and Solution," p. 168.

42. Textiles actually refers to a complex of industries, including upstream (raw materials and fiber production), midstream (spinning, weaving, and dyeing/finishing), and downstream segments (garments). For the purposes of this chapter, we refer to this complex as textiles. On the role of textiles in Taiwan's business groups, see Thomas B. Gold, "Entrepreneurs, Multinationals and the State," Winckler and Greenhalgh, eds., *Contending Approaches*, p. 188.

43. Unless otherwise noted, this paragraph is drawn from Kuo, "Economic Regimes," Chapter 4.

44. Wade, *Governing the Market*, pp. 204, 281.

45. Haggard, *Pathways from the Periphery*, p. 89.

46. Ibid., p. 98.

47. On leadership and followership, see Wade, *Governing the Market*, pp. 28–29. On bureaucratic consolidation around export policies, see ibid., p. 392; and Haggard, *Pathways from the Periphery*, pp. 90–93.

48. Kuo, "Economic Regimes," p. 118.

49. Thomas B. Gold, "Dependent Development in Taiwan" (Ph.D. diss., Dept. of Government, Harvard University, 1981), Chapter 5, p. 276. The rest of this paragraph also draws on Haggard, *Pathways from the Periphery*, p. 89.

50. On the state's imposition of this scheme, see Kuo, "Economic Regimes," p. 113.

51. Evans, "The State as Problem and Solution," p. 161.

52. Thus, Kuo notes that the state could enforce interfirm agreements, through threats to cut off loans and electricity, and could compel firms to join the cotton spinners' associations. "Economic Regimes," pp. 106–107.

53. Evans, "The State as Problem and Solution," p. 179.

54. Cheng, "Political Regimes and Development Strategies," p. 154.

55. This paragraph draws on Kuo, "Economic Regimes," Chapter 5.

56. According to Cheng, labeling the move to new stages of development in East Asia as a "strategic choice" is "a post facto conceptualization." Cheng, "Political Regimes and Development Strategy," p. 141. According to Wade, the shift toward the view of economic development as the priority led the president to change leading personnel, "and the change in strategy came along with the new personnel." *Governing the Market*, p. 392.

57. Kuo, "Economic Regimes," p. 94. See also idem., "Still the Decade of the Developmental State," paper presented to the 1991 Annual Meeting of the American Political Science Association.

58. This characterization applies only until the mid-1980s. Wade, *Governing the Market*, p. 282.

59. Kuo, "Economic Regimes," p. 113.

60. Kuo, "Economic Regimes," Chapter 5.

61. Wade, *Governing the Market*, p. 281.

62. On the extensive linkages among business groups and between the Taiwan Cotton Textile Association and Taiwan Synthetic Fibers Association, see Ichiro Numazaki, "Networks of Taiwanese Big Business," *Modern China* 12, no. 4 (October 1986): pp. 487–534, especially p. 511.

63. Wade, *Governing the Market*, p. 281.

64. The Ministry of Economic Affairs convened six formal meetings with producers between 1959 and 1960. The important Foreign Exchange and Trade Control Commission held monthly meetings with textile producers during the early 1960s. After the FETCC was dissolved in 1970, consultations continued between the producers and two bureaus in the Ministry of Economic Affairs. Kuo, "Economic Regimes," pp. 115–119.

65. Kuo, "Economic Regimes," pp. 83–84, 115. This discussion runs only through the early 1970s. Subsequent network development is unclear. Wade (*Governing the Market*, pp. 293–295) argues for the economy that the government responded to increasing economic complexity, including shady financial dealings, by strengthening the policy network and institutionalizing decisionmaking inputs from the private sector as a whole. It is unclear whether this has been the trend in textiles.

66. Pack and Westphal, "Industrial Strategy," p. 99.

67. Ibid., p. 99. The citation on the Korean auto industry is from Soek-Jin Lew, "Bringing Capital Back In: A Case Study of the South Korean Automobile Industrialization" (*sic*), Ph.D. diss., Yale University, Department of Government, 1992, pp. 329–330 (emphasis in original). On Korean autos, see also Doner, "Limits of State Strength."

68. In a 1983 study of thirty-one countries. Thailand, South Korea, Malaysia, the Philippines, and Indonesia ranked in the eleven countries with the least price

distortion (World Bank, 1983: pp. 60–61). Singapore, Hong Kong, and South Korea were the only countries judged to have practiced strongly outward-oriented trade regimes from 1973–1985; Malaysia and Thailand were among the seven moderately-outward-oriented, while Indonesia and the Philippines were judged moderately-inward-oriented.

69. For export figures see Table 6.4; and James et al., *Asian Development*, p. 40. Unless otherwise noted, information on economic policy is drawn from James et al., *Asian Development,* and Noland, *Pacific Basin Developing Countries,* Chapter 3.

70. Tariff levels in 1992 are 15.64 percent for Malaysia, 21.68 percent for Indonesia, 25.96 percent for the Philippines, and 43.83 percent for Thailand. Eric Stone, "Trading on ASEAN's Future," *Asian Business* (July 1992), cited in Linda Lim, "The Role of the Private Sector in ASEAN Regional Economic Cooperation," OECD Development Centre, Paris, 1992.

71. Robert Dohner and Stephan Haggard, "The Political Economy of Adjustment in the Philippines," paper prepared for OECD study on the Political Economy of Adjustment, April 1992, p. 16.

72. Until very recently, Thai monetary authorities have maintained lending and deposit rate ceilings and limited entry by new firms into the financial sector. See the country studies in Stephan Haggard, Chung Lee, and Sylvia Maxfield, eds., *The Politics of Finance in Developing Countries* (Ithaca: Cornell University Press, 1993).

73. The reforms also overlapped with a devaluation of the Japanese yen that stimulated a search by business there to find cheaper platforms for export to industrialized world markets.

74. See especially Richard Stubbs, "Geopolitics and the Political Economy of Southeast Asia," *International Journal* 44, no. 3 (summer, 1989): pp. 517–540, especially pp. 524–525. Note that U.S. defense and security aid to Thailand from 1950–1975 amounted to over half of Thai government defense expenditures during the same period. J. L. S. Girling, *Thailand: Society and Politics* (Ithaca, N.Y.: Cornell University Press, 1981), p. 96.

75. See, for example, Narongchai Akrasanee, David Dapice, and Frank Flatters, *Thailand's Export-Led Growth: Retrospect and Prospects,* Policy Study No. 3 (Bangkok: Thailand Development Research Institute, 1991), p. 23. On broader shifts, see Richard F. Doner, "Japanese Foreign Investment and the Creation of a Pacific-Asian Community," in Miles Kahler and Jeffrey Frankel, eds., *Regionalism and Rivalry: the US and Japan in Pacific Asia* (Chicago: University of Chicago Press for the National Bureau of Economic Research, 1993).

76. On the Philippines, see Noland, *Pacific Basin Developing Countries,* p. 82. On Malaysia, see James et al., *Asian Development,* pp. 46–47.

77. Akrasanee et al., *Thailand's Export-Led Growth Retrospect,* p. 23.

78. Devaluations took place in Indonesia in 1978, 1984, and 1986; in Thailand in 1981 and 1984; and in the Philippines in 1983 and 1984. On inflation offsetting devaluations in the Philippines, see James et al., *Asian Development,* p. 118; and especially Robert Dohner and Stephan Haggard, "The Political Economy of Adjustment in the Philippines," paper prepared for OECD Study on Political Economy of Adjustment, April 1992.

79. Ruth McVey, "The Materialization of the Southeast Asian Entrepreneur," in McVey, ed., *Southeast Asian Capitalists* (Ithaca: Cornell University Southeast Asia Program, 1992), p. 16. See also Fred W. Riggs, *Thailand: The Modernization of a Bureaucratic Polity* (Honolulu: East-West Center Press, 1966); Donald K. Crone, "State, Social Elites and Government Capacity in Southeast Asia," *World*

Politics 40 (January 1988); and Harold Crouch, *Domestic Political Structures and Regional Economic Co-Operation* (Singapore: Institute of Southeast Asian Studies, 1984).

80. Richard Robison, *Indonesia: The Rise of Capital* (North Sydney: Allen and Unwin, 1986); Ozay Mehmet, *Development in Malaysia: Poverty, Wealth and Trusteeship* (Kuala Lumpur: Insan, 1988); and Kevin Hewison, *Bankers and Bureaucrats: Capital and the Role of the State in Thailand*, Southeast Asia Monograph Series, No. 34 (New Haven, Conn.: Yale University Press, 1989).

81. Yoshihara Kunio, *The Rise of Ersatz Capitalism in South-East Asia* (Singapore: Oxford University Press, 1988), Chapter 4.

82. On Thailand, see, for example, Ian Brown, *The Elite and the Economy in Siam c. 1890–1920* (Singapore: Oxford University Press, 1988). On the Philippines, see Gary Hawes, *The Philippine State and the Macros Regime* (Ithaca: Cornell University Press, 1987); and Paul Hutchcroft, "Oligarchs and Cronies in the Philippines State: The Politics of Patrimonial Plunder," *World Politics* 43, no. 3 (April 1991), p. 421; idem., "Booty Capitalism: An Analysis of Government-Business Relations in the Philippines," unpublished ms., p. 6; and Frederic Deyo, "Social Bases of Development Strategy: The Latin American and East Asian NICs," unpublished ms.

83. William S. Borden, *The Pacific Alliance: United States Foreign Economic Policy and Japanese Trade Recovery, 1947–1955* (Madison, Wis.: University of Wisconsin Press, 1984), Chapter 3.

84. See, for example, Hutchcroft, "Oligarchs and Cronies in the Philippine State," p. 416.

85. McVey, "The Materialization of the Southeast Asian Entrepreneur," pp. 20–21.

86. On Thailand, see Anek Laothamatas, *Business Associations and the New Political Economy of Thailand: From Bureaucratic Polity to Liberal Corporatism* (Boulder: Westview Press, 1991). On Indonesia, see Andrew MacIntyre, *Business and Politics in Indonesia* (Sydney: Allen and Unwin, 1990).

87. See, for example, Noland, *Pacific Basin Developing Economies*.

88. On Thailand, see Richard Doner and Patcharee Siroros, "Technology Development and Collective Action in Southeast Asia: Notes from the Thai Case," paper presented at the Annual Meeting of the Association for Asian Studies, Washington, D.C., 1992.

89. The pioneering work on this subject is Nathaniel Leff, "Entrepreneurship and Economic Development: The Problem Revisited," *Journal of Economic Literature* 17 (March 1979): pp. 46–64. See also Richard F. Doner, "Approaches to the Politics of Economic Growth in Southeast Asia," *Journal of Asian Studies* 50, no. 4 (November 1991), especially pp. 832–835.

90. It is interesting to speculate on why these operations remained in private sector hands in, say, Malaysia, as opposed to their domination by state marketing boards in Africa. One reason may have to do with the nature of the transition to independence. In Malaysia the independence process was a relatively peaceful shift of control from Britain to a coalition that included Malay teachers and civil servants on the one hand, and Chinese and Indian business interests on the other. Under this agreement, the politically dominant Malays had no reason to subvert the country's economic stability and thus their own revenue sources by taking direct control of plantation agriculture, then in the hands of large British firms, or of domestic and foreign commercial operations dominated by the Chinese. Also, given its rural political base, the Malay elite had no strong pressure to pay off urban

supporters with surpluses from the countryside. Finally, the subsequent discovery of oil reserves moderated any possible pressure to obtain financial reserves from the raw materials sector. On marketing boards in Africa, see Robert H. Bates, *Markets and States in Tropical Africa: The Political Basis of Agricultural Policies* (Berkeley: University of California Press, 1981). On Malaysia, see Alasdair Bowie, *Crossing the Industrial Divide: State, Society and the Politics of Economic Transformation in Malaysia* (New York: Columbia University Press, 1991).

91. McVey, "The Materialization of the Southeast Asian Entrepreneur," p. 21.

92. See Akira Suehiro, "Capitalist Development in Postwar Thailand: Commercial Bankers, Industrial Elite, and Agribusiness Groups," in McVey, ed., *Southeast Asian Capitalists*; and Richard Doner and Daniel Unger, "The Politics of Finance in Thai Economic Development," in Haggard, Lee, and Maxfield, *The Politics of Finance in Developing Countries*. On Thai business associations, see Laothamatas, *Business Associations and the New Political Economy of Thailand*.

93. Hutchcroft, "Oligarchs and Cronies," p. 426.

94. On Indonesia, see Richard Robison, *Indonesia and the Rise of Captial* (London: Allen and Unwin, 1986); and McIntyre, *Business and Politics in Indonesia*. On Malaysia, see Heng Pek Koon, "The Chinese Business Elite of Malaysia," in McVey, ed., *Southeast Asian Capitalism;* and Richard Doner and Alasdair Bowie, "Business Associations in Malaysia: Communalism and Nationalism in Organizational Growth," unpublished ms. On Chinese networks in general, see Linda Y. C. Lim and L. A. Peter Gosling, *The Chinese in Southeast Asia,* Vol. 1 (Singapore: Maruzen Asia, 1983).

95. Our impressionistic conclusion, based on a limited number of interviews, is that the strongest public-private links regulating commodity exports operate in Malaysia.

96. Laothamatas, *Business Associations and the New Political Economy of Thailand*.

97. See, for example, the special issue of the ASEAN *Economic Bulletin* 5, no. 3 (March 1989); and R. S. Milne, "Privatization in the ASEAN: Who Gets, What, Why, and With What Effect," *Pacific Affairs* 65, no. 1 (spring 1992): pp, 7–29.

98. Laothamatas, *Business Associations and the New Political Economy of Thailand*.

99. Author interviews, Kuala Lumpur, summer 1991.

100. Support for general liberalization and coordination was high during the two leadership periods of Anand Panyarachun (February 1991–March 1992, and May 1992–September 1992). Anand, a retired civil servant and former head of both a large textile group and the country's largest business association, was first appointed interim prime minister in February 1991 after a military coup overthrew the allegedly corrupt elected prime minister, Chatchai Choonhavan. After elections, Anand was succeeded by General Suchinda Krapayoon, under whom support for policy and administrative reform weakened. Suchinda was forced to resign after the military attacked street demonstrators, and Anand was reappointed by the king. See, for example, Linda Lim, "The Role of the Private Sector in ASEAN Regional Economic Cooperation," (Paris: OECD Development Centre, 1992), p. 8. According to interviews, political uncertainty has also blocked progress on the BUILD program. The National Agricultural Council, proposed to encourage greater agricultural diversification and processing, also seems to be dead in the water. The council was widely criticized as a tool of large agribusiness against small farmers. See, for example, *Bangkok Post*, May 22, 1991, p. 28.

101. Alasdair Bowie, "Dynamics of Business-Government Interaction in Industrializing Malaysia," unpublished ms.

102. Hadi Soesastro, "The Political Economy of Deregulation in Indonesia," *Asian Survey*, p. 869.

103. Hutchcroft, "Oligarchs and Cronies," p. 447, emphasis in original.

104. Unlike the Taiwan case, the Thai textile industry as discussed here includes the garment, as well as other more mid- and upstream sectors such as dyeing, spinning, and weaving. Information for this case study is drawn from Richard Doner and Ansil Ramsay, "Postimperialism and Development in Thailand," *World Development* (May 1993), and idem., "Thailand in the Pacific Rim Garment Industry," paper prepared for conference on the Globalization of the Apparel Industry in the Pacific Rim, UCLA, 1992.

105. Paul Handley, "Cuts from Different Cloth," *FEER* (October 27, 1988): pp. 88–89. On the growth of another textile conglomerate, the TBI group, see Doner and Ramsay, "Postimperialism."

7

The Changing Political
Economy of China

Robert E. Gamer

This chapter focuses on factors affecting current changes in China's economy, politics, and society. It argues that China's Confucian political culture provides a stable climate for economic growth, but at the same time slows the development of democracy and a fully free market. However, that will not prevent intellectuals and business people from expanding their career and investment opportunities. History holds the key for understanding this. The chapter begins with a brief discussion of ancient China, then analyzes the development of communist China, and finally focuses on nuances of modern China, providing a context for the comprehension of Chinese political economy.

This book has been analyzing regional and national political economies in terms of paradigms. Instead of using a paradigm developed among Western social scientists to analyze China, we turn here to a social theory developed within China itself. That social theory is Confucianism, the value system that has guided Chinese thinking for over 2,000 years. It provides a practical paradigm for analyzing China because it is the basis for China's political culture, the values that underlie its political habits. We shall especially focus on those values as they were practiced during the Song dynasty, from the tenth to thirteenth centuries A.D. That period in China's history—like the present—was one of rapid social reorganization, economic change, and opening to the outside world. We are not suggesting that history is repeating itself, but the limits that China's political culture placed upon China's society and economy in the past still apply today. First we shall examine what those limits are. Then we shall explore how they might modify Chinese communism and affect China's move into the international market-oriented economy.

The relationships between business and government are very different in China from what they are in the post-Soviet republics or in the North Atlantic nations and the other regions they penetrated during the period of colonialism. To understand China, one must first examine the nature of those merchant-government relations. This understanding begins with the discovery that unlike the West, where intellectuals have often been deemed "eggheads" divorced from the world of business, China's intellectuals have been the cement bonding merchants with the imperial rulers. Since the founding of the Han dynasty in 206 B.C. (after the dramatic seizure of centralized control fifteen years earlier by Chin Shih Huang-di, ending the feudalism that prevailed during the prior millennium under the Zhou dynasty), that symbiosis among political leaders, intellectuals, and merchants has endured. The Han emperors adopted the precepts of Confucius, a philosopher born in the sixth century B.C. The values he espoused have become the basis of Chinese political culture, the Confucian paradigm that still guides China's daily behavior. Confucianism clearly defines the roles of the emperor, intellectuals, and merchants. It can be summarized as follows:

Confucius saw the moral order centering around an emperor, whose mandate to rule (the "Mandate of Heaven") is proven by the existence of peace, good weather for crops, and harmony among his subjects. That social harmony depends on subjects living up to their obligations within five basic relationships: affection between parent and child, distinction between husband and wife, order between older and younger brothers, sincerity between specially selected friends, and righteousness between ruler and subject. The principal obligation in all these relationships is for the inferior party to obey the superior party (wives obey husbands, subjects obey rulers) and for the superior party to be worthy of that absolute obedience.[1] Society itself was divided into superior and inferior orders, with the emperor and his scholar-officials at the top, followed by peasants, artisans, and, at the bottom, merchants.

Those relationships and rank orders have undergone subtle changes over time; they still underlie all political and economic behavior in China. In the next section we shall pause for some historical perspective, to see how these relationships and rank ordering evolved and especially how they maintained themselves during the Song dynasty. Following that, we shall examine the rise of communism in China. Then we shall look at three somewhat contradictory economic policy initiatives of the current regime in China and how they are affected by China's political culture. This will provide a perspective on China's prospects for adapting to Asia and the world's economy.

Emperors, Intellectuals, and Merchants

Confucius deemed peasants, as the suppliers of food and the predominant social group, an especially estimable part of society. So are artisans, who make goods needed for carrying on everyday life. Confucius viewed the countryside as a place of moral value, where man and nature find harmony; that is where those of highest social rank ideally resided. Special deference was to be given to those who had studied the teachings of Confucius and the arts (such as calligraphy and painting natural objects), which allowed them to give personal embodiment to his ideals of personal harmony with man and nature. The imperial court held periodic examinations for the best and brightest of these students; the small percentage of those who passed would achieve the title of *literatus,* scholar-official. The scholar-officials formed the highest level of the government bureaucracy and were charged with assuring that all individuals and ranks in society carried out their obligations. They collected taxes, oversaw the administration of the laws, and held court to punish those charged with breaking the laws and carrying on incorrect relationships. Sons of scholar-officials often studied to take the imperial civil service exams, as did bright sons of peasants and artisans. But only those who passed the exams could become officials; their status was based on merit and could even be achieved by those from poor families.[2]

The system, of course, made it easy for the emperor to control intellectuals since the highest intellectuals thus became closely allied with the emperor. The freedom of intellectuals to experiment with ideas, the arts, and social programs waxed and waned with the objectives and temperaments of individual dynasties and emperors. But intellectuals were assured of social and political prominence. Merchants were another matter entirely. They resided in towns and cities. They traveled from place to place, which took them away from regular day-to-day relationships. They produced nothing on their own but profited from the labor of others. They focused on buying and selling, rather than perfecting moral relationships. And, with their money, they threatened to become independent of the power of the state. Hence their activities were strictly supervised by the scholar-officials, though they were free to buy and sell in markets. The Tang dynasty (which ruled from A.D. 618 to 907) forbade its sons to take the civil service examinations. The Tang dynasty discouraged contact with the outside world and sought to maximize centralized power.

Though the state distrusted the merchants, it also benefited from their activities. Taxes on their commerce were a major source of income both for the state and (often under the counter) for the scholar-officials. The Tang dynasty, needing extensive revenue for its military conquests of outlying regions, taxed merchants and peasants heavily. This helped spur a civil war, which eventually left that dynasty weak, divided, and at the mercy of barbarian invaders. The Song Empire (A.D. 907–1278), which replaced it, managed to unite the southern part of China while leaving the north and west to other rulers.[3]

The Song emperors increased the number of scholar-officials, rewarding them with land and large retinues of helpers.[4] As China has again been doing since 1978, those rulers welcomed traders from the outside world to live and trade in the port cities, and they encouraged specialization of agricultural products that could then be shipped about on the Grand Canal. That enriched many merchants, who joined the scholar-officials and absentee landlords in moving to the cities and engaging in lavish spending, which, in turn, supported new artisan ventures.[5] All these activities were taxed by the state, which accumulated large revenues. State-owned mines, armament plants, mints, breweries, shipyards, and textile plants employed tens of thousands of workers. All this parallels activities in contemporary China.

As a result of this new productivity and opening to the outside world, China's ships carried pottery and textiles as far as the African coast. Merchants assisted the government in provisioning troops with rice and in operating its factories and monopolies on goods like iron, salt, tea, frankincense, and liquor. They were allowed to purchase official titles for their sons, who could also take the civil service examinations and thus achieve higher social status. Merchant guilds proliferated and could regulate prices and control markets. All this complicated the relationship between officials and merchants. Some merchants had become officials. Officials, whose pay was low, were tempted to involve themselves in commerce; because this was not an honorable endeavor, their involvement had to be kept behind the scene. Many officials used their positions to demand a percentage from merchants on their transactions, and they even used government funds, boats, and labor to invest in commercial ventures for their own profit. Officials also lent money at high interest and rented out urban property. This, too, as we shall see later, parallels activities in contemporary China.

While the system enriched merchants and officials and improved living standards for some other members of the populace, it did not create an independent middle class, encourage investment in new technologies and consumer goods, or provide the basis for a self-sustaining industrial revolution. If China today is to become part of a modern consumer economy, all three of those things must happen. So before we examine the current scene, it is instructive to take note of what inhibited these developments during the Song dynasty. Then we can see how contemporary China mimics, and diverges from, that era. During the Song dynasty, three main trends held back such consumer-oriented development:

A. The state retained control over the activities capable of generating the most income and technological advance. Those who prospered during Song, whether merchants or officials, had direct ties to the state, which demanded political cooperation in exchange for the right to make money. The state retained control over advanced technology; while guild leaders could use simple technology to set up bakeries with dozens of ovens, the state controlled hydraulics, mining, metallurgy, armaments, shipbuilding, textile manufacture, and other enterprises where independent investors would later spur innovation in Europe. China's rulers were conservative about any technological advances that might upset the agrarian-based Confucian social order.

B. Peasants did not constitute a new market for consumer goods. Under the Tang dynasty the state presumably owned all the land, which it distributed to individual families. When most peasants died, their land reverted to the state. But scholar-officials and others with political influence were allowed to retain their land and to escape taxation as well. Gradually, the countryside was divided into large landed estates. High taxes and landlessness drove most peasants to work on these estates, for low wages or as tenants receiving a small percentage of the yield. The Song dynasty tried reforms of this system, which freed some peasants who had been virtual slaves to leave the land. But it did nothing to increase peasant income or relieve them of paying taxes from which the large landowners (who now came to include additional officials and merchants) remained exempt. Merchants and officials were tempted to invest extra income in new land, which enhanced their status as Confucian gentlemen, but did not add to peasant buying power.

C. There was little basis for an expansion of manufacturing and trade or the social mobility that would naturally accompany it. The most lucrative businesses catered to the extravagant tastes of the urban officials and merchants. Foreign trade largely exported gold, coins, and fabrics made in state factories and imported luxury goods. Some artisan-made goods like lacquerware, pottery, nails, silk, and leather goods did sell abroad, as well as to a wider domestic market. Guild merchants could become wealthy by controlling local prices on rice, water carrying, or manure collection. This income came from monopoly, rather than an expansion of competition. The foreign trade was dominated by a few merchants. Since most households had little money to spend, the small list of necessities and luxuries mentioned here consumed much of it; in each town and city a few guilds controlled much of this trade.

So, the Song dynasty generated much income for a few people closely allied with the state. It did little to enrich or improve the living standards of other portions of the populace.

In 1278 Genghis Khan overthrew the Song dynasty.[6] The Yuan dynasty he founded brought a century of even more intense foreign trade in these luxury goods. The Ming dynasty, which overthrew the Yuans in 1368, and its successor, the Qing dynasty, three centuries later, reversed these trends. In 1436, the building of ocean-going ships was banned. The government frowned on ostentatious displays of personal wealth and foreign trade. Intellectuals retained their stature as leaders of the bureaucracy and gatekeepers of national norms. Their ties with merchants declined. Merchants retreated back to their place at the bottom of the social hierarchy, keeping their wealth as hidden as possible from the tax collectors who still depended on it to enrich state coffers. Scholar-officials often seized assets and closed businesses—especially those without a scholar-official in the family. Until Portuguese ships and other European powers in the nineteenth century forced open her ports, China turned her back on world trade and politics. In doing so, she decreased the prosperity of merchants and intellectuals and did little to enhance the well-being of peasants and laborers.

The arrival of the Europeans once again opened opportunities for Chinese and foreign merchants. Weakened by British invasion in the Opium War (1839–1842) and the Taiping Rebellion, the emperors had to let foreigners set up trading enclaves in "treaty ports." In those coastal cities foreign investors set up factories that competed with artisans inland and built neighborhoods with fine European houses. The warlords who came to dominate various regions used foreign-built railroads to transport agricultural products out of the country. British opium imports created addicts—and great wealth for those who sold it; when scholar-officials tried to block its sale, the British swept them aside by military force, further weakening the imperial court and strengthening the regional warlords. Contrary to Chinese traditions, merchants and warlords were enriching themselves against the wishes of both the emperor and the scholar-officials. They were also opening the way for missionaries, who introduced young Chinese to foreign education and ideas.

It was apparent that neither the emperor nor the scholar-officials could withstand the power of the foreigners. When the Republic took the place of the Qing dynasty in 1912 it threw out the system of choosing scholar-officials through Confucian examinations and allowed the introduction of Western-style universities. Many young students began to question traditional values. But, as we are about to see, the events that followed did not radically alter the hierarchy of emperor, intellectuals, peasants, and merchants or free any of those groups from dominance by the emperors' successors. Merchants today experience many of the same opportunities and restraints as their predecessors in the Song dynasty, though the restraints on intellectuals may more resemble those in the Qing dynasty, when intellectuals were less free to explore new ideas. The state retains control over the most advanced income-generating technology. While the role of peasants and urban workers as consumers is growing (especially for clothing, home electronics, and appliances), they do not constitute a market that can absorb a great volume of output; market expansion largely depends on sales abroad. And both freedoms and job opportunities are tightly controlled by the state, which uses intellectuals to help retain its command over the marketplace.

While circumstances differ, the same restraints that held back the growth of a middle class and technological innovation during the Song dynasty apply today. The state retains control over the activities capable of generating the most income and technological advance. Peasants constitute a limited market for consuming goods. The most lucrative incomes derive from monopoly, rather than competition. And intellectuals find that to benefit from the market they must serve the state. But before we look at contemporary China, we must first examine the rise and character of China's communism.

China's Return to Outward-Reaching Centralization

From the White Lotus rebellion in 1796 to the ascension of the Communists in 1949, centralized power declined in China. Both the White Lotus and Taiping (1851–1864) rebellions were fueled by peasants angry over high taxes and low incomes. The Taiping rebellion denuded entire regions of the countryside and caused millions to die of disease and starvation. The regional armies organized to fight this rebellion failed to disband after it was suppressed, staying on to support warlords who became the true governing powers. Even after the declaration of the Republic, these warlords resisted all attempts to establish centralized rule. They enriched themselves by heavy taxation of crops, which they exported for profit.

Meanwhile, new generations of graduates from missionary schools and universities grew restless. Some established successful businesses in the cities or entered medicine and other professions. More sought careers in the new bureaucracy established by the Republic. There they found chances to enrich themselves in ways similar to the scholar-officials of the Song dynasty. Or they found themselves disgusted with China's division, corruption, and submission to foreign powers, and the contrast between the excesses of the rich and the plight of the poor. In 1921 some members of the Guomindang, the movement that brought the Republic into being, founded the Chinese Communist Party on a platform of returning China to the control of its own citizens; many students and young intellectuals joined it. In 1927 the Guomindang began armed conflict with the Communists, which would continue even after Japan invaded Manchuria and

China. Mao Zedong, not one of the innermost circle of the original Communist Party, succeeded in seizing large segments of the countryside from the warlords and placing it under the control of his Red Army and peasants.[7] By the end of World War II he was positioned to lead his army against the remnants of the Guomindang in southern coastal provinces. Many warlords and merchants fled with their wealth to Formosa, thereby reducing the Republic of China to one small island, what we know today as Taiwan.

When Mao Zedong entered Beijing in 1949, China was once again returned to centralized rule without foreign intervention. The new regime pledged that peasants would regain control of the land. The People's Republic of China is administered by a civil service under the supervision of cadres, who form the core of the Communist Party and the principal intelligentsia; unlike the *literati,* their numbers include many who lack education. Heavy industries manufacturing essential goods are operated by the state; unlike those in the Song dynasty, they also produce many common household items used by ordinary peasants and workers.

The Communist regime has passed through four principal phases. All four have emphasized the responsibility of the subject to obey the ruler without question. All have left the merchant and entrepreneur subordinate to other social classes, yet entwined with the interests of the cadres. Like the entire century that preceded the Communist takeover, none have been comfortable times for the one percent or less of the population with higher education. First, during the years from 1949 to 1956 the regime gradually took control of the economy and the reins of power. Then the "Hundred Flowers" and "Great Leap Forward" campaigns of 1956–1960 greatly accelerated centralized control while weakening both merchants and those with higher education, who initiated their own countermoves until 1965. Following that, from 1966 to 1976 the Great Proletarian Cultural Revolution was a time of intense hardship for all educated Chinese. Most recently, the period of reform since 1978 has seen a steady rise in economic indexes, but only halting moves toward political liberalization.

Phase One

Between 1949 and 1952 the regime redistributed land in the countryside. Depending on the extent to which they were deemed to have been exploiting tenants and laborers, and to which they cooperated with the Communists, former owners were allowed to keep portions of their land, while landless peasants received new plots. Then, between 1953 and 1955, groups of peasant families were forced to pool their land and implements within collectively owned cooperatives. In the cities, other political parties that had cooperated with the Communist Party were allowed to stay organized in a "united front." The state compensated them for their property when it was nationalized and often kept them on as managers. Some firms stayed under joint state-private ownership. Those who did not cooperate were executed. Small artisans were allowed to merge into cooperatives that they ran themselves. Many large industries had either been seized from the Japanese after World War II or were owned by the nationalist government, and hence simply stayed in government control. Together, these accounted for over a third of industrial output. Businesses not nationalized were often forced to close by high taxes and price competition from government-run enterprises; these might then be purchased by the government. Many of the families who received money from those transactions continued to live in China's cities, retaining homes and assets that let them live better than most cadres.[8]

Phase Two

In 1956, Mao Zedong invited intellectuals to criticize the Party so it could improve itself: "Let a hundred flowers bloom, let a hundred schools of thought contend." When this unleashed a flood of complaints, he responded with an "Anti-Rightist Movement." Intellectuals accused of having right-wing class tendencies were transferred to menial jobs, often in distant provinces, and were sometimes imprisoned. Then, under the Great Leap Forward, rural cooperatives were merged into enormous communes encompassing entire townships. All private plots were eliminated, and peasants were ordered to give the communes all their animals, eat in communal mess halls, and melt down all available metal in backyard smelters as a contribution to industrial production.[9] Both the communes and urban industries were ordered to speed up production. In an effort to meet unrealistic quotas, cadres ruined land and equipment and lied about output. Coinciding with the withdrawal of Soviet aid and unfavorable weather, the moves resulted in starvation for millions of people. Those who objected were purged from the Party. In 1960, Mao relinquished control of the bureaucracy to leaders who sought a retreat from class warfare and these economic policies, but he continued to purge cadres from the Party and tightened his political control of the army. Still, peasants were returning to production on private plots, cadres profited from state enterprises, and bureaucrats worked with cadres to resist egalitarian initiatives.

Phase Three

Mao countered by organizing young "Red Guards" to do an end run around the Party's establishment by marching in public demonstrations opposing them. In May of 1966 they forced the mayor of Beijing to resign and ushered in the Great Proletarian Cultural Revolution.[10] Soon the Red Guards had closed the universities and many factories, parading public officials through the streets in dunce caps and subjecting them to "people's trials," and they were even fighting one another like street gangs. By January of 1968 the chaos had become so great that Mao ordered the Red Guards to join Party officials and the army in "revolutionary committees" to restore order. While the Party now officially proclaimed the Cultural Revolution, its older leaders gradually regained control. Meanwhile millions of uneducated Red Guards were recruited as Party cadres. It took several years to reopen the universities, rebuild Party organizations and government bureaucracy, and put the economy back on track.

Phase Four

In 1978, Deng Xiaoping recaptured power and allowed China to move in the direction of economic reforms.[11] His declaration that "to get wealth is glorious" might have been a throwback to the Song dynasty. By promoting private industry and a new generation of students much better educated than the old leadership, those reforms threaten the positions both of older cadres and those recruited during the Cultural Revolution, who now have a common fear of having their power usurped by this new generation.

Some of the reforms have aided social stability; ironically, they may also threaten further reforms. The "household responsibility system" allows peasants to lease land from the former communes. The state agrees to buy a portion of their output at fixed prices and then lets them sell the remainder in free markets. This has brought prosperity to great portions of the countryside, accompanied by new houses, small "Trag" minitractors, electrification, and some consumer goods.[12] Millions of peasants and urbanites have united with neighbors to form small profitsharing "cooperative" businesses that produce more than a fourth of China's industrial output.[13] So, both rural and urban workers, to a greater extent than was the case under the Song dynasty, have experienced a level of economic comfort. But, as during the Song, the chief beneficiaries have been among the officials, intellectuals, and merchants. Municipal and provincial leaders set up "joint ventures" with foreign corporations. Through foreign exchange and output derived from these new businesses, homes all over China are acquiring growing numbers of color television sets, stereos, refrigerators, computers, air conditioners, VCRs, washing machines, and other prized consumer goods.[14] With memories of the chaos wrought by the Cultural Revolution fresh in their minds, those experiencing this new prosperity do not tend to welcome social disruption that might threaten to interfere with it, even if the disruption is aimed at giving them greater freedom. And those profiting most have been cadres, bureaucrats, and other families who have acquired political status under the Communist regime; as in the Song dynasty, they use their special social connections within the Party to make lucrative deals and acquire consumer goods. A further extension of economic and political reform could interfere both with their political status and their special connections.

Some conditions threaten social stability; they, too, cause the leadership to hesitate about further reforms that, ironically, may be the only way to correct them. The corruption by those using their positions to make special deals is resented by those who are left out of them. Many of those cadres are among the uneducated recruits of the Cultural Revolution who, threatened by the rise of a new educated generation, use their influence to hold back the advancement of university graduates. Since the corruption is within all ranks of the ruling party, it is hard for party leaders to control.[15] Inflation increases each year. State industries, forced to compete with competitive and profit-conscious cooperatives and joint ventures, find it hard to guarantee universal employment to oversized work forces.[16] Perhaps a hundred million of China's 1.2 billion people are already unemployed, with few government programs to give them a safety net, and greater freedom to travel lets people move from the countryside to cities. Those with grievances supply a tinderbox for political dissent, and leaders fear that once ignited it could explode into chaos.

Modern China

Since 1978, China's annual growth in industrial output has consistently topped 10 percent; much of this growth has occurred in the "special economic zones" along the coast. By 1990 there were about 20,000 joint ventures with foreign firms in China, with $22 billion invested. In 1991, $3.5 billion was invested, and over $60 billion in 1992—more than all prior years combined.[17] China, which had little foreign trade in 1978, now has the world's eleventh largest volume of trade. In 1990, China exported ten billion dollars more to the United States than it imported: in 1992, fifteen billion.[18] The European Community is experiencing similar deficits. Further development, however, may be slowed by the lack of political reform. Businesses require new roads, airports, petroleum, telecommunications, convertible currency, banking and securities trading, legal protection of contracts, and other infrastructure, which can place great financial and political strains on China's government. The road connecting Shenzhen with Hong Kong was built by a Hong Kong billionaire who could not attract outside financing because it was considered so speculative. The Chinese government lacks a tax base to build internal modern highways within the provinces; the roads now being built at a frantic pace simply link cities with their suburbs. Without the assurance of political stability, outside investors and lenders remain cautious about providing funds for such roads, pipelines, and other expensive public works. European and American firms are improving telecommunications; the government remains cautious about extending fiberoptics and other modern means of allowing uncontrolled communication with foreign media and governments. The government continues to experiment with ways to provide foreigners convertible currency while keeping Chinese citizens tied to currency that is easy to regulate. Such duality lets the black market in currency thrive and hampers efforts to create a predictable foreign exchange. Investors need assurances that their business contracts will be protected by law, but legal protection of contracts would hamper the current ability of cadres and bureaucrats to profit by threatening to delay and obstruct business deals until they receive a cut in them.

Chinese remember that before the Communist regime little industrial production catered to domestic needs; between 1949 and 1973 the percentage of industrial output devoted to producing factory machinery, iron, fuels, and other materials needed to make China's industry self-sufficient rose from 28 percent to 65 percent.[19] Following that, production of consumer goods for local consumption rose markedly. At the same time, peasants who had formerly been tenants or without jobs came to share in the income of agricultural production and were able to buy affordable bicycles, watches, radios, and other goods they never dreamed possible. Before 1949, savings represented 5 percent to 7 percent of gross domestic product; by 1992 they were over 40 percent of GDP.[20] Furthermore, state-run factories were deliberately spread throughout the countryside, rather than being concentrated in a few coastal cities.[21] Prices charged by state factories were kept low to benefit consumers. Now, they hire more workers than they need, to keep employment high. When they lose money, the government gives them subsidies. The government also gives the peasants high prices for grain and then sells it to urban consumers at low prices. Families receive coupons that assure them basic rations of low-cost rice, cooking oil, matches, meat, and other necessities. In 1991 those subsidies to peasants, factories, and consumers used up 24 percent of the national government's revenues, causing it to resort to borrowing. To save money, it is gradually lowering these subsidies. That can force state factories to reduce the number of job positions they guarantee, lower peasant incomes, and raise the cost of living for consumers—all unpopular moves. While the reforms are welcome, the social security guarantees of jobs and low-cost food and goods, created during the 1950s and 1960s, remain popular. People are not keen to see them dismantled.

The national government used to derive most of its revenues from the state industries. Increasingly, revenues are flowing to more local levels of government from their involvement in joint ventures and cooperatives. The latter make use of personal savings and must compete or go out of business; hence, they have learned to use fewer workers to produce better products at lower cost. The state industries, bloated with excess staffs who are guaranteed jobs for life and secure in the knowledge that government will subsidize them if they lose money, are becoming more of a drain on the national treasury than a source of it. The government is threatening to cut off their subsidies unless they reduce their staffs and become more efficient.

After a century of disintegrating authority, China returned to centralized control during the 1950s. During the 1980s it sought to retain that control, while once again reaching out to the rest of the world for trade, technology, and exchange of ideas. Like imperial dynasties, it does so with caution. Old cadres fear losing the income they receive from tight domination over politics and the economy. They fear political revolt by the unemployed, rural migration to cities, or those angry at rising prices deriving from a loosening of subsidies and price controls. They are unwilling to give up their control of planning agencies and joint ventures that force investors to deal with them and share profits with them. For the same reasons they hesitate to make currency fully convertible on international exchanges; as it is, they control both the open market and the black market for currency. And, so long as there is no legal protection for contracts, they can demand bribes to assure foreign investors that promises will be kept. Economic reform continues to bring pressures to loosen those controls and unleash those forces.

Yet the cadres also feel strong pressure to continue economic reform. They have personally profited from their involvement in cooperatives and joint ventures. So have large portions of the populace, who are therefore willing to bestow the Mandate of Heaven on the leadership, so long as the prosperity continues. The tax base remains weak, and this makes it hard to build the infrastructure of roads, bridges, power lines, airports, and other facilities needed for economic growth. It also makes it hard to continue providing subsidies for food prices and state factories necessary to guarantee prosperity to farmers and low prices to urban dwellers. Outside investment provides cadres with the income they need to deal with those social needs and jobs to replace those lost at failing state enterprises, as well as opportunities for personal profit. But increasing numbers of people will be without jobs or sufficient income to purchase necessities. At the same time, economic reform unleashes demands for political and legal reforms that threaten the power of cadres. That is their dilemma.

The same restraints that held back the growth of a middle class and technological innovation during the Song dynasty still apply. The state retains control over the activities capable of generating the most income and technological advance. Peasants constitute a limited market for consuming goods. The most lucrative incomes derive from monopoly, rather than competition. And, to benefit from the market, intellectuals must serve the state. The challenge is to remove those restraints while still recognizing these realities.

Three Policy Initiatives

Already, the outside contacts are hard to contain. In Guangzhou, Shenzhen, and Shanghai contacts with outsiders grow increasingly frequent. Trains and boats along the Pearl River carry daily loads of People's Republic citizens and outsiders—often from Taiwan—between Guangzhou and Hong Kong. Roof antennas outlawed immediately following the 1989 events at Tiananmen Square have reappeared in abundance, providing clear signals from Hong Kong television stations. Many now eat out in the Pizza Huts, Kentucky Fried Chickens, McDonalds, and the tens of thousands of restaurants proliferating in the cities; portable telephones and beepers are a common sight around restaurant tables. Karaoke clubs play Michael Jackson, Madonna, and other Western music on their dance floors; so do popular sound tape shops and millions of personal stereos all over China. Modern dance troupes, modeling agencies, boutiques, and other private businesses run by Chinese introduce both capitalism and Western ways. Pay scales in Shenzhen are many times those of interior cities. Floods of peasants enter the new economic zones, only to find themselves displaced from the land and without a job; with passing months, it becomes harder for them to return to the countryside. Some 70 million peasants now move from city to city as migrant occasional laborers in construction or doing odd jobs. About a tenth of university graduates are now finding jobs with joint ventures. Investing in the new stock markets has become a national craze. Since land leases were opened to foreign investors in 1988, billions of dollars have flowed into land speculation; many well-placed officials have grown rich on this. Government offices demand "service charges" for services that are supposed to be free; such charges account for up to 5 percent of the operating costs of some foreign businesses.[22] Even academic departments of universities (which now charge tuition and will allow entry of underqualified students in exchange for a higher fee) are raising money by doing business deals.

Among Guangzhou's trendiest karaoke clubs is Putong 100. Its fashions, music, lighting, and ambiance give it the look, sound, and feel of similar establishments in Hong Kong, New York, or Paris. On stage, members of the audience[23] chant lyrics about personal choice, generational change, freedom of expression—interspersed with songs praising the owners of the club and the People's Liberation Army.[24] Those in and around coastal cities exposed to this fare are likely to resist attempts to cut it off.[25] That does not mean they have fundamentally changed their political behavior. Like marchers and the millions of onlookers to the 1989 street demonstrations, they may decry corruption, nepotism, boredom, limited earnings horizons, cramped housing, and lack of job choice. Yet for them, as for the 70 percent of the populace who live in the countryside and lack exposure to these new scents and sounds, Confucian precepts about the obligation of subjects to give their rulers absolute obedience in times of peace and prosperity still remain deeply ingrained. Immediately following the 1989 crackdown at Tiananmen Square, parents all over China called their children home, and the students who had been involved in demonstrations returned there. [26] Press criticism was silenced, and even the most modern Chinese returned to a stance of avoiding public political discussion. The Chinese talk about change after the death of Deng Xiaoping, implying the ascendance of another ruler to take his place, as in former dynastic traditions. Such new leaders may be more inclined to own, or even visit, a karaoke club; that does not mean they would condone free elections, a free press, or legal protection of personal dissent. In the spring of 1993 students and academics were primarily interested in only one issue: would the United States give China most-favored-nation status in trading? They frequently questioned why civil rights was a factor in this issue, despite the fact that dissidents are still being harshly treated.

State enterprises lose millions of yuan each year. They find it hard to adapt to new technology. Families all over China demand consumer goods based on technology imported or adapted from abroad. Urban Chinese demand contact with Western fashions, music, video, and ideas. Governments need foreign joint ventures to acquire revenue; cadres have found them a source of personal enrichment. Sons and daughters of even conservative, reform-wary, members of the Party's Politburo have studied in universities all over the world. No giant socialist power stands ready to fill in for lost contacts with capitalist countries. Therefore, even conservatives within the Communist hierarchy find themselves reluctant to discontinue the experiments with cooperatives, joint ventures, the rural household responsibility system, and other free market initiatives. Yet even the most reform-oriented leaders want to keep the Communist Party the dominant authority in the nation. No alternative party has been allowed to organize. Attempts by exiled dissidents to create an opposition party have been scuttled by factional bickering. Even among reform-minded intellectuals there is little talk about transforming China into a free-market democratic country. Instead, the focus is on how to emulate the progress of the four "little dragons": Hong Kong, Taiwan, South Korea, and Singapore.

Hong Kong has a legislature but is still (until it becomes part of China in 1997) under the rule of a British governor. South Korea, Taiwan, and Singapore have each been under the control of a single ruling party, which, while challenged by other parties, has not yet lost to them. The press is strictly controlled. Formation of interest groups is regulated. Personal liberties are curtailed.

In Singapore, littering, failure to queue or flush a toilet, chewing gum, or driving an automobile downtown during rush hours can bring heavy fines. Men can not wear their hair beyond a certain length. Leading foreign periodicals have been banned from selling after running articles unfavorable to the regime. The daily newspaper, *The Straits Times,* consults with government officials each day about the stories it runs; government-controlled television gives extensive coverage to government leaders and little access to opposition views. Gatherings of more than ten people need government permission. Leaders of opposition parties have been harassed with lengthy and expensive lawsuits accusing them of economic improprieties. Some Catholic priests and lay workers have been arrested for treasonable activities. All books, movies, videotapes, audiotapes, and CDs are censored upon their arrival on the island.

Meanwhile, Singapore prospers. Grand hotels, shopping malls, night entertainment spots, and office complexes abound. Investors from around the world run state-of-the-art factories that employ large numbers of workers. These workers can purchase modern government-built apartments at subsidized prices, drawing on their government-managed provident funds. An ultramodern subway system provides cheap, clean, and efficient transportation. All workers are covered by health insurance; the provident fund for retirement comes from employee deductions and employers' contributions. The government provides industries with industrial parks containing buildings with rental space for factories, control over labor unions, tax benefits, containerized wharfs, and considerable additional amenities. Parks, beaches, and playgrounds abound. The universal education system is free up to the level of secondary school or university that a student is capable of achieving.

These systems with tight central governance and immersion in the world economy inspire many Chinese. They have retained Confucian tendencies for citizens to obey the state, while at the same time opening to world markets and nourishing a flourishing capitalism. They differ from China in an important aspect. None of the four little dragons has been ruled by Chinese emperors who excluded foreign investors and supervised control of commerce through scholar-officials, not to mention a communist regime that ended free capitalist investment. Three of the four (Taiwan, Hong Kong, and Singapore) have, in fact been created as zones where international capitalists can invest with considerable freedom. While South Korea and Taiwan, imitating Communist China's reforms under Mao, have carried out land reform, neither has made all land the property of the state. None of the four give their citizens guaranteed jobs combined with monthly coupons to buy inexpensive food, fuel, and other necessities from government shops. And none has China's giant population, making such programs so costly. Like imperial China, but unlike the "four little dragons," Communist China retains heavy state control over investment and land. Even China's reform-minded cadres are wary about abandoning all those features. They want to retain the balance between political control and economic growth found in the "little dragons" without becoming as fully capitalistic as those republics.

China can take at least three approaches to emulate the little dragons without moving fully into capitalism. One is to extend into all of China contract and civil law formal consultation between government and professional groups, creation of investment groups, currency convertibility, and improved commercial access. Another is to keep Guangzhou, Shenzhen, Hong Kong, Shanghai, and other special cities along the coast separated from the rest of the country. A third is to reemphasize reliance on state and cooperative industries and party cadres. All three approaches let leaders retain political control while opening to outside commerce, in the tradition of the Song dynasty. None of these approaches can be applied entirely in the absence of the other two. All have precedents. The first remains a goal for reform-minded Chinese, while the second and third are already in progress and probably cannot be turned back.

Improving China's Business Climate

While the four little dragons have not adopted American-style values of individualism, personal liberty, and constitutional democratic government, they have absorbed (from British colonialism and the American economic presence) the capacity to guarantee contracts and assure free passage of goods and currency. Their ability to do so has some precedent in the Song dynasty and its brief successor, the Yuan dynasty, which flowered under Kublai Khan. Prior to the Song dynasty, cities had been divided into *fang*—areas that were surrounded by walls. Trade could only be transacted within each fang at certain hours, under the strict supervision of officials. That encouraged corruption and restrained intra-city, inter-city, and international trade. The Song emperors opened these walls and let merchants form guilds, which could move goods from city to city. Private shops appeared widely, open at all hours and accessible to customers from all over the city and countryside. This did not end monopoly and corruption, but it moderated those practices.

All merchants were required to join the guild pertaining to their trade. The leaders of these guilds had some power to control prices, corner markets, get the most lucrative government contracts, and squeeze out smaller competitors, cutting down on competition. But the guilds could use their collective force to keep commerce flowing, resist some demands for bribes from officials, make government pay market prices for goods and charge predictable taxes, and legally challenge competitors who might try to undercut their prices once contracts were made.

In the Song dynasty, as today in China, merchants needed certificates and vouchers to complete transactions with state-owned businesses.[27] But these were cross-filed at different offices, making it harder for individual bureaucrats to change them. Vouchers contained the names of those to whom they were issued, and they were frequently reissued, forcing their holders to trade in old ones; this helped regulate the black market and the value of vouchers. Government officials still managed to extract high bribes, illegal commerce continued to flow, and many monopolies remained intact, but commerce at home and abroad could expand in an atmosphere that gave at least larger merchants some guarantee of a return on their investments and allowed new entries into the marketplace.

The Ming and Qing dynasties brought greater uncertainty to merchants. Foreign trade was curtailed. The scholar-officials frowned on ostentatious spending and sometimes confiscated the property of merchants they did not trust. Paper currency was discontinued. Canals were poorly maintained. Technological innovation and investment by merchants focused on agriculture. State businesses held monopolies on the heaviest industry and agricultural trade. Private merchants producing cloth, wine, or other basic goods often were established as social elites in their villages, broaching little competition.

China's reforms since 1978 have returned some of the freedoms found during the Song dynasty. Officials can create joint ventures with foreign concerns. Citizens can join together in cooperatives to manufacture and sell goods. Private stores and markets can operate independently of those run or controlled by government. Heavy restrictions still apply. Peasants must sell a certain percentage of their crops through government agencies. Vendors and merchants need vouchers. Businesses are limited in the number of their employees. Obtaining raw materials may require elaborate negotiations with government officials. And political currents may quickly alter the channels through which those negotiations take place as well as the results of prior negotiations. All this makes investment uncertain. Nothing comparable to the Song dynasty's guilds or cross-filing of vouchers has emerged to reduce that uncertainty.

Western-style democracy can not easily adapt to China's political culture. Rulers still demand absolute obedience. Merchants are still subject to the dictates of officials. Harmony and prosperity remain stronger social goals than individual liberty or freedom of commerce. But China has always been willing to absorb those conventions it deems compatible with its own norms. The student demonstrations of 1986 and 1989 revealed widespread frustration among many urban dwellers. They also clearly showed the limits on the extent of political change China's government might tolerate. The demonstrators were clamoring for a greater degree of freedom than they have known. Most of the demands they articulated fell short of pluralism, competitive elections, and unrestricted press freedom.[28] In fact, most of their demands were not highly controversial. They asked for a share in the prosperity emanating from the economic reforms, citing nepotism, corruption, and lack of consultation with intellectuals as abuses that hold back the spread of affluence. They expressed a desire to acquire more control over their choice of jobs and to gain greater personal income. All that is rhetoric that can be embraced by Chinese leaders from a great variety of factions; in fact, since 1989 the chance for students to obtain lucrative jobs has grown. More controversial were posters and speeches that specifically criticized Deng Xiaoping and hence showed a failure to obey the top leader of the country.[29] The few specific suggestions for reform that were made by intellectuals in the debate over whether and how a neoauthoritarian leader might bring improvements fell far short of a call for democracy, but did constitute a frontal assault on some powerful centers of privilege.[30]

Those suggestions included firmer legal support for contract and civil law, formal consultation between government and professional groups, creation of investment groups and stock markets, currency convertibility, and improved commercial access. These recall some of the powers of the Song guilds to enforce contracts and hold government to its commitments. The common problem with the proposals is that they would interfere with corruption, from which many cadres benefit. Like scholar-officials before them, they profit from their ability to demand money in exchange for granting privileges to merchants and businesses. When merchants can seek redress in the courts or through formal channels of communication, they achieve their goals without paying bribes.[31] As it is, China's International Economic and Trade Arbitration Commission handles more cases than any other arbitration panel on Earth, but its decisions can not be enforced in court because the courts refuse to issue orders against Chinese citizens. If China's yuan can be exchanged in international banks at uniform rates that rise and fall on international currency markets, China's bureaucrats lose considerable control over the marketplace. China has maintained a system of dual currencies; her citizens carry on their business transactions with a currency different from that used in international trade. While both currencies are traded on the black market, from which some officials also benefit, both are controlled by Chinese officials who remain the sole legitimate dispensers of either currency. Stock markets pose the possibility that individuals could amass investment capital without reliance on either foreigners or public officials; the stocks issued in China's new stock exchanges are firms partly controlled by public officials.

During the Vietnam War, many Americans saw the nations of Southeast Asia stacked up like a row of dominoes; the fall of Vietnam to Communism might topple the remaining Southeast Asian governments into the Communist camp. Today, many Westerners join some in the leadership circles of China's Communist Party in espousing a new dominoes theory; reforms like those above will activate (depending on one's point of view) democratic chaos or liberalization. Some Chinese elites fear that the breakup of the Soviet Union calls for resistance to reform in China if the Communist regime is to stay in power. In America, Francis Fukuyama sees world events leading to an "unabashed victory of economic and political liberalism."[32]

The shakeout of events in the former Soviet Union and in Eastern Europe already provides evidence that we might have reason to rethink such bipolar views of a world tipping either in one direction or the other. For centuries, Chinese scholar-officials have feared the fragility of their system in the face of outside forces. While Europe headed into the era of the discovery of America, the Reformation, and the Renaissance, Ming China closed its doors to the outside world. But the Song and Yuan dynasties before it, like the economies of Taiwan and South Korea today, show that reforms in this direction can be effected without radical moves toward democracy; rather than turning aside the ruling elite, they offer chances for officials to enrich themselves. Such reforms would be hard to implement because of resistance by cadres and bureaucrats, but would attract new foreign investment and trade that would raise China's overall level of wealth. These reforms, in short, might be assimilated into China's present system of rule.

By further increasing unemployment, making taxes harder to collect, and giving rich peasants advantages over the poor, they might also endanger the standard of living attained by both peasants and workers in China. Eastern European nations and the former republics of the Soviet Union have been hesitant to dismantle economic and social systems that have provided them at least a safety net. In China, where the system of guaranteed jobs, subsidized food and housing, and peasant control over land and crops has worked well, that hesitancy is even greater.[33] The "four little dragons" offer evidence that reforms that strengthen, rather than weaken, such guarantees can be effected. Those economic and social guarantees, together with opportunities for profit, probably have higher priority among China's intelligentsia than guarantees of personal liberty or participatory democracy. And faced with a choice of endangering social peace (especially after the turmoil of the Cultural Revolution) and economic security by experimenting with new reforms, many Chinese might choose to slow down the reforms. These reforms may not, in fact, pose such danger, but many Chinese perceive that they do.

Separate Enclaves

There is a way for China to open up commerce with even less extension of liberties. During the eighteenth and nineteenth centuries the Qing dynasty created treaty ports where, in zones socially isolated from the rest of China, foreign businessmen might carry on their activities. That allowed for new types of commercial transactions in a setting that did not endanger China's traditional ways. So long as officials in all provinces are free to create such zones, it is easier to find consensus on this path to reform than one that allows reform to proceed everywhere in the realm.[34] Deng Xiaoping began reform in this mold in 1991, urging these coastal enclaves—and the smaller special economic zones in cities across China—to catch up with the four "little dragons" in the next twenty years.

Just inland from Hong Kong is the city of Guangzhou (Canton) and three special economic zones in the province of Guangdong (Shenzhen, Shantou, and Zhuhai). Northward along the coast is the city of Xiamen, which faces the island of Taiwan. Shanghai lies farther up the coast, while Shenyang rests to the north of Korea. These are the sites of special economic initiatives.[35] Shanghai and Shenzhen have had stock markets since 1990,[36] and stock markets are scheduled to open in the rest of these areas by 1994. As has been the case in Guangdong, Shanghai in 1992 was given permission to grant enterprises easier export-import rights, lowering government control over their foreign exchange, and to approve production-oriented projects without permission from Beijing. Shanghai may also sell stocks and bonds to raise money for development. The special economic zones have attracted industrial parks, where industrial output grew at a rate of 40 percent in 1990–1992;[37] all over China, officials are creating these zones. During the first five months of 1993, output of joint ventures rose 73 percent beyond that of the comparable period in the prior year.[38] Many of these new factories are little more than sweat shops, where young, poorly educated girls toil long hours for low wages; most make use of considerable hand labor. That helps to create employment. While these firms are required to provide housing and other social services to employees, they do not always match the services provided by state industries to their workers, and they do not hire as many workers as a comparable state industry.

Officials in these zones have unusual autonomy over economic planning. Shenzhen officials are planning to turn it into a complete free trade zone. Zhuhai is building a new deepwater port, an enlarged airport, a power station, and a superhighway linking it with Guangzhou and Macau.

Hainan Island has been given permission to create a free-port development zone. In Shanghai's Pudong development zone a whole new city the size of Hong Kong is rising out of farmland. All this building employs thousands of laborers using little machinery and a lot of farmland (often, because of local corruption, more than the amount authorized by Beijing). Some of the companies in these areas have been granted greater autonomy than others; most are still run by county governments as joint ventures with foreign firms. No foreign firms in China can operate as entirely independent companies, like those incorporated in the little dragons or North Atlantic democracies.[39]

These projects have rapidly enlarged China's industrial output. They involve the danger that inhabitants will demand freedoms too rapidly and spread these demands into the rest of China. So far, the British authorities have worked with the Chinese to keep demands for further democratization of Hong Kong under control;[40] this has been limited to allowing free elections for eighteen of the sixty members on the Legislative Council. Hong Kong continues to lack a popularly elected chief executive and legislature or guarantees for the right of dissent. Despite some vocal demands from inside and outside the legislature, the government has failed to even promulgate a Freedom of Information Ordinance, which would give citizens access to official information. Hence Hong Kong—with its years of exposure to British culture—lags behind even the other three little dragons on its road to democratization. There seems no impelling reason to believe that such forces will move faster in the coastal provinces only recently exposed to Western influences.

Emphasizing State Industries and Party Cadres

The rapid development of the coastal provinces has caused frustrations among officials of inland provinces, who feel left behind. But they, too, have found ways to promote development. Today, China's government lets local governments all over China create joint ventures with foreign enterprises. It is lifting price controls on grain and oils, ending central price subsidies to farmers. In a few years, peasants will no longer be required to sell a portion of their grain to government marketing agencies. By 1993, only eighty-nine raw materials, agricultural and mined, were subject to price controls. The many state industries that currently operate at a loss are being encouraged to initiate measures that will make them less unprofitable. Managers are being chosen on the basis of their commercial, rather than political, capabilities. They are given performance targets, based on sales and profits, and may forfeit pay and their jobs if they do not meet them. In 1993, each province was allowed to select one or two state companies to issue stock on the Shanghai and Shenzhen exchanges. Foreign firms are converting some state factories into joint ventures. These moves will strengthen the influence of local officials, while retaining state industries and the "household responsibility system" in the countryside.

Upon first perusal, moves to end price controls and mandatory sales to government marketing agencies might seem to weaken the purview of government officials and party cadres. When such moves are not combined with passable roads, private land ownership, convertible currency, independent stock markets, and guarantees for contracts they do not open the door to independent outside investors. Peasants and small cooperatives attempting to sell crops in cities will still need to deal with local authorities. So will foreign investors seeking to create investment opportunities; any companies they form are likely to be joint ventures with local officials. China's railways have been neglected, and they form a small network in relation to people and land. There will be need for passable waterways, which have traditionally been the principal means for moving crops. During the Song dynasty, prefects sometimes diverted money from state monopolies and combined it with their own funds and money raised from merchants to make river improvements that aided the flow of commerce. Then they could share in the profits. Police and officials, now as then, may also ask bribes or just help themselves to part of shipments in exchange for letting cargo pass though their regions. The state marketing agencies controlled by central government authorities are likely to be replaced by cooperatives and joint ventures from which local authorities can benefit. Already trade is handled by some 3,700 general trading companies, in which local officials play major roles. State infrastructures are likely to be increasingly underwritten by cadres working with foreign investors. Regarding the reforms in the countryside, Jean Oi observes:

> The power that cadres have over peasants is no longer direct but informal, created by their influence over economic opportunities. The existing structure leaves them in a position to grant licenses, distribute key inputs, act as the middlemen between peasants and the state market, and regulate the open market. This half-planned half-market economy makes peasants, as individuals, more vulnerable to a wider range of corruption outside the village while continuing to subject them to village cadre power.[41]

This combination of reforms can cause considerable economic distress. Inflation is well over 10 percent annually. An end to government subsidies that currently keep up the peasants' income from crops and vouchers that lower the cost of food purchases for urban dwellers may simultaneously lower peasant income and further raise the cost of living for urbanites.[42] Since urban employers are meanwhile being asked to control costs, wages may stay low[43] and layoffs increase. Within villages, both economic and political control is falling into the hands of the best-connected families. Peasant incomes in poor provinces are only half those on the coast. Over 200 million people will be without regular employment by the end of the 1990s; they will increasingly be dependent on government for unemployment compensation and social services.

During 1993, in hundreds of villages around China, peasants, complaining that their income is stagnant while the cities boom, rioted. Their complaints were aimed at local officials who charged them for services, raised taxes to build roads, and paid them for crops with IOUs while diverting the cash into land speculation and economic development zones. Thousands threw rocks at the police called in to quell the disturbances. The government responded by initiating an anticorruption campaign (some show trials of corrupt high level officials) and a slowdown in investment.

If these problems grow, the pendulum could swing to those party cadres who advocate the return of controls and the strengthening of administration and technological innovation in the state industries. That, too, would require cooperation with the outside world, to input the latest technological advances and maintain the capital infusion provided by the development within the coastal provinces. So much power has now shifted to municipalities and provinces, it is probably already impossible for central officials to regain the economic control they once enjoyed. Based on purchasing power parity (what goods earnings will buy within the country) the International Monetary Fund now classes China's economy the third largest in the world, behind only the United States and Japan. Whether controls continue to loosen or once again tighten, mainland development will remain closely allied with cadres and state industries, and outside investment and trade will continue.

State industries also produce arms for export.[44] Those exports, too, require doors open to the world.

Above all, further development depends on increased electrical power. Current growth has demanded a remarkable increase in electrical output, which grew by 57 percent between 1986 and 1990 alone.[45] Still, the capacity falls far behind what is needed to keep up growth at the present pace. Many regions have had to hold back air conditioner sales due to inadequate generating capacity; factories are forced to shut down up to three days a week, and offices are without lighting. Generating equipment operates nearly twice as many hours a year as is considered optimal. Even if Guangdong meets its present goals for increasing generating capacity, it will only produce 0.2 kilowatts of electricity per capita by 1995, as opposed to Hong Kong's present 1 kilowatt.[46] Interior provinces are far behind that. The massive, environmentally controversial Three Gorges Project to tame the Yangtze River, now approved and in early phases of construction, is only projected to produce 17,000 megawatts—a third of the 1986–1990 growth in capacity. Planned nuclear facilities will create even less.

Most new generating capacity must be fueled by coal. China has abundant bituminous coal in the north, but water is lacking for cooling electrical plants, and new roads and railroads are needed to transport the coal to other regions. The abundant, soft, high-sulfur coal found toward the west and east produces intense air pollution. Because the decentralization has reduced the central government's revenues, most new capacity must be created by provincial governments and state-owned factories. The provinces with the coal are distant from the coastal enclaves experiencing the greatest growth; they depend for income on the very state industries that are losing money. Most of China's technical capacity in this field is of 1970s vintage. All this creates the need for a strong infusion of foreign capital, while retaining the need for considerable low-wage, unskilled labor.

The Himalayas and surrounding ranges contain enormous water resources capable of generating vast amounts of hydroelectric power, but the costs of producing and transmitting it to the more populous regions are enormous. China must have financial and technical assistance from the outside world to construct these facilities. Foreign consortiums are already providing much such assistance to the coastal areas. To extend their operations inland, they need assurance of freedom from crippling bureaucratic interference and of recovering their investment.

Conclusion

Chinese intellectuals have an aphorism to describe its current political economy: "loosening up on the outside, clamping down on the inside."[47] While production by foreign joint ventures climbs, political restrictions on China's citizenry tighten. Applications to study abroad are harder to obtain. Press censorship is alternatively relaxed and rigid.[48] Even workers at cooperative and private businesses are being drawn into the government-dominated union federation, so as to control strikes and resistance to measures aimed at eliminating redundant employees and increasing production and to keep smaller businesses under the same restrictions as state enterprises.

Cadres include people with little education. The opening of university education to sons and daughters of prominent peasants and of workers has created intellectuals who, unlike peers from better-connected families, will have little chance to rise into prominent positions. Most of the new batch of students seek careers in business rather than bureaucracy. Yet the most choice business opportunities are open only to those who are well-connected politically. Some of these intellectuals correctly sense that they have little chance to advance in this system unless it loosens, rather than further tightens, its political grip. They are socially isolated from peasants and workers, without (as in past centuries) having inherently greater power than those groups. The Song dynasty witnessed the simultaneous flowering of commerce and artistic and intellectual expression. Today's officialdom, comprised both of educated and uneducated cadres, is also overseeing a flowering of commerce and artistic expression; it is being more cautious about allowing freedom of speech. But intellectuals from less-well-connected families benefit from little of this. They are in the ironic position of being lower on the social scale than merchants. This irony is brought home to them every day by their awareness that many peasants, street vendors, people pedaling bicycle carts, and even bicycle repairmen—taking advantage of their right to buy and sell small items—earn many times more and often live in better housing than a university graduate assigned to a government job and apartment. Meanwhile, even those intellectuals who are part of officialdom have found that factionalism among themselves prevents the ministry of culture from maintaining any consistent policy on artistic or intellectual expression; this month's approved fare may be banned next month. And the new graduates finding career opportunities in business can find themselves last hired, first fired when reins are once again placed on economic growth.

Between 1989 and 1991, China's citizens (responding to uncertainty in much the same way as Americans during a period of recession and lowered consumer confidence) found a nonpolitical way to resist government initiatives: they slowed their spending on goods produced by the state-run factories and increased their savings.[49] That had the beneficial effect of slowing the inflation that had been heating up too rapidly in prior months. The resultant losses by those industries induced government to declare a year of emphasis on quality, highlighted by daily journalistic investigative reports of shoddy goods and poor services to consumers. Electronics manufacturers set up a nationwide network of maintenance centers, and firms concentrated on improving product quality. By 1992, sales of consumer goods once again boomed, with rural dwellers increasingly joining the market as well. Brand name products by foreign joint ventures have high favor with consumers.[50] The decade of the nineties will increasingly place state enterprises into competition with joint ventures and cooperatives. As that improves public access to consumer goods, the results may again prove ironic. So long as consumerism can flourish without political reform, the access to capitalism may reduce the impetus for such reform rather than increase it.[51] If unemployment rises above its present official 3 percent rate (with unofficial estimates running over 15 percent) at the same time prosperity is growing among the employed, those with work and benefits may acquiesce in suppressing the liberties of the latter to keep them politically quiet. If, on the other hand, inflation reduces buying power for the new goods, the public may condone efforts by conservative cadres to slow reforms so as to keep prices in line and return a greater measure of social security through subsidies. In either case, political re- ⌋ form will be set back.

The children of Communist China's founding fathers are now middle aged, often educated abroad, and well placed to move into prominent positions in the Politburo and Central Committee. Conservatives from that generation of octogenarians have determinedly blocked the elevation of reformers to positions of party leadership; pressured to do so, they are more inclined to allow in members of the leading families, which have often intermarried. In 1992, Deng Xiaoping succeeded in adding the Party secretaries of Guangdong, Tianjin, and Shanghai, and at least seven other reform-minded individuals to the now twenty-member Politburo.[52] About half the 189-member Central Committee was replaced, mostly with technocrats. Many of these new members are from or have connections with those leading families. Deng's successor is likely to come from within these circles. Whether that person has Qing tendencies to withdraw from the world or Song tendencies to embrace what can be safely absorbed from outside, he will be balancing the need to keep inflation and unemployment under control against the desire to increase consumption.[53]

All the families in this ruling circle have personally profited from the reforms, which have also helped bestow the "Mandate of Heaven" on these leaders by providing peace and prosperity. The first of these policy initiatives (extending a better business climate into all of China) is more likely to appeal to those cadres with a strong yen for reform, while those most wedded to Mao Zedong's egalitarian communism may feel more comfortable with the third set of initiatives (revolving around regional cadres and state industries).

Yet all three of these initiatives have their own dialectic that is unlikely to stop; continuance of peace and prosperity depends on interaction among them. Unrestricted growth would endanger that interaction as much as withdrawal from world trade. Unless officials, merchants, and the populace all benefit, China's social peace has always been hard to maintain. China's next leader is likely to try to continue that balance, which depends both on holding together centralized rule and bringing in wealth from abroad. Singapore, Hong Kong, Taiwan, and South Korea, like the Song dynasty before them, have experience at that from which the new leader is likely to draw. They have combined market reforms with tight control over politics. But China's political culture and economic pressures are likely to cause it to lag behind the "little dragons" in extending either economic or political freedom. That means capitalists can continue to site joint venture production facilities there and sell single units of some consumer goods to its large populace (one television set x 300 million families = a lot of sets). Yet China's capacity to absorb investment and provide markets will remain limited by an imperative to exert political control over infrastructure, technology, and marketing. Free market capitalism must learn to live with that. Then the frustrations expressed by one of the biggest financiers of power projects along the coast will at least become more understandable and at best (as some additional legal and monetary reforms emerge) more manageable:

> The biggest problem is that you've always got to get 29 different committees to put their chop on every project. Then you get them sticking their noses in all the time. You've just got to tell them to go to hell, or you never get anything done.[54]

These chops are more than bureaucratic rubber stamps. We can view them, like the vouchers of the Song dynasty, as "big character posters" certifying the Confucian nexus among emperors, scholar-officials, and merchants that underlies China's political economy—a centralized system of ranking, privileges, control, and material rewards. This nexus, with the strength of millennia behind it, protects China's social and economic structure from outside disruption.

China is not on the road to unrestricted free-market capitalism. Neither is it becoming a dependent Third World country. It continues to largely feed its own people. It is not selling land or natural resources to private investors. Its farmland remains in the hands of the tiller. Its mines and factories stay under the control of its own leaders. Its overall balance of trade is favorable to itself. China's government still assures its citizens food, clothing, shelter, and basic social services. Its political economy resists becoming a supplier of raw materials and manufactured goods to the rest of the world at the cost of its own social integration and well-being, even if that slows growth. And, even with that, its economy is growing faster than any other on Earth.

China is not embracing Western democracy. But the Mandate of Heaven—with its imperative to provide peace, good crops, and social harmony before thinking about commercial gain—will give it incentive to abandon communist experiments that hamper these goals, retain those that aid them, and keep capitalist experiments in line with them. China's leaders know they can ignore this imperative only at the risk of losing the Mandate of Heaven. If that were to happen, a new White Lotus or Taiping rebellion could sweep them from power. That is China's democratic approach.

Notes

1. Donald J. Munro, *The Concept of Man in Early China* (Stanford: Stanford University Press, 1968) and Richard H. Solomon, *Mao's Revolution and the Chinese*

Political Culture, Parts 1 & 2 (Berkeley: University of California Press, 1971), discuss this heritage.

2. For an introduction to all this, see Etienne Balazs, *Chinese Civilization and Bureaucracy* (New Haven, Conn.: Yale University Press, 1967).

3. For an overview of the Song dynasty, see Robert P. Hymes and Conrad Schirokeuer, eds., *Ordering the World: Approaches to State and Society in Sung Dynasty China* (Berkeley: University of California Press, 1993).

4. See Brian E. McKnight, *Law and Order in Sung China* (Cambridge, Mass.: Cambridge University Press, 1992); idem., *Village and Bureaucracy in Southern Sung China* (Chicago: University of Chicago Press, 1971); E. A. Kracke, Jr., *Civil Service in Early Sung China, 960–1067* (Cambridge, Mass.: Harvard University Press, 1959).

5. Lawrence J. C. Ma, *Commercial Development and Urban Change in Sung China (960–1279),* Michigan Geographical Publication No. 6 (Ann Arbor: University of Michigan Department of Geography, 1971) offers an overview of these commercial activities.

6. See Jennifer W. Jay, *A Change in Dynasties: Loyalism in Thirteenth-Century China* (Bellingham, Wash.: Western Washington, 1991).

7. See Edgar Snow, *Red Star Over China* (New York: Random House, 1938); A. Doak Barnett, *China on the Eve of Communist Takeover* (New York: Praeger, 1963); Chalmers Johnson, *Peasant Nationalism and Communist Power* (Stanford: University of California Press, 1962); Benjamin I. Schwartz, *Chinese Communism and the Rise of Mao* (Cambridge, Mass.: Harvard University Press, 1964).

8. See Alexander Eckstein, *China's Economic Revolution* (Cambridge, Mass.: Cambridge University Press, 1977); Doak Barnett, *Communist China: The Early Years, 1949–55* (New York: Praeger, 1964); Richard C. Walker, *China Under Communism: The First Five Years* (New Haven, Conn.: Yale University Press, 1955).

9. Anita Chan, Richard Madsen, and Jonathan Unger, *Chen Village: The Recent History of a Peasant Communist in Mao's China* (Berkeley: University of California Press, 1984) give a fascinating account of how one village fared during this period into the Cultural Revolution.

10. On this subject, see Stanley Karnow, *Mao and China: From Revolution to Revolution* (New York: Viking, 1972); Ezra Fogel, *Canton Under Communism* (Cambridge, Mass.: Harvard University Press, 1969); Lee Hong Yung, *The Politics of the Chinese Cultural Revolution* (Berkeley: University of California Press, 1978); Roderick MacFarquhar, *The Origins of the Cultural Revolution,* 2 vols. (New York: Columbia University Press, 1974 and 1983).

11. For overviews of the reforms, see John Woodruff, *China in Search of its Future: Years of Great Reform* (Seattle: University of Washington Press, 1989).

12. See Simon Powell, *Agricultural Reform in China: From Communes to Commodity Economy 1978–1990* (Manchester, U.K.: Manchester University Press, 1992); Xu Guohua and L. J. Peel, *The Agriculture of China* (New York: Oxford University Press, 1991).

13. In 1991, the nineteen million rural cooperatives, employing ninety-six million people, accounted for 40 percent of industrial employment and a quarter of industrial output and exports. "Down Off the Farm," *The Economist,* November 28, 1992.

14. In 1987, 64 in 100 urban households had a black and white TV, and 34 a color TV, 75 in 100 had a sewing machine, 103 an electric fan, 20 a refrigerator,

and 57 a tape recorder. China had 293 million bicycles, up from 75 million in 1978. *China Statistical Abstract 1990.* Those numbers have been growing rapidly. The 30 percent of China's population living in the city, who own 60 percent of the personal money deposited in banks, are especially well positioned to make these purchases. "Soaking the Rich," *The Economist,* November 28, 1992.

15. On corruption, see Alan P. L. Liu, "The Politics of Corruption in the People's Republic of China," *American Political Science Review* 77 (1983): pp. 602–623; James T. Myers, "China: Modernization and 'Unhealthy' Tendencies," *Comparative Politics* 21 (1989): pp. 193–213; Jean C. Oi, "Market Reforms and Corruption in Rural China," *Studies in Comparative Communism* 22 (summer-autumn 1989): pp. 221–233; Michael Johnston, "The Political Consequences of Corruption: A Reassessment," *Comparative Politics* 18, vol. 4 (July 1986): pp. 459–477.

16. The *People's Daily* estimates that ten to fifteen million of the eighty million workers in state firms are not needed. Sheila Tefft, "China's Workers Seek Anchors in Swiftly Changing Economy," *Christian Science Monitor,* August 20, 1993.

17. In 1992, this represented 40–50 percent as much as was invested in the United States, and 15 percent of the total investment in poorer countries. "Sino Xenophobia," *The Economist,* November 28, 1992; "Yuan a Debased Currency?" *The Economist,* April 24, 1993.

18. On China's exports, see Wang Hong, *China's Exports Since 1979* (New York: St. Martins, 1992); Nicholas R. Lardy, *Foreign Trade and Economic Reform in China* (Cambridge, Mass.: Cambridge University Press, 1992).

19. Gilbert Rozman, ed., *The Modernization of China* (New York: Macmillan Free Press, 1981), p. 328.

20. Idem., p. 327; "Still the Middle Kingdom," *The Economist,* December 12, 1992.

21. See Tung Fu-jeng, *Industrialization and China's Rural Modernization* (New York: St. Martins, 1992).

22. Lena H. Sun, "Widespread Graft Prompts Chinese Anti-Corruption Drive," *Washington Post,* September 7, 1993.

23. A karaoke club provides music, written lyrics on television screens, and microphones. Members of the audience sing along. Guangzhou was less active in the 1989 demonstrations than Shanghai and many other cities. While karaoke is a craze in cities throughout China, Guangzhou night life is among the most active. Expressions of this type do not necessarily translate into political activism.

24. The five-star Palace Hotel and a number of other hotels in Beijing are also owned by the PLA. Norinco, an arms-dealing outfit connected with China's defense industry, owns Guangzhou's Cathay Hotel. Army-owned enterprises produce over U.S.$4 billion worth of civilian products, including over 60 percent of China's motorcycles. "The Army That Makes Money," *The Economist,* October 5, 1991. The army earns about $6 billion each year from its investments in enterprises. It spends much of this on perks for officers. "Asia's Arms Race," *The Economist,* February 20, 1993.

25. See Andrew Watson, ed., *Economic Reform and Social Change in China* (London: Routledge, 1992); *State and Society in China: the Consequences of Reform* (Boulder: Westview Press, 1992).

26. The Sunday following the midnight crackdown at Tiananmen Square, we rose for an early morning bus trip to the village where Lu Xun, the noted novelist, was born. People were on Sunday strolls. We chatted with patrons of a noodle shop and our boatman at the grotto there. Everything appeared normal, and no one in

our party had an inkling that events had occurred in Beijing until our return to Hangzhou that night. On Monday morning in Hangzhou we found street dividers were ripped out and buses abandoned, cutting off motor traffic to the center for three days. But most students left campus almost immediately. Rumors abounded that Shanghai was immobilized by demonstrations. My wife and I took a ferry to Suzhou and discovered that we could take a train home through Shanghai; the railway station there was entirely tranquil. But we were met by disbelief when we reported this in Hangzhou to people still convinced that rail traffic was cut off. The following week we stayed at a university hostel in Shanghai, attended a dance with the ambiance of a 1950's prom in America, and I gave a lecture to an attentive class of urban commuter students. The Bund was filled with strollers, and older people doing their tai-chi exercises. There was no sign that this had been the site of massive demonstrations during the prior two months. Outward appearances can easily be deceiving in China. And opposition political organization is always highly tenuous.

27. See Edmund H. Worthy, "Regional Control of the Southern Sung Salt Administration," in John Winthrop Haeger, ed., *Crisis and Prosperity in Sung China* (Tucson, Ariz.: University of Arizona Press, 1975), pp. 101–142.

28. For discussion of this, see Lin Nan, *The Struggle for Tiananmen: Anatomy of the 1989 Mass Movement* (New York: Praeger, 1992); Shen Tong, *Almost a Revolution* (New York: Harper Perennial, 1991); Roger V. Des Forges, Luo Ning, Wu Yen-bo, *Chinese Democracy and the Crisis of 1989: Chinese and American Reflections* (Albany: State University of New York Press, 1993); Rai Shirin, *Resistance and Reaction: University Politics in Post-Mao China* (New York: St. Martins, 1992); Jeffrey N. Wasserstrom and Elizabeth J. Perry, *Popular Protest and Political Culture in Modern China* (Boulder: Westview Press, 1992); Thomas Jordan, *Chaos Under Heaven: The Shocking Story Behind China's Search for Democracy* (Secaucus, N.J.: Carol Publishing Group, 1991).

29. "One of the most incredible aspects of the Peking insurrection is that despite the rapid expansion of the movement, at times involving more than a million people—far beyond the capacity of the initial leadership to effectively discipline— at no time did the demonstrators openly oppose or call for the overthrow of the communist party." Robert Delfs, "The People's Republic," *Far Eastern Economic Review*, June 1, 1989. Posters on the campuses of Qinghua and Beijing universities on March 1–3 called for dismantling the Communist Party, and a shout of "Down with the Communist Party" on April 18 caused police to force demonstrators onto buses to return to campus. Frederic E. Wakeman Jr., *Items*, Social Science Research Council 43, vol. 3 (September 1989): p. 59. Subsequent to that, such attacks ceased. In Hangzhou, where I observed the marches on a daily basis, banners and "big character posters" did not attack Deng or the Party's domination. Jonathan Unger, ed., *The Pro-Democracy Protests in China: Reports from the Provinces* (Armonk, New York: M. E. Sharpe, 1991) reports on demonstrations and slogans on banners throughout China. With the exception of "Hang Deng Xiaoping" cartoons (p. 194) and the breaking of glasses (p. 189) in Shanghai, none of the articles report on slogans denouncing Deng Xiaoping or the Communist Party. My own students in Hangzhou had heard about the breaking of glasses (*xiaoping* means small glass) and were concerned that it was too disrespectful. For more on that, see Robert E. Gamer, "From Zig-Zag to Confrontation at Tiananmen: Tradition and Politics in China," *University Field Staff Reports* 10 (November 1989).

30. For more on that debate, see Robert E. Gamer, "Can China Modernize Without a Fight for Democracy? Samuel P. Huntington and the 'Neo-Authoritarian'

Debate," *Crossroads: A Socio-Political Journal,* (Jerusalem and Moscow), 33 (1994), and Gamer, "From Zig-Zag to Confrontation."

31. For present legal guarantees, see Zhang Danian, Milton R. Larson, and Dong Shizhong, *Trade and Investment Opportunities in China: The Current Commercial and Legal Framework* (New York: Quorum Books, 1992); Pitman B. Potter, *The Economic Contract Law of China: Legitimation and Contract Autonomy in the PRC* (Seattle: University of Washington Press, 1992); Robert C. Goodwin Jr., "The Evolving Legal Framework," *The China Business Review* (May–June 1983), pp. 42–44.

32. For further extrapolation on how these American and Chinese arguments relate, see Robert E. Gamer, "Helping History Find Its Way: Liberalization in China," *Crossroads: A Socio-Political Journal,* (Jerusalem and Moscow), 32 (1991).

33. For more on this, see Robert E. Gamer, "East Europe's Search for Freedom Without Disruption: Avoiding the China Syndrome," *University Field Staff Reports* 3 (October, 1990).

34. Some members of the Central Advisory Commission, the council of elders, denounced the special economic zones as "capitalist beachheads." Lincoln Kaye, "Leaning to the Right," *Far Eastern Economic Review*, March 26, 1992. Most leaders younger than eighty probably remain more open to these experiments.

35. See *China's Coastal Cities: Catalysts for Modernization* (Honolulu: University of Hawaii Press, 1992).

36. Neither operates under comprehensive securities regulations to protect investors or indicate how companies are to be formed; many Chinese investors have lost money buying these stocks. The first three offerings to foreigners, in 1992, immediately raised U.S.$140 million from foreign investors eager for a way to enter the China market; they were underwritten by foreign banks. Jonathan Friedland, "Bulls in a China Shop," *Far Eastern Economic Review*, April 9, 1992. See also Yi Gang, *Money, Banking, and Financial Markets in China* (Boulder: Westview Press, 1993); Xia Mei, Lin Jian Hai, and Phillip D. Grub, *The Reemerging Securities Market in China* (New York: Quorum Books, 1992).

37. "A Great Leap Forward," *The Economist*, October 5, 1991. After Deng Xiaoping's endorsement of Guangdong's reforms in January of 1991, officials there said "It's much easier to talk about high growth now" and indicated that the whole province had 1991 industrial growth above 27 percent, with 35 percent expected in 1992. Carl Goldstein, "Under Licence," *Far Eastern Economic Review*, April 23, 1992.

38. "China Records 27 Percent Industrial Growth in First Five Months," *The Straits Times*, June 11, 1993.

39. For an interesting case study of a joint venture, see William H. Newman, *Birth of a Successful Joint Venture* (Lanham, Md.: University Press of America, 1992). Phillip Donald Grub and Jian Hai Lin, *Foreign Direct Investment in China* (New York: Quorum Books, 1991) provide a good overview of joint ventures.

40. There seems to be considerable evidence that when the treaty was signed in 1985 to return Hong Kong to China in 1997, a secret deal was struck to give China's leaders some control over political reform in Hong Kong prior to 1997. No Hong Kong newspapers have investigated or published the story. John Walden, "Knowledge Is Power," *Far Eastern Economic Review*, April 9, 1992. For an overview, see Sung Yun Wing, *The China Hong Kong Connection: The Key to China's Open Door Policy* (New York: Cambridge University Press, 1991).

41. Jean C. Oi, *State and Peasant in Contemporary China: The Political Economy of Village Government* (Berkeley: University of California Press, 1989), p. 232.

42. In 1991, the government spent U.S.$9.3 billion on subsidizing the probably 70 percent of state industries that were losing money (official government figures say 40 percent in 1991, 30 percent in 1990), and U.S.$6.8 billion on food, housing, and other subsidies paid to private citizens, resulting in a budget deficit of U.S.$3.9 billion, according to China's finance minister. These two expenditures used up 24 percent of government revenue. "Catching the Tide," *The Economist,* March 28, 1992.

43. While 1991 wages had risen to four times their 1979 level, they still do not always keep up with inflation; new austerity programs to cut costs of production could increase that disparity. For an introduction to these problems see Michael Korzec, *Labour and the Failure of Reform in China* (New York: St. Martins, 1992).

44. In 1989, China concluded agreements for U.S.$1.8 billion in arms sales; in 1990, U.S. $2.5 billion. "Gun Diplomacy," *The Economist,* October 26, 1991.

45. From 87,000 megawatts to 138,000 megawatts. Carl Goldstein, "China's Generation Gap," *Far Eastern Economic Review,* June 11, 1992.

46. Carl Goldstein, "Southern Acumen," *Far Eastern Economic Review,* June 11, 1992.

47. John Woodruff's *China in Search of Its Future: Reform vs. Repression, 1982–1989* (Secaucus, N.J.: Carle Publication Group, 1990) deals with this theme.

48. To appease the Clinton administration, which advocates human rights in China, the government released some leaders of the 1989 demonstrations and cut back on day-to-day supervision of newspapers. At the same time, it increased threats of lawsuits for articles it deems improper and stripped some 1989 dissidents of their citizenship.

49. Lin Bih-jaw et al., eds., *The Aftermath of the 1989 Tiananmen Crisis in Mainland China* (Boulder: Westview Press, 1992) discusses this period.

50. Philips, the Dutch electronics firm, has opened nine joint-venture manufacturing plants in China and expects close to $1.5 billion in sales of television sets, television tubes for television sets made in state factories, hair driers, irons, and radios within China by 1996. The Japanese firms of Hitachi, Matsushita, and Toshiba also manufacture television tubes for the Chinese market. Mark Clifford, "The Big Picture," *Far Eastern Economic Review,* September 24, 1992.

51. The *Economic Daily* wrote in November 1991, quoting from Deng Xiaoping: "So long as economic work is done well and we have an adequate material base, all issues will be settled." Reported in "China Swings Back to Reform," *The Economist,* February 1, 1992.

52. The seven-member Standing Committee of the Politburo, which has the highest power, remains evenly balanced between reformers and conservatives.

53. For a very interesting personal account of where China's reforms are leading see Gu Zhibin, *China Beyond Deng: Reform in the PRC* (Jefferson, N.C.: McFarland and Co., 1991). Also see David S. G. Goodman and Gerald Segal, eds., *China in the Nineties: Crisis Management and Beyond* (Oxford: Clarendon Press, 1991); Susan L. Shirk, *The Political Logic of Economic Reform in China* (Berkeley: University of California Press, 1993).

54. Goldstein, "Southern Acumen," *Far Eastern Economic Review,* June 11, 1992.

Part 2

ISSUES IN
POLITICAL ECONOMIES OF
THE THIRD WORLD

8

◆

Foreign Aid in the 1990s:
The New Realities

John W. Newark

The Changing World of Development Assistance

Major changes have recently taken place in the organization and delivery of foreign aid, or official development assistance (ODA).[1] These changes are related, in one way or another, to the debt crisis of the 1980s and to the winding down of the Cold War and superpower rivalry.

In the 1980s, the World Bank, USAID, and the other major aid agencies began to look not just at costs and benefits of specific projects, and perhaps the political orientation of recipient governments, but at whether or not a recipient nation was reducing the role of the state in promoting economic development and relying, to a much greater extent than had hitherto been the case, on unfettered market forces to determine both the pace and the pattern of economic development. This new "conditionality" represents a fairly dramatic break with the past.

The origins of this new conditionality lie in the development experience of the 1970s and 1980s. The 1980s are widely regarded as a "lost decade" for most of the developing countries in Latin America and Africa. Between 1980 and 1989 real GDP increased by only 1.6 percent per annum in Latin America, and by only 1.0 percent per annum in sub-Saharan Africa. Over the same period Latin America's population was growing by 2.2 percent a year, and in Africa the figure was closer to 3 percent per year.[2] Rising unemployment, falling real wages, and often drastic reductions in government expenditures on health care, education, and food subsidies contributed to an intensification of poverty.

In Asia, on the other hand, particularly in the East Asian economies of Taiwan, South Korea, Singapore, Hong Kong, Thailand, and Malaysia, economic growth was strong. Wages were rising, investment levels were high, and most of these countries managed to avoid the debt crisis that was debilitating so many African and Latin American economies.

The economic failures of the 1980s are closely related to the debt crisis that affected so many Latin American and African countries. The debt crisis, which emerged with much fanfare in 1982 when Mexico declared that it was unable to meet its debt service obligations, was an announcement that the economic structures in the highly indebted countries, which had been created with the important assistance of external borrowing, were essentially unviable.

In principle, a nation that borrows abroad does so on the assumption that borrowed resources will be invested wisely, whether in education, road building, or other activities. Productive capacity will be increased, and investments will produce returns that will more than allow the interest on the loan to be paid. As nation after nation declared itself unable to meet its debt service obligations, the donor community raised a fundamental question: What had gone wrong? Why had so much investment, in so many countries, failed to earn a sufficient return to allow the debt to be serviced on time?

The development experience of the late 1970s and early 1980s has led to what has been called a "quiet revolution" in development thinking.[3] This revolution has been led by the World Bank, USAID, and the major Western aid agencies, and its philosophy can be observed both in policy statements and lending practices.[4] Within the major aid agencies it is not an exaggeration to state that a new consensus had emerged by the early 1980s, both as to the reasons for recent development failures and, more importantly, as to what should be done to revive development prospects.

Development plans throughout Latin America and Africa prior to the early 1980s had been based on the assumption of widespread market failure. Market forces (and the legacy of colonialism), it was argued, had produced an international economic structure that left these regions as providers of raw materials to the industrial nations. This international division of economic activity had condemned Third World regions to underdevelopment and persistent poverty. During the 1950s, 1960s, and 1970s, it was widely assumed that the state in developing countries must take a directing role in the raising and allocating of capital, operating productive enterprises in key sectors, and extensively regulating the private sector to ensure that development objectives were met.[5]

This new orthodoxy focused on the argument that many developing countries have asked more of government than government could reasonably be expected to deliver. "Government-led" development, it was argued, (for example, see Krueger, 1986[6]) too often frustrated the working of market forces; instead of competitive markets allocating resources efficiently, the state was doing so inefficiently, either directly or indirectly with a host of trade and exchange controls, price controls and subsidies, and other regulatory practices. Government enterprises were generally highly inefficient, required massive subsidies, were seriously overstaffed, and paid wage rates well in excess of market rates.

Government was seldom the benign seeker of the general public good. Too often it tended to promote the particular interests of those who controlled the levers of power, be they generals, members of a wealthy urban elite, or an ethnic group. The myriad of economic controls possessed by government gave those whose hands were at the levers of the controls unprecedented opportunity to increase their own wealth. Corruption within state organizations was often a key contributing factor to poor economic performance in many countries.[7]

This new orthodoxy promotes a development strategy that, relative to previous development fashions, foresees a drastically reduced role for the state in promoting economic development. Sweeping economic liberalization and privatization are viewed as central initiatives that are prerequisites to renewing growth prospects.[8] Unfettered market forces are to become the main forums in which prices are determined and resources allocated. Investment levels and allocations are to be made primarily by private sector firms responding to market opportunities. Government enterprises are to be eliminated or substantially scaled back, subsidies eliminated, and, most importantly, trade and capital flows are to be deregulated.

The collapse of Soviet communism and the decline in superpower rivalries is also having a major impact on development assistance. McGuire and Ruttan[9] and Griffin[10] have noted that USAID often provided development assistance to notoriously corrupt regimes as long as those regimes were sufficiently anticommunist. Such aid frequently only lined the pockets of those in power. Numerous regimes played on this rivalry to gain access to Western aid coffers. But as Smith Hempstone, U.S. ambassador to Kenya, has recently observed, "With the Soviets out of the game, we can no longer be blackmailed into giving money to projects which we know are not beneficial to the countries concerned."[11]

The major donor agencies of the OECD (Organization for Economic Cooperation and Development) have recently confirmed that they intend to give higher priority to supporting the efforts of developing countries that have demonstrated a strong commitment to democracy, participatory development, good and efficient governance, and a respect for human rights. The 1991 annual High Level Meeting of DAC (Development Assistance Committee) members produced a communique to this effect.[12] It is too early for a definitive assessment of this potentially most important initiative.

A decade ago, such pronouncements would surely not have been made, or they would widely have been condemned as acts of political interference and imperialism on the part of the developed nations. That there has been no great outcry, or as yet, wavering from this position, is an indication of how things have changed.

Early indications suggest that efforts in these new directions may be significant. Haiti, Kenya, Thailand, Peru, Malawi, Zaire, and Indonesia, to name only a few, had assistance programs suspended or terminated in 1991 as a result of human rights or corruption problems.[13]

There are hopes[14] that the end of the Cold War will lead to a "peace dividend" for development assistance, although there is no evidence as yet of such a dividend emerging. On the other hand, there are skeptics such as Keith Griffin[15] who expect major reductions in development assistance now that superpower conflict is in decline.

The relationship between the developing world and the donor nations is undergoing rapid and significant change. The debt crisis has given the developed nations unprecedented leverage over the indebted nations of the south. In sub-Saharan Africa, for example, development assistance now accounts for over 82 percent of all net resource flows to the region. As the 1992 OECD report of the Development Assistance Committee, *Development Co-Operation,* notes, sub-Saharan Africa has developed "a near total dependence on official aid flows to meet its basic foreign exchange needs, most domestic investment requirements, and, increasingly, recurrent costs" (p. 5). As the Cold War no longer inhibits the donor community from actively promoting its political and economic agendas, many developing nations, effectively trapped by their external debt environment, have accepted that they must march to the new tunes.

Trends in Aid Flows

Total Official Development Assistance (ODA)[16] from the OECD countries in 1991 amounted to (U.S.) $54 billion. As Table 8.1 indicates, real ODA has been increasing steadily, if not dramatically, over the past two decades. Over the 1980s real ODA expenditures increased by 25 percent.[17] After falling slightly in 1990, real ODA expenditures increased by 3.3 percent in 1991.

The United States was the largest single donor in 1991, with aid expenditures amounting to $10.8 billion. Japanese aid, which amounted to $9.98 billion, has been increasing rapidly (7 percent per annum in real terms) in recent years, and the Japanese overtook the United States as the world's largest donor in 1992.

Table 8.1   Net ODA Flows, 1970–1991 (net disbursements at 1990 prices and exchange rates in billions of dollars)

Year	ODA flows
1970	34.7
1975	36.9
1980	43.1
1988	52.9
1989	53.7
1990	52.7
1991	54.0

Source: OECD/DAC, *Development Co-Operation, 1992* (Paris: OECD, 1992) Table 1V-1.

Development assistance effort is usually measured by a donor's ODA/GNP ratio. Despite some significant changes in individual donor's contributions, aggregate ODA/GNP has remained remarkably stable between 1970 and 1991 at 0.33 percent. There is, however, substantial variation around that average figure. At one end of the spectrum, with ODA/GNP ratios in excess of 0.75 percent, are Denmark, Finland, the Netherlands, Norway, and Sweden. France, Canada, Germany, and Belgium record ratios between 0.4 percent and 0.74 percent, and Australia, Austria, Italy, Japan, Portugal, Switzerland, and the United Kingdom report ratios between 0.25 percent and 0.39 percent. At the bottom of the list are Spain (0.23 percent) the United States (0.20 percent), and Ireland (0.19 percent).

The United States, the United Kingdom, Australia, and France all experienced constant or declining aid expenditures in the 1980s (and falling ODA/GNP ratios), but this was more than compensated by substantial expenditure increases in Japan and the Nordic countries.

Since 1980, renewed efforts were made to concentrate more development expenditures in the poorer of the developing countries. Some success was achieved; over 85 percent of the increase in ODA in the past decade was spent in nations defined by the World Bank as being "least developed."[18]

The share of development assistance received by sub-Saharan Africa has increased, and the share received by South Asia decreased since 1970. By 1991, sub-Saharan Africa was receiving 32 percent of development assistance expenditures, the Middle East and North Africa 28 percent, South Asia 12 percent, Latin America and the Caribbean 11 percent, and other Asia 17 percent. The large share accounted for by the Middle East and North Africa is largely due to USAID's large bilateral programs in Israel and Egypt.

There is little evidence to date that the volume of aid is likely to change dramatically in the near future. Japan, France, Denmark, Norway,

Sweden, and the Netherlands have made relatively firm commitments to increase development assistance.[19] The United States remains a major question mark; if the new Democratic leadership is able to resist calls to further reduce the American aid effort, then it is likely that modest increases may be realized over the next few years.

Foreign Aid: A Historical Perspective

The provision of ongoing economic assistance to promote development in the Third World is a relatively recent phenomenon. Indeed, it may be argued that the first major "aid" program was the Marshall Plan, under which the United States provided over $60 billion (1987 dollars) to aid in the reconstruction of war-torn Europe after 1945. Under the Marshall Plan, capital, food aid, technical skills, and other assistance were provided on generous terms. The war-ravaged European economies rebuilt their infrastructure in a remarkably short time, and the Marshall Plan was credited with being an important element in the post-war economic boom.

The primary post-war foreign policy objective of the United States was the containment of communism. The Marshall Plan (and subsequent U.S. aid efforts in the Third World) were, to a great extent, implemented in an effort to realize this objective. As the Cold War rivalry spread from Europe to the Third World, the United States and its Western allies initiated bilateral aid programs. By promoting pro-Western, capitalist economic development in the Third World, the donor nations could both make a contribution toward overcoming the poverty and stagnation that appeared widespread and, by doing so, make communism less attractive to Third World populations.

In the 1950s and 1960s, the donor community encouraged development strategies that emphasized formal economic plans and large-scale public sector investments, particularly to promote import-substituting industrialization. The state was to take a leading and directing role.[20]

Curiously, structural change was not viewed in the early 1950s as being critical to development, as it is now, but had a different meaning. There was less faith in the magic of the market; participation in world markets had been associated with economic stagnation, not growth. Market imperfections and rigidities appeared to be widespread, and very low incomes meant low savings, which in turn meant that the economy could not generate internally the levels of investment needed to make a break with existing economic structures that were only reproducing poverty and stagnation.

Walt Rostow[21] captured much of the early thinking within the donor community with his stages theory of economic growth. A stagnant economy needed a shock, which most likely required external intervention. Such an economy must manage to boost its savings rate from less than 5 percent of income (typical of a stagnating economy) to at least 10 percent. International capital markets were not directing sufficient volumes of capital to the less-developed world, and this suggested key roles for development assistance and government planning. The economic structures within the developing nations sought such capital; these structures had to be changed in order to stimulate the demand for capital. The dominant ideas of the day emphasized that development required a concerted, deliberate, and large-scale effort to break existing patterns of stagnation. These ideas included: "big push," "take-off," and "minimal critical effort," and all assumed a key role for an activist state in the promotion of economic development.

By most conventional measures, economic development accelerated rapidly in all developing regions between 1950 and 1975. Despite rapid population growth, real per capita income in all developing regions increased at an average annual rate of 3.4 percent over this period.[22] Life expectancy increased, and child and infant mortality rates declined substantially in all regions. Literacy rates more than doubled in Africa and Asia.[23]

Important lessons were being learned, and these helped to shape ideas within the donor agencies. Despite historically unprecedented improvements in most aggregate measures of economic development, closer examinations too frequently revealed that the very poor often had benefited only marginally from the economic development taking place.[24]

Robert McNamara, then chairman of the World Bank, shocked the bank's board of governors in 1972 when he told them that:

> Increases in national income—essential as they are—will not benefit the poor unless they reach the poor. They have not reached the poor to any significant degree in most developing countries in the past, and this in spite of historically unprecedented average rates of growth throughout the sixties.[25]

In the 1970s the donor agencies "dethroned" GNP as a development indicator. Direct assaults on poverty and inequality were now being emphasized. The World Bank was promoting a strategy of "redistribution with growth," and the International Labour Organisation was advocating a "basic needs" approach.[26] Aid philosophy was changing; aid lending was now to be targeted at the poor. Aid investments were aimed at raising the productivity of poor households, often by projects in the areas of health care, primary education, and the promotion of small-scale agriculture through integrated rural development projects. Highly capital-intensive industrialization efforts were now questioned, and "appropriate" technology, which in practice meant more labor-intensive methods, were being advocated.

In the United States, the Foreign Assistance Act of 1973, known as the Basic Human Needs Mandate, or New Directions, formally redirected U.S. development assistance efforts toward directly improving the circumstances of the poorest segments of the populations in the developing countries. Most OECD nations had made similar declarations by the mid-1970s.[27]

The Rise of Market Fundamentalism

The early 1980s witnessed neoconservative governments sweep to power in the United States, Great Britain, Canada, Germany, and elsewhere. The shared experience of stagflation and rising public sector deficits in the 1970s had everywhere shaken confidence in the ability of government to solve many of our persistent economic woes. These new regimes shared the view that governments had tried to accomplish far too much in the past and had taken on too many activities that were much more efficiently handled by competitive private markets.

This general thrust of greater reliance on market forces and reducing the role of the state in economic activity was quickly and strongly reflected in aid philosophies. In a remarkably candid telegram, then U.S. Secretary of State George Schultz identified the new aid objectives:

> Policy dialogue should be used to encourage LDCs [less developed countries] to follow free market principles for sustained economic growth and to move away from government intervention in the economy. . . . To the *maximum* extent practical, governments should rely on the market mechanism.[28]

After specifying a number of areas in which regulation should be minimized or eliminated, Schultz launched a broadside on the parastatals that are so prevalent in many LDCs:

> Parastatals are generally an inefficient way of doing business. They usually require subsidies and/or preferential treatment. . . . In most cases public sector firms should be privatized.[29]

Many neoclassical economists had never been comfortable with the highly interventionist thrusts of aid efforts in the previous decades. Their views increasingly came to dominate the thinking in the aid agencies and in the World Bank.[30] The World Bank began to take a leading role in coordinating aid donor efforts to make aid contributions conditional upon acceptance of the new wisdom emanating from Washington. The new consensus identified domestic policy failures within the developing countries as the overriding reason for poor economic performance.[31]

It was the debt crisis, however, that ensured that this new orthodoxy was to have a far greater influence on domestic policies within the LDCs than had earlier ideas that had been prominent within the aid agencies. The debt position of most African and Latin American nations in the 1980s forced them to seek external finance from the International Monetary Fund (IMF), the World Bank, and the donor community. The absence of any viable alternative to IMF and World Bank financing ensured that the indebted nations would respond positively to the new conditionality being imposed by the international financial institutions.

In the 1960s and 1970s the acquisition of external debt was encouraged by the international community. Most developing countries were growing rapidly but had low saving rates. External finance was needed to sustain the high growth rates. Developing countries tended to run deficits on the current account, as high growth strategies were usually import intensive. This was matched, however, by surpluses on the capital account, as foreign loans, investment, and development assistance helped to finance rapid growth. As long as export receipts continued to increase, problems in servicing the debt did not arise.

External borrowing is not without risk. The finance provided can accelerate growth, but it also creates debt service obligations, usually denominated in hard currencies. The two great oil shocks of 1973 and 1979, and the reaction of the international financial community, fundamentally altered the economic environment within which developing countries operated. The first oil shock greatly increased the import bill of oil-importing developing nations. In order to achieve external balance, a developing country could impose restrictive economic policies to depress incomes and imports, but this would greatly restrict economic growth. The other alternative, which was in fact adopted by most developing countries, was to attempt to increase external borrowing in order to sustain economic growth and pay for the increased borrowing out of future export earnings. Total external debt of all developing countries increased by 353 percent between 1975 and 1980.[32] The international banks served as financial "recyclers," as petrodollar surpluses were deposited in the international commercial banks and subsequently lent to developing countries. Economic growth continued to advance at a brisk pace, as did exports, and the ratio of debt service payments to exports for all developing countries actually declined slightly from 13.5 percent to 13.2 percent between these two years.[33]

This strategy began to unravel with the second oil price shock of 1979. By the late 1970s inflation had a strong grip on most industrial countries. The conservative governments of the West responded to this threat with highly restrictive monetary policies. Inflation was eventually wrung out of the industrialized economies, but not before interest rates were pushed to record highs, often approaching 20 percent. In 1981/82 these restrictive policies produced the most severe recession the industrialized world had witnessed since the 1930s.

The global recession in the early 1980s reduced the demand for exports from the developing nations. Commodity prices declined steeply; in sub-Saharan Africa the terms of trade deteriorated by over 30 percent between 1980 and 1987.[34] As export earnings fell, debt service obligations rose with skyrocketing interest rates. The current account balance for all developing countries deteriorated rapidly, from an annual deficit of $32 billion in 1978 to an annual deficit of $87 billion in 1982.[35]

This time, however, the developing nations as a whole were not able to produce surpluses on the capital account to finance the growing deficits on the current account. On the contrary, past surpluses disappeared and were replaced by mounting deficits on the capital account. The capital account balance of all developing countries declined from a $38 billion surplus in 1978 to a $35 billion deficit by 1984.[36] International bank lending collapsed after Mexico declared its inability to service its obligations on time. As external payments accounts began to deteriorate, developing countries also had to deal with massive capital flight, as investors sought to protect their wealth by shifting it to more stable economies and currencies. It has been estimated that approximately $200 billion fled the highly indebted countries between 1976 and 1985.[37] This amounts to over 50 percent of total borrowing by all developing countries over the same period.

Faced with this critical payments situation, indebted developing countries had few options. Continued borrowing was no longer an option. For most indebted nations the magnitude of the external account imbalance had increased dramatically, and neither foreign loans nor foreign investments were forthcoming in sufficient amounts. Structural adjustment, to restore equilibrium in the external accounts, would now have to become the top priority of the indebted developing countries.

Deficits on the external account that cannot be financed by increased capital inflows necessitate action to reduce imports and augment the capacity to export. At this level, there is little disagreement that some structural adjustment is needed. Indeed, the International Monetary Fund (IMF) was created in large part to provide short-term external finance in order to allow an orderly flow of essential imports to continue while domestic policies were adjusted to correct the payments disequilibrium.

By the mid-1980s almost all Latin American and African nations had been forced to seek IMF financing, and most had also entered into structural adjustment programs with the World Bank. The magnitude of the debt crisis, however, quickly made it clear that the resources of the IMF and the short-term loans offered (usually twelve to thirty-six months) were inadequate to meet the challenges faced by the highly indebted nations. The World Bank began to provide longer-term financial assistance, with its

Structural Adjustment Loans (SALs) and Sector Adjustment Loans (SECALs). Access to this essential source of finance was made conditional upon acceptance of a "Structural Adjustment Program" designed to restore equilibrium to the external accounts. In practice, the terms of the World Bank SALs were remarkably similar to those demanded by the International Monetary Fund.

Although there is some variety in the detail of the prescriptions offered by the World Bank, nearly all entail elements of the following:

1. A depreciation in the real exchange rate. This is to boost exports and reduce imports by making them more expensive.

2. Opening up the economy to international trade. Import licensing systems are to be dismantled, quantity restrictions on imports are to be substantially reduced or eliminated, and tariffs are to be reduced.

3. Significant reductions in the level of government expenditures to reduce budget deficits. Layoffs and wage cuts are often prescribed. These often entail significant expenditure reductions in the areas of health care, education, social services, and subsidies on basic food items.

4. Systems of price controls are to be scaled back or eliminated. Price controls on agricultural products are to be removed to provide greater incentives to producers. Consumer subsidies, which often comprise a major part of fiscal deficits, are to be reduced or eliminated.

5. Foreign investment codes are to be liberalized.

6. The privatization of government owned operations.

7. The government should examine the regulatory framework it has erected with an eye to scaling back or eliminating those regulations that impede private markets and the free flow of private capital.

8. The growth of the money supply should be constrained to dampen inflation and provide a more secure investment environment. Real interest rates should be allowed to rise to reflect the scarcity of price of capital, and governments should refrain from allocating subsidized credit to favored sectors or firms.

The reforms promoted under such programs are truly breathtaking in their scope. They go far beyond requiring a recipient nation to demonstrate that it has or will undertake a set of initiatives that can reasonably be expected to address a deficit in the external account. What is being required is across-the-board liberalization, increasing external openness with respect to both trade and capital, and a significantly reduced role for the state in promoting economic development.

It should be acknowledged that the critics of excessive government intervention have identified numerous examples of government actions that harmed development prospects by catering to powerful interest groups, invested in politically prestigious white elephants, overemphasized industrial development, and neglected agriculture (see, for example, the annual reports of the World Bank, *World Development Report*, 1981, 1984, 1986). As Peter Timmer has remarked: "Getting prices right is not the end of economic development, but getting prices wrong frequently is."[38] The assumption that government and bureaucracies are disinterested, efficient organizations pursuing the public interest now appears, with the benefit of hindsight, as somewhat naive.[39]

Many LDCs have indeed suffered from excessive protection of industrial sectors, highly overvalued exchange rates, and regulatory frameworks that discouraged competition and productive investment.[40] Prices are important; producers and consumers do respond in a predictable fashion to price changes.[41] There are important lessons to be learned from the 1980s, and policy "errors" should be high on the list.

What is questionable, however, is the somewhat simplistic over-reliance on a single answer: reduce the role of the state, as opposed to correct the policy errors, and rely to the *greatest extent possible* on free market solutions to development problems.

We should place the current enthusiasm for state minimalism in proper historical perspective. By virtually any measure, economic development was much more rapid in the 1950 to 1975 period in almost all regions of the Third World than development had been prior to 1950. Per capita incomes during this period also advanced much more rapidly than has been the case in the 1980s.[42] Social indicators, including life expectancy, infant and child mortality rates, and literacy rates, all improved dramatically between 1950 and 1975.[43]

If state intervention in the economy produced the disastrous results claimed, it is difficult to explain why it should have taken over a quarter century of excessive interventionism before the negative effects manifested themselves. As has already been discussed, it was in fact unforeseen, and to a great extent unforeseeable, *external* events that produced the dramatic deterioration in the external accounts of many LDCs that led to the economic difficulties of the 1980s. A poor policy environment doubtless made the economic difficulties of the early 1980s worse for some LDCs, but it can hardly be blamed for the dramatic change in the fortunes of so many LDCs all at the same time.

Market Fundamentalism and Poverty

When land, wealth, and access to political power are all highly concentrated, as they are in many LDCs, then relying on market forces merely means that the purchasing power of the wealthy minorities will drive market forces. One of the most important lessons that emerged from the 1970s was that under such circumstances an activist state, particularly in the

areas of primary education, rural health promotion, small farm development and land reform, is essential if the benefits of economic growth are
not to be entirely captured by the wealthy elites.[44] Across Africa and Latin
America, and from Jamaica to the Philippines, the adoption of Structural
Adjustment programs has been accompanied by falling wages, incomes,
rising infant mortality rates, and worsening poverty.[45] In Latin America
and the Caribbean, real wages were lower in 1989 than in 1980, and by
some estimates the incidence of poverty has risen to 50 percent of the population and continues to rise.[46]

Education and health services have been allowed to deteriorate
steadily. According to the United Nations Educational, Scientific, and Cultural Organization (UNESCO), education budgets shrank by more than 25
percent in the 1980s in two-thirds of the developing countries. Three-quarters
of the nations in Latin America reported substantial declines in health
spending per capita, and the Pan-American Health Organization (PAHO) reports that the incidence of malaria is rising.[47] Several Latin American
countries are now attempting to deal with cholera outbreaks, which health
officials fear imperil 300,000 lives.[48]

Nor were the urban poor spared. Food subsidies, which often made the
difference between getting by and going hungry, were frequently eliminated overnight. In Sri Lanka, scaling back on food subsidies has led to a
rise in infant mortality rates. From Venezuela to Zambia, the lifting of food
and transportation subsidies has led to riots, deaths, and the destruction of
property. The poor live at the margin of survival; strategies have been
worked out that allow life to continue at the current set of relative prices.
It is often simply beyond the capacity of many to adjust effectively to a
large rise in the price of an essential commodity in the short run. The combination of deflationary macroeconomic policies and consequent rising unemployment and the price increases associated with adjustment policies
have had a devastating effect on the poor in many developing countries.[49]

According to the United Nations Development Programme (UNDP)
Human Development Report (1990), women have been particularly hard
hit by the structural changes introduced. As incomes fall, the report notes,
"Female members of a poor household are often worse off than male members because of gender-based differences in the distribution of food and
other entitlements within the family."[50] Food production in Africa has
failed to keep up with population increases over the 1980s, and women
and children tend to be the first victims of food shortages.

Market Fundamentalism and Restarting Economic Growth

It is becoming increasingly apparent that Structural Adjustment lending is
failing to meet its own prime objective, that is to restart economic growth

in the indebted low-income countries. Real GDP growth has averaged only 1.6 percent per annum in Latin America and the Caribbean between 1980 and 1989, and only 1.0 percent in sub-Saharan Africa. In Africa, population growth is in excess of 3 percent per annum. A recent (partially World Bank funded) study[51] examined economic performance before and three years after Structural Adjustment programs had been completed. The study found that the budget deficit/GNP ratio had increased, and the Investment/GNP ratio had declined in the "adjusting" countries. Another recent study by Faini, De Melo, Senhadji, and Stanton (1991) provides a comparative analysis of the economic performance of adjustment loan recipients and the performance of LDCs that did not receive adjustment loans. Overall, the authors concluded that: "The positive effects on growth and resource mobilization expected from adjustment with growth packages had not yet occurred."[52]

The Côte d'Ivoire, for example, which had long been regarded as one of the better-managed, more market-oriented African economies, witnessed private sector investment fall from over 15 percent of GDP in 1981 to only 2 percent in 1986. External debt as a percentage of GDP had risen from 59 percent in 1980 to over 182 percent by 1989.[53]

Looking at sub-Saharan Africa as a whole, real GDP declined by 12 percent between 1980 and 1985 and then declined by a further 13 percent between 1985 and 1989. Net exports from the region, which had been marginally positive between 1980 and 1985, has been negative in each year since 1985. Gross Domestic Investment as a share of GDP declined from 25 percent in 1980 to only 18 percent in 1989.[54] Despite rising real interest rates, the proportion of national income saved fell by 50 percent between 1980 and 1989.

Clearly the African economies are not structurally adjusting as expected. But significant output and export increases in other parts of the Third World contributed to a decline in the terms of trade facing African countries of 6 percent per year between 1980 and 1988.

The only important economic variable that continues to grow rapidly is debt outstanding. Official debt was increasing at a rate of 22 percent per year over the 1980s. The aggregate ratio of external debt to GDP increased from 27 percent in 1980 to 97 percent in 1989. The total debt service payments of the developing countries in 1989 amounted to almost $160 billion, representing a massive flow of capital from the developing world to the developed world. Between 1988 and 1992 total external debt of all developing countries increased from $1,397 billion to $1,703 billion.[55] After a decade of deflation, stagnation, rising poverty, and unprecedented capital flows out of the developing countries, the level of outstanding debt continues to rise, and thus claims that the debt crisis is "over" are false, at least for the developing world.

The deflationary policies that were recommended in the early 1980s brought with them the inevitable output and employment contractions, which the IMF and the World Bank assumed would be short term in nature. But the economies have not stabilized. Budget deficits have not been reduced, and balance of payments deficits have only been slightly reduced at a cost of a huge drop in investment. Stagnation, deteriorating health and educational systems, falling incomes, and rising debt have been the lasting result of Structural Adjustment lending programs in too many countries.

Market Fundamentalism: A Reassessment

Market fundamentalism has failed to deliver on its promises. We need to recognize that for markets to function effectively, strong, and in some instances, expanded state intervention is required, although frequently intervention of a different sort than the kind practiced in the past.

This is particularly evident in rural areas. Most of the very poor in the Third World live in rural areas and are employed in the agricultural sector. Development has frequently passed the rural poor by. In the 1970s, efforts to reach the poor were reflected in a much higher priority being attached to agricultural development projects to help landless agricultural laborers and small farmers. Irrigation projects, agricultural research and extension projects, rural road building, and land reform were all on the agenda. Crucial public sector investments in these areas allowed food supply to increase more rapidly than population in most regions.

These important public sector activities have received short shrift from the new orthodoxy with its emphasis on "getting prices right" in agriculture. This is reflected in changes in the World Bank's own allocation of funds. Over the 1980s, the share of World Bank expenditures allocated to agricultural projects declined by almost 50 percent.[56] Structural Adjustment lending on the other hand, which had been virtually nonexistent in the late 1970s, accounted for 36 percent of World Bank lending to the highly indebted countries by 1988.[57]

The decline in World Bank agricultural lending has to be viewed in light of the budget changes that Structural Adjustment programs were requiring of indebted countries. As Michael Lipton has often pointed out,[58] the rural poor typically have the least political influence. When budget cuts are required, it is not surprising that the rural poor are often hit the hardest. In Jamaica, for example, which has been attempting to follow either an IMF or a World Bank program since the late 1970s, public sector investments to promote food production collapsed. Expenditures by the Ministry of Agriculture declined, in real terms, by 40 percent between 1982 and 1988; agricultural research expenditures on food crops declined by over 60 percent. Three-quarters of the extension workers were laid off, and agricultural credit for food production declined by 50 percent. Not surprisingly, food production, which had increased by 36 percent over the 1960s and by 52 percent over the 1970s, failed to increase at all over the 1980s and declined by 22 percent on a per capita basis.[59] The reductions in important public sector investments have led to declines in food production and falling incomes for the rural poor in Jamaica.

In much of the Third World, total agricultural output can not rise until improved farming practices are developed, tested, and introduced. Farmers also need reliable and timely access to inputs, access which they often do not have at present. Improved agricultural research and extension efforts may allow output to rise, but this requires substantial government investment and support.

In many regions rural roads need to be improved, and labor input will not likely increase until there are improvements in rural health and nutrition. Education is important in promoting more effective diets and healthier lifestyles. Education is also important if farmers are to take advantage of improved farming practices as they are developed.[60] Streeten[61] cites extensive evidence from South Korea, Taiwan, India, Bangladesh, and elsewhere documenting the positive supply response produced by well-designed public sector investments in these activities.

The World Bank stresses the importance of the positive supply response of individual commodities to rising prices.[62] This is true, but not the entire story. Small farmers are quick to respond to changes in *relative* prices. With a relatively fixed supply of land and traditional technology that has not changed significantly, the output of one crop can usually only be increased by reducing production of another crop. This indeed appears to be what has happened; estimates of supply response indicate that if all farm prices doubled (and no other changes were made) agricultural output would increase by only between 6 percent and 16 percent.[63] Estimates of the supply response of a single crop to a change usually do not take into account the fall in output of other crops.

Several authors[64] have expressed alarm at the World Bank's advice to a number of countries to increase production of the same export crop at the same time. Many of these commodities are characterized by low income and price elasticities of demand, and increased supplies offered on the market from a number of countries simultaneously is likely only to lead to falling prices and benefits to the consumers in the north.

The promotion of agricultural exports also fails to take into account the highly interventionist, protectionist policies that the EEC (European Economic Community), the United States, and Canada adopted in the 1980s, contributing to falling grain and rice prices. In Thailand, for example, USAID and the World Bank had led donor efforts to introduce new high-yield varieties of rice and to raise levels of rice production. These efforts were immensely successful; between 1978 and 1984 rice exports trebled. But in 1985 the United States passed a new Farm Act, which provided large subsidies to U.S. rice growers. The price of U.S. rice exports fell by 50 percent, and Thai exports to the United States alone fell by 40 percent.[65]

Nor has trade liberalization brought the turnaround that had been expected. Supporters of the market fundamentalism often point to the success stories in East Asia, particularly South Korea and Taiwan, but also to a lesser extent Hong Kong, Singapore, Indonesia, Malaysia, and Thailand. These economies are export oriented, do not have seriously overvalued exchange rates, and rely primarily on private sector firms to take the leading role in promoting economic development.

But all of the above countries, with the partial exception of Hong Kong, began with import-substituting industrialization, overvalued exchange rates, massive government involvement in the economy, and indeed in the investment decisionmaking processes of major firms. After a period of inward-looking development, during which basic infrastructure was established and governments allocated credit and technical advice, subsidized key firms, and provided tariff-protected markets, these economies made, to varying degrees, successful transitions to more export-oriented structures.

The governments in Taiwan and South Korea, for example, were highly dirigiste regimes[66] that, even after moving toward more export-oriented economic structures, managed and controlled imports (to promote targeted sectors), subsidized favored industries and firms, allocated subsidized credit, purchased or aided in the development of new technologies, coordinated suppliers, and provided export subsidies. Selective export subsidies were a key element in South Korea's successful penetration of export markets. Sachs concludes that the essential lesson to be drawn from the East Asian experience is that the public sector is likely to play a major role in supporting export promotion via a host of trade, capital, technology, and industrial policies, and that raising the quality of public sector management (where it is obviously poor) may be essential.[67]

Helleiner[68] suggests that the evidence from East Asia confirms that import liberalization will only follow success at export promotion, and it is unlikely to precede export promotion. Helleiner also observes that import liberalization can only be successful after the economy has been stabilized. Liberalization efforts during macroeconomic instability are not likely to succeed. The World Bank itself has acknowledged that "Countries which have tried to liberalize trade in the midst of macroeconomic crisis have failed."[69]

Finally, the debt overhang itself constitutes a major barrier to increased private sector investment. When outstanding debt is rising, investors will tend to assume that a rising proportion of future income streams will be taken by the government as taxes in order to meet external debt obligations. This can be a powerful barrier to investment, and there is some evidence that a number of countries are facing this constraint.[70]

Conclusion

The overreliance on a single approach, which had been pursued by the donor community over the 1980s, has clearly been costly. The pendulum has swung too far in one direction, and the correction, which may be only just now beginning, is long overdue. Nevertheless, some important lessons have been learned, which hopefully will guide development advice and practice in the future. The donor community is no longer willing to turn a blind eye to inefficient, wasteful, or excessively corrupt regimes. In recent years, for example, Japan, currently the world's largest donor, has suspended aid to Myanmmar, Zaire, Haiti, Sudan, Sierra Leone, and Guatemala because of human rights violations.[71] North American and European donors have also suspended aid in a number of instances. Hopefully, these actions should improve the efficacy of aid expenditures in the future.

The donor community has, belatedly, taken some action to reduce the debt burden for some of the poorest, most indebted countries. The extent of debt forgiveness, which had been virtually nonexistent in 1982, rose from $196 million in 1985 to $1.5 billion in 1989 and $5.7 billion in 1991.[72] Falling interest rates have also eased the debt burden in many developing countries. In sub-Saharan Africa the debt service to exports ratio (an indicator of "burden" insofar as it measures the difficulty of meeting debt service obligations out of export earnings) fell from 28 percent in 1986 to 19 percent in 1991. In Latin America the debt service to export ratio fell from 44 percent to 30 percent.[73]

We need to remember the essential, important roles government must play in promoting development, while taking necessary action to avoid some of the wasteful practices of the past. The record of the past decade should point in the direction of a retreat from market fundamentalism and support for a more mixed economy.

Notes

1. Official Development Assistance (ODA) is comprised of official flows that have a grant element of at least 25 percent. The definition has been adopted by the Development Assistance Committee (DAC) of the OECD. OECD aid now accounts for

over 95 percent of global aid. Aid from eastern Europe and the former Soviet Union have all but disappeared, and aid from the Arab world has steeply declined in the past ten years.

2. World Bank, *World Development Report,* (Washington: Johns Hopkins University Press, 1991).

3. The Inter-American Development Bank was one of the first institutions to employ this term. See, for example, Nicholas Raymond, "The Lost Decade of Development: The Role of Debt, Trade, and Structural Adjustment," in Robert M. Jackson, ed., *Global Issues, 93/94* (Guilford, Conn.: The Dushkin Publishing Group, 1993).

4. This is most apparent in the Structural Adjustment Loans (SALS), which have been developed by the World Bank to deal with the foreign exchange shortages that plague the highly indebted developing countries. In exchange for the badly needed foreign exchange the borrower must agree to adopt a host of economic policies that essentially align domestic macroeconomic and development policies with the new orthodoxy. Most donor agencies have, in recent years, committed themselves to move toward allocating their bilateral assistance according to the willingness of the recipient country to adopt policies compatible with this new orthodoxy. See, for example, the most recent annual review of OECD development assistance activity, *Development Co-Operation, 1992* (Paris: OECD, 1992).

5. H. W. Arndt, *Economic Development: The History of an Idea* (Chicago: University of Chicago Press, 1987), Chapters 2, 3.

6. Anne O. Krueger, Constantine Michaelopoulos, and Vernon W. Ruttan, *Aid and Development* (Baltimore: Johns Hopkins University Press, 1989).

7. Deepak Lall, *The Poverty of Development Economics,* Hobart Paperback No. 16. (London: Institute of Economic Affairs, 1983).

8. See Anne O. Krueger, "Aid in the Development Process," *Research Observer* (Washington, D.C.: World Bank, 1986).

9. Mark McGuire and Vernon W. Ruttan, *Lost Directions: U. S. Foreign Assistance Policy Since New Directions* (Minneapolis: Economic Development Center, University of Minnesota, 1989).

10. Keith Griffin, "Foreign Aid After the Cold War," *Development and Change* 22, no. 4 (1991): pp. 645–685.

11. As reported by Henrik Bering-Jensen, "Africa in the Balance," *Insight,* August 24, 1992.

12. OECD/DAC, *Development Co-Operation, 1992* (Paris: OECD, 1992).

13. Ibid.

14. Joseph C. Wheeler, "The Critical Role of Official Development Assistance in the 1990s," *Finance and Development* (September 1989): pp. 38–40.

15. Keith Griffin, "Foreign Aid After the Cold War," *Development and Change* 22, no. 4 (1991): pp. 645–685.

16. All ODA figures refer, unless otherwise specified, to OECD aid.

17. All figures in this section are from the statistical appendix to the 1992 annual report of the OECD's Development Assistance Committee: *Development Co-Operation* (Paris: OECD, 1992).

18. OECD/DAC, *Development Co-Operation, 1992* (Paris: OECD, 1992), p. 88.

19. Ibid., p. 95.

20. R. C. Riddell, *Foreign Aid Reconsidered* (Baltimore: Overseas Development Institute, 1987).

21. Walter Rostow, *The Stages of Economic Growth* (Cambridge, Mass.: Cambridge University Press, 1971).

22. David Morawetz, *Twenty-Five Years of Economic Development* (Baltimore: Johns Hopkins University Press, 1977).

23. World Bank, *World Development Report, 1982* (Washington D. C.: World Bank, 1982), Table 3. 3.

24. See, for example, H. Chenery, M. S. Ahluwalia, C. L. G. Bell, J. H. Duloy, and R. Jolly, eds., *Redistribution with Growth* (London: Oxford University Press, 1974).

25. Robert McNamara, *Address to the Board of Governors* (Washington, D.C.:World Bank, 1973).

26. For a defense of the "redistribution with growth" strategy, see H. Chenery, M. S. Ahluwalia, C. L. G. Bell, J. H. Duloy and R. Jolly, eds., *Redistribution with Growth* (London: Oxford University Press, 1974). For the classic argument in favor of a "basic needs" approach, see International Labour Office, *Employment, Growth, and Basic Needs* (Geneva: ILO, 1976).

27. Paul Mosley, *Foreign Aid: Its Defense and Reform* (Lexington, Ky.: University of Kentucky Press, 1987).

28. Reported in Tony Killick, "Twenty-Five Years in Development: The Rise and Impending Decline of Market Solutions," *Development Policy Review* 4 (1986): p. 101.

29. Ibid., p. 102.

30. See, for example, any of the annual reports of the World Bank, *World Development Report* (Washington, D.C.: World Bank), published since 1985, or any of the annual reports of the OECD/DAC (Development Assistance Committee), *Development Co-Operation* (Paris: OECD), since 1985. For a spirited defense of the new orthodoxy, see Anne O. Krueger, Constantine Michaelopoulos, and Vernon B. Ruttan, *Aid and Development* (Baltimore: Johns Hopkins University Press, 1989.)

31. See, for example, B. Balassa, "Adjustment Policies in Developing Countries: A Reassessment," *World Development* 12 (1984): pp. 955–972, or Anne O. Krueger, Constantine Michaelopoulos, and Vernon Ruttan, *Aid and Development* (Baltimore: Johns Hopkins University Press, 1989). For a discussion of the need for policy reform in Africa, see the World Bank's influential *Towards Sustainable Development in Sub-Sahara Africa, A Joint Program for Action* (New York: Oxford University Press/World Bank, 1984).

32. OECD, *Debt Survey* (Paris: OECD, 1992), Table 9.

33. Ibid., Table 9.

34. World Bank, *World Development Report* (Washington, D.C.: World Bank, 1991), p. 189.

35. International Monetary Fund, *World Economic Outlook, 1988* (Washington, D.C.: International Monetary Fund, 1988), Table A.33.

36. Ibid.

37. John Charles Pool and Steve Stamos, *The ABCs of International Finance* (Lexington, Mass.: Lexington Books, D. C. Heath and Co., 1987).

38. Reported in Tony Killick, "Twenty-five Years in Development: The Rise and Impending Decline of Market Solutions," *Development Policy Review* 4 (1986): p. 103.

39. See, for example, Robert H. Bates, *Markets and States in Tropical Africa* (Berkeley: University of California Press, 1981).

40. Leroy P. Jones, in *Public Enterprises in Less Developed Countries* (Cambridge, Mass.: Cambridge University Press, 1983), discusses the rather mixed record of parastals. Jagdish Bhagwati examines the problems and costs associated with inappropriate exchange rate regimes in *Anatomy and Consequences of Exchange Control Regimes* (Cambridge, Mass.: Ballinger, 1978).

41. Numerous studies have confirmed this argument. H. Askari and J. Cummings, in *Agricultural Supply Response: A Survey of the Econometric Evidence* (New York: Praeger, 1976), examine a number of well-documented case studies from the agricultural sectors of many countries.

42. See, for example, Simon Kuznets, *Modern Economic Growth: Rate, Structure, and Spread* (New Haven and London: Yale University Press, 1966), and D. Morawetz, *Twenty-Five Years of Economic Development* (Baltimore: Johns Hopkins University Press, 1977).

43. World Bank, *World Development Report, 1982* (Washington, D.C.: World Bank, 1982), Table 3. 3.

44. Hollis B. Chenery, M. S. Ahluwalia, C. L. G. Bell, J. H. Duloy, and Richard Jolly, eds., *Redistribution with Growth* (London: Oxford University Press, 1974).

45. See, for example, B. K. Campbell and John Loxley, eds., *Structural Adjustment in Africa* (London: Macmillan, 1986), and G. Cornea, Richard Jolly, and Frances Stewart, eds., *Adjustment with a Human Face* 1,2 (Oxford: Oxford University Press, 1987).

46. Reported in Nicholas Raymond, "The 'Lost Decade' of Development: The Role of Debt, Trade, and Structural Adjustment," in Robert M. Jackson, ed., *Global Issues 93/94* (Guilford, Conn.: Dushkin, 1993).

47. Ibid., p. 113.

48. Ibid., p. 113.

49. G. Cornea, Richard Jolly, and Frances Stewart, eds., *Adjustment With a Human Face* 1,2 (Oxford: Oxford University Press, 1987).

50. Reported in Daphne Topouzis, "The Feminization of Poverty," *Africa Report* (July/August 1990): pp. 60–63.

51. Dani Rodik, "How Structural Adjustment Programs Should be Designed," *World Development* 18, no. 7 (1991): pp. 933–947.

52. R. J. Faini, Jaime de Melo, A. Senhadji, and J. Stanton, "Growth Oriented Adjustment Programs: A Statistical Analysis," *World Development* 19, no. 8 (1991): pp. 957–968.

53. World Bank, *World Development Report,* Statistical Annex, (Washington, D.C.: World Bank, 1991).

54. Ibid., p. 182.

55. World Bank, *World Debt Tables, 1992/93,* 1 (Washington, D.C.: World Bank, 1993).

56. World Bank, *Fiscal Year 1989, Annual Sector Review: Agriculture* (Washington, D.C.: World Bank, 1989).

57. World Bank, *Adjustment Lending: An Evaluation of Ten Years Experience* (Washington: World Bank, 1988).

58. Michael Lipton, *Why Poor People Stay Poor: Urban Bias in World Development* (London: Temple Smith, 1977).

59. John Newark, *Canadian Food Aid to Jamaica* (mimeo, Athabasca University, Alberta, Canada, 1992).

60. R. Albert Berry, "Agricultural and Rural Policies for the Poor," in Richard M. Bird and Sue Horton, eds., *Government Policy and the Poor in Developing Countries* (Toronto: University of Toronto Press, 1989).

61. Paul Streeten, *What Price Food* (Ithaca, N.Y.: Cornell University Press, 1987).

62. See, for example, World Bank, *World Development Report, 1986* (Washington, D.C.: World Bank, 1986).

63. Michael Lipton, *Why Poor People Stay Poor: Urban Bias in World Development* (London: Temple Smith, 1977).

64. See, for example, Paul Streeten, *What Price Food? Agricultural Price Policies in Developing Countries* (Ithaca, N.Y.: Cornell University Press, 1987).

65. R. C. Riddell, *Foreign Aid Reconsidered* (Baltimore: Overseas Development Institute, 1987), p. 212.

66. See, for example, Tony Mitchell, "Administrative Traditions and Economic Decision Making in South Korea," *IDS Bulletin* 15, no. 2 (1984): pp. 32–38, and Robert Wade, "Dirigisme Taiwan-Style," *IDS Bulletin* 15, no. 2 (1984): pp. 65–70.

67. G. K. Helleiner, "Conventional Foolishness and Overall Ignorance: Current Approaches to Global Transformation and Development," *Canadian Journal of Development Studies* 10, no. 1 (1989): pp. 107–120.

68. Ibid., p. 112–114.

69. World Bank, *World Development Report, 1987* (Washington, D.C.: World Bank, 1987), p. 107.

70. E. Borensztein, "The Effects of External Debt on Investment," *Finance and Development* (September 1989).

71. *Economist*, October 9, 1993, p. 35.

72. World Bank, *World Debt Tables, 1992/93* 1, (Washington, D.C.: World Bank, 1993), p. 20.

73. World Bank, *World Debt Tables, 1992/93* 1, (Washington, D.C.: World Bank, 1992), Table 1.4.

9

◆

The Third World Agenda in Environmental Politics: From Stockholm to Rio

Marian A. L. Miller

The global environment has moved to the forefront of world politics; increasingly, it is the subject of international negotiations. Both the North and the South have significant stakes in global environmental politics, but they often bring different interests and agendas to the bargaining table. These differences are largely a result of their roles in the global economy. Global environmental politics cannot be divorced from North-South economic issues. An inequitable global economic system and the internationalization of economies reduce Third World countries' control over the disposition of their resources. These circumstances reduce their environmental options and affect their strategies in global environmental negotiations.

As the global community attempts to steer development along an environmentally responsible path, developing countries fear that they will bear the brunt of the change. Increasingly, they see constraints imposed on their growth, and they are banding together to negotiate for conditions with which they can live.

This chapter identifies the Third World's interests in global environmental politics, and it assesses how the evolving environmental regime has affected those interests. It highlights the biodiversity regime, and it focuses on the period from 1972 to 1992. Nineteen seventy-two marks the date of the United Nations Conference on the Human Environment, which was held in Stockholm; twenty years later, Rio de Janeiro was the venue for the United Nations Conference on Environment and Development. The

Stockholm conference highlighted the different interests of the developing countries and the developed countries in environmental politics; many of these differences had been exacerbated by the time of the Rio conference. Biodiversity became an issue of concern at the Stockholm conference, and by the time of the Rio conference it had such a prominent place on the international agenda that a separate convention was negotiated on this issue. Negotiations on the biodiversity regime underline the differences between developed and developing countries. As the biodiversity regime has developed, developing countries have identified three issues as being crucial: sovereignty over their natural resources, financial assistance for conservation purposes, and technology transfer. This chapter examines how these issues have been affected as the regime has evolved in the period from Stockholm to Rio.

The Emergence of Global Environmental Politics

Environmental degradation is not a twentieth-century phenomenon. Air pollution and soil erosion have been occurring for centuries. But changes in recent decades have made an international environmental movement and international environmental politics possible. One prerequisite was a change to a conception of the environment that had universal applicability. It was necessary to go beyond the traditional perception of the environment as a local or national concern and to transcend the economic focus. Historically, environmental concerns had focused on national resource needs, rather than on conservation of the global environment. "Before a comprehensive international environmental movement could occur, the interactive, life-sustaining processes of the biosphere had to be perceived as a concern common to all mankind."[1] The change in the perception of the environment was reflected in public and international policy. Consequently, an Intergovernmental Conference of Experts on the Scientific Basis for Rational Use and Conservation of the Biosphere was convened in Paris in 1968. It was organized by UNESCO (United Nations Educational, Scientific, and Cultural Organization) with assistance from other international agencies. The final report of the conference underlined the fact that exploitation of the earth had to "give way to recognition that the biosphere is a system all of which is widely affected by action on any part of it."[2] That conference proved to be a threshold in terms of the treatment of the environment in international policy. From 1968 onward, the biosphere, explicitly or implicitly, was treated as a holistic, integrated system.[3]

The second change had to do with how governments dealt with environmental policy at the domestic level. The environment could not become an international policy issue if governments did not regard it as a legitimate area for national policymaking. They had to treat environmental issues as areas of regular and official concern. Only then were they likely to be willing to cooperate on this issue at the international level.[4] This legitimization of the environment as a national policy issue began to take place in the decades leading up to the Stockholm conference. Citizens of many countries began to express serious concerns about the deteriorating environment. These concerns embraced a wide range of issues, including the endangering of ecosystems, depletion of resources, misuse of technology, and pollution of environments. The decade of the sixties saw a series of books addressing these issues. These included Rachel Carson's *Silent Spring,* Jean Dorst's *Before Nature Dies,* and Rolf Edberg's *On the Shred of a Cloud.* The books were well received by the public because they expressed some widely felt concerns. By the end of the sixties, national environmental laws and policies were being developed in response to these issues. At this time, the biosphere concept was also gaining acceptance. Consequently, people began to see their environmental concerns as no longer merely local or national, but as matters with global implications.

Widespread acceptance of the biosphere concept did not mean that countries discounted national interest. On the contrary, they were quick to identify differences in national interest among themselves. Developing countries found that their developmental and environmental priorities were different from those of developed countries. These differences have been played out in the global environmental politics of the period from Stockholm to Rio, 1972 to 1992.

Environmental Politics: From Stockholm to Rio

The Stockholm conference was the result of efforts to place the protection of the biosphere on the official agenda of international policy. It drew twelve hundred diplomats from 112 nations, several thousand experts from 550 nongovernmental organizations, and a wide variety of environmental activists. Although the focus of the conference was environmental politics, it could not divorce itself from its Cold War context: the Soviet Union, Poland, Hungary, Czechoslovakia, and Bulgaria boycotted the conference because the German Democratic Republic had not been invited as a full participant. The People's Republic of China played up the issue of imperialism, and that delegation wanted to replace the conference declaration with a statement placing all the blame for pollution and exploitation on imperialism.[5] In addition, the United States was accused of ecocide in Vietnam because of its use of defoliants and saturation bombing.[6]

North-South differences over global economic relations dominated the conference and affected developing countries' positions. Developing countries feared that commitments to conserve natural resources or protect the environment would interfere with their prospects for economic growth, and they began to express this fear in the preparatory meetings for the conference. At the conference, there was a focus on the fact that the United States, which had less than 6 percent of the world's population, consumed about 40 percent of the world's goods, and as a result caused by far the greatest environmental damage.[7]

One of the major disputes at Stockholm involved the provision of financial assistance. Developing countries felt that they should not pay the cost of cleaning up the pollution caused by developed countries. Additionally, they did not have the resources to do so. They were also aware that some environmental measures were likely to penalize them, directly or indirectly. Intensive recycling of used goods, for example, would likely cut the demand for their raw materials. In addition, pollution control measures at factories in the industrialized countries would inevitably increase the cost of finished goods imported by the developing nations. Because of these impacts, developing countries pressed for financial assistance from the developed world.

This political and economic context affected environmental politics at the Stockholm conference. The conference had to address two conflicting perspectives regarding the environment: the North emphasized pollution control and resource conservation, and the South focused on social and economic development. To bridge these differences, the conference advanced the concept that environmental protection was an integral dimension of development.[8]

The Stockholm conference resulted in two major documents: the Declaration of the United Nations Conference on the Human Environment, and the Action Plan for the Human Environment. The declaration contains twenty-six principles addressing the behavior and responsibility of the community of nations. It provides a basis for the establishment of new codes of international conduct. The Action Plan of 109 recommendations calls for specific actions by national and international bodies. It addresses provisions for a comprehensive international ban on dumping toxic wastes in the oceans, for tightening up international law on oil pollution at sea, for a moratorium on commercial whaling, for the preservation of important ecosystems, and for the establishment of genetic banks. The plan also provides for an Earthwatch program of global assessment and monitoring. The information gathered is to be evaluated by scientists and then disseminated to policymakers.

One of the lasting results of the Stockholm conference was the establishment of the United Nations Environment Programme, which is headquartered in Nairobi, Kenya. This location was a result of developing countries' determination to have a significant United Nations body headquartered in the developing world. It was the first global intergovernmental body to be headquartered outside of North America and Europe.

In the years between Stockholm and Rio, scores of environmental treaties have been formulated, dealing with issues such as biodiversity, marine pollution, hazardous waste disposal, and ozone depletion. But this cooperation in the establishment of regimes did not significantly narrow the divide between the developed and the developing countries in global environmental politics. This was again reflected in the preparations for the Rio conference and in the proceedings of the conference itself.

The issue of inequity was still a major concern at the Rio conference in 1992. For Rio, the developing and developed country groups had suggested agendas that reflected their differences at the Stockholm conference. The developed countries wanted to address ozone depletion, global warming, acid rain, and deforestation, while the developing countries were more interested in examining the relationship between developed countries' economic policies and developing countries' sluggish economic growth. Although the title of the conference embraced both concepts—environment and development—the focus of the preparatory meetings was on the concerns of the developed countries.

In 1990, at the first preparatory meeting for the Rio conference, the developing country group once more presented its agenda. This included technology transfer on preferential, noncommercial, and concessional terms, and additional financial assistance. The latter was seen as important because many developing countries were unable to bear the costs of environmental protection. The industrialized countries were split on this issue: the Nordic countries sought to set up a working group on the transfer of technology and resources, but the United States and the countries of the European Community opposed this move. The latter position prevailed. As a result, North-South economic issues were not considered by the working group and could only be raised in plenary sessions. Developing countries, therefore, focused on trying to link technology transfer and demands for additional financial resources to their participation in the major environmental agreements being proposed by developed countries.

The Rio conference demonstrated the higher political profile that the environment had assumed over the preceding twenty years. More than 170 nations sent delegations, and there were representatives from thousands of nongovernmental organizations. But the major difference between Stockholm and Rio was in the attendance of heads of states. About 118 heads of state were present at this conference, the largest gathering of world leaders up until then.[9] The conference also drew about nine thousand members of the media, so it received extensive media coverage.[10] The attendance of the heads of state and the attention of the media reflected the fact that, with the end of the Cold War, environmental issues were receiving greater international attention.

During the preparatory sessions and the conference proceedings, leaders of developing countries insisted that environmental protection alone was not enough. They argued that agreements about global environmental issues should include measures for their economic development. They insisted that the developed countries had to help the poor countries in their struggle to develop, if the environment was to be protected. The North acknowledged the connection between environment and development in the conference documents, and some industrial countries did commit themselves to increased monetary aid. However, environmental priorities reflected each group's development concerns: the developed countries refused to commit to specific steps to reduce their own industrial pollution; at the same time, they pressed the developing countries to protect forests and wildlife. Beyond the North-South tension, however, the Rio conference confirmed a position taken at the Stockholm conference: that protecting the environment and promoting economic growth are not opposed to each other, but rather are ultimately inseparable actions. This dialogue on environment and development produced international treaties on climate and on biodiversity, a statement on forests, the Rio Declaration, and an action plan for sustainable development known as Agenda 21.

The United Nations Framework Convention on Climate Change does not establish any legal obligations. Instead, it sets out broad principles, and it requires countries to use their best efforts to reduce emissions of climate-altering greenhouse gases. The convention mentions a target of stabilizing emissions at 1990 levels. Developing countries would have liked the treaty to require industrialized countries to share with them the technology for controlling greenhouse emissions, but the treaty does not do this. The treaty, however, establishes in international law the principle that nations must take into account the global environmental consequences of their economic and technological decisions. Although the treaty is relatively weak, it does allow for later strengthening by protocols. The second treaty is the United Nations Convention on Biological Diversity. It calls for the development of national strategies for the conservation and sustainable use of biological diversity. But like the climate treaty, it does not set any deadline or other definite legal obligations. Nor does it set any clear obligations for sharing the fruits of genetic engineering between the countries that exploit genetic knowledge and the countries in which the genes are discovered. This treaty will be addressed in greater detail when we focus on biodiversity.

The conference produced a statement on forests, in lieu of a convention. Hopes for an agreement in this area were dashed by disagreements between the North and the South. Developing countries took the position that forests were subject only to the sovereign decisions of the nations in which they are located, and therefore their uses and their management could not be regulated by an international treaty. The developing countries insisted on retaining the option to use their forests to enrich themselves, in the same way that developed countries had profited from their forests in the past.

Both developed and developing countries expressed their support of sustainable development and the eradication of poverty in the Rio Declaration, a twenty-seven-point, nonbinding statement. Among the new principles enunciated are the special responsibility of developed countries for global environmental restoration because of their technological and financial capabilities and their major contribution to pollution and resource consumption.

The conference also produced Agenda 21. It contains recommendations designed to guide countries toward sustainable development and protection of the global environment. It also is nonbinding, but it contains a number of ideas and provisions. A Commission on Sustainable Development is also being established to ensure effective follow-up to the Rio conference and to report on progress in implementing Agenda 21.

Focus on Biodiversity

Biodiversity is but one of the environmental issues that the community of nations brings to the negotiating table, but negotiations dealing with the biodiversity regime have highlighted many of the issues separating the developed countries and the developing countries in global environmental politics.

Developing countries have attempted to use linkage politics in the negotiations dealing with biological diversity. They see global environmental negotiations as opportunities to advance a broader agenda of change in the structure of North-South economic relations. Toward this end, they are linking environmental issues in which developed countries have an interest with issues in North-South economic relations. This strategy is based on the assumption that the environment and natural resources can only be conserved under conditions of sustainable global development. Specifically, over the last two decades, a major demand by developing countries has been to link the North's access to biological resources in developing countries to the South's access to the resulting biotechnology. Biotechnology has been increasing the value of genetic resources, and developing countries want reimbursement for the use of their natural resources. They have also requested increased financial assistance to help them conserve their biological diversity. They believe that the present world economic system makes sustainable development impossible, and that economic adjustments are crucial if their economies are to have the chance of surviving the changes imposed by environmental constraints. Developing country demands have generally been met by systematic resistance from developed countries.

Defining Biodiversity

Biodiversity, or biological diversity, refers to the variety of life on earth. The term encompasses three categories: genetic diversity, species diversity, and ecosystem diversity. Genetic diversity describes the variation of genes within a species. Species diversity describes the variety of species within a region, and ecosystem diversity refers to the number and distribution of ecosystems. The increasing interest in biodiversity results from concerns regarding species extinction, depletion of genetic diversity, and disruptions to the atmosphere, water supplies, fisheries, and forests. This growing awareness on the part of both governments and the general public has resulted in a desire to protect the world's natural heritage. Biodiversity brings together a variety of constituencies, including forestry, agronomy, biotechnology, pharmaceuticals, and international trade. While they may have different perspectives on biodiversity, they all see it as an important resource.

Approximately 1.4 million species of plants and animals have been identified, but scientists believe that between 10 million and 80 million species exist.[11] Species are disappearing rapidly, and there is growing consensus in the international community that a system should be put in place to slow or halt the process of extinction. Arguments in favor of species preservation include the perspective that a species has a right to exist because of its own unique nature. But self-interest is also a strong motive; given the interdependent nature of the ecosystem, the extinction of some species diminishes the well-being of the remaining species, including human beings. Consequently, it is important to protect species and threatened ecosystems such as forests, wetlands, and coastal waters.

Central to the concern about biological diversity is the shrinking genetic pool. It is estimated that tropical forests contain "at least 50 percent and perhaps 90 percent of the world's species."[12] According to one estimate, twenty to seventy-five species per day are becoming extinct because of deforestation in the tropics.[13] Traditionally, the genetic character of the many species of plants and animals were considered a part of the common heritage of mankind, but increasingly they are the objects of an enclosure movement, which is seeking to enclose, privatize, and reduce the building blocks of life to marketable products.

The Third World's Biodiversity Agenda

Stockholm was not the first time that issues related to biodiversity were placed on the international agenda. A variety of legal instruments existed. Some were regional, such as the Convention on Nature Protection and Wildlife Preservation in the Western Hemisphere (Washington, 1940) and the African Convention on the Conservation of Nature and Natural Resources (Algiers, 1968). Other measures dealt with specific species, such as birds and marine and polar region species. Before Stockholm, the only major international legal instrument for conserving biodiversity was the 1971 Convention on Wetlands of International Importance, especially regarding waterfowl habitat. But there was no comprehensive international treaty addressing the problem of biological diversity. Although Stockholm did not produce such a document, the issue of biodiversity was debated, and the nation-states of the South began to link the issue of technology transfer with the issue of biodiversity and the related genetic resources and to push for financial assistance. They felt that if the issues of sovereignty, financial assistance, and technology transfer were not appropriately addressed, the resulting regime would be weak and ineffective.

The sovereignty issue. For developing countries, the recognition of sovereign rights over all of their natural resources, including genetic resources, is important. That recognition underscores their right to control access to these resources and legitimizes demands for reimbursement for the use of these resources and for the product of research resulting therefrom. Industrial interests have been rushing to gain access to the shrinking gene pool, and developing countries that are the repositories of the bulk of these genetic resources are seeking compensation for the use of these resources. Although most of the world's biological wealth is concentrated in the Third World, it is the industrialized countries that have the capital and technological capability for transforming that wealth into commercial products. Northern institutions hold the patents and other intellectual property rights on the products of their research, and the Third World receives little benefit from this research.

Gene technology has implications for fields ranging from medicine to agriculture; the United Nations estimates that medicines from plants are worth about U.S.$40 billion per year, and a single gene from an Ethiopian barley plant has been used to protect California's U.S.$10 million annual barley crop.[14] Corporations are searching the shrinking gene pool for genetic traits that are commercially valuable. This strategy has increased tensions between the industrialized nations of the North and the developing nations of the South. The latter see these biological resources as part of their national heritage, and they believe that they should receive compensation for the use of these resources. Developing countries want legal recognition of their rights to indigenous knowledge of their local plant and animal species. In exchange for allowing the North access to these species, the South wants access to the resulting biotechnologies. But the countries and companies of the North believe that these resources only gain value with the application of their technology, so many of them do not believe that compensation is justified.

Two examples of the use of genetic technology illustrate the dimensions of this issue. The first example involves the discovery by scientists of a rare perennial strain of maize in a mountain forest in Mexico. Only a few thousand stalks of this existed. Tests have shown that this strain is resistant to a leaf fungus that had devastated the United States' corn crop in 1970, costing farmers more than two billion dollars. Consequently, the commercial value of this variety could be several million dollars per year. The other example deals with the rosy periwinkle from Madagascar's tropical rain forest. The plant contains a rare genetic trait that has been used to develop pharmaceuticals to treat childhood leukemia. While the pharmaceutical companies are making windfall profits, Madagascar has received nothing from the use of this resource.[15]

In the industrial age, the political and economic forces that controlled access to fossil fuel have been able to exert tremendous economic control; in the new age of biotechnology, the forces that control access to genetic resources will exercise tremendous power over the world economy. Unfortunately, the South is at a technological disadvantage.

Access to technology. Technology transfer has long been an issue for developing countries. In the 1970s, it was an important item on the agenda of the New International Economic Order. Almost all advanced technology originates in industrialized countries. Consequently, nearly all of the world's patents are registered in the industrialized states and are in the hands of the transnational corporations.[16] The issue of access to science and technology has been under international discussion for years, mostly in United Nations bodies. Countries of the South have adopted a common position in negotiating with the North on technology matters. Lack of access to technology was addressed in a series of negotiations in the 1970s and 1980s. Considerable progress toward facilitating the South's access to technology was made during the 1970s in negotiations in the United Nations Conference on Trade and Development (UNCTAD) on an International Code of Conduct on the Transfer of Technology and on a revision of the intellectual property system. There was also some progress on the revision of the Paris Convention for the Protection of Industrial Property, but stalled negotiations prevented its revision.[17] Developing countries find the issue of access to technology extremely relevant to the debate about biodiversity. They believe that access to technology would help them conserve their biodiversity, and they also want access to the biotechnology that results from the use of their natural resources.

Financial assistance. Developing countries see as their first priority pulling their countries out of poverty. In their opinion, poverty is a significant cause of pollution. They believe that it would be counterproductive to pull resources away from basic needs projects in order to use them for the conservation of biodiversity. Therefore, they need financial assistance for their conservation projects. They argue that since conservation of their biodiversity will benefit the whole community of nations, developing countries should not have to bear the entire financial burden of resource conservation.

The Evolution of the Biodiversity Regime from Stockholm to Rio

The area of genetic resources and biotechnology was already a controversial one in 1972. Developing countries were concerned about their lack of access to the biotechnology that was developed from the use of their resources, and they tried to use linkage politics to gain access to this technology. At Stockholm, developing countries pressed their demand for the transfer of technology on noncommercial terms. This demand was rejected by the countries of the industrialized world. The final statement of the conference diluted the language that addressed this linkage between economics and environment.

Both the Declaration of the United Nations Conference on the Human Environment and the Action Plan for the Human Environment include language addressing biodiversity. Principles 2, 4, and 6 of the declaration include provisions for the safeguarding of flora and fauna and the preservation of ecosystems.[18] The action plan generally addresses the importance of protecting forests, which, among other things, were important habitats for wildlife;[19] wildlife should be monitored to assess the impact of pollutants on them,[20] and their economic value should be assessed;[21] governments were also to take steps to protect ecosystems of international significance.[22] Recommendations 39 to 45 deal generally with the issue of preserving genetic resources.[23]

In the period between the Stockholm and Rio conferences, the body of legislation concerning biodiversity continued to grow. Relevant major international legislation includes the Convention Concerning the Protection of the World Cultural and Natural Heritage (1972), the Convention on International Trade in Endangered Species of Wild Fauna and Flora (1973), and the Convention on Conservation of Migratory Species of Wild Animals (1979).

In the aftermath of Stockholm, developing countries continued their push for greater access to the biotechnology resulting from their biological wealth. A nonbinding Undertaking on Plant Genetic Resources (Resolution 8/33) was passed by the Food and Agriculture Organization of the United Nations (FAO) in 1983. It stated that access to genetic resources should not be restricted, and it declared that all seed resources were the common property of humanity. Both primitive stocks and those developed by proprietary means should be free to all. Developed world producers were opposed to this undertaking, and many industrial countries were not parties to this declaration because it was incompatible with their patent rights.[24] However, Third World members accepted its provisions.[25]

In 1989, the FAO Commission proposed the concept of farmers' rights. The international community was seen as the trustee for present and future farmers. This concept was to be the basis for helping farm communities all over the world to benefit from the improvements in plant genetic resources. But no funding mechanism was set up to transfer resources to the developing countries. Developing countries were also no longer endorsing the common heritage concept with regard to their plant resources. They wanted access to their resources to be on the basis of bilateral arrangements.

A 1991 Costa Rican deal is considered one possible model for future arrangements. The parties to the deal were the National Biodiversity Institute, a nonprofit Costa Rican research center, and Merck and Company, the world's largest pharmaceutical company. Merck agreed to pay the institute U.S.$1 million, as well as royalties from any product developed. In return, the institute is to provide Merck with plant, insect, and microbe samples from all over Costa Rica.[26] Costa Rica is estimated to have about 5 percent of all plant and animal species on the planet. Ten percent of the upfront money and 50 percent of any royalties go directly into conservation. Although this agreement provides for compensation, some critics say that it gives away Costa Rican resources for too little money. Nevertheless, many developing countries are studying this arrangement with interest.[27]

The years between Stockholm and Rio show incremental progress with regard to the items on the Third World's biodiversity agenda. On the sovereignty issue, developing states wanted to make their own arrangements with regard to resource access, and there was some movement in this direction among developed country actors, as the Merck deal illustrates. The slow process of norm change had begun. But there was less movement in the areas of transfer of technology and financial assistance. Although developing countries continued to push for changes in these areas, developed countries continued their determined resistance. Their conflicting perspectives were reflected in the preparatory negotiations for the Rio conference.

Unlike Stockholm, Rio produced a separate document addressing biodiversity. Negotiations on the Convention on Biological Diversity began in 1991. The complexity of issues such as access, financial assistance, and technology transfer made negotiations difficult. The convention provides a comprehensive framework for the conservation of biodiversity. The convention includes the following commitments:

1. national identification and monitoring of biological diversity;[28]
2. the development of national strategies and programs for conserving biological diversity;[29]
3. national *in situ* and *ex situ* conservation measures;[30]
4. environmental assessment procedures to take into account the effects of projects on biological diversity;[31] and
5. national reports from parties on measures taken to implement the convention and the effectiveness of the measures.[32]

The language of the convention is general. It is liberally sprinkled with qualifiers such as "as far as possible and as appropriate" and "in accordance with its particular conditions and capabilities." In spite of the general language and all the qualifiers, the specific issues of interest to developing countries proved to be controversial.

In the period spanned by the Stockholm and Rio conferences, the countries of the Third World made uneven progress with regard to their agenda items. The following discussion focuses on the consequences of the evolution of the biodiversity regime for Third World interests related to sovereignty, technology transfer, and financial assistance.

The sovereignty issue. The Stockholm convention addressed the issue of sovereignty in a general manner. Principle 21 of the declaration recognizes that states have sovereignty over their own resources and that they should manage the resources in keeping with their own environmental policies. This right of sovereignty is restricted only by the responsibility not to "cause damage to the environment of other States or of areas beyond the limits of national jurisdiction."[33] Two decades later, the biodiversity convention (Article 15) also recognizes the sovereign rights of states over their natural resources. But it goes further than the Stockholm declaration; its language indicates that states have the authority to grant access to their resources on mutually agreed terms.[34] Developed countries and their institutions are concerned about the implications of this article. It might indicate that the days of free scientific and commercial access are ending and that foreign enterprises will have to come to terms with developing country institutions before collecting specimens. The Merck deal in Costa Rica illustrates the kind of arrangement that can be made.

Access to technology. The declaration and the action plan from the Stockholm conference contain several references to transfer of technology or the use of technology to address environmental concerns. In the action plan, the relevant parts are Principles 12, 18, and 20. The principles dealt generally with the use of science and technology "for the common good of mankind,"[35] they encouraged the free flow of up-to-date scientific information, and they addressed the issue of making environmental technologies available to developing countries on terms that they could afford.[36] Principles 26 and 27 of the action plan recommend that the United Nations Food and Agriculture Organization coordinate research and information exchange and transfer on forest-related issues, while Principle 108 recommends studies "to find means by which environmental technologies may be made available for adoption by developing countries under terms and conditions that encourage their wide distribution without constituting an unacceptable burden to developing countries."[37]

At Rio, technology transfer is dealt with in more detail. The Rio Declaration encourages exchanges of scientific and technological knowledge, and development, adaptation, diffusion, and transfer of technologies, including new and innovative technologies.[38] However, the articles addressing science and technology in the convention are ambiguous, with some provisions seeming to be aimed at satisfying the interests of the developing countries and others seeming to target developed countries' concerns.

Articles 15, 16, 17, 18, and 19 address exchange and cooperation with regard to science and technology. Scientific research based on genetic resources is to be carried out with the full participation of the countries providing the resources. These states should also share equitably in the results and benefits of the research.[39] Access to these benefits should be on mutually agreed terms.[40] Technologies should be transferred under fair and favorable terms, including concessional and preferential terms where mutually agreed. However, where patents and intellectual property rights are involved, access and transfer should be provided on terms consistent with the protection of these rights.[41] Article 17 calls for the exchange of information, including results of technical, scientific, and socioeconomic research,[42] and Article 18 calls for technical and scientific cooperation in conservation and sustainable use of biological diversity.[43] The language in these articles attempts to satisfy the interests of both the developing and the developed countries; the language calling for transfer of technology was used to satisfy the developing countries, and the qualifiers dealing with mutual agreement and intellectual property rights were included to satisfy the developed countries.

Financial assistance. The Stockholm documents made several references to the matter of financial assistance for developing countries.[44] Recommendation 45 of the action plan was the only one that made specific reference to financial assistance for the purpose of conserving genetic diversity.[45] The declaration recognized that because of their underdevelopment and the "costs which may emanate from their incorporating environmental safeguards into their development planning,"[46] developing countries would need assistance. The action plan made the point that developed countries' preoccupation with their own environmental problems should not be an excuse to slow the flow of assistance.[47]

Nevertheless, at the Rio conference two decades later, this preoccupation did contribute to the contentious nature of the debate over financial assistance. The biodiversity convention had to address two primary issues related to financial assistance: the amount of money to be contributed by the developed nations, and the financial mechanism to administer the funds. Article 21 addressed the latter, and Article 20 addressed the former.

According to Article 20, the developed country parties should fund the "agreed full incremental costs" to developing countries of meeting the obligations of the convention. It makes the point that the provision of this assistance will determine whether developing countries can meet their commitments, since developing countries' priorities are "economic and social development and eradication of poverty."[48] Arriving at the figure for the agreed costs is likely to be a challenging task.

Article 21, which addresses the financial mechanism, is controversial. The mechanism, policy, strategy, program priorities, and eligibility criteria were to be determined by "the Conference of Parties"[49] within a year of the time the treaty enters into force. Will the financial institution be run by majority rule, or will it be donor-controlled? No doubt, developing countries would prefer the former, but developed countries would be less willing to contribute funds to an institution that they do not control. Until the activation of the convention's treaty, the Global Environment Facility of the United Nations Development Program, the United Nations Environment Programme, and the World Bank will operate the financial mechanism.[50] This interim financial arrangement will be weighted toward donor control.

A related issue was the funding of Agenda 21, a blueprint that suggested how the world might enrich itself without destroying the environment. The debate over the funding of Agenda 21 was extremely contentious. Third World countries at Rio wanted a commitment that would have almost doubled aid to developing countries by the year 2000. They felt that the increase was needed to guarantee that the Third World countries' development would be environmentally sound. This kind of incentive was used to encourage developing countries' participation in the Montreal Protocol on Substances that Deplete the Ozone Layer. A U.S.$240 million fund was created in order to help developing countries make the switch from chlorofluorocarbons to chlorofluorocarbon substitutes. Without this provision, key developing countries would not have supported the protocol. However, at Rio, less than twenty-four hours before the end of the conference, the developing countries were forced to compromise on the aid issue. They had faced strong resistance from some industrialized countries: the United States refused to be bound by a longstanding United Nations' goal of raising aid levels to 0.7 percent of the country's economic output, and several other large donors refused to commit themselves to the target by any specific date. The developing countries had to compromise by agreeing to language that encouraged richer countries to increase their aid to the Third World. The countries of the industrialized North only committed themselves to reach the 0.7 percent target "as soon as possible."

Prospects for the Third World's Biodiversity Agenda

Of the three agenda items under discussion, the sovereignty issue is the one on which there has been the most movement. Even before the Rio conference, small changes in practice had taken place that were sure to have significant implications for international norms regarding access to, and reimbursement for, natural resources. The convention itself underscores the sovereignty of countries over their resources, and it legitimizes restrictions of access to their natural resources. The implications of this are most important with regard to genetic resources, which have been increasing in economic value as the genetic pool shrinks. Merck's arrangement with the Costa Rican institute is a recognition of these changes. The combination of new patterns of behavior and the language in the convention will help to usher in new norms regarding access and reimbursement.

Developing countries were less successful with regard to the issue of technology transfer. In Rio, as in Stockholm, they sought to use linkage politics. In convention negotiations, they tried to use access to plant genetic resources to bargain for technology transfer. And they did achieve some limited success in this area: according to the biodiversity convention, research, profits, and technology should be shared with the nations whose resources are used. But the language is not strong enough to make this mandatory. It can be interpreted to mean that companies do not have to turn over technologies or pay royalties unless they agree to. But even this weak language can help to establish new norms for the relationship between companies and developing countries in the area of genetic reserves.

The United States was critical of the treaty provisions addressing technology issues. It was the only major country not to sign the biodiversity convention. President George Bush claimed that accession to the convention was impossible because the country could not make commitments for private industry to transfer protected technology. He said that doing so would retard biotechnology and undermine the protection of ideas. Some developing countries provided a rapid response to President Bush's decision.

For example, several Central American presidents signed a resolution encouraging the enactment of laws regulating access to genetic resources. Other countries have already strictly regulated the export of genetic resources. It is likely that when these countries are faced with requests for permits to collect specimens, preference will be given to signatory countries.

Although the biodiversity pact would be effective once it had been ratified by thirty nations, it would be legally binding only on signatory nations.[51] Consequently, if the United States was not a signatory state, it would not apply to United States' corporations. However, even though the United States has not officially accepted the convention, there is nothing to prevent the United States' institutions and companies from working within its framework.

With regard to the third agenda item, financial assistance, progress was more symbolic than real. Although the convention, as well as Agenda 21, dealt with the issue of financial assistance, the developing countries did not get the financial commitments they wanted. They certainly did not receive a commitment for the transfer of a specific amount of funds. The likely result is that any financial assistance will be less than the Third World's perceived need and that it will be controlled by the donor countries.

Conclusion

The outcome at the Rio conference for the developing countries' biodiversity agenda has been mixed. But that is reflective of these countries' short- and medium-term prospects in global environmental negotiations. Developing countries are at a disadvantage because global environmental politics reflect the structure of the global economy, and that is clearly controlled by the North; but, by adopting a common position, they have been able to induce incremental changes in global environmental politics. Although they fell short of their goals, they clearly succeeded in making the issue of development as prominent as that of environmental protection. One key objective of the proposals before the conference was to merge the UN environment and development capacities in a new institution in order to take account of the linkages between them and promote sustainable development. The conference did indeed come up with a plan for a Commission on Sustainable Development. It would monitor the follow-up to the Rio conference, including the progress toward the aid target.

Developing countries need to adopt a two-fold strategy for their participation in global environmental politics. This strategy would have both a short-term component and a longer-term component. In the short term, they need to continue to use linkage politics. Their right to control access has been legitimized. But effective environmental governance also depends in large measure on access to financial assistance and technology, and progress in this area is likely to be only incremental. In the short term, it is unlikely that developed country actors will feel inclined to dispense large amounts of charity toward developing countries. Significant changes in developed country behavior is dependent on a perception of self-interest. And the perception of self-interest is dependent on two factors: a recognition that the transfer of resources is necessary to maintain a healthy world environment, and the assurance that the resources will indeed be used toward that end.

In the medium and long term, developing countries' strategies should focus on the development of their own capabilities. This could be facilitated by the pooling and sharing of scientific and technological resources. Not all Third World countries are at the same stage of technological development. Venezuela and Thailand are examples of countries that have established a biotechnology infrastructure. Others such as China, Thailand, the Philippines, Kuwait, Mexico, Brazil, and India are in the process of establishing the requisite infrastructure.[52] A Centre for Science and Technology of the Non-Aligned and Other Developing Countries has been set up in India.[53] It could work with other Third World scientific institutions to coordinate joint research and development in the cutting edge area of biotechnology. Such a strategy could increase developing countries' capacity to benefit from their own genetic resources. Even more importantly, it would increase their ability to set the terms of their own development.

Notes

1. Lynton Keith Caldwell, *International Environmental Policy* (Durham, N.C.: Duke University Press, 1990), p. 23.

2. UNESCO, "Final Report of the Intergovernmental Conference of Experts on the Scientific Basis for Rational Use and Conservation of the Resources of the Biosphere, held at UNESCO house, Paris, 4–13 September 1968," Paris, January 9, 1969, p. 5.

3. Caldwell, p. 28.

4. Ibid., p. 23.

5. "The Stockholm Conference: The Chinese Foiled," *The Economist*, June 24, 1972, p. 28.

6. "Woodstockholm," *Time*, June 19, 1992, p. 55.

7. Ibid.

8. Caldwell, p. 56.

9. The 1993 Information Please Environmental Almanac, p. 9.

10. Ibid.

11. John C. Ryan, "Conserving Biological Diversity" in Lester R. Brown, *State of the World* (New York: Norton, 1992), p. 9.

12. World Resources Institute, *World Resources 1992–93* (New York: Oxford University Press, 1992), p. 130.

13. Ibid., p. 128.

14. Mostafa Tolba, *Earth Audit* (Nairobi: UNEP, 1972), p. 15.

15. Jeremy Rifkin, *Biosphere Politics* (New York: Crown Publishers, 1991), p. 66–67.

16. Willy Brandt, *North-South: A Program for Survival* (Cambridge, Mass.: MIT Press, 1980), p. 194.

17. The South Commission, *The Challenge to the South* (Oxford: Oxford University Press, 1990), p. 254.

18. United Nations, *Report of the United Nations Conference on the Human Environment held at Stockholm 5–16 June 1972*, reprinted in *International Legal Materials*, Vol. 11 (November 1972), p. 1418.

19. Ibid., Recommendations 24–25, pp. 1431–1432.

20. Ibid., Recommendation 29, p. 1433.

21. Ibid., Recommendation 30, p. 1433.

22. Ibid., Recommendation 38, p. 1435.

23. Ibid., pp. 1435–1441.

24. Canada, France, West Germany, Japan, and the United States initially withheld their membership in the FAO Commission on Plant Genetic Resources.

25. Thomas C. Wiegele, *Biotechnology and International Relations: The Political Dimensions* (Gainesville: University of Florida Press, 1991), p. 113.

26. World Resources Institute, p. 138.

27. "Chemical Prospecting: Hope for Vanishing Ecosystems?" *Science* 256 (May 22, 1992): p. 1142.

28. United Nations Environment Programme, *United Nations Conference on Environment and Development: Convention on Biological Diversity*, 1992, Article 7, reprinted in 31 *International Legal Materials* (1992), p. 825.

29. Ibid., Article 6, p. 825.

30. Ibid., Articles 8 and 9, pp. 825–826.

31. Ibid., Article 14, p. 827.

32. Ibid., Article 26, p. 834.

33. United Nations 1972, p. 1420.

34. United Nations Environment Programme 1992, Article 15, p. 828.

35. United Nations 1972, p. 1420.

36. Ibid.

37. Ibid., pp. 1463–1464.

38. United Nations Environment Programme, *The Rio Declaration on Environment and Development*, June 14, 1992, Principle 9, reprinted in *International Legal Materials*, Vol. 31 (July 1992), p. 877.

39. United Nations Environment Programme, *United Nations Conference on Environment and Development: Convention on Biological Diversity*, 1992, Article 15, reprinted in 31 *International Legal Materials* (1992), p. 828.

40. Ibid., Article 19, p. 830.

41. Ibid., Article 16, p. 829.

42. Ibid., p. 829.

43. Ibid., pp. 829–830.

44. These references were in Principles 9 and 12 of the declaration, and Recommendations 45, 107, and 109 of the action plan.

45. United Nations 1972, pp. 1439–1441.

46. Ibid., p. 1419.

47. Ibid., p. 1464.

48. United Nations Environment Programme 1992, *United Nations Conference*, Article 20, pp. 830–831.

49. Ibid., Article 21, pp. 831–832.

50. United Nations Environment Programme, *Resolutions of the Conference for the Adoption of the Agreed Text of the Convention on Biological Diversity,* May 22, 1992, reprinted in *International Legal Materials,* Vol. 31 (July 1992), p. 843.

51. United Nations Environment Programme, *United Nations Conference on Environment and Development: Convention on Biological Diversity,* 1992, Article 36, reprinted in 31 *International Legal Materials* (1992), p. 837.

52. Wiegele, p. 119.

53. The South Commission, p. 209.

10

♦

Women Under Layers of Oppression: The (Un)Changing Political Economy of Gender

Zehra F. Arat

Despite the tendency to treat women as a homogenous and unified group, they hardly constitute a monolithic group with identical problems. They live in countries with diverse historical experience and development levels; within each country, the issues pertaining to women vary according to race, ethnicity, class, religion, tribe, residence, and educational levels. Nevertheless, despite this diversity, the common denominator of women in all societies, including the industrialized ones, is their subordinate status. Women compose the poorest and the least powerful segment of the population throughout the world. The oppression of Third World women is even more intense due to the legacy of Western imperialism, which culminated in economic dependency and crises. Moreover, the economic and political structural changes introduced by colonial powers, and later imposed by international lending and development agencies, have further widened the gender gap in these countries. Unrecognized as full partners either in the family or in society, women have been denied equal access to education, job training, employment, health care, ownership, and political power.

As indicated in Table 10.1, only 55 percent of women in developing countries are literate, compared to 75 percent of men. Even if the literacy rate is considered for the younger population (ages 15–19), the progress is marginal for the female population, which still has a literacy rate of only 65 percent. Similarly, female educational enrollment rates are far below those of males at all levels. The average years of schooling for the adult

Table 10.1 Literacy and Education in Developing Countries

		Total	Male	Female	Gap
Enrollments (as % of the age group)					
Primary	1988–1990	83	—	86	94
	1960	—	—	—	61
Secondary	1988–1990	48	49[a]	36	74
Tertiary	1988–1990	7	10.2[a]	5	51
Primary intake rate (% of age					
group in first grade)	1988	91	—	76	—
Tertiary science and engineering					
enrollments (% female)	1987–1988			20	
Adult literacy rate					
(as % of age 15+)	1990	65	75	55	72
	1970	46	—	—	54
Literacy rate					
(as % of age 15–19)	1990	82	—	65	—
	1985	60	71	50	70[a]
	1970	43	53	33	62[a]
Mean years of schooling					
(for age 25+)	1990	3.7	4.6	2.7	58

Note: a. Average values are estimated by using gap values, and vice versa.
Source: Human Development Report 1993, United Nations Development Programme, (New York: Oxford University Press, 1993).

population are 2.7 years for women and 4.6 years for men. The corresponding values for industrial countries are 9.6 and 10.4, with a female-male gap figure of 92; it is much higher than the gap figure in developing countries, which is 58.[1] When the low level of first grade female enrollments is taken into account (76 percent), the gap is not likely to be closed in the near future.

Women in many developing countries are denied the right to inherit property, and in some places where they have property rights they cannot control the land to which they have title or manage the shops they own. In Lesotho, for example, a woman cannot borrow money, sign contracts, or slaughter cattle without her husband's consent.[2]

According to official statistics, men constitute two-thirds of the paid labor force in developing countries and slightly more than half in industrial societies (see Table 10.2). Unemployment statistics, on the other hand, are higher for women. The representation of women in administrative and managerial positions is low in all countries, regardless of their development level, and marginal in developing countries where the average is only 8 percent. Since they tend to hold lower positions, women's wages

Table 10.2 Employment and Wages

	Developing Countries			Industrial Countries		
	Male	Female	Gap	Male	Female	Gap
Percent in labor force						
1990	67.4	32.6	52	57.6	42.4	77
1988	67.9	32.1	48[a]	58.9	41.1	70[a]
Percent of administrative and managerial staff						
1988–1989	92.0	8.0	9[a]	76.0	24.0	32[a]
Parliaments Percent of seats occupied						
1991	88.0	12.0	14[a]	91.0	9.0	10[a]
1988	87.2	11.8	14[a]	74.0	16.0	22[a]
Percent unemployed						
1989	8.7	11.6	140	5.9	8.3	140
Wages 1990	—	—	70	—	—	70

Note: a. The gap figures are calculated as female averages as a percentage of male averages by the author.
Source: Human Development Report 1993, United Nations Development Programme, (New York: Oxford University Press, 1993); and *Human Development Report 1990.* Unemployment statistics and wage gap are calculated by using data reported by ILO in *Yearbook of Labor Statistics 1992* (Geneva: International Labor Organization, 1992), for a limited number of countries.

and salaries are also low. Moreover, even for the same or comparable work, women are consistently paid less, 50 to 80 percent of what is paid to men.

In some countries women still can not enjoy full citizenship rights; they are denied the right to vote or run for office. Where women's political rights are recognized by statute, their de facto denial is common. Consequently, only approximately 10 percent of the world's parliamentary representatives are women, and women have never held more than 4 percent of cabinet offices or other positions of executive authority.[3] Moreover, the progress in this area has been unsteady (see Table 10.2).

Women lag behind in all indicators of human development. Even in many industrial countries, the female human development index appears to be only about 80 percent that of males, and in developing countries it is lower, only 60 percent.[4]

The neglect of the female population becomes most obvious when health indicators are examined. In addition to the health problems they share with men, "since women [also] face such physical changes as menarche, menstruation, pregnancy, childbearing, lactation, and menopause," it is stated that "the crisis in world health is a crisis of women."[5] Yet, women's health receives very little medical attention, they lack equal access to the health care system, and their health suffers from physical hardships and malnutrition. In developing countries 50 percent of all women of child-bearing age and 60 percent of pregnant women suffer from nutritional anemia, compared with less than 7 percent of their counterparts in industrial countries.[6] Statistics from some countries are more alarming: In India, 50 percent of all women "gain no weight during the third trimester of pregnancy, owing to malnourishment," and 80 percent of "pregnant and nursing rural women in Java have anemia."[7]

Biologically, females have an advantage over men. Theoretically, if there were no favorable treatments of males, females would be more likely to survive early childhood and apt to live longer as adults. Male children are more vulnerable than female children to diseases of infancy and childhood, and in old age women tend to live longer since "women's hormones protect them from atherosclerotic diseases; their lower metabolic rate and higher proportional body fat content may also make them less vulnerable to a range of other chronic and critical conditions."[8] In developing countries, however, statistics on life expectancy at birth do not manifest a significant female advantage. In fact, the female child mortality rate is higher (see Table 10.3). Both indicators, which should normally be in favor of females, reflect the social biases against women. Due to the low value assigned to female children and women, female infanticide (and abortion of female fetuses where the sonogram technology that identifies the sex is available) has been high; both nutritional quality and quantity of food for the female—throughout her life—have been poor; and the females have been less likely to receive preventive health care or curative medicine when they have fallen ill. In the 1980s in Bangladesh, malnutrition was about three times more common among young girls (14 percent) than boys (5 percent); in rural Punjab of India, families spend more than twice as much for their male infants' care than for the care of female infants.[9] In these countries, and others where these social biases have been stronger, life expectancy and child survival rates for males have been higher than those for females. Consequently, despite their natural disadvantages, males outnumber females by 100 to 99, globally, and by 100 to 96 in developing countries (Table 10.3). For 114 countries for which the population data are available, forty-eight countries had masculine sex ratios in 1990, and in some countries the female-male gap (the number of females per hundred males) was as low as forty-eight.[10]

The female deprivation leads to the deprivation of future generations and feeds the poverty cycle. Children of malnourished and uneducated mothers are more likely to suffer from malnutrition, more susceptible to diseases, and more likely to die. Pointing to "the health problems of infants born to women who had been underfed as children," a research team

Table 10.3 Mortality and Population

	Developing Countries				Industrial Countries			
	Total	Male	Female	Gap	Total	Male	Female	Gap
Life expectancy at birth								
1990	62.8	—	64.2	104	74.5	—	77.9	110
1960	46.2	—	—	—	69.0	—	—	—
Child mortality rate[a]								
(per 1000 live births)								
1980–1987	104.0	3.4	3.1	90	16.0	.7	.6	90
Population	—	—	—	96	—	—	—	106

Note: a. Male and female average rates and the gap values are calculated by employing the data for a small number of countries reported in *Statistical Yearbook,* 1988/89, no. 37, (New York: United Nations, 1992); total values are for 1990 and from *Human Development Report 1993.*

Source: Human Development Report 1993, United Nations Development Programme, (New York: Oxford University Press, 1993).

in Guatemala concludes that "it would really take two generations of improved female nutrition to bring down the infant mortality rate."[11]

Although employment statistics indicate that only 32.6 percent of women in developing countries were employed in 1990, and only 11.6 percent were looking for a job (official definition of unemployment) in 1989 (Table 10.3), in reality women are far from idle, working for more days and longer hours than men. "Women in developing countries produce, process and market up to 80 percent of the food," and in Africa "88 percent of rural African women work in agriculture . . . [and] 80 percent of the family's food is produced, processed and stored by women."[12] According to the United Nation's estimates, "to transport water, fuel and goods to and from market, women [in developing countries] spend 2,000 to 5,000 hours a year or the equivalent of an eight-hour job . . . [and they] run 70 percent of micro-enterprises."[13] It is estimated that women typically work about 25 percent longer hours than men.[14] Survey research reveals that in rural areas of the dry zone of Sri Lanka, women work for 560 hours during the peak season and 530 hours during the slack season, while the respective work hours for men are 426 and 350. The time women can spare for leisure activities or sleep, on the other hand, is half of that for men, for both seasons.[15] Women's workload does not show much of a decline during the slack seasons, and women have practically no leisure time because they are held responsible for household activities and domestic chores throughout the world. Even in Cuba, where men are required by law to share household responsibilities with women, "82 percent of women in the capital city, Havana, and 96 percent of women in the countryside have sole responsibility for domestic chores."[16]

Although the household tasks performed by women—such as cooking, cleaning, child care, horticulture, husbandry, food processing, sewing, collecting fuel, and carrying water—and their community functions—such as carrying out ceremonial and social obligations and maintaining social linkages and networks—are essential for the survival and operation of family and community as functional units, they are not assigned a high value and not included in labor statistics. For example, in Sri Lanka, while according to the official statistics "women constituted only 26 percent of the total labor force," in the early 1970s a survey that included housewives and counted their "home-based and part-time work" found the proportion to be 44.9 percent.[17] The gap appears because women's work is defined as "reproductive" as opposed to "productive," and its social and economic worth is completely undervalued.

Reproductive labor—biological (childbirth and care), economic (collecting fuel, sewing, and producing and processing food for household consumption), or social (care and maintenance of the house and family affairs)—takes place in the domestic sphere of life and meets the subsistence needs of the family. Although it contributes to the family budget, its contribution is not monetary but in kind, and thus has a use-value. Productive labor, on the other hand, has an exchange value in the market and usually generates cash income. Thus, most of the female labor that takes place in the domestic sphere and the wealth that it generates are not included in official statistics. A 1973 survey indicates that only six out of seventy developing countries "counted the value of carrying water to its point of use in the GNP's [*sic*]."[18] According to a UN survey of 1990, however, if women's unpaid work in house and family care were counted as productive output in national income accounts, global output value would increase by 20 to 30 percent.[19]

The vicious cycle of women's subordination began with the patriarchal creation of gender roles in the society. First the biological differences between sexes were used as the basis for a social division of labor. The female, as the one who is physically capable of childbearing, was pushed to the domestic area to perform reproductive functions and denied access to productive labor. Then, her contribution was devalued. The separation between the sexes and their labor as reproductive and productive led to further segregation of life into the private and public domains for women and men, respectively.[20]

When and why such a separation took place and resulted in a male dominant society (patriarchy) instead of a matriarchy constitute puzzling questions without definite answers. What we know is that all civilizations—characterized by the specialization of labor, social stratification, and institutionalization—have been patriarchal.[21] Although some precivilized societies demonstrate more egalitarian gender relations, even in those societies the power balance is usually tilted in favor of men.[22]

The State Strength and the Patriarchy

Although all civilizations have been patriarchal, the form and strength of patriarchy vary. In some societies women have enjoyed more freedom and opportunities than others. The strength of patriarchy largely depends on the extent of the centralization of property relations and power or the strength of the state. Thus, the form of the state and the extent of its permeation into different spheres of life are important in analyzing gender relations.

Most Third World countries experienced colonization by the Western powers. Others that escaped direct Western rule were subject to Western political control and economic domination through the establishment of spheres of influence (e.g., China during the late nineteenth century), unequal treaties (the Ottoman Empire between the eighteenth and twentieth centuries), and mandates and protectorates (e.g., Iraq, Kuwait, Jordan, Palestine, and the other former Ottoman land in the Middle East between the two world wars). All of these arrangements made these lands open markets for Western commodities, sources of cheap raw materials, and profitable investment domains.

Prior to the Western conquest and penetration, some societies had developed agrarian economies along with viable cities of commerce, were highly stratified and organized under strong state structures, and followed influential patriarchal religions and philosophies such as Islam, Hinduism, and Confucianism.[23] Women in such societies (mostly in North Africa, the Middle East, Asia, and parts of sub-Saharan Africa) were expected to remain in the private domain and take care of the household affairs. Although these women received respect as mothers and acquired more influence within the family and community as they gained seniority and gave birth to male children, they were largely separated from the productive labor and public life, and they depended on men as providers.[24]

Compared to these societies, in some regions of Africa and the Americas—where the economy was based on subsistence agriculture, the money economy was not developed, and the separation between the ruler and the ruled was not as sharp—women played a larger role both in the production process and public affairs.[25]

Depending on the structure of the indigenous economy and politics, the impact of the Western penetration on the status of women and gender relations varied. In those societies where women had already been subject to considerable state authority and economic subordination, the impact of colonization had been mainly further deterioration of women's economic status. In the process of issuing titles and licenses, women lost their traditional rights to the land they cultivated, and the flow of Western manufactured products ruined the handcrafts and cottage industries that had involved female labor. In other societies, especially in Africa and the

Americas, in addition to these economic encroachments, colonial rule introduced Western Christian morality, state authority, cash crops, and a money economy. The discriminatory economic policies and Western patriarchy, added to the existing patriarchal practices of the land, had a more inhibiting impact on the African and American women who had been enjoying some visibility and mobility in public life as active participants in agriculture, commerce, and community affairs—the areas that had been often more restricted to their sisters elsewhere.

Since the main concern of the colonial powers was their economic gain, the traditional economy, culture, and even political boundaries were completely undermined. Some colonial decrees that were against the tradition appeared to be favorable to women (e.g., repudiation of polygamy). Such changes were introduced, however, at those historical junctures when they could best serve the economic or political purposes of the colonialists rather than those of women. In fact, the traditional patriarchal institutions and values were recognized, and even reinforced, when they coincided with colonial interests. An examination of the colonial record as a whole, nevertheless, would reveal that while their policies displayed some vacillation in the face of changing social conditions, colonial governments maintained a patriarchal attitude toward the native women. For example, when the British imposed a hut tax on Africans to force the men to leave their villages to work at the colonial enterprises such as mines, plantations, and railbuilding, they limited the residence in these areas and cities to single men only. A restricted number of women (prostitutes, beer brewers, and so on) were allowed in those areas to perform certain "womanly" services for the male laborers. When these self-employed women started to accumulate some capital, however, the colonial state interfered by restricting prostitution and taking over brewing. In their effort to limit the activities of these independent women, the state reinforced the power of the local chiefs to contain women and restored some confining traditional practices as the law.[26]

Regardless of whom the colonial power was and the variations in its polices toward women, we can argue that the overall impact of Western domination was negative for women. The capitalist mode of production introduced by the West facilitated private ownership, nonagricultural employment, waged labor, money economy, replacement of food crops with cash crops, and the concentration of the land and capital (especially in the hands of the colonists). All of these changes crystallized the division of labor between the two sexes and sharpened the distinction between reproductive and productive labors. Women's labor, especially in horticulture and food processing, was crucial for the survival of the family in the face of meager wages earned by men. Since women lacked access to the labor market and could not generate cash income, however, their labor continued to be devalued. Since the colonial governments recognized men as the heads of the households and relied upon mainly male labor, the economic position of women was marginalized. Moreover, regulations and taxes imposed by the colonial governments established centralized state control over people, which has been more suppressive for women.

Although women were mobilized and played active roles in independence movements and revolutions, national liberation did not bring about the emancipation of women. Women were complimented on their sacrifices and their contributions to the liberation movements and expected to join their male compatriots in the national struggle for development, but they were not given equal power and responsibility to be full partners in the formation or operation of the new state.[27]

Regardless of the variation in the ideologies of the nationalist leaders, an analysis of the content of state policies that pertain to gender relations and women's lives would identify three main strategies: traditionalism, Westernization, and socialist revolution. As the victims of the Western capitalist and imperialist ambitions, the leaders who followed traditionalism identified the Western culture as an immoral one that had not only retarded their economic development but also distorted their culture and social fabric. Thus, the new state was committed to follow a new path of development, distinct from that of the West. Western institutions and values were rejected, precolonial beliefs and practices were revived, and women were summoned to assume the roles prescribed by tradition and embrace subjugating practices, such as genital mutilation and polygamy, to prove their patriotism (e.g., Eastern Africa and parts of the Middle East).

The second strategy, Westernization, was based on the belief that the ability of the West to conquer and rule the rest of the world was due to its modernity. Thus, the future society was designed to incorporate the political, educational, technological, and cultural characteristics of the West. The goal set for women by this strategy was to be like the Western women who were more visible in the public life but still lacked social and economic equality with their men (e.g., Turkey, India, and most of the Latin American and Caribbean countries).

The third path, socialist revolutionary strategy—incorporated either into the independence movements (e.g., China) or pursued by the new leadership long after independence (e.g., Cuba)—accepted the equality of male and female labor and promised the liberation of women along with all oppressed groups.

All new states, however, regardless of their attitude toward the West or their perception of its capitalist structures, acknowledged Western economic and technological success. Thus, even if the acceptance was residual, they all adopted the Western concept of development as industrialization. In order to achieve industrialization, a new society had to be created as a new dynamic work force; thus, new generations had to be given the education appropriate for a modern economy. Therefore, the new regimes encouraged women's participation both in education and employment, though not to the extent they did for men. As reported in Table 10.1, although female literacy and enrollment in primary education has increased since the 1960s and 1970s, there is still considerable discrepancy between female and male levels. The employment situation has not been any better, since women were not fully integrated into the work force and were mostly pushed into the so-called informal economy where they are unprotected workers who work under most brutal market conditions as street vendors, casual or seasonal laborers, and domestic servants. For example, according to the International Labor Organization (ILO) estimates for 1970, the female economic activity rates were approximately 32, 27, and 25 percents in Ghana, Kenya, and Zambia, but the figures from the formal sector indicate that women wage earners constituted a small minority of all economically active women—2.7 percent in Ghana, 8.7 percent in Kenya, and 5.7 percent in Zambia, circa 1970.[28] Female employment in developing countries, as will be illustrated and discussed in the following pages, has demonstrated sectoral fluctuations rather than a major net gain during the last four decades.

Again, mostly for development purposes, the new governments in countries that pursued the Westernization or socialist strategies adopted secularization and introduced some social reforms that eliminated or modified some traditional practices that were restrictive for women. Setting a minimum age for marriage, introducing marriage licenses, recognizing women's right to divorce, establishing monogamy as the norm, and banning bridal wealth, dowries, and foot-binding were changes favorable to women. The overall content of the reform codes, however, were far from liberating. They included several clauses that restricted women's rights (e.g., the right to work depended upon the husband's permission, and the father's primacy was recognized for child custody), and statutes favorable to women were not fully enforced. Moreover, persecution of violators was relaxed, and verdicts reached by the courts controlled by male justices and juries tended to favor men. Consequently, the legal struggle often became a frustrating, ineffective, and, therefore, not a very inviting option for women. Furthermore, since women were not granted equal access to education, job training, and employment in the formal economy, left without financial resources and independence, women were forced to accept their fate and seldom sought to enforce their legal rights. Thus, the utilization of these reforms has been limited to the upper- and middle-class, urban, educated women. It can be concluded that the overall impact of reforms has been the replacement of the traditional family authority and religious patriarchy with the authority and control of the state organized as a secular patriarchy.[29]

Moreover, since men continued to be recognized as heads of households, women were seldom included in development projects and could hardly be beneficiaries. The land reforms and cooperatives that were established through government subsidies have been open only to men. Similarly, fertilizers, irrigation, high-yielding crop seeds, and new technology have not been available to women. While women are usually denied access, recent World Bank studies "found that women farmers with the same access as men to agricultural inputs (credit and extensive services) produced around 7 percent more food per hectare."[30]

Until the 1980s, both the national development planners and international agencies held the view that all households are male headed and women are not producers—or subscribed to patriarchal ideologies that prescribe such gender roles—and ignored women. Believing that the increased household income would benefit everybody in the family, they focused on increasing male employment and productivity to foster development and reduce poverty.[31] Consequently, women's needs and input were not incorporated into the development plans and their participation in projects was kept minimal. A four-country study of the degree of female involvement in technical cooperation, capital, and food aid projects sponsored by the United Nations' organizations reveals that in 1984, out of a total of 254 such projects undertaken in Rwanda, Democratic Yemen, Indonesia, and Haiti, only 9 were projects that exclusively concerned women, 33 were designed to include women, 152 included activities that would affect women but involved no provision to include women's participation, and 60 projects had no immediate interest to women. Their budgetary allocations constituted 3.5, 13, 59.8 and 23.6 percents, respectively.[32] Some other studies have found the patriarchal attitudes and policies of development agencies to be ineffective and counterproductive in fighting poverty or promoting growth and show that it is the mother's income, rather than the overall household income, that is significantly related to the children's well-being and nutrition intake.[33]

As a result of the misdirected efforts, the high economic growth rates that most developing countries experienced in the 1960s had diminutive positive impacts for women. In fact, in some cases, economic growth and modernization eroded the little power and few opportunities that the women had had. In Indonesia, for example, due to rapid industrialization and increased imports, the traditionally female occupations (i.e., harvesting, rice pounding, weaving and batiking, handicraft manufacturing, and small-scale marketing and trade) have been diminished.

> Rice-hulling machines have cut women's income by $55 million and reduced half-time employment by more than 8.3 months for 1 million women; yet income for men who work in the new mills has increased by $5 million. . . . Rural women lost their major source of income when

high-yield rice was introduced (1972); men working with scythes for wages replaced women working with *ani-ani* knives for a portion of their harvest. Imports and mechanization have forced 90% of women weavers (over 1 million women) out of work. Batik-making has been mechanized, with men who operate machinery earning 400–500% more than women in labor intensive jobs.[34]

The same pattern is observed in Nepal:

An increase in imports and mechanization has resulted in a decline in village and cottage industries, and thus a displacement of many women from the monetized sector. Between 1952–54 and 1971 the rate of employed women declined from 3.75% to 1.83% in the non-agricultural sector, 34% to 13% in the industrial labor force, and 59.4% to 35.1% in the total labor force.[35]

Similar changes experienced by women in other developing countries led some feminist analysts to denounce development, calling it "a form of patriarchal colonialism" or "women's worst enemy."[36]

The incomplete legal reforms that extend some rights to women without full equality with men, combined with the lack of economic independence, resulted in gender-biased systems where women are pushed back to second-class citizenship. In fact, it can be argued that while women were mobilized for development, a conscious effort was made to maintain their dependency on men.

In their development efforts, Third World governments have also taken measures to curtail population increase. Receiving considerable support from foreign governments and international agencies for this purpose, many countries managed to reduced their fertility rates significantly.

While the average fertility rate for developing countries is still nearly twice the industrial world's average, a considerable decline is noted between 1960 and 1991 (Table 10.4).

The decline in fertility rates is a change favorable to women because it means a reduced burden of extra pregnancies, prolonged breastfeeding, and other child-rearing activities. In addition to improving women's conditions and health, lower fertility rates may also lead to lower maternal mortality rates.[37] The population control policies, however, have been employed with a concern for economic development and ecological conservation rather than the welfare of women. Governments "give" women the right to use contraception or employ abortion when high fertility rates and overpopulation are considered to be obstacles to development by the male leadership. Then, various birth control devices and medications, some of which are inappropriate or unsafe and thus banned in industrialized countries, are pushed in developing countries by Third World governments and

Table 10.4   Fertility and Maternity in Developing and Industrial Countries

	Developing	Industrial
Total fertility rate, 1991	3.8	2.0
Ratio of 1991 fertility rate to 1960	60.0	65.0
Contraceptive prevalance[a] Rate, 1985–1990	49.0	59.0
Maternal mortality rate (per 100,000 live births)		
1988	420.0	26.0
1980–1987	290.0	24.0
Average age of female at first marriage		
1980–1985	20.7	23.5
Infant mortality rate (per 1000 live births)		
1991	71.0	14.0
Percent of pregnant women with prenatal care		
1989–1990	63.0	—
Percent of births attended by health care personnel		
1988–1990	66.0	—
Percent of children breastfed at 12–15 months		
1986–1991	68.0	—

Note: a. The percentage of married women of childbearing age who are using, or whose husbands are using, any form of contraception; that is, modern or traditional methods. In many countries the rate is less than 1 percent, and the average for poorest countries is 19 percent.

Source: Human Development Report 1993, United Nations Development Programme, (New York: Oxford University Press, 1993).

foreign agencies, regardless of how women feel about them.[38] On the other hand, women's right to reproductive freedom is denied if the labor force is considered to be shrinking too much or women are acting "too free" to sustain the traditional family structure. Then, women are forced to bear unwanted children in wretched conditions or endanger their lives by seeking illegal abortions.

Thirty percent of all "maternal" deaths in Latin America are due to improperly performed illegal abortions or to complications following abor-

tion attempts. . . . Every ten minutes in 1980, an Indian woman died of a
septic abortion. . . . Illegal abortion is the leading cause of female deaths
in Caracas.

In Peru, 10 to 15 percent of all women in prison were convicted for
having had illegal abortions: 60 percent of the women in one Lima prison
were there for having had or performed illegal abortions.[39]

In Brazil, a country where abortion is illegal, each year about 1.5 million women undergo clandestine abortions. But the government continues
to block all possible safe means of inducing abortion, and all methods of
artificial contraception are condemned as ethically unacceptable by the
National Confederation of Bishops of Brazil.[40]

International Dimension

After the Second World War a renewed period of decolonization began.
By the end of the 1960s, most nations were sovereign states; Latin American countries had been independent since the nineteenth century. Political
autonomy, however, did not result in complete independence for the new
states—most of them have maintained their dependency on Western capital and technology. The post–World War II trend in the international economy has been a rapid expansion and consolidation of both financial and
product markets.

> Each of the postwar decades has seen a different major source of international capital flow appear. Immediately postwar, the United States was
> the wellspring through the Marshall Plan. In the 1950s, private corporations supplied most of the capital to developing countries for investment
> in wholly owned industrial plants, mines, and plantations. . . . The 1960s
> were the heyday of official development assistance (international aid).
> . . . In the 1970s, private banks emerged for the first time as a major
> channel for international financial transfers [loans]. Private international
> financial transfers increased by about twenty percent each year, considerably faster, even allowing for inflation, than the growth in the volume
> of total world trade. The nominal value of capital flow increased more
> than ten times between the beginning and the end of the decade, from $9
> billion in around 1970 to $115 billion in 1980. . . . Developing countries
> were the destination for about sixty percent of the total amount.[41]

The capital transferred to the developing countries as foreign aid, investments, or loans, however, did not necessarily foster the recipient
economies. Multiples of the original amount went back to the West in the
form of profits from investments, payments of principle and interest on
loans, and import payments as well as foreign bank deposits and spending
on Western products by the domestic elite. "Whereas in 1980, the net trans-

fer of funds from the North to the South totalled $19.1 billion, by 1990 the flow was the other way—$27.5 billion flowed from South to North."[42]

The consolidation of markets and penetration of transnational corporations in developing countries encouraged, if not pushed, the commercial banks to lend to developing countries to facilitate their purchase of Western products.[43]

The impact of international economic integration on women is complex. The impact on female employment varies among economic sectors and from one region to another. In general, however, we can argue that the integration that facilitated mechanization and commercialization has reduced and further marginalized female labor within the agricultural sector—women constitute the bulk of the migrant workers and seasonal laborers—and pushed them into the service sector and informal economy. The direction of change in employment opportunities for women in the industrial sector is related to the capital- or labor-intensive nature of the industrialization process; women are usually hired for routine production line work in labor-intensive industries.

In countries where agriculture is the main economic sector (e.g., most of Africa), women's economic status has been deteriorating, while in countries where industry is more dynamic (mostly Asia), women have made some marginal gains. However, where integration resulted in capital-intensive production, either in agriculture or industry, both men and women faced increasing unemployment and were forced to move to the service sector and informal economy (e.g., most Latin American countries). Moreover, it should be noted that where an increase in the female participation in the industrial and service sectors did occur, it did not necessarily improve women's lives, since they were employed in mostly unskilled, low-wage jobs. A preference exists among transnational corporations for female labor. However, since it was the low value of her labor and her docility that attracted the cost-minimizing employer to the woman worker, this preference did not reverse the sex wage differential; rather, it reinforced it. Indonesia is an illustrative case of the export-processing zones of Southeast Asia where women provide up to 80 percent of the work force in industries such as electronics, food processing, textiles, and footwear:[44]

In 1978, 8000 women were working for multinational companies for $0.17 per hour. Young women, hired mostly on a daily or probationary basis, earned Rp.200–350 per day; women were paid 30% less than men for comparable work. Cost of in-factory food and transportation (Rp.250) is often deducted from wages, and consequently a woman takes home approx. $0.25 per day.[45]

Along with the growth of female industrial employment comes sexual specialization of labor and "feminization" of certain industries. As female

Table 10.5   Patterns of Female Participation in the Labor Force

	Developing countries	Industrial countries	Africa	Latin America & Carribean	Middle East	Asia[a]	China	India
Total								
1960	32.7	38.1	32.9	18.9	24.5	34.1	38.4	31.3
1970	32.9	39.7	32.7	21.2	22.3	34.2	37.9	32.6
1980	32.4	40.2	32.0	23.0	22.9	33.6	37.6	31.7
1990[b]	32.6	42.4	33.9	31.8	13.3	30.7	43.0	26.0
Agriculture								
1960	36.7	46.1	35.1	9.4	30.7	38.8	45.0	35.4
1970	36.5	44.4	34.8	8.1	28.1	38.7	34.8	37.9
1980	36.4	43.3	34.4	9.3	30.3	38.5	44.1	37.7
Industry								
1960	21.0	26.7	17.2	16.9	14.4	22.0	20.0	24.6
1970	25.7	28.8	19.7	16.7	14.3	27.6	28.7	26.1
1980	26.5	29.2	19.7	15.8	14.5	28.8	30.6	27.1
Service								
1960	32.1	42.6	28.9	34.3	8.6	19.3	16.3	15.8
1970	25.9	47.2	31.5	38.4	13.9	21.8	20.5	16.2
1980	26.9	48.7	31.6	38.8	15.8	23.2	22.7	17.4

Notes: a. Excluding China and India.

b. From *Human Development Report 1993*, United Nations Development Programme (New York: Oxford University Press, 1993). The statistics for the Middle East are limited to Arab states. Asia value is a crude estimate obtained through averaging the values reported for three regions: South Asia (excluding India) is 22.0; East Asia (excluding China) is 42.9; and South East Asia is 40.8.

Source: World Survey on the Role of Women in Development, Department of International Economic and Social Affairs (New York: United Nations, 1986) p. 70.

representation within an industry increases, the wage graphics draw a decline. Furthermore, feminized industries, both in the formal and informal sectors, also tend to occur at sites that escape labor and occupational safety laws and provide few or no benefits and no job security.[46] These conditions are difficult to improve. In a hurry to attend to their domestic chores after work, or afraid of being labeled loose women, female workers are less likely to establish unions or participate in union activities, and their needs and demands are likely to be neglected or ignored by male co-workers who control unions.

In addition to its marginalizing impact on female employment, international economic integration, via increasing dependency on foreign capital and indebtedness, has created more burdens for women. Given their disadvantages in the world trade market—being dependent on primary goods for exports, facing low and fluctuating export prices, and having a high level of concentration both in exports and trade partners—and dependency on the Western world for technology and capital, developing countries encounter major balance of payment problems. Development requires industrial technology. This technology is offered by the Western corporations, but at a high price. Unable to pay for the technology by its limited export earnings, the developing country buys the Western products via capital borrowed from the West. Most of the foreign currency earned by the country is used to pay back its debt, and the profits are taken out of the country by the foreign companies or domestic speculators. Thus, to finance new investments or to refinance its debt, the country finds itself in need to obtain more foreign currency. Once again, it turns to Western lenders. An international agency, the International Monetary Fund (IMF), plays an important role in this process.[47]

Established after World War II to stabilize domestic economies and stimulate international trade (to avoid another world depression and war), the IMF lends money to its member nations. With narrow concerns and commitment to the principles of free market and trade, the IMF sets certain conditions and requires the applicant country to make adjustments in its economic structure. These structural adjustments, expected to increase the country's exports and reduce its aggregate demand, include reductions in government spending through cuts in welfare services, removal of government subsidies on basic goods (e.g., flour, bread, kerosene, public utilities, and so on), wage cuts, devaluation of the national currency, and privatization. These measures, often referred to as austerity measures due to their high social costs, have their most catastrophic impact on the poor and women. Since these adjustments often result in a rapid increase in unemployment and decline in wages, moving the burden of welfare from the state to families, women try to make up for the lost family income and government services by adjusting their lives and living conditions.[48]

Through their "invisible adjustment," Momsen says, women make the austerity measures "socially possible by increasing their own economic activity, by working harder and by self-abnegation."[49] During the world economic crisis of the 1980s, women's usual hardships were both multiplied and intensified due to these adjustments.

The world economic crisis has been caused by multiple and interrelated factors that have been precipitating since the 1970s and led to a global stagnation in economic production and development in the 1980s. A major world recession expedited by the rise in oil prices in 1978–1979 and the decline in the economic growth rates of the industrialized countries further depressed the economies of developing countries that could not sell their products. Thus, export prices in developing countries fell rapidly, and they found themselves paying more for imports while receiving lower prices for exports. The protectionist policies of the industrialized countries further compressed the export markets for developing countries. With diminishing incomes, developing countries had to turn to borrowing, but borrowing was not a viable option. The interest rates had soared, reaching as high as 18–20 percent. Many countries were already in deep debt and unable to pay back what they had borrowed in the 1970s when Western banks had been pushing loans. In order to be able to qualify for loans within the tightened financial market, developing countries were forced to agree to the IMF conditionalities.[50]

Research indicates that during the economic crisis of the 1980s, the removal of food subsidies resulted in both qualitative and quantitative reductions in the food intake of poor families, especially for female members, who are traditionally fed last and least.[51] Women were forced to take jobs, where available, regardless of the pay and working conditions. Many of those who used to be employed in the formal sector lost their jobs. Especially where industrial output and employment showed the lowest rates of increase and employment conditions tightened (e.g., Sri Lanka, Taiwan, Venezuela, Jamaica, and Haiti), "women were squeezed out of industrial jobs."[52] Some of these women joined the informal sector, others felt the pressure to migrate.

Moreover, the cutbacks in government services and investments in health care and education resulted in reductions in women's already limited access to these services. A study of seventeen countries that had implemented the structural adjustment programs identified "a clear tendency for a deterioration in the ratio of girls to boys in secondary education after the onset of recession, reflecting decisions by families to remove girls from schools at a faster rate than boys."[53]

In addition to these economic hardships and decline in their status, women have had to face increasing levels of violence by men who reacted to the crisis and their own marginalized position by increasing their alcohol consumption.[54]

As global integration progressed and the economic and military dominance of the West accelerated again during the postcolonial era, women became commodities themselves. The oldest profession, prostitution, gained momentum with international dimensions, especially in the 1980s, and became an economically more viable job for women. Entertainment centers serving U.S. military bases, foreign investors, and tourists attracted young peasant girls (e.g., Thailand and Philippines).[55] The red-light districts of European cities (e.g., Amsterdam) were filled with women of color. The oil-rich countries of the Middle East recruited female domestic servants from Asia (e.g., Sri Lanka, Philippines) with ambiguous, albeit broadly interpreted, job descriptions. This migration process is accelerated by the economic crisis. Bernabe Paguio's report on the female immigrant workers from the Philippines is quite telling:

> There are about 26,000 women workers in the Middle East and 20,000 more in Japan, Hong Kong and other Asian nations, the great majority classified as domestic helpers. According to a recent study. . . they suffer extreme degradation, humiliation, sexual harassment and even rape. In addition, they are often faced with hazardous working conditions, including contract substitution, wage discrimination, ill-treatment by employers and other degrading factors.[56]

Women's Movements and Global Efforts

Women have not passively accepted their position. They have always sought survival strategies, individually or collectively. In her anthology of the international women's movement, Robin Morgan declares that "an indigenous feminism has been present in every culture in the world and in every period in history since the suppression of women began."[57]

To solve their immediate problems and meet their practical needs, women have been organizing among themselves for mutual help. Through cooperation, women are trying to diminish the burden of the international economic integration and crisis, as well as the patriarchal restrictions.

Ad hoc and informal organizations of poor women in the capital cities of Peru and Jamaica, as well as in some other major cities of the developing world, have attempted to reduce the cost of food and the burden of cooking and child care. In these neighborhood organizations, women take turns in preparing meals for multiple households; they save time and money by cooking in large volumes and shopping for sizeable amounts.

Established in 1972, the Self-Employed Women's Association (SEWA) in India serves as a trade union for the poor women who work in the informal sector as vendors, home-based producers, and casual laborers. SEWA (meaning "service" in Hindi) provides its members with credit, producer cooperatives, training, legal services, and some social welfare assistance such as maternal protection, widow's benefits, child care, and midwife training.

Many of these collaborative efforts by women, originally planned to address their practical needs, contributed to the development of women's organizational skills and a sense of solidarity among them and, consequently, led to more ambitious movements and organizations geared toward addressing the strategic interests of women.

The Women's Networking Association in Cameroon brings together fifty women's groups, and it undertakes literacy campaigns, establishes purchasing cooperatives to buy women's produce, and organizes seminars and conferences to raise and address women's issues.

The Alliance of Costa Rican Women aims at improving the status of poor women; it publishes information on issues of health, legal rights, and violence against women and provides health and legal services to more than four thousand low-income women.

Kenya has twenty-three thousand women's groups with activities ranging from eliminating environmental degradation and poverty (e.g., the Green Belt Movement) to providing legal assistance to the poor.

Educated and professional women, who had been the beneficiaries of the postindependence reforms, have cooperated with their less-advantaged sisters to help them in solving their problems, and they have also mobilized women from all classes to put pressure on governments for social and economic change. Women lawyers in India and Kenya, for example, assist and encourage poor women to seek their currently recognized rights, and they also strive to expand the scope of women's rights.

Centro de Investigación para la Acción Feminina of the Dominican Republic, by mobilizing middle-class women, offers programs of research, education, training, and public information, all geared toward promoting lasting social change in the status of women. It also organizes activities and seminars in Honduras and Panama.

The Indonesian Women's Congress (KOWANI), established in 1929, grew into an umbrella organization that embodies fifty-two member organizations, and its individual membership included more than ten million women in the early 1980s.

In El Salvador, there has been a strong tradition of female activism—the market women protested the government and demanded freedom of political prisoners in 1922. More recently, the Women's Front (Frente Femenino), formed in 1977, became a national organization with a national political agenda of democratization and over 150,000 members from all classes.

Authoritarian, especially military, regimes have been more hostile and cruel to women. Women under such regimes were subject to torture and forced to go back to traditional roles. The brutality and repression directed at them or their family members, however, facilitated the development of women's political consciousness, which stimulated organization, protest, and struggle. Consequently, the decline of the military regimes in the 1980s in Chile, Argentina, Turkey, and elsewhere also corresponded to the birth of several women's movements and feminist organizations in those countries.[58]

International Solidarity: Efforts and Organizations

Although Article 8 of the United Nations Charter, the Universal Declaration of Human Rights, recognized equality between men and women in 1948, like its many other clauses, the equality principle of the charter was not enforced to accomplish any improvements in the status of women.[59] However, the rising women's movements in several countries and international women's organizations pushed the United Nations to undertake women-specific revisions and measures.

In 1972, the president of the Women's International Democratic Federation, Hertta Kuusinen, a Finnish parliamentarian, along with some other NGO (nongovernmental organizations) observers of the UN Commission on the Status of Women, drafted a proposal for the commission. The proposal, presented by the Romanian representative and seconded by the Finnish one, was accepted by the commission, which, in turn, recommended the UN General Assembly to declare 1975 as the International Women's Year. The recommendation was accepted by the General Assembly in December 1972. Also in 1972, the UN Secretary-General, Kurt Waldheim, who was pressured to increase the presence of women in top positions of the UN, appointed the Finnish representative at the commission, Helvi Sipila, to the post of Assistant Secretary-General.

The International Women's Year Conference at Mexico City in 1975 was flooded by over nine hundred proposals and amendments presented by countries and delegates. The conference led the UN General Assembly to approve its World Plan of Action and to declare the period of 1976–1985 to be the United Nations Decade for Women. These changes initiated within the UN context—the most visible and comprehensive intergovernmental organization—put women on the agenda of other conferences and organizations.

Following the passage of the International Women's Year resolution, Assistant Secretary-General Sipila organized the International Forum on the Role of Women to incorporate women into the agenda of the World Population Conference in 1974—the conference originally had made no connection between women and population issues. Similarly, the forum emphasized women's contribution to food production at the World Food Conference. The Mexico conference raised the problem of the lack of data on women and stressed the need to establish a research and training institute for women. To fill the information gap, "during the first five years of the Decade, the UN system undertook systematic collection of data on the situation and circumstances of women all over the world."[60]

As a result of the awareness raised by the International Year of Women and the following Decade of Women, several conferences that focused on issues pertaining to women were organized and the agendas of other conferences were broadened to include women. The UN itself created specialized agencies to foster the programs and policies developed at these conferences.

Seventeen months after the Mexico conference, the Voluntary Fund for the United Nations Decade for Women was established by the UN General Assembly. The fund's name was changed to UNIFEM in 1985. Working in association with the United Nations Development Programme (UNDP), UNIFEM "provides direct financial and technical support to low-income women in developing countries, who are striving to raise their living standards. It also funds activities that bring women into mainstream development decisionmaking."[61]

The flow of new information on the extent of social and economic contributions of women, as well as on their detrimental conditions and subjugation, expedited the ratification of the "Convention on the Elimination of All Forms of Discrimination Against Women." Approved by the UN General Assembly in 1979, the convention was signed by sixty countries during the mid-decade conference in Copenhagen in 1980. The Committee on the Elimination of Discrimination Against Women (CEDAW) was established and charged with the responsibility of supervising the implementation of the convention through the evaluation of periodic required reports on the status of women and the interrogation of reporting governments about their efforts and policies at public hearings.

A specialized research and training institute, however, was not achieved until 1985 when the statute of INSTRAW (United Nations International Research and Training Institute for the Advancement of Women) was endorsed by the General Assembly.

Until 1975, the UN had only one small secretariat to handle issues affecting women, the Branch of the Advancement of Women within the Centre for Social Development and Humanitarian Affairs, which, in turn, is a part of the Department of International Economic and Social Affairs. In 1988, the department decided to elevate the branch to the status of a division. Thus, the Division for the Advancement of Women emerged and became the central unit within the UN for all issues pertaining to women.

> It is the unit which prepares the drafts for all new plans and programmes, acts as the secretariat for the Commission on the Status of Women, follows up implementation of resolutions concerning women, acts as informal source and contact point for the national machineries for the advancement of women in member states, etc. In principle, the Division covers the whole field.[62]

The elevation in the status, however, did not correspond to any increase in the staff or other resources of the division.[63]

The consciousness and awareness raised by the women's organizations and conferences led to the inclusion of women in the agendas of other development agencies within the UN, other intergovernmental organizations such as the World Bank, and governmental organizations that focus on foreign aid and international development.

The International Development Strategy for the Third United Nations Development Decade, issued in 1980,[64] endorsed the programs of the Mexico and Copenhagen conferences and indicated that "a substantial improvement in the status of women will take place during the Decade" and "women should play an active role in that [development] process."[65] The Percy Amendment of 1973 required the inclusion of women in all projects of the United States Agency for International Development (USAID), and the agency developed several training sessions and manuals to meet the requirement. In 1980, the British Commonwealth established a Women and Development Program that was supported by all member countries.

A global financial organization, the Women's World Bank, was established, also in 1980. Distinct from the World Bank, the Women's World Bank, with its nonprofit banking affiliates in some forty countries, tries to create credit opportunities for female owners of microenterprises. By serving as a guarantor, the bank encourages commercial banks to lend to women who lack property or collateral and are thus normally denied credit.

Although all of these changes and adjustments to include women in development are impressive and promising, the poor record of the United Nations and other international agencies in solving other global problems, such as human rights violations or poverty, calls for prudence rather than excitement. Following the declaration of the development decade, for example, elimination of poverty was included in the programs of abovementioned agencies, but even though the Third United Nations Development Decade concluded in 1990, findings indicate that the extent of poverty, disease, illiteracy, and unemployment in the Third World had increased over the decade. Moreover, the agency that makes this negative assessment, the World Bank, continues to push for structural adjustment programs that devastate the poor and women.

Similarly, the preliminary assessments of the UN Decade of Women present a grim outlook on the impact of the integration of women in development. While several UN surveys and reports conclude that the integration has been slow and inadequate,[66] some women researchers and activists from the Third World question the "nature of the development process into which women were to be integrated."[67]

In 1985, the concluding Conference of the Untied Nations Women's Decade in Nairobi took a critical view of the UN activities and accomplishments of the decade and produced a document, *The Forward-Looking Strategies for the Advancement of Women,*[68] that was unanimously accepted at the conference. The objectives of this document are the same as those of the decade—"Equality, Development and Peace"—but the document clarifies the meaning of these concepts. Paragraph 12 defines development:

> Development means total development, including development in the political, economic, social, cultural, and other dimensions of human life as well as development of the economic and other material resources and the physical, moral, intellectual and cultural growth of human beings. Development also requires a moral dimension to ensure that it is just and responsive to the needs and rights of the individual and that science and technology are applied within a social and economic framework that ensures environmental safety for all life forms on our planet.

To achieve such development goals, the document states demands for an increase in funding for UNIFEM and INSTRAW and suggests the adoption of a women's perspective on development.

> The need for women's perspective on human development is critical, since it is in the interest of human enrichment and progress to introduce and weave into the social fabric women's concept of equality, their choices between alternative development strategies and their approach to peace, in accordance with their aspirations, interests and talents. These things are not only desirable in themselves but are also essential for the attainment of the goals and objectives of the Decade (Paragraph 16).
>
> What is now needed is the political will to promote development in such a way that the strategy for the advancement of women seeks first and foremost to alter the current unequal conditions and structures that continue to define women as secondary persons and give women's issues a low priority. Development should now move to another plane in which women's pivotal role in society is recognized and given its true value. That will allow women to assume their legitimate and core positions in the strategies for effecting the changes necessary to promote and sustain development (Paragraph 21).

Conclusion

The Third World woman has been discriminated against in all aspects of life, and throughout her life. Although she was forced to carry a heavier burden, her social and economic contributions are continually ignored and seldom acknowledged.

The female labor force has been kept marginal: unpaid at home and at family farms and shops; barely compensated in commercial agrarian economies where they are hired as migrant laborers and seasonal workers; underpaid in the informal economies of urban sectors as street vendors, cleaning women, domestic help, and so forth; and exploited as unskilled workers in the industrial sweatshops. Treated as a reserve labor force, women are mobilized when there is a labor shortage and pushed back home at times of economic decline and unemployment.

The global evidence from the last four decades implies that even when there is economic growth, it is not certain that women will be a part of it and receive an equal share. At times of economic stagnation or decline, however, the burden of adjustment falls on women, and the poor women in developing countries suffer more.

Third World women have been subject to gender oppression that is exacerbated by class, race, and international exploitation. The years of struggle, however, have resulted in some steps in the 1970s and 1980s toward raising global awareness and establishing national and international solidarity among women with different socioeconomic backgrounds. Partly due to national women's movements, partly due to the pressure by international groups such as the United Nations' CEDAW (as of December 2, 1993, the convention was ratified by 129 countries), most countries today have a cabinet ministry, department, division, or bureau that focuses on women's issues and affairs. They are also forced to undertake some legislative reforms and make legal adjustments to curb patriarchal injustices. Some countries passed affirmative action legislation or adopted quota systems to guarantee female representation in the legislative and executive branches of government. The full impact of these changes on the lives of Third World women is yet to be seen. The success, as argued in the *Forward-Looking Strategies for the Advancement of Women,* "will depend in large measure upon whether or not women can unite to help each other" (Paragraph 33) and, we can add, if they manage to reverse or redirect the course of global economy and the terms of integration.

Notes

Gratitude is extended to my assistants Anastasia Martin and Jenny Parker for collecting the data and responding to the preliminary drafts, and Eric Jaffa for his help in data analysis, preparation of the tables, and editing. I am most grateful to my colleague, Kim Christensen, and will-be colleague, Liena Gurevich, for their extensive and invaluable comments.

1. Gap figures are expressed in relation to the male average, which is indexed to equal 100. The smaller the figure, the bigger the gap; the closer the figure to 100, the smaller the gap; and the figure above 100 indicates that the female average is higher than the male. *Human Development Report 1993*, United Nations Development Programme (New York: Oxford University Press, 1993).

2. Daphne Topouzis, "The Feminization of Poverty," *Africa Report* (July/August 1990): pp. 60–63.

3. *Human Development Report 1993*, p. 25.

4. *Human Development Report 1993*, pp. 25–26.

5. Robin Morgan, ed., *Sisterhood is Global: The International Women's Movement Anthology* (New York: Anchor Books, 1984), p. 2.

6. UNIFEM 1988–1989, "Strength in Adversity: Women in the Developing World," Report on the United Nations Development Fund for Women, p. 4.

7. Morgan, *Sisterhood is Global*, p. 7.

8. Susan Joekes, *Women in the World Economy*, An INSTRAW Study, United Nations (New York: Oxford University Press, 1987), p. 14.

9. *Human Development Report 1990*, United Nations Development Programme (New York: Oxford University Press, 1990), p. 31.

10. The gap is particularly large for the oil-rich Gulf states. In 1990, the number of females per 100 males was 48 in the United Arab Emirates, 60 in Qatar, 73 in Bahrain, 76 in Kuwait, 84 in Saudi Arabia, and 91 in Oman (*Human Development Report 1993*).

11. Kathleen Newland, "Infant Mortality and the Health of Societies," Worldwatch Paper 47 (Washington, D.C.: Worldwatch Institute, December 1981), p. 30.

12. UNIFEM, 1988–1989.

13. UNIFEM, 1988–1989, p. 5.

14. *Human Development Report 1990*, p. 32.

15. Janet H. Momsen, *Women and Development in the Third World* (London: Routledge, 1991), p. 58.

16. Ibid., p. 38.

17. Morgan, *Sisterhood is Global*, p. 639.

18. Ibid., p. 15.

19. *Human Development Report 1993*, p. 45.

20. See Linda Nicholson, ed., *Feminism/Postmodernism* (New York: Routledge, 1990); Sheila Ruth, *Issues in Feminism* (Mountain View, Calif.: 1990); Carole Pateman, *The Sexual Contract* (Stanford, Calif.: Stanford University press, 1988); Selya Benhabib and Drucilla Cornell, eds., *Feminism as Critique: On the Politics of Gender* (Minneapolis, Minn.: University of Minnesota Press, 1987); Alison M. Jaggar and Paula S. Rothenberg, eds., *Feminist Frameworks: Alternative Theoretical Accounts of the Relations Between Women and Men*, 2nd ed., (New York: McGraw-Hill, 1984); Nancy Chodorow, *Reproduction of Mothering* (Berkeley: University of California press, 1978); Rayna R. Reiter, ed., *Toward an Anthropology of Women* (New York: Monthly Review Press, 1975); Frederick Engels, *The Origin of the Family, Private Property and the State* (New York: International Publishers, 1972).

21. The six member nations of the Iroquois Confederacy constitute a curious case. The extent of power that the Iroquois matrons had over public affairs astonished their nineteenth-century observers and even led some of them to classify these societies as "matriarchy." Although the Iroquois matrons enjoyed an authority more than women have ever had in history, they could not be chiefs or serve on the Council of Elders, the highest ruling body of the Confederacy. Women mainly maintained a veto power and exercised an indirect influence due to their control of food and other supplies.

22. Reiter, *Toward an Anthropology of Women*.

23. Carol Mukhapadhyay, "Sati or Shakti: Women, Culture and Politics in India," in Jean F. O'Barr, ed., *Perspectives on Power: Women in Africa, Asia, and*

Latin America (Durham, N.C.: Duke University Press, 1982), pp. 11–26; Evelyn P. Stevens, "Marianismo: The Other Face of Machismo in Latin America," in Ann Pescatello, ed., *Female and Male in Latin America* (Pittsburgh: University of Pittsburgh Press, 1973), pp. 89–102; Margaret Strobel, "Women in Religion and in Secular Ideology," in Jean Margaret Hay and Sharon Stichter, eds., *African Women South of the Sahara* (London: Longman, 1984), pp. 87–101; Fatima Mernissi, *Beyond the Veil: Male-Female Dynamics in Modern Muslim Society,* revised edition (Bloomington: Indiana University Press, 1987); John L. Esposito, *Women in Muslim Family Law* (Syracuse, N.Y.: Syracuse University Press, 1982).

24. Leila Ahmed, *Women and Gender in Islam* (New Haven, Conn.: Yale University Press, 1992); Deniz Kandiyoti, ed., *Women, Islam and the State* (Philadelphia: Temple University Press, 1991); Nikki R. Keddie and Beth Baron, eds., *Women in Middle Eastern History: Shifting Boundaries in Sex and Gender* (New Haven, Conn.: Yale University Press, 1991); Vanaja Dhruvajan, *Hindu Women and The Power of Ideology* (Granby, Mass.: Bergin and Garvey Publishers, Inc., 1989); Kumari Jayawardena, *Feminism and Nationalism in the Third World* (London: Zed Books, 1986); Jean F. O'Barr, ed., *Perspectives on Power: Women in Africa, Asia, and Latin America* (Durham, N.C.: Duke University Press, 1982).

25. O'Barr, *Perspectives on Power;* Jane L. Parpart and Kathleen A. Staidt, eds., *Women and the State in Africa* (Boulder: Lynne Rienner Publishers, 1989); Pat Ellis, ed., *Women of the Caribbean* (London: Zed Books, 1986); Jean Margaret Hay and Sharon Stichter, eds., *African Women South of the Sahara* (London: Longman, 1984).

26. Margot Lovett, "Gender Relations, Class Formation, and the Colonial State in Africa," in Jane L. Parpart and Kathleen A. Staidt, eds. *Women and the State in Africa,* pp. 23–46.

27. Kandiyoti, *Women, Islam, and the State;* Jayawardena, *Feminism and Nationalism in the Third World;* Hay and Stichter, *African Women South of the Sahara*; Zehra Arat, "Kemalism and Turkish Women," *Women and Politics* 14, no. 4 (fall 1994), pp. 57–80; Sue Ellen M. Charlton, Jana Everett, and Kathleen Staudt, eds., *Women, the State, and Development* (Albany, N.Y.: State University of New York Press, 1989); Carol Wolkowitz, "Controlling Women's Access to Political Power: A Case Study in Andhra Pradesh, India," in Haleh Afshar, *Women, State, and Ideology* (Albany: State University of New York Press, 1987), pp. 204–224.

28. Hay and Stichter, *African Women South of the Sahara,* pp. 190–191.

29. Socialist countries have been more successful in the process of secularization and integration of women into the productive forces. Overall they have higher representation of women in the labor force and positions of authority. During the 1990–1991 period, Chinese women constituted 43 percent of the labor force and held 21 percent of the seats in the legislature. The corresponding percentages were 46 and 20 for the Democratic Republic of Korea, 32 and 34 for Cuba, 45 and 2 for Mongolia, 47 and 18 for Vietnam, 21 and 37 for Guyana, and 34 and 16 in Nicaragua (despite the change in the regime), as compared to 33 and 12 for all developing countries, 29 and 9 for the least developed countries, and 42 and 9 for industrial countries. *Human Development Report 1993,* pp. 150–151. It should be noted, however, that opening employment opportunities has not eliminated the subjugation of women in these countries, since the other patriarchal norms and values have prevailed. See Maxine Molyneux, "Women in Socialist Societies: Problems of Theory and Practice," in Kate Young, Carol Wolkowitz, and Roslyn McCullagh, eds., *Of Marriage and the Market: Women's Subordination Internationally and Its Lessons* (London: Routledge, 1984), pp. 55–90; and Lydia Sargent,

ed., *Women and Revolution: A Discussion of the Unhappy Marriage of Marxism and Feminism* (Boston: South End Press, 1981).

30. UNIFEM Annual Report 1990 (New York: United Nations Development Fund for Women, 1990), p. 7.

31. Gita Sen and Caren Grown, *Development, Crises, and Alternative Visions: Third World Women's Perspectives* (New York: Monthly Review Press, 1987).

32. *Women's Participation in Development: An Inter-organizational Assessment,* Evaluation Study No. 13 (New York: United Nations Development Programme, June 1985), p. 42.

33. Art Hansen et al., *Food in Sub-Saharan Africa* (Boulder: Lynne Rienner Publishers, Inc., 1986).

34. Morgan, *Sisterhood is Global*, p. 312.

35. Ibid., p. 455.

36. Ibid., p. 18.

37. Maternal mortality rates have been increasing in developing countries due to the malnutrition and inadequate health care. About 63 percent of women do not receive prenatal care, and 66 percent of births are not attended by any kind of trained (traditional or modern) health care personnel (Table 10.4).

38. Carole J. L. Collins, "Women as Hidden Casualties of the Cold War," *Ms.* 3, no. 3 (November/December, 1992): pp. 14–15; Ammu Joseph, "India's Population 'Bomb' Explodes Over Women," *Ms.* 3, no. 3 (November/December, 1992): pp. 12–14.

39. Morgan, *Sisterhood is Global*, p. 7.

40. James Brooke, "Ulcer Drug Tied to Numerous Abortions in Brazil," *New York Times*, May 19, 1993, p. C13.

41. Joekes, *Women in the World Economy*, pp. 29–30.

42. UNIFEM, 1990, p. 6.

43. Susan George, *A Fate Worse than Debt*, revised and updated edition (New York: Grove Weidenfeld, 1990).

44. *Human Development Report 1993*, p. 45.

45. Morgan, *Sisterhood is Global*, p. 313.

46. Joekes, *Women in the World Economy*.

47. The IMF loans constitute only a small portion of total lending, but the agency's approval allows the applicant country to acquire loans from other states and commercial banks.

48. *Human Development Report 1990*, p. 32.

49. Momsen, *Women and Development in the Third World*, p. 97.

50. George, *A Fate Worse Than Debt*. Jeanne Vickers, *Women and the World Economic Crisis* (London: Zed Books, 1991).

51. Momsen, *Women and Development in the Third World*, pp. 98–99.

52. Joekes, *Women in the World Economy*, p. 96.

53. Vickers, *Women and the World Economic Crisis*, p. 29.

54. Momsen, *Women and Development in the Third World*, p. 99.

55. Cleo Odzer, "Patpong Prostitution: A Look at the Gender Relationships Involved in, and Affected by, the Sex Industry in Thailand," paper prepared for the Gender and Industrialization in Asia Conference, State University of New York–Purchase, May 3–4, 1991; Cynthia Enloe, *Bananas, Beaches and Bases: Making Feminist Sense of International Politics* (Berkeley: University of California Press, 1989).

56. As quoted in Vickers, 1991; Hilkka Pietilä and Jeanne Vickers, *Making Women Matter: The Role of the United Nations* (London: Zed Books, 1990).

57. Morgan, *Sisterhood is Global*, p. 5.

58. Elizabeth Jelin, ed., *Women and Social Change in Latin America* (London: Zed Books, 1990).

59. In fact, the organization itself reflects a patriarchal structure and andro-centric values. Since its establishment in 1945, it has never had a woman in the Secretary-General position. According to the Ad Hoc Group for Equal Rights for Women at the United Nations, as of February 1993, out of the 21 Undersecretaries-General, only 3 are women. Compared to 11 male Assistant Secretaries-General, there is only 1 woman Assistant Secretary-General. Among Division Directors, while there are 64 men as First Directors and 209 men as Second Directors, there are only 9 women First Directors and 30 women Second Directors. In the five pro-fessional categories the ratios of men to women are 378 to 100, 472 to 206, 395 to 245, 234 to 194, and 3 to 8 for levels five to one, respectively. As reported in the *1989 World Survey on the Role of Women in Development*, United Nations Office at Vienna, Centre for Social Development and Humanitarian Affairs (New York: United Nations, 1989), out of 106 members of the UN for which data were avail-able, 38 countries had no female professional staff in the UN Secretariat in 1987 (Table 2, pp. 337–340).

It is clear that there has not been much progress since 1983 when out of 26 Undersecretaries-General, only 1 was a woman. Out of 22 Assistant Secretaries-General, 3 were women. Out of 316 Division Directors, 16 were women. Out of a total of 2,582 persons in the professional category, 959 were women. In the gen-eral service category, which covers secretarial and clerical work, however, women outnumbered men by 4,591 to 3,450. Moreover, although the UN has advocated equal pay for equal work, the average annual salary for professional and general service categories was $44,000 for men and $27,000 for women (Morgan, 1984), p. 691.

60. Pietilä and Vickers, *Making Women Matter*, p. 77.

61. UNIFEM, 1990.

62. Pietilä and Vickers, *Making Women Matter*, p. 100.

63. Ibid.

64. Published by the Department of Public Information (New York: United Nations, 1980).

65. See especially Paragraphs 8, 51, and 168.

66. See the *Women's Participation in Development* as well as *1989 World Survey of the Role of Women in Development; World Survey on the Role of Women in Development*, Department of International and Economic Social Affairs (New York: United Nations, 1986).

67. Sen and Grown, *Development, Crisis, and Alternative Visions*, p. 16. For a brief review of the assumptions and implications of development goals and ac-tivities, see Deniz Kandiyoti, "Women and Rural Development Policies: The Changing Agenda," in Charles K. Wilber and Kenneth P. Jameson, eds., *Political Economy of Development and Under-development*, 5th ed. (New York: McGraw-Hill, Inc., 1992), pp. 516–531.

68. *The Nairobi Forward-Looking Strategies for the Advancement of Women*, Department of Public Information (New York: United Nations, 1985).

Index

The Contributors

◆

Zehra F. Arat is associate professor of political science at State University of New York at Purchase. She is the author of *Democracy and Human Rights in Developing Countries* (Boulder: Lynne Rienner Publishers, 1991). She has also contributed several articles on development, human rights, and gender in the Third World.

Margaretta DeMar is assistant professor of political science at North Dakota State University with specialization in political economy of development in the Caribbean and Central America. She is the author of several articles and book chapters on political economy of the Third World and the Caribbean.

Richard F. Doner is associate professor of political science at Emory University with specialization in political economy of Southeast Asia. He is the author of *Driving a Bargain: Automobile Industrialization and Japanese Firms in Southeast Asia* (Berkeley: University of California Press, 1991). He has also contributed numerous articles on different aspects of political economy of growth in Southeast Asia to leading professional journals.

Manochehr Dorraj is associate professor of political science at Texas Christian University with specialization in Third World and Middle Eastern development. He is the author of *From Zarathustra to Khomeini: Populism and Dissent in Iran* (Boulder: Lynne Rienner Publishers, 1990). Dorraj has also contributed numerous articles and book chapters on Third World and Middle Eastern developmental issues.

Michael W. Foley is associate professor of political science at Catholic University of America with specialization in the political economy of development in Latin America. He is the coeditor of *State, Capital, and Rural Society: Anthropological Perspectives on Political Economy in Mexico and the Andes* (Boulder: Westview Press, 1989). Foley has also contributed numerous articles and book chapters on the political economy of Latin America.

Antony T. K. Gadzey is assistant professor of political science at Auburn University with specialization in international political economy and African political economy. He is the author of *Political Economy of Power: Hegemoney and Economic Liberalism* (New York: McMillan Publishers, 1994). He has also contributed several articles on international political economy and African political economy.

Robert E. Gamer is professor of political science at the University of Missouri–Kansas City with specialization in Asian development. He is the author of *The Politics of Urban Development in Singapore* (Ithaca: Cornell University Press, 1972), *The Developing Nations: A Comparative Perspective*, 3d ed. (Madison, Wis.: Brown & Benchmark, 1993), and *Government and Politics in a Changing World* (Madison, Wis.: Brown & Benchmark, 1992). He has also contributed numerous articles on Asian development to professional journals.

Gary Hawes is associate professor of political science with specialization in the political economy of East Asia. He is the author of *The Philippine State and the Marcos Regime: The Politics of Exports* (Ithaca: Cornell University Press, 1987). He has also contributed a number of articles on East Asian political economy.

Marian A. L. Miller is assistant professor of political science at University of Akron. She is the author of *The Third World in Global Environmental Politics* (Boulder: Lynne Rienner Publishers, 1995). She has also contributed several articles on development and environment in the Third World.

John W. Newark is associate dean, Faculty of Arts, at Athabasca University in Alberta, Canada. Professor Newark has published several articles in the area of development assistance and education.

About the Book and Editor

◆

The tumultuous events of the past decade have significantly altered economic and political power structures worldwide, though perhaps most profoundly in the developing nations. This book presents a historical and theoretical appraisal of the new realities facing the Third World, introducing students to a uniquely Third World perspective that shows not only how the *governments,* but more importantly the *people* of the Third World are affected by recent international events.

Through case studies of regional political economies and discussions of such pertinent issues as foreign aid, environmental policy, and the condition of women, the authors provide a lucid portrayal of the increasing complexity and polarization that has engulfed the Third World. Analyzing the disparities among countries in terms of strategies of growth and development, the role of the state and its policies, and the nuances of the democratization process, they offer new insights into the changing character of Third World political economies.

Manochehr Dorraj is associate professor of political science at Texas Christian University. He is author of *From Zarathustra to Khomeini: Populism and Dissent in Iran* (Lynne Rienner Publishers 1990).